D1084782

RUSSIAN LITERATURE, MODERNISM AND THE VISUAL ARTS

In the Russian modernist era, literature threw itself open to influences from other art forms, most particularly the visual arts. Collaborations between writers, artists, designers, and theatre and cinema directors took place more intensively and productively than ever before or since. Equally striking was the incursion of spatial and visual motifs and structures into verbal texts. Verbal and visual principles of creation joined forces in an attempt to transform and surpass life through art. Yet willed transcendence of the boundaries between art forms gave rise to confrontation and creative tension as well as to harmonious co-operation.

This collection of essays by leading British, American and Russian scholars draws on a rich variety of material – from Dostoevskii to Siniavskii, from writers' doodles to cabarets, from well-known modernists such as Akhmatova, Malevich, Platonov and Olesha to less well-known figures – to demonstrate the creative power and dynamism of Russian culture 'on the boundaries'.

CATRIONA KELLY is Reader in Russian at New College, Oxford. She is author of *Petrushka, the Russian Carnival Puppet Theatre* (1990), *A History of Russian Women's Writing* (1994), editor of *An Anthology of Russian Women's Writing* (1994), and of *Utopias: Russian Modernist Texts 1905–1940* (1999) and co-editor of *Constructing Russian Culture in the Age of Revolution* and *An Introduction to Russian Cultural Studies* (1998).

STEPHEN LOVELL is a Junior Research Fellow at St John's College, Oxford. He is author of *The Russian Reading Revolution: Print Culture in the Soviet and Post-Soviet Eras* (2000) and co-editor of *Bribery and Blat in Russia: Negotiating Reciprocity from the Middle Ages to the 1990s* (2000).

Recent titles in this series include

The Last Soviet Avant-Garde: OBERIU – Fact, Fiction, Metafiction
GRAHAM ROBERTS

Literary Journals in Imperial Russia
edited by DEBORAH A. MARTINSEN

Russian Modernism: The Transfiguration of the Everyday
STEPHEN C. HUTCHINGS

Reading Russian Fortunes
Print Culture, Gender and Divination in Russia from 1765
FAITH WIGZELL

English Literature and the Russian Aesthetic Renaissance
RACHEL POLONSKY

Christianity in Bakhtin: God and the Exiled Author
RUTH COATES

The Development of Russian Verse: Meter and its Meanings
MICHAEL WACHTEL

Nabokov and his Fiction: New Perspectives
edited by JULIAN W. CONNOLLY

A complete list of titles in the series is given at the back of the book

RUSSIAN LITERATURE, MODERNISM AND THE VISUAL ARTS

EDITED BY

CATRIONA KELLY
New College, Oxford

STEPHEN LOVELL
St John's College, Oxford

CAMBRIDGE
UNIVERSITY PRESS

PUBLISHED BY THE PRESS SYNDICATE OF THE UNIVERSITY OF CAMBRIDGE
The Pitt Building, Trumpington Street, Cambridge, United Kingdom

CAMBRIDGE UNIVERSITY PRESS
The Edinburgh Building, Cambridge CB2 2RU, UK   http://www.cup.cam.ac.uk
40 West 20th Street, New York NY 10011–4211, USA   http://www.cup.org
10 Stamford Road, Oakleigh, Melbourne 3166, Australia

First published 2000

Typeset in 11/12.5pt Baskerville   [CE]

A catalogue record for this book is available from the British Library

Library of Congress cataloguing in publication data

Russian literature, modernism and the visual arts / edited by
Catriona Kelly and Stephen Lovell.
p.   cm. – (Cambridge studies in Russian literature)
Includes bibliographical references and index.
ISBN 0 521 66191 9 hb
1. Russian literature – 20th century – History and criticism.
2. Modernism (Literature) – Russia.
3. Modernism (Literature) – Soviet Union.
4. Arts in literature.
1. Kelly, Catriona.   11. Lovell, Stephen.   111. Series.
PG3020.5.M6R79   2000
891.709'112 – dc21   99–23185   CIP

ISBN 0 521 66191 9 hardback

Contents

Illustrations

Illustration credits

F. Dostoevskii, pages from notebooks to *Crime and Punishment* and *The Idiot*, Russian State Archive of Literature and Art, Moscow. Anon, *The Dying Lioness*, © The British Museum, London; reprinted by permission. Anon, Gargas Hand, from Abbé H. Breuil, *Four Hundred Centuries of Cave Art*, trans. Mary E. Boyle, New York, 1979 © Hacker Art Books, New York, reprinted by permission. G. de Chiorico, *Ettore e Andromache* © Fondation Giorgio di Chirico. N. Goncharova, *Posadka kartofelia*, M. Larionov, *Siniaia svin'ia*, © 1999 Artists Rights Society (ARS), New York/ADAGP, Paris. F. Goya, *El Ritual de las Brujas* and *La Romaria de San Isidro* © Museo del Prado, Madrid; reprinted by permission. M. V. Iakunchikova and V. V. Vul'f, *Vecher na balkone*, V. Perov, *Portret F. M. Dostoevskogo*, Tret'iakov Gallery, Moscow. K. Malevich, *Krest'ianka* and *Tri zhenskikh figury*, I. Repin, *Barsuki na Volge*, I. Shishkin, *Khvoinyi les v solnechnyi den'*, Russian Museum, St Petersburg. H. Matisse, *Le Peintre et son modèle* © Succession H. Matisse/ARS New York. N. Rerikh (Nicholas Roerich), *Drevniaia zhizn'*, Radishchev Art Museum, Saratov. V. Tatlin, *Portret moriaka* © DACS.

The editors are grateful to the above for permission to reproduce works in copyright. Every effort has been made to trace the copyright-holders of all works included. The publishers would be pleased to rectify any omission brought to their notice at the earliest opportunity.

Note on conventions

Transliteration is according to the Library of Congress system, except in the case of émigré artists who themselves preferred an alternative spelling of their own names, or in the cases of well-known individuals whose names have an established alternative form in English (Gorky, Mandelstam, Gogol).

Unless indicated in the Notes, all translations are the work of the authors of essays. Konstantin Barsht's essay was translated into English by Stephen Lovell.

Notes on contributors

KONSTANTIN BARSHT is Professor in the Philology Department of the Russian State Herzen University in St Petersburg. Among his numerous publications in the fields of the theory and history of nineteenth- and twentieth-century Russian literature are a study of Dostoevskii's *The Possessed*, published in 1994, a history of twentieth-century Russian literary criticism, and various writings on the subject of non-verbal signs in writers' manuscripts, including his pioneering *Risunki v rukopisiakh Dostoevskogo* (Drawings in the Manuscripts of Dostoevskii, 1996).

PAMELA CHESTER, an Associate at the Davis Center for Russian Studies, Harvard University, is an independent scholar with interests in Russian women's writing, especially autobiography, and in the connections between literature and the visual arts. Her publications include 'Engaging Sexual Demons in Tsvetaeva's "Chert"', in *Slavic Review*, and 'Landscape of Recollection: Tolstoy's "Childhood" and the Feminization of the Countryside', in *Engendering Slavic Literatures* (1996), which she co-edited with Sibelan Forrester. She is just completing work on a book analysing Tsvetaeva's autobiographical prose.

JANE GRAYSON, Lecturer in Russian Language and Literature at the School of Slavonic and East European Studies, University of London, is a specialist in twentieth-century Russian literature, particularly prose fiction. Her publications include *Nabokov Translated: A Comparison of Nabokov's Russian and English Prose* (1977), *Nikolai Gogol: Text and Context* (1989: co-edited with Richard Freeborn), and numerous articles on twentieth-century Russian and Soviet literature. In 1999 she organised a Nabokov Centenary Conference at Jesus College, Cambridge. She is currently completing work on a study of the reception of Gogol and Pushkin in three twentieth-century Russian writers: Bulgakov, Nabokov and Siniavskii.

BARBARA HENRY, Max Hayward Fellow, St Antony's College, Oxford, has interests in twentieth-century Russian literature and culture, particularly theatre; her study of the 'Crooked Mirror' cabaret in St Petersburg is forthcoming from Oxford University Press. She is the author of articles on Bulgakov's dramas and on the Russian cabaret; she is now working on a general study of the Jewish theatre in the early twentieth century.

CATRIONA KELLY is Reader in Russian, New College, University of Oxford. Her publications include *Petrushka, the Russian Carnival Puppet Theatre* (1990), *A History of Russian Women's Writing, 1820–1992* (1994), *An Anthology of Russian Women's Writing* (1994), and numerous articles on Russian literature and cultural history; she is co-editor of *Constructing Russian Culture in the Age of Revolution* and *An Introduction to Russian Cultural Studies* (both 1998). Her current project is *Refining Russia: Gender and the Regulation of Behaviour from 1760*, a study of gentility in Russian culture.

STEPHEN LOVELL is a Junior Research Fellow at St John's College, Oxford. Besides several articles on the history of reading and print culture in twentieth-century Russia, he is author of *The Russian Reading Revolution: Print Culture in the Soviet and Post-Soviet Eras* and co-editor of *Bribery and Blat in Russia: Negotiating Reciprocity from the Early Modern Period to the 1990s* (both forthcoming). His current project is a social and cultural history of the dacha.

CYNTHIA MARSH, Senior Lecturer in Russian, University of Nottingham, is the author of *Maksimilian Voloshin: Artist-Poet* (1983), and compiler of *The File on Gorky* (1993), and also of various articles on Russian drama and theatre. She is currently working on a large-scale study of Gorky's plays. Besides her academic interest in the theatre, she has also directed many productions of plays by Russian, and other, writers for the live theatre.

MILENA MICHALSKI, School of Slavonic and East European Studies, University of London, is just completing her PhD thesis on Soviet literature and film. She is the co-translator, with Silva Rubashova, of Lydia Chukovskaya's *The Akhmatova Journals* (1994), and is currently working on a book about Abram Room.

ROBIN MILNER-GULLAND is Professor Emeritus of Russian and East European Studies at the University of Sussex. He is the author of many studies of Russian culture, especially modernist literature and painting, including *Cultural Atlas of Russia* (1980) and *The Russians* (1997), and of *An Introduction to Russian Art and Architecture*, which he co-authored with John Bowlt. He translated and edited N. N. Zabolotsky, *The Life of Zabolotsky* (1994), and has published many articles on Russian modernist literature, particularly Kharms, Zabolotsky and Yevtushenko.

ANDREW WACHTEL is Herman and Beulah Pearce Miller Research Professor in Literature and Chair of the Department of Slavic Languages and Literatures at Northwestern University. Wachtel is the author of a wide variety of books and articles on Russian literature and culture of the nineteenth and twentieth centuries, including *The Battle for Childhood: Creation of a Russian Myth* (1990) and *An Obsession with History: Russian Writers Confront the Past* (1994). He is the editor of two collections of essays: *Petrushka: Sources and Contexts*, as well as *Intersections and Transpositions: Russian Music, Literature, and Society* (both 1998). Apart from Russian literature, he also maintains a strong, and increasing, interest in South Slavic culture: *Making a Nation, Breaking a Nation: Literature and Cultural Politics in Yugoslavia* was published in 1998.

ALEXANDER ZHOLKOVSKY is Professor of Slavic Languages and Literatures at the University of Southern California. His publications include: *Themes and Texts: Toward a Poetics of Expressiveness* (1984); *Text Counter Text: Rereadings in Russian Literary History* (1994); *Babel'* (with Mikhail Iampolsky, Moscow, 1994); *Inventsii* (Moscow, 1995); *Raboty po poetike vyrazitel'nosti* (Essays on a Poetics of Expressiveness (with Yuri Shcheglov), 1996); and *Mikhail Zoshchenko: poetika nedoveriia* (Mikhail Zoshchenko: A Poetics of Mistrust, 1999). In 1998, he was awarded the Severnaia Pal'mira Prize for an article on Boris Pasternak published in *Zvezda*, December 1997.

Acknowledgements

The original inspiration for this book was a series of seminars under the title 'Russian Literature and the Other Arts', held at the School of Slavonic and East European Studies, University of London, in the academic year 1996–1997. Though the seminar series was much broader in scope than the volume that has emerged (it included papers on Romanticism and on nineteenth-century realism as well as on Modernism), and although most of the essays in this book were specially commissioned, rather than being presented as papers in the series, we would like to thank the organisers of the seminars, Arnold McMillin and Faith Wigzell, and the participants and audience, for their significant contribution to the broader context in which the book took shape. The two anonymous readers at Cambridge University Press made a valuable contribution at a later stage of this book's preparation.

We would also like to thank our own institutions, New College and St John's College, Oxford, for providing us with a congenial environment in which to carry out the editing, and for providing funds towards the cost of colour printing on the cover; and to express our gratitude to the staffs of the Taylorian and Bodleian Libraries.

Introduction: boundaries of the spectacular

Catriona Kelly and Stephen Lovell

The Russian modernist era was remarkable not only for the extraordinary energy that infused all the arts, but also for the fact that this energy was so often generated by collaboration between artists working in different media – poetry, drama, film, painting and music. To date, however, the interaction of the arts as such has rarely been the subject of special study: most analyses have concentrated on well-known figures or groups (Maiakovskii, Pasternak, Diaghilev's Ballets russes) rather than attempting a broader picture.[1] This collection of essays aims to widen the discussion, not only by introducing some less familiar artists and writers (including women as well as men) alongside major names, but also by raising questions about the general principles of collaboration, adaptation and appropriation that operated in the age of Modernism, and about the relationship between Modernism and other artistic schools (in particular realism) so far as the interaction of the arts is concerned. It concentrates on 'spectacular' art forms (painting and theatre) not only because the early twentieth century was the time at which Russia first attained international standing as a producer, rather than a consumer, of top-quality work in these forms, with artists such as Bakst, Goncharova and later Malevich, Eisenstein and Lissitsky enjoying the respect and indeed awe that had been extended to their literary predecessors Tolstoi and Dostoevskii, but because the modernist era did so much to revise the relationship between the visual arts and Russian literature (a relationship that had traditionally been rather distant, as will be argued in more detail below).

The second element in the title of our introduction, 'boundaries', with its apparent emphasis on divisions and constraints, might appear to do little justice to the spirit of Modernism in its Russian variant, which was dominated by a neo-Romantic view that the purpose of boundaries was to be surmounted. In her 1934 poem,

'Vskryla zhily' (I opened my veins), for example, Marina Tsvetaeva drew a parallel between blood-letting and the poetic utterance, both of which overflow the limits of everyday vessels and measures, just as the actions of their originator in mutilating her body transgress customary notions of self-preservation and self-restraint.[2] Boris Pasternak, whose second collection bore the programmatic title *Poverkh bar'erov* (Over the Barriers), was equally, though less flamboyantly, concerned with the theme of the dissolution of self. Poems such as 'Margarita' (1919) dissolve the boundaries between human and natural worlds, between subject and object, and in 'Gorod' (Town, 1916), from the cycle *Epicheskie motivy* (Epic Motifs), the lyric subject, identified at first as a passenger upon a train, slips at the end of the poem beyond the figuration of personal identity, as observed and observer shift places, and the speaker imagines himself *outside* the train:

> Где горизонт, как рубикон,
> Где сквозь агонию громленой
> Рябины, в дождь бегут бегом
> Свистки и тучи, и вагоны.

> [Where the horizon is a rubicon,
> And through the death-agony of the thunderstruck
> Rowan, into the rain rush at full pace
> Whistles, clouds, and carriages.][3]

The traditional hierarchy of 'foreground' and 'background', of 'animate' and 'inanimate' is disrupted, and viewing-points are combined, as in a post-impressionist painting.

As this second example illustrates, boundaries between different art forms were as subject to assault as any other kind; indeed, here the assault upon the traditional divisions of 'self' and 'other', 'narrator' and 'narrated', is also dependent upon a substitution of the representative principles of painting for the traditions of lyric poetry. As Robin Milner-Gulland reminds us in the introduction to an essay included here, 'Khlebnikov's Eye', 'the period of the European "Modern Movement" (*c.* 1880–1930) witnessed close interaction between the various forms of art: a Mallarmé and a Debussy, a Schoenberg and a Kandinskii, a Picasso and an Apollinaire could be linked not only by ties of friendship and co-operation, but by a feeling of common purpose across normal generic boundaries'. Milner-Gulland goes on to mention one manifestation of artistic syncretism during the 'Modern Movement', the fact that 'practitioners of one art frequently operated at a serious level in other territories': to the Russian artists that he cites, Filonov, Kandinskii, Pasternak and Maiakovskii, might be added Leonid Andreev (writer and pioneer of photography), Kuz'ma Petrov-Vodkin (painter and memoirist), Sergei Eisenstein (film director, artist and writer), Mikhail Kuzmin (composer and poet), Elizaveta Kuz'mina-Karavaeva (poet and creator of religious embroideries), Elena Guro (writer and painter), Varvara Stepanova and Ol'ga Rozanova (painters and writers) – and the list is still by no means exhaustive. In some cases, the engagement with alternative forms was to prove personally liberating, as in the case of Kuzmin, a minor composer turned major poet, or of Leonid Andreev, whose photographs display 'a lyrical sensitivity to physical beauty unexpected in one whose writings concentrate almost exclusively on philosophical and psychological probing and make minimal use of external description'.[4]

The crossing of boundaries by artists who were on the whole more prominent in one art form than the other or others is, however, only one way in which the convergence among different art forms during the modernist period made itself manifest. The Russian Romantics, who took their models above all from French contemporaries such as Lamartine, and from Byron, did not share the predilection of German writers of their era for synaesthesia, the blurring of sense impressions such that, say, sounds acquire colour value, or tactile impressions musical note values. But for modernists such as Belyi and Nabokov, the fusion of perception was fundamental to artistic creation.[5] Synaesthesia was more than a trope; it was intimately connected with the creation of multi-genre texts in which verbal, musical and visual texts were integrated in ways directly inspired by Wagner's theories of *Gesamtkunst*, or 'total art':[6] here the *son et lumière* orchestral works of Skriabin, such as *Prometei* (Prometheus), were particularly important. Post-Nietzschean appreciations of Greek tragedy through the prism of Wagner also prompted the composition and staging of neo-classical dramas with emphasis on musical and visual spectacular: one significant contribution to this direction was Tairov's production of Innokentii Annenskii's 'satyr-play' *Famira-kifared* (Thamyris the Citharist) in 1916. Other contributions to the convergence of the art forms included the increasing use of verbal commentaries on visual texts. As Ol'ga Rozanova pointed out in her essay of 1913, 'Osnovy novogo iskusstva i prichiny ego neponimaniia' (The Principles of Contemporary Art and the Reasons Why it is Misunderstood), avant-garde groups such as the Suprematists used titles which drew attention to the technical devices employed in works of art; a more jaded observer, Maksimilian Voloshin, was to insinuate, in a critique of the avant-garde 'The Donkey's Tail' exhibition, that the titles of the neo-primitivist works on show were often more provocative than the contents of the paintings themselves.[7] Conversely, verbal texts were often accompanied by illustrations, ranging from the spidery vignettes of Konstantin Somov and other 'World of Art' painters, to the dramatic ink and charcoal sketches of Natal'ia Goncharova, while adventurous typography and book production (the use of multiple typefaces, sometimes within one word, and of unorthodox papers and bindings) was to be exploited to its limits in the early books of the cubo-futurist movement.[8]

Another important area for collaboration was the theatre. There are few countries that can boast such a distinguished tradition of stage design as Russia between 1880 and 1940. The many artists who worked in the medium included Goncharova, Larionov, Bilibin, Korovin, Aleksandra Ekster, Bakst, Benois, Tatlin and Liubov' Popova; artists such as these collaborated on every detail of a production, designing everything from drop-curtains to shoe-buckles and stockings. And in the 1920s, as the constructivist movement gained ground, stage design moved from two into three dimensions, dictating movement as well as satisfying the decorative principle, and absorbing textual elements into the visual structure by means of such devices as the display of banners and notices. In Konstantin Khokhlov's staging of Aleksei Tolstoi's play *Bunt mashin* (Mutiny of the Machines), for example, slogans appeared both as exhortations, rupturing the illusion of direct communication between actors and audience, and as symbolic significations of theatrical space (one part of the huge cage-like structure that formed the set was labelled 'hotel').[9] At the same time, directors such as Meierkhol'd boldly and controversially remade dramas to suit a new view of the theatre as above all a visual medium: a signal event was the performance of Gogol's classic stage comedy *Revizor* (The Government Inspector), played on a claustrophobically cluttered stage, where 'characterisation' was sacrificed to identification by visual cues: petitioners clutched letters decorated with grotesque blobs of sealing wax, and Khlestakov, in Gogol's version an amiable buffoon, loomed in heavy glasses and a tall hat like a Dostoevskian devil.[10] And the arrival of the cinema offered new possibilities of dramatising verbal texts (an important early example being Iakov Protazanov's extraordinarily rich version of Tolstoi's *Otets Sergii* (Father Sergius, 1918), still one of the most impressive translations of Tolstoyan narrative to the screen).

One could also mention the imitation of one art form in another. In literature, the modernist concepts of 'collage' or 'montage', and cinematic devices such as the close-up, or use of film segments run in reverse, facilitated the invocation of visuality in extremely diverse ways.[11] Resources now extended far beyond the traditional trope of ekphrasis (the citation of painting in poetry or narrative fiction), and suggested a unity of artistic vision that was quite different from the Aristotelian appreciation that painting and writing were united by their joint striving for mimesis, the exact imitation and reproduction of life (a project that was dismissed with typically modernist scorn by Ol'ga Rozanova as 'plagiarism of nature'), or the Horatian definition, *ut pictura poesis*.[12] As traditional narrative was dethroned in literary texts, and painters became involved in performance (such as the notorious experiments of Goncharova and Larionov in face-painting) the traditional division between literature as temporally defined and art as spatially defined began to be eroded.[13] Nor should one forget the importance of artistic cross-fertilisation in modernist literary theory: the terminology applied to compositional principles in painting, cinema and music began to be used as the basis of Russian Formalists' innovative and rigorous discussions of literary texts in terms of 'viewpoint' (*tochka zreniia*), 'dominant' (*dominanta*) and 'facture' (*faktura*), while later on the performance arts inspired Mikhail Bakhtin's brilliant contextualisations of literary strategies via the concept of 'carnival' in *Tvorchestvo Fransua Rable* (Rabelais's World, 1965). The application of terms originating in the criticism of other arts to literary texts could not but heighten the convergence of artistic principles between visual and verbal texts.

In a sense, then, the modernist movement can be seen as an era at which the preference manifested in nineteenth-century Russian culture for the word over the visual image was swept away. No doubt partly because of the predominance of the visual image in religious culture, on the one hand, and because of the Enlightenment's assertion of the primacy of the verbal on the other,[14] the secular intelligentsia that began emerging in the 1840s had regarded painting as an inferior art form. The Peredvizhniki (Wanderer) movement that emerged in the 1860s was an attempt by painters to lay claim to the high seriousness and the political and moral commitment of literary realism, to a tradition defined by Belinskii as the 'expression of ideas'. As Igor Golomstock has argued, the literariness of Russian landscape painting in the second half of the nineteenth century was evident not only in its choice of subjects (with, for example, Shishkin's paintings of fields and woods recalling the lyrical scenes in Turgenev's novels), but also in its intonation, its preference for the intuitive colour-world as seen by an eye uneducated in landscape painting over the counter-intuitive world of a close observer of nature.[15] An outstandingly gifted example of such a close observer, Vladimir Nabokov, was later to provide his American annotator, Alfred Appel, with a useful tutorial in how to see in the new way. When Appel, following Humbert Humbert's temporary mistress Rita, queried a line in Humbert's 'wistful French ballad', 'a very / blood bath of trees before the blue hotel', with the question, 'Why blue when it is white, why blue for heaven's sake?', Nabokov explained, 'What Rita does not understand is that a white surface, the chalk of that hotel, does look blue in a wash of light and shade on a vivid fall day, amid red foliage. H.H. is merely paying a tribute to French impressionist painters.'[16] In contrast, the paintings of even the most talented Russian realists, Repin and Levitan, evoke the russets, duns, chocolate browns, sandy yellows and sere beiges that harmonise with a lay person's perception of the steppe landscape.

Yet if the modernist era saw painting break from the tyranny of commonsensical observation, and literature in turn absorbing the insights of painting, it also saw something of a backlash on the part of writers against the visual, a contradictory assertion of the uniqueness of literature, its independence from art and music. For some modernist writers, any painting was too literal compared with the cerebral world of verbal creation. Innokentii Annenskii, for example, wrote in 'Chto takoe poeziia?' (What is Poetry?):

A poet does not create images: he presents problems that resound down the centuries. A vast gulf lies between Dante's Beatrice and Fra Beato's Madonna of the Stars, for all the similarity of the concepts that inspired them. Have you ever pondered the question of why it is impossible to illustrate poetry? Of course, Botticelli's pencil drawings are far more interesting than Gustave Doré's luxurious banalities, every one of which has the same tempest raging in the background. But even in the exaggeratedly stern lines of the quattrocentista we see not so much Dante as Botticelli's love for Dante. And if Dante Gabriel Rossetti himself had tried to capture Ophelia for us with his brush, though he might make you succumb to the enchantment of his vision, would he really stop you from taking offence on account of that eternal Ophelia who can exist only symbolically, in the immortal illusion of words?[17]

It was not only painting, but also performance, which excited suspicion. The emphasis in Russian realism on the ideal, on literature as the expression of a possible as well as (or sometimes rather than) a plausible world meant that the direct audience response to which theatrical performance exposed itself was seen as constraining rather than enabling. Twelve years after Griboedov had lamented 'the fussy suit of clothes' – that is, the dramatic form – in which he had been forced to dress the 'magnificent' idea behind his comedy of Moscow manners, *Gore ot uma* (*Woe from Wit*, 1824),[18] Gogol had the anti-hero of his play *Revizor* turn to the audience and denounce them for their delight in the spectacle with the famous line, 'Why are you laughing? You are laughing at yourselves.' A similarly coercive attitude to the audience (inimical to the spirit of the traditional theatre, with its emphasis on audience collaboration) is evident in Meierkhol'd's productions of the 1920s, with their hortatory banners and restructuring of the stage as a tribunal. And, as Barbara Henry reminds us in her study of the concept of 'theatricality' in modernist culture, the modern movement in Russia was not entirely free of the hostility to spectacle which had char-acterised puritan sensibilities since the Middle Ages. Even after 1905, when Symbolists and post-Symbolists alike became interested in the theatre as a means of reaching a broader audience, tension between poetry and performance remained. Meierkhol'd's 1906 production of Blok's *Balaganchik* (The Little Fairground Booth) was controversial for the freedoms that it took with the original text, as were the same director's later adaptations of Gogol and Griboedov.[19] It is signifi-cant that some of the most successful modernist theatrical spectacles were wordless (for example, the Stravinsky–Benois *Petrouchka*) and that cases where writers employed the dialogue form for plays that were never intended to be staged were far from unknown (a case in point being Gumilev's neo-classical drama *Actaeon*).[20]

The essays in this collection accordingly deal not only with

harmonious co-creation, the fusion of artistic resources, but also
with tension; with the reinforcement of boundaries as well as with
challenges to these. Such areas of conflict are reflected in numerous
studies of the 'sister arts' in European culture. In recent decades, the
anti-syncretic orthodoxy, with its resistance to 'interart' perspectives,
has been challenged by structuralism, semiotics and intertextuality –
new approaches which tend to treat a culture broadly as one large
field of meanings where no *essential* difference between verbal and
visual art forms can be discerned.[21] That is not, of course, to say
that distinctions cannot be made between the verbal and the visual,
or that there is any generalisable method for analysing the shared
cultural code within which (let us assume) literature and the visual
arts operate. As many works on European literature and art have
shown, the most rewarding method of investigating this relationship
is to study the ways in which the boundary between the verbal and
the visual is drawn and redrawn in a particular culture of a
particular era. On the level of close formal analysis, much has been
done to interrogate – and in large part to undermine – the
privileging of the literary and the temporal over the visual and
spatial in literary and art criticism, and in cultural theory more
generally.[22]

This book does not claim to make a major new contribution to the
above theoretical debates. But it undoubtedly draws on the insights
they have generated, assuming, first, that 'interart' investigations of a
culture must cast their imaginative net wide, to include not only
studies of adaptations (the reworking of a text from one medium in
another), but also artistic affinities and cross-fertilisation more
generally; second, that attempts to demonstrate the superiority, or
indeed inferiority, of verbal media to visual forms of representation
deserve cultural–historical deconstruction rather than intellectual
credence; and, third, that artistic inter-relationships are profitably
regarded as demonstrations of the dynamic relationships between
genres, as manifestations of intertextuality.

In the first section of the book, 'The Arts Reflected in Literature',
our contributors examine how Russian literature of the modernist
era reflects the visual and performance arts. Konstantin Barsht's
essay, 'Defining the face: observations on Dostoevskii's creative
processes', analyses the importance of painting in the work of a
writer who was seen by many important Russian modernists (among
them Viacheslav Ivanov, Innokentii Annenskii, Anna Akhmatova,

Dmitrii Merezhkovskii, Zinaida Gippius, and not least Mikhail Bakhtin) as ancestor and inspiration. In his pioneering analysis of the sketches with which Dostoevskii adorned the manuscripts of his fiction, Barsht shows that for Dostoevskii, drawing was an embodiment of the verbal text, an essential parallel to and expression of the compositional instinct. (One might contrast the significance of illustration for Pushkin, for whom 'doodling' and 'scribbling', to evoke the poet's own ironically self-deprecatory terminology, were complementary rather than intimately associated forms: to quote *Evgenii Onegin*:

> Пишу, и сердце не тоскует,
> Перо в забытьи не рисует
> Близ неоконченных стихов
> Ни женских ножек, ни голов.

> [I write and my heart no longer feels anguish,
> My pen does not draw in forgetfulness
> Next to the unfinished verses
> Women's little feet or women's heads.][23])

But Barsht goes further than simply pointing out the relevance of Dostoevskii's doodles to the progress of his literary composition. He also sets out a wide-ranging and extremely thought-provoking analysis of Dostoevskii's interest in the visual arts (which is clear, for example, in his travel writings), and of the visual domain in Dostoevskii's fiction. He deals not only with the citation of paintings (a famous example is Holbein's *Crucifixion*, which plays a pivotal role in *The Idiot*), but also with the ways in which Dostoevskii's handling of the visual differs from classic realism. Barsht suggests that Dostoevskii's characters are *liki* (a term borrowed from Orthodox theology) rather than types; their physical features are intended not so much to be mimetically suggestive as to reflect a psychological and metaphysical existence beyond the obvious. It was this aspect of Dostoevskii's art which was to prove attractive to such visually rich Russian modernist writers of a later generation as Andrei Belyi, above all in his great novel *Peterburg* (St Petersburg).

The next essay, Catriona Kelly's 'Painting and autobiography: Anna Prismanova's *Pesok* and Anna Akhmatova's *Epicheskie motivy*', examines a number of different areas in the relationship between modernist poetry and the visual arts. These include the circulation of portraits of poets, and the way that these established a canonical view of the modernist poet's physical appearance; the importance, for marginal figures in the modernist movement, of painting as a mediating source for methods of representing biographical realia not hallowed in literary tradition; and the relationship between cubist painting and visual punning in modernist poetry. The essay examines two contrasting approaches to self-portraits in verse, as manifested in Anna Akhmatova's *Epicheskie motivy* and Anna Prismanova's *Pesok*. Born, unlike Akhmatova, in a town that had not captured the mind of earlier writers, and so did not allow her access to the poetic topoi that were available to Akhmatova writing of St Petersburg, and without Akhmatova's reputation as a famous beauty, Prismanova did not see painting as the mere material of poetry. Instead, she employed references to, and artistic methods taken from, the contemporary arts in order to break with the constraints of the acmeist aesthetic which dominated the émigré literary circles in which she moved, and to find an original and effective way of representing a landscape that had been a blank space in Russian literary culture: the Baltic coast.

If Prismanova's *Pesok* (first published in 1946) is an illustration of how the impact of the modernist movement was felt in émigré Russian culture well beyond the 1920s, the next essay deals with the revival of Russian Modernism in the Soviet Union after Stalin's death. During the early 1960s, modernist trends in literature and the visual arts, for many years treated as highly disreputable, were rehabilitated (albeit partially and temporarily). One of the more prominent figures in this revival was Andrei Siniavskii, a writer for whom the visual arts were always vital to literary enterprises. As Jane Grayson shows in her essay, this special relationship of the visual and the verbal, as reflected notably in imagery and metaphor, is a structuring principle of much of Siniavskii's work. For Siniavskii, art always presents reality filtered through a particular human consciousness, or, to put it another way, reality 'seen' through a particular pair of human eyes. This 'situated' quality, in Siniavskii's view, gives art an ethical as well as a human charge – but it is also connected to a specifically modernist subjectivity, an emphasis on the breakdown of totalising views (omniscience), a rebellion against the socialist realist myth of a unified nation and unified viewing-point.

Not only painting, but performance, was crucial to literary representations in the modernist era. Alexander Zholkovsky's study of Zoshchenko's 'Monter' (The Electrician) and 'El'vira', 'Mikhail

Zoshchenko's Shadow Operas', illustrates that this writer, often read 'sociologically' as a depictor of *homo sovieticus* in the making, and of early Soviet *byt* (daily life/private life), was in fact a sophisticated modernist whose literary representations of theatrical spectacle make 'the problems of the self's fluid boundaries, author's/character's masks, and role-playing take centre stage'. Zholkovsky shows that Zoshchenko's apparently inconsequential tales of a recalcitrant electrician and an importunate singer emerge, once their dense allusiveness is appreciated, as parallel masterpieces of complex intertextual play. Operatic texts – Mozart's *Don Giovanni*, Glinka's *Ruslan and Liudmila* – are intertwined with autocitation and the employment of archetypal 'Zoshchenkovian' themes, so that in the end Zoshchenko's dissimulating 'performances' can be seen as revealing much not only about his literary methods, but also about how performance texts supply 'scripts, roles, and masks for [the] aggressive–defensive dissimulation' of Zoshchenko's protagonists, and in turn for the author's own psychological preoccupations.

The second part of the book, 'Adaptations, collaborations, disputes, rapprochements' takes a rather different focus from the first, addressing relationships between literature and other art forms rather than portrayals of those art forms in the literary text. Some contributions explore ways in which artists working in different media have attempted to overcome the borderlines between different art forms. Barbara Henry's chapter, ' "Theatricality" as a Concept in the Russian Modernist Movement' begins by surveying the ways in which Russian theatre of the early twentieth century was heir to the long tradition of suspicion of 'spectacle' in literary culture. However, she also shows that literary parody was a case where theatre sometimes exacted revenge on literature for this history of prejudice. The central section of her essay, based on unpublished original scripts and scenarios, is a case-study of one of the most important artistic cabarets in St Petersburg, the 'Krivoe Zerkalo' (Crooked Mirror), whose repertoire made an especial feature of satirical representations of fashionable literary texts, as well as of meta-theatrical performances.

In 'Design on Drama: V. A. Simov and Chekhov' Cynthia Marsh analyses an important and often neglected element of the Moscow Arts Theatre productions of Chekhov's plays: the set designs of V. A. Simov. Drawing on Mikhail Bakhtin's concept of the 'chronotope', Marsh shows that the course of Chekhov's work with the Moscow

Arts Theatre 'displays [his] increasing awareness of the stage chronotope', as opposed to the chronotope of narrative fiction, a process generating in its turn 'a striking unmasking of the authenticity implied by the realist/naturalist style of theatre, core to the work of MAT'. Fundamental to this process was Chekhov's engagement – sometimes an irritable engagement – with the work of Simov, whose stagings of the plays prompted Chekhov to address the performative aspects of drama with growing clarity and urgency.

If Chekhov could be described as a writer who evolved into a modernist, Velimir Khlebnikov spent his entire career as a member – indeed, perhaps the most genuinely colourful member – of the Russian avant-garde. Robin Milner-Gulland's chapter, 'Khlebnikov's eye' is an overview of the visual concerns in the work of a poet popularly (and rather misleadingly) famed above all for his contributions to sound poetry, *zaum'*. Alongside an account of the extraordinarily rich presence of visual elements in Khlebnikov's own writing – from sketches to visual tropes, from the evocation of sculpture and visonary architecture to the use of hieroglyphics and portraits in letters of the alphabet – this essay is a sketch of the poet's associations with modernist painters, in particular Kazimir Malevich, Pavel Filonov and Vladimir Tatlin. These close and warm relations between like-minded artists not only produced some of the most remarkable illustrated books of the modernist era, but also (particularly in the case of Khlebnikov and Tatlin) had creative effects on both sides – in Khlebnikov's remarkable tribute to Tatlin on the one hand, in a debt to Khlebnikov for the germ of the idea that led to Tatlin's famous Monument to the Third International on the other. The essay ends by considering the central role played in Khlebnikov's work by 'eye' in another sense: the word *oko*, central to his symbolic and verbal system.

A collaboration of a rather different kind is analysed in Milena Michalski's study, 'Cinematic literature and literary cinema: Olesha, Room and the search for a new art form'. Michalski begins with an analysis of the 'cinematic' qualities in Olesha's fiction, manifested in particular by the employment of lighting effects in his fiction and essays. However, she goes on to show how the citation of cinematic texts as a literary strategy did not prove a good practical preparation for Olesha's work on the 1930s film *Strogii iunosha* (A Strict Youth), since 'the cinematic' could not be evoked in the same manner within a filmic text, where it was the 'given' narrative mode rather than marked as 'other'. Rather, the film's brilliantly adventurous cinematography (a factor in its suppression when Socialist Realism again asserted the hegemony of the verbal text that had been questioned by Modernism) was derived from the ability of Olesha's collaborator, Abram Room, to translate Olesha's ideas into specific techniques and images.

The discussions of Khlebnikov, Chekhov and Olesha concern historically documented instances of cross-fertilising relationships between writers and other artists. Andrew Wachtel, on the other hand, in 'Meaningful Voids: Facelessness in Platonov and Malevich', presents an imaginative, rather than a biographical, comparison of an important writer and painter, both of whom are often represented as having embraced more 'traditional' modes of representation during the rise of Socialist Realism. Wachtel suggests that there are, in fact, more interesting resemblances between the two, and, more particularly, that they are allied in their eerie insistence on human presence as absence. Wachtel fruitfully relates discussion of these two Russian cases of 'faceless' representation to general tendencies in international Modernism, evoking parallels in, for example, the work of Matisse and Picasso, though he also suggests the very different resonance that such representations could have in the context of changing cultural politics in the late 1920s and early 1930s.

Similar to Wachtel's essay in its emphasis on imaginative affinities is Pamela Chester's 'Painted mirrors: landscape and self-representation in women's verbal and visual art'. Chester argues that the landscapes of two pivotal women modernists, Tsvetaeva and Goncharova, may be interpreted not only in terms of their relationship to the formal preferences of Modernism, but also as inheritors of a tradition established by nineteenth-century women painters and writers. A crucial factor is the 'anti-Edenic' character of these landscapes, a character evident in the work of, for example, the mid-nineteenth-century realist writer Evgeniia Tur, and the painter Mariia Bashkirtseva, but not in the work of their male contemporaries, such as Savrasov and Shishkin. Chester traces this 'anti-Edenic' tradition through pre-modernist painters such as Iakunchikova (whose work again contrasts with that of male contemporaries such as Levitan and Polenov) up to the modernist era. She argues that Tsvetaeva and Goncharova's 'sense of their ambiguous femininity, of the constraints as well as the rewards of this constricted domain, shapes their representation of a space physically narrow but opening into other, non-material worlds'. The essay suggests that in some cultural contexts affinities of gender may be more significant than the medium of expression selected by a creative artist; however, avoiding any facile polarisation of 'masculine' and 'feminine' painting, it also emphasises that the modernist era offered women, including Tsvetaeva and Goncharova, a chance to move away from 'feminine' tradition as well as embracing this.[24]

Between them, the essays here cover over a century of literary history, from the pre-modernism of Dostoevskii in the 1860s and 1870s to the 1960s revival of Modernism, with its rediscovery of artistic principles buried, if not abandoned, in the face of Socialist Realism. The wide time-span covered has allowed us to test the boundaries of the artistic direction known as Modernism as well as relations between the arts in the modern era. The case of Dostoevskii, as we argued earlier, raises the question of how far Russian realism ever was a form of mimetic and detail-saturated 'classic realism' as defined by Barthes. It has become customary to trace the hegemony of Socialist Realism to the utilitarian theories of nineteenth-century radical critics such as Belinskii, Chernyshevskii and Pisarev,[25] but it might be just as valid to explore the ancestry of Russian Modernism in the nineteenth century as well, to explore the pre-history of fragmentary modes of composition such as montage and bricolage in the episodic structure of nineteenth-century novels, for example Goncharov's *Oblomov*. It must, moreover, be acknowledged that musical and spatial structuring principles made an incursion into Russian literature well before Belyi's *Peterburg*.[26] Yet at the same time, the discussions in this book indicate that Modernism did represent a break with the nineteenth-century past in terms of an at least partial re-establishment of the dignity of visual imagery and of performance, reduced to marginal status in post-1840 Russian culture: as in medieval Russian culture and in the Russian Baroque, verbal and visual texts now had a productive, often rather complex and far from hierarchical relationship.[27]

However, the 'shock of the new' that Modernism brought cannot be understood simply in terms of a revival of the pre-Petrine past, any more than it can in terms of mere imitation of Western modernist practices. If the overcoming of boundaries that is the most striking feature of Russian Modernism is related to the determination of many artists to live life 'beyond barriers', the tensions between different art forms which this book lays bare can be related to other important conflicts in the Russian modernist movement: most particularly, perhaps, to the debates over the division between 'art' and 'life' that one recent commentator, Stephen Hutchings, has seen as particularly characteristic of Modernism in its Russian variant. If Western Modernism 'counts as among the last-ditch attempts to shore up representationalism and stave off the abyss; a world torn loose from its moorings, hopelessly stranded on an ocean of pure signification', Russian Modernism was especially characterised by the employment of what Hutchings himself has termed 'the verbal icon', a sign that attempts to fuse 'art' and 'daily life', rather than simply mediating between these. The result is that 'Russian turn of the century fiction aims to supplant the West's alienated representations of the everyday with its individualized icons of the ordinary.' According to this interpretation, trends as different as Viacheslav Ivanov's mystical anarchism and 1920s Constructivism have in common their desire to unite art and reality, to inscribe upon reality a meaning that can be derived only from artistic form. But the underlying foundation of Russian Modernism was itself friable, and not only because of the incursion of Western trends that Hutchings himself acknowledges.[28] For example, the functionalism that was essential to constructivist models of reality had only distant and inexact analogues in the world of writing: a memoir may pretend to documentary reality, but it cannot be 'used' in the same way that Rodchenko's library chairs may be. In this way, even the forces that pushed hardest towards integration within the modernist movement were themselves pushed apart again: the frustration of the desire to unite different art forms (apparently a less ambitious one than the desire to unify art and life) became a demonstration of the modernist movement's entropy, its condemnation to that very abyss that it had sought to avert.

As the different contributions to this book show, fusion and the frustration of fusion were equally characteristic of modernist cross-art collaborations. The writings of Iurii Tynianov, one of the most original and fertile minds of the modernist period, help to explain why this should be so. In a 1923 article on illustrations to literary texts, he noted the 'vulgarity' (*poshlost'*) of any attempt to visualise characters from, say, a Gogol story. The extreme 'concreteness' of Gogol's depictions, he observed, makes some readers imagine that visual art must be able to offer a corresponding, satisfyingly illustrative concreteness; but this is a false assumption. In reality, verbal art escapes realisation in visual form:

you feel that speech is leading you to gestures, and that gestures can lead you to an almost tangible physical appearance [*oblik*], but this tangibility is elusive, it is concentrated in articulated speech, as if it's there on the end of your lips – and slips away as soon as you try to pin the character down [visually].[29]

In a slightly later article, Tynianov defended the aesthetic autonomy of the cinema in similar terms: for him, attempts to define cinema in terms of other art forms were just as absurd as defining painting as 'immobile cinema'. Uncharacteristically, he even went so far as to issue a negative prescription for the future development of the newest art form: for 'silent' cinema to acquire speech would result in a 'mongrel cross-breed of theatre and cinema, a pathetic compromise'.[30]

With hindsight, we can see that Tynianov was quite wrong about this last point.[31] But he, better than anyone else, should have understood why he was likely to be proved wrong – why it is that the boundaries between art forms, although they surely exist, are far from immutable. In much of his writing he drew attention to the ways in which 'material' and 'constructive principles' from one genre or art form could be reappropriated and re-marked in another. In the article on illustrations, for example, he noted the continuing sequence of 'rapprochements and divergences' in the historical relations of the different arts.[32] As Tynianov well understood, to examine the relationship between literature and the other arts is to expose onself to the temptation of casual, allusive homologising, yet it is also to investigate an enduringly dynamic and creative factor in cultural history. To elaborate this point, here, finally, we quote one of the most fertile minds of the decades *following* the modernist era:

One must not imagine the realm of culture as some sort of spatial whole, with boundaries but also with internal territory. The realm of culture has no internal territory. It is distributed entirely along the boundaries: boundaries pass everywhere, through its every aspect, the systematic unity of a culture extends into the very atoms of cultural life, it reflects like the sun in each drop of that life. Every cultural act lives essentially on the boundaries: in this is its seriousness and its significance; abstracted from boundaries, it loses its native soil, it becomes empty, arrogant, it degenerates and dies.[33]

NOTES

1 See for example A. Ripellino, *Majakovski et le théâtre russe d'avant-garde* (Paris, 1965); B. Jangfeldt, *Majakovskij and Futurism, 1917–1921* (Stockholm, 1977); J. R. Stapanian, *Mayakovsky's Cubo-Futurist Vision* (Houston, 1986); Christopher Barnes, *Boris Pasternak: A Literary Biography: Volume 1 1890–1928* (Cambridge, 1989).

2 Marina Tsvetaeva, 'Vskryla zhily', *Stikhotvoreniia i poemy* (Leningrad, 1990), p. 436.

3 Boris Pasternak, 'Gorod', *Stikhotvoreniia i poemy* (Moscow, 1965), p. 217.

4 See R. Davies in his edition of Leonid Andreev's photographs, *Leonid Andreyev: Photographs by a Russian Writer* (London, 1989), p. 10.

5 For Nabokov, of course, synaesthesia was more than just an artistic strategy; as the writer records in *Speak, Memory* (Harmondsworth, 1969), p. 29, 'colored hearing' was a sensation to which he was innately subject. However, the fact remains that a Nabokov born a century earlier would not have found so ready an expression for his synaesthetic powers as he did in the early twentieth century.

6 See Rosamund Bartlett, *Wagner in Russian Culture* (Cambridge, 1994).

7 O. Rozanova, 'Osnovy novogo tvorchestva i prichiny ego neponimaniia', *Soiuz molodezhi* 1 (1913), reprinted in V. Markov (ed.), *Manifesty i programmy russkikh futuristov* (Munich, 1972), 168–72; M. Voloshin, 'Oslinyi khvost', *Apollon* 7 (1912), reprinted in Voloshin, *Liki tvorchestva* (Leningrad, 1988), p. 288. An extract from the text appears in Catriona Kelly (ed.), *Utopias: Russian Modernist Texts 1905–1940* (London, 1999).

8 See G. Janecek, *The Look of Russian Literature: Avant-Garde Visual Experiments 1900–1930* (Princeton, NJ, 1984); S. Compton, *The World Backwards: Russian Futurist Books 1912–16* (London, 1978) and *Russian Avant-Garde Books 1917–34* (London, 1992). The preference for *zaum'* (transrational language) among some of the Russian Futurists (notably Kruchenykh) was a further contribution to the fusion, yet also to the differentiation, of the arts, since it assaulted not only the referentiality of language, but also the traditional subordination of language to conventionalised figuration, in which the visual element of a letter is taken as a given. *Zaum'* cannot be effortlessly decoded; it can only be recited aloud or, alternatively, admired as a pure visual image for its graphic qualities.

9 See the set photograph in K. Rudnitsky, *Russian and Soviet Theatre* (London, 1988), p. 134.

10 Performance photographs appear in Rudnitsky, *Russian and Soviet Theatre*, pp. 125–6, and also in R. Fülöp-Miller and P. Gregor, *The Russian Theatre: Its Character and History* (London, 1930), figs. 364–9. See also E. Braun, *Meyerhold: A Revolution in Theatre* (London, 1995).

11 See especially Yury Tsivian's brilliant discussion of this topic in *Early Cinema in Russia and Its Cultural Reception*, trans. A. Bodger (London, 1994).

12 Rozanova, 'Osnovy', p. 169. A study dealing with ekphrasis in the context of nineteenth-century Russian literature is A. Mandelker, *Framing Anna Karenina: Tolstoy, the Woman Question, and the Victorian Novel* (Columbus, Ohio, 1993).

13 The classic analysis of the division between 'spatial' visual arts and 'temporal' verbal arts (poetry) is Gottfried Lessing's *Laokoon, oder über die Grenzen der Malerei und Poesie* (1766). On modernist face-painting, see J. Bowlt, 'Body Beautiful: The Artistic Search for the Perfect Physique', in J. Bowlt and O. Matich (eds.), *The Laboratory of Dreams: The Russian Avant-Garde and Cultural Experiment* (Stanford, 1996), pp. 52–4.

14 It should be remembered that Lessing not only defined the 'boundaries' between painting and poetry, he also regarded poetry as superior to the visual arts thanks to its much greater proximity to the sphere of ideal meanings (its spirituality, or Geistigkeit). Here he was blazing an intellectual trail that would have enormous influence on nineteenth-century aesthetics – and perhaps nowhere more so than in Russia. For more detail on Lessing's 'metasemiotic', see David E. Wellbery, *Lessing's Laocoon: Semiotics and Aesthetics in the Age of Reason* (Cambridge, 1984), esp. pp. 228–47.

15 Golomstock made these observations in an informal talk given in the series 'Russian Literature and the Other Arts' at SSEES, Spring 1996. Our discussion here ignores the question of the extent to which Russian realism was itself mimetic in intention or effect, on which see more below.

16 V. Nabokov, *The Annotated Lolita*, ed. Alfred Appel Jr. (London, 1995), p. 437 (n. 3 to p. 263).

17 I. Annenskii, 'Chto takoe poeziia?', *Knigi otrazhenii* (Leningrad, 1979), p. 205.

18 A. Griboedov, 'Po povodu "Goria ot uma"' (c. 1824), *Sochineniia v stikhakh* (Leningrad, 1987), p. 387. See also Barbara Henry's comments on Griboedov's note in her essay below.

19 On *Balaganchik* see, for example, J. Douglas Clayton, *Pierrot in Petrograd: The Commedia dell'arte/balagan in Twentieth-Century Russian Theatre and Drama* (Montreal, 1994).

20 N. Gumilev, *Akteon, Sobranie sochinenii* vol. III (Washington, 1966), pp. 28–32; see also M. Basker, 'Gumilev's *Akteon*: a forgotten manifesto of Acmeism', *Slavonic and East European Review* 63 (1985), 498–517.

21 Note for example W. J. T. Mitchell, 'Going Too Far with the Sister Arts', in James A. W. Heffernan (ed.), *Space, Time, Image, Sign: Essays on Literature and the Visual Arts* (New York, 1987), pp. 1–11. Similar ground is covered less controversially, but also less incisively, in Ulrich Weisstein, 'Literature and the (Visual) Arts: Intertextuality and Mutual Illumination', in I. Hoesterey and U. Weisstein, *Intertextuality: German Literature and Visual Art from the Renaissance to the Twentieth Century* (Columbia, SC), pp. 1–17. Mario Praz's *Mnemosyne: The Parallel Between Literature and the*

Visual Arts (Princeton, 1970) is, as its title implies, one of the more ambitious attempts to argue the connection between verbal and visual arts: see esp. ch. 7, on 'spatial and temporal interpenetration' in the modernist period. For much fuller listings, see 'A Bibliography on the Relations between Literature and the Other Arts' (founded in 1952 under the auspices of the Modern Language Association of America).

22 For a robust refutation of 'the implied primacy of the literary' among critics dealing with the visual arts, applied to the case of filmic adaptations of literary texts, see B. McFarlane, *Novel to Film: An Introduction to the Theory of Adaptation* (Oxford, 1990). The literature on 'space' in the humanities and social sciences is now vast: for a polemical critique of the marginalisation of 'spatiality' by 'temporality' in Western thought since Lessing, see E. Soja, *Postmodern Geographies: The Reassertion of Space in Critical Social Theory* (London, 1985), esp. ch. 1.

23 Pushkin, *Evgenii Onegin* chapter 1, stanza 59, lines 5 to 8, *Polnoe sobranie sochinenii* vol. VI (Leningrad, 1937), p. 30.

24 Chester's essay is also an important corrective to the general neglect of the visual in Tsvetaeva's work, and according lack of interest in her important memoir of the painter Nataliia Goncharova. Viktoria Schweitzer, for example, argues that 'Tsvetaeva was an aural rather than a visual person, and she was indifferent to the visual arts' (see *Tsvetaeva*, trans. Robert Chandler and H. T. Willetts, ed. Angela Livingstone (London, 1992), p. 301). Yet Tsvetaeva's study contains sophisticated readings of such paintings as *The Haymakers* and *The Vintage*, as well as an attempt to site Goncharova's work in the history of twentieth-century painting, the occasional errors in which are traceable to her reliance on the dubious testimony of Goncharova's partner, Mikhail Larionov.

25 See for example Régine Robin, *Socialist Realism: An Impossible Aesthetic*, trans. C. Porter (Stanford, 1992).

26 Note here the work of the 'Moscow semiotic circle', for example T. V. Tsiv'ian, 'O strukture vremeni i prostranstva v romane *Podrostok*', in T. M. Nikolaeva (comp.), *Iz rabot moskovskogo semioticheskogo kruga* (Moscow, 1997), pp. 661–706. Tsiv'ian argues convincingly that Dostoevskii's novels are characterised by their 'recursiveness', as opposed to the linear 'discursiveness' that is commonly attributed to the nineteenth-century novel.

27 On the homology of medieval writing and painting, see particularly the famous and influential studies of D. S. Likhachev, such as *Poetika drevnerusskoi literatury* (3rd edn, Moscow, 1979), ch. 1, and *Chelovek v literature drevnei Rusi* (Moscow, 1958). As Dimitri Obolensky points out in 'Medieval Russian culture in the writings of D. S. Likhachev', Oxford Slavonic Papers 9 (1976), 13, Likhachev's comparisons of verbal and visual suffer from a certain impressionism and lack of specificity; one could add that visual materials were cited by Likhachev above all as a

didactic strategy (because icons were more familiar to the non-specialist reader anticipated by him than were hagiographies). The use of the known as analogy for the unknown inevitably provoked him to give little attention to features differentiating verbal and visual in medieval culture, for example, the existence of a theological tradition emphasising mystic experience that cannot be captured in ordinary articulate speech. To the extent that Likhachev's 'homology' did obtain in medieval Russian culture, however, it was undermined from the mid-seventeenth century onwards, when visual and verbal cultures began to diverge with secularisation: the emerging non-religious visual culture emphasised the portrait – that is, the secular icon – while narrative gained prominence in the new prose forms. But for all that a strong link between the verbal and the visual persisted through emblematism (that is, the use of common symbols across different forms of cultural expression). The late seventeenth century has, not without reason, been called the period of 'Russia's belated "Renaissance"'. See Lindsey Hughes, *Sophia, Regent of Russia 1657–1704* (New Haven and London), esp. ch. 7 (this quote on p. 178). The significance of European post-Renaissance influence following Tsar Aleksei Mikhailovich's Polish adventures in the 1650s is explained in Lydia Sazonova's introduction to Simeon Polotskii, *Vertograd mnogotsvetnyi*, ed. Anthony Hippisley and Lydia I. Sazonova (Cologne, 1996).

28 Stephen C. Hutchings, *Russian Modernism: The Transfiguration of the Everyday* (Cambridge, 1997), *passim*: the passages quoted are on pp. 228 and 230.

29 Iu. N. Tynianov, 'Illiustratsii', in idem, *Arkhaisty i novatory* (Leningrad, 1929), pp. 503–4. (This comment refers specifically to Leskov, but it has more general import.)

30 Iu. N. Tynianov, 'Kino – slovo – myzyka' (1924), in idem, *Poetika. Istoriia literatury. Kino* (Moscow, 1977), p. 322.

31 Contrast the line taken here by Tynianov with Eisenstein's later writings on montage (see *The Film Sense* (London, 1968), chs. 2 and 4), which present sound cinema not as a compromise, but as a synthesis of verbal, visual and musical: Eisenstein sees the soundtrack as counterpointing and challenging the visual representations.

32 Tynianov, 'Illiustratsii', p. 509.

33 Mikhail Bakhtin, 'Problema soderzhaniia, materiala i formy v slovesnom khudozhestvennom tvorchestve', in *Voprosy literatury i estetiki* (Moscow, 1975), p. 25. This passage is also quoted in the finale to Caryl Emerson's *Boris Godunov: Transpositions of a Russian Theme* (Bloomington and Indianapolis, 1986), pp. 210–11, but bears repeating here because the point made is so important.

PART I

The arts reflected in literature

CHAPTER I

Defining the face: observations on Dostoevskii's creative processes

Konstantin A. Barsht

The visual aspects of Dostoevskii's creation have often been neglected in critical writings. This is partly because of the post-Bakhtinian emphasis on multiplicity of voicing and instability of meaning in Dostoevskii, and partly because the conventional polarisation between Tolstoi and Dostoevskii as opposites has meant that 'spectacularity' in Dostoevskii has been associated above all with the dramatic force of his fiction (as opposed to the obviously 'visual' qualities of Tolstoi's). Yet Dostoevskii's diaries and manuscripts reveal that the visual arts were extremely important for the writer both as consumer and as practitioner; while references to paintings and to visual representations have a pivotal role in his works. More generally, a familiarity with Dostoevskii's interest in the visual, and with the iconic aspects of his imagination, is vital to interpretation of his fiction, as will be demonstrated here.

ENVISAGING THE HUMAN PERSONALITY: DOSTOEVSKII AND THE *LIK*

For Dostoevskii, the writer's main task was to create a 'face' that expressed an 'idea'. This 'personalised image of the idea', or *lik*, comes to take a central place in his aesthetic credo; it was with it in mind that he created the heroes of his own works and assessed the literary characters of other writers. For Dostoevskii the supreme value was not simply 'human life' in any form, but the 'human facial image' (*chelovecheskii lik*) in particular, its quality of single and unrepeatable individuality: the unity, in other words, of the internal (the 'idea') and the external (the face) in man – the unity of the facial image (*lik*). 'A man's face is the image of his personality, his spirit, his human worth.'[1] These words of Dostoevskii could stand as an epigraph to any of the portraits he created, be they literary or visual.

Each of the writer's works is in essence composed of a number of portraits drawn by literary means, a number of 'faces' facing each other, each one fronting its own 'idea'. Contemporaries of Dostoevskii felt this more acutely than the modern reader: they saw *The Brothers Karamazov*, for example, as a 'whole little gallery of family portraits'.[2] The scope of this practice is all-encompassing: Dostoevskii was constantly turning over in his imagination the images (*liki*) of various ideas, even when he was examining the works of professional painters.

In his comments on the face of Christ in Ge's painting *Tainaia vecheria* (The Last Supper) Dostoevskii noted that 'Titian . . . would have given this Teacher a face like the one he gave him in his famous picture "Render Unto Caesar"; then many things would have become clear at once.'[3] Although in this particular case Dostoevskii is talking about painting, as he 'fits' an image created by Titian to a subject depicted by Ge, he viewed not only painted portraits but also the faces of the people around him in exactly the same way. Gazing intently at faces was one of the writer's favourite activities and formed an important part of his creative processes. Prefacing a whole series of street sketches drawn 'from nature' in his 'Little Pictures' (*A Writer's Diary*, 1873), Dostoevskii states quite clearly how they were done: 'When I wander about the streets I enjoy examining certain total strangers, studying their faces and trying to guess who they are, how they live, what they work at, and what is in their minds at this particular moment.'[4] He immediately offers the portrait of an artisan and his apprentice as a practical example of this 'gazing' and 'divining': in the character's face the writer sees his life, his personal tragedy, his personality. In the way he perceived reality Dostoevskii was uniquely close to a painter: he tried to grasp the essence, spirit and 'idea' of a man through his external features, his face; he always conceptualised the object of his attention from two points of view – both as something universally human, typical of everyone, and as something profoundly original and unusual. The crucial factor in this 'image-ining' (*obrazhenie*) of man is the portrait painter's ability to look deeply into a face and read it like an open book. In essence, this is also the work of a physiognomist, who employs a particular method to divine the secrets of the human personality that are somehow concealed in the features and expression of a face. Dostoevskii was no less preoccupied than any portrait painter by the relationship between human character and its embodiment in portraits. The greatest difficulty was that man is constantly changing and at any moment of his existence is not identical to himself, is 'not like himself'. Straightforward documentary accuracy does not necessarily render adequately the human image: it is not often that we are happy with photos taken of us, and we often 'do not recognise ourselves'.

With this in mind, it is interesting to note that Dostoevskii did not himself like viewing his own face in the mirror. He seemed to dissolve his appearance in his view of the world, a view whose intensive actuality did not allow him to switch to a 'view of himself from outside'. This apparent paradox is explained by the essentials of the writer's artistic credo. When he looks in the mirror, a person sees only the reflection of his external *oblik*, which is not at all the expression of the *lik* that Dostoevskii's heroes (and the writer himself) were searching for. A person cannot from within look at himself from outside: an ethical 'short circuit' takes place, and the only way out of this is to create a special external point of view on oneself and the world which by definition cannot coincide with the 'I-for-myself'; to create, in other words, a literary hero. A beautiful woman who spends hours sitting in front of the mirror, whether she is doing her make-up or not, is carrying out – albeit for a different purpose – the same work as a poet: she is creating a special 'ideal' view of herself from outside by moulding an ideal object (creating a 'face', to use Dostoevskii's term). The difference is that the beautiful woman sitting in front of the mirror aims to make her own individual face identical with a model selected according to a particular set of aesthetic norms; the writer, on the contrary, creates the face of a hero by making it as dissimilar as possible to all the models he knows, by searching for a 'face of uncommon expressions'. A second distinction is that a person sitting in front of the mirror regards the face as the end meaning of their activities; the artist regards the face as a means to an end, and aims to find a connection between the human face and the Face of the universe. This explains the strange feeling a person experiences when standing in front of a mirror: he tries to view his expression as a 'sign of himself' (and the more he gazes at his own reflection, the more this feeling intensifies). The skill of a make-up artist working on himself is to view the world from within, using face-paint to bring his appearance, which he treats as something quite separate from his *lik*, as close as possible to a hired model. The position of a writer is diametrically opposed to this: he must go beyond the limits of his existential location and try to see the world from the viewpoint of another being. For this reason the mirror no longer remains essential and in fact the reality it presents becomes rather terrifying; at the same time, the hero's identity becomes defined autobiographically as his 'I' is displaced in time and place.

For Dostoevskii, the creation of a literary hero is an attempt to see the world through the eyes of another person who feels his tragic separateness from the world, while at the same time this hero is (being) defined through the eyes of yet another, third, person, who views him sympathetically from a position alongside him, and inhabits the same chronotope. Thus both the hero of the novel and the narrator (chronicler) are born.[5] The writer absolutely had to *see* his hero. The secret of Dostoevskii's envisioning of his heroes opens up a little when he describes how *seeing* the hero was a precondition for *hearing his voice*; the one was impossible without the other. Not for nothing does Ivan Karamazov, in notes Dostoevskii wrote for *The Brothers Karamazov*, complain to the devil that 'I sometimes no longer see you, but only hear your voice.'[6] The visual image of what was to be embodied ('the individual face' or 'the face of the idea') prepared the ground for Dostoevskii's utterance of the 'individual word', as opposed to the 'general word'.

Dostoevskii's extremely concrete aesthetics was never a pretext for abstract philosophical speculation: it expressed urgent and essential questions which defined the course of his existence both as a man and as an artist and provided a foundation for the encoding of his own texts and his perception of art in general. It is hard to speak of Dostoevskii's literary portraits: there are no portraits as such, there is just the impression made by one man in the eyes of another, as they together make contact with and/or are repelled by Beauty/Truth. The description of the hero's portrait is based on the Old Russian *zhitie* which presents the 'face (*lik*) of a man' who has made contact with Truth (or, as often happens in Dostoevskii, rejected it); in just the same way the writer's drawings on his manuscripts are based on the icon, as a genre that evokes the likeness of man and God. According to Dostoevskii, art, by requiring of the artist love for the subject of depiction irrespective of the morality of the face being depicted, places him in the position of the Christian obliged to love his enemy. This idea, which is highly revealing of the national specificity of Russian art, figured large in the writer's reflections, and made it possible for him to link art with Christian morality.

The recollection of a 'face' that he had once seen and been impressed by was the writer's starting-point when he came to create artistic form. Dostoevskii often has recourse to this technique in his works, thereby revealing to us the particular features of his creative process. Characters systematically hang portraits of each other on the walls of their flats, and the semantic context of their locations is no less important than the domestic environment of the hero himself.[7] It should be noted that the hero of any Dostoevskii novel always sets great store by the depiction of a woman (and never that of a man). We may see this as a 'cryptogram' of Dostoevskii's own habits: he himself treasured several portraits of this kind, including a medallion with a depiction of his first wife, M. D. Dostoevskaia.[8] More often than not Dostoevskii expressed the idea of the suffering of good and beauty in this world in the form of the sufferings of a beautiful woman. He conveyed this by leaving his hero in front of her portrait; the word 'obraz' thus took on a dual meaning, and every portrait of this kind has something of the Orthodox icon – a window on to Truth, which guarantees Good and the path to which is Beauty.

In the novel *A Raw Youth* Dostoevskii does not restrict himself to reflections on the 'principal feature' of a face but also feels the need again to make sense of a *lik*. He suggests the connection between man and the universe through the reflection of the Divine Face in man:

It was also a photograph, very much smaller, in a delicate oval wooden frame – the face of a girl, thin and consumptive yet, despite that, beautiful, a pensive face and at the same time oddly devoid of ideas [. . .] as if this were a case of a person suddenly seized by some fixed idea which was tormenting for the very reason that it was beyond the power of that person to comprehend it.[9]

The highest expression of love in Dostoevskii is to gaze lovingly into the face of a person, to seek spiritual communion with his or her *lik*. On the other hand, the highest expression of hatred is to destroy a portrait (or else to treat it outrageously, or to slap someone in the face). In *The Insulted and the Humiliated*, the incensed old Ikhmenev 'snatched up the locket, threw it violently on the floor, and started trampling it with his foot in a frenzy'.[10] To destroy someone's image is, in the understanding of Dostoevskii's heroes, equivalent to murder. After disfiguring the medallion, the old man 'stopped short, horrified at what he was doing. Suddenly he snatched up the locket from the floor and rushed towards the door, but he had not taken two steps when he fell on his knees, and dropping his arms on the sofa before him, let his head fall helplessly on them.'[11]

For this reason, a crucial role in Dostoevskii's works is allotted to visual depictions of people, all kinds of portraits and especially photographs. It is with a photograph that Prince Myshkin begins his acquaintance with Nastas'ia Filippovna in *The Idiot*: staggered, he whispers quietly about 'beauty that can overturn mountains' (both consciously and involuntarily he refers us back to the formula in the Gospels about Christian faith with which one can move mountains). In *The Insulted and the Humiliated*, when Katia arrives to meet Natasha, she tells her that she has seen her photograph, whereupon an ethical and aesthetic comparison of two expressions of the 'human face' immediately ensues:

'Well, is it a good likeness?'
'You're better.' Katia replied resolutely and gravely. 'But I was quite sure you would be.'[12]

Dostoevskii uses this motif persistently. In *A Raw Youth* Arkadii, when he meets the heroine, already knows her by her portrait:

'I can't stand your smile any more!' I screamed out suddenly. [. . .] 'When I got here I spent a whole month before you arrived gazing at your portrait in your father's study and not making any sense of it. [. . .] You've got a full figure and you're of medium height, but you've got the full, light plumpness of a healthy country girl. Yes, and you've got a country girl's face, the face of a country beauty [. . .] a round, red-cheeked, clear-skinned, bold, laughing and . . . and unassuming face!'[13]

It is hard to imagine a situation where these remarks on a woman's 'full plumpness' could be addressed to her without violating nine-teenth-century norms of decent behaviour. Such a situation would in practical terms be impossible. But this description is not intended to be heard by the heroine: in essence, it is the transcript of the writer's internal monologue as he formulates the portrait of his heroine's 'face' – it is directly analogous to the sketch created by Dostoevskii as he planned the novel.

A low parodic variation of this technique of revealing the meaning of an event through a 'face' is found in the story 'The Crocodile', where Elena Ivanovna, the wife of a man who has just been swallowed by a crocodile, is distraught that she has no photograph of her spouse. Dostoevskii's thought about the 'principal feature' can therefore take many different forms in his artistic practice.

THE VISUAL IMAGE AS PART OF DOSTOEVSKII'S CREATIVE PROCESSES

When he puts something down on paper, the writer does not simply fix something he has thought over during the artistic gestation period, but also establishes a connection between this thought and its future artistic form. For this purpose Dostoevskii created his own kind of 'mediating language' which helped him to connect the 'input' language of his internal speech and the language of artistic form that he created. The writer must carefully cultivate the linguistic form of his future work. An idea which has been prematurely and inadequately embodied in a word, turn of phrase or expression does not assist but rather hinders the further progress of artistic creation. Of course, this 'pre-verbal' possession of an idea varies from one writer to another depending on the particularities of their education, upbringing, era and creative style; and, naturally, by no means all of them assisted this process by drawing sketches as Dostoevskii did. Indeed, Dostoevskii went even further than sketching by creating his own special 'ideography': it was characteristic for him to 'sketch in his mind', to use the words of the writer himself, the 'full image' of the artistic idea, and to accompany this mental sketch with movements of the pen on paper which reflected the processes of creative thought. We know that Dostoevskii, while engaged in 'the poet's work', often gave free rein to his fantasy with interesting results: images succeeded one another at lightning speed, but sometimes the writer stopped to 'gaze into' the hero he had created at length. We also know that it was precisely while he was taking this extended look at the personality and *lik* of his character that he usually sketched out his 'portraits'. But what was going on in the writer's consciousness at these moments? Did he pause to consider the meaning of a technique of literary creation that had become the norm for him?

We find interesting evidence on this question in *The Diary of a Writer*, where Dostoevskii recounts that as a convict, though he was deprived of the opportunity for normal literary activity ('with a pen in my hand'), he still could not check the impulse to make an artistic response to his environment and began to 'sketch pictures' in his mind. Dostoevskii recalls this as follows:

Little by little I lost myself in reverie and imperceptibly sank into memories of the past. All through my four years in prison I continually thought of all my past days, and I think I relived the whole of my former life in my memories. These memories arose in my mind of themselves; rarely did I summon them up consciously. They would begin from a certain point, some little thing that was often barely perceptible, and then bit by bit they would grow into a finished picture, some strong and complete impression. I would analyze these impressions, adding new touches to things experienced long ago; and the main thing was that I would refine them, continually refine them, and in this consisted my entire entertainment.[14]

We see here that the 'full picture' grows out of a 'point' or 'feature', but the means by which the writer achieves success in the 'work of a poet' is still far removed from his operations with words and verbal expressions: it more closely recalls the technique of a professional painter who 'corrects' his picture with calculated light strokes and thereby brings his work to a peak of artistry and authenticity. One feature of graphic art – of any type or level of professional expertise – is that it is operated by a particular kind of 'retrospective connection': every stroke, feature and line defines the following ones, just as words are defined by their context as they enter speech or writing. The process of drawing is thus not a simple transferral on to paper of some picture formed in the mind's eye, but rather a constant 'correction', the careful examination and completion of what has been drawn earlier, an analysis that continues even as the image is being realised.

    Professional artists and photographers, to continue the above analogy, are remarkable for their ability to create precisely *portraits* of people where the subjects open up in the fullness of their internal essence. Dostoevskii penetrates deeply into this problem decades in advance of the appearance of art photography in its present form. One of the heroes of the novel *A Raw Youth*, Versilov, remarks as he holds in his hands a daguerrotype of his wife Sonia:

You know . . . photographs are only very rarely good likenesses, and one knows why. It's because the original, I mean each one of us, is only rarely a good likeness of himself. Only at rare moments does a human face express its chief feature, its most characteristic idea. An artist can study a face and gauge its main idea, though at the moment he copies it it might not be on the face at all. A photograph captures a person as he is at one moment, and it's very likely that Napoleon at such a moment could appear stupid and Bismarck kindly. In this particular portrait the sun deliberately seemed to catch Sonya at the moment when her chief feature was visible, her shy, timid love and her rather challenging, fearful chastity.[15]

The essence of the discovery made by Dostoevskii is that the creation of an individual portrait is also a quest for the typical, but the portrait conceals not a multitude of similar people united by a single fate, but a multitude of different faces belonging to one and the same *person*.

To be able to glimpse man at this characteristic moment, when his internal and external aspects, his personality and biography are united, is the main task facing a portraitist, both in painting and in literature. This is why Dostoevskii accords such an important role to the *liki* of his main characters, who gaze into each other just as intesely as their author with exactly the same aim – to 'divine' the meaning of the 'idea' concealed in a person. In *The Brothers Karamazov*, after Dmitrii's disgraceful sally in the Elder Zosima's cell, Zosima puzzles the assembled company by bowing down before him. When asked by Alesha about the meaning of this bow, Zosima explains: 'I sensed something terrible yesterday . . . it was as though the look in his eyes had revealed his whole destiny. [. . .] my soul shuddered momentarily at what the man was laying in store for himself. I have seen that kind of expression on people's faces once or twice before in my life . . . as though it revealed the whole of their destiny, and their destiny, alas, came to pass.'[16] Dmitrii's face expressed the 'chief feature' of his life and his fate, both of which the Elder is able to 'read' just as Versilov 'reads' the face of his wife on a photograph. The 'terrible fate' imprinted on Dmitrii's face could only be overcome with the help of the fraternal *lik* of Alesha Karamazov. 'I sent you to him, Aleksei, because I thought that the sight of a brother's face would help him.'[17]

Any novel or story by Dostoevskii is crammed with physiognomical investigations of this kind. There are quite a few of them in *The Diary of a Writer* as well. Whenever Dostoevskii in his articles raises the question of how to create a literary depiction of man, he invariably touches on this area. Not only that, if his characters demonstrate the ability to 'read people by their faces', this is an important indication of their spiritual development and moral qualities. For Dostoevskii's 'author-heroes', 'chroniclers' and narrators, a constant and careful study of the faces around them provides the absolute foundation for their view of the world. The discoveries made by the 'author-heroes' are of course a reflection of their creator's opinions. The 'Dreamer' in *White Nights* confesses that:

whether I walked on the Nevsky, went to the garden or sauntered along the embankment, there was not one face of those I had been accustomed to meet at the same time and place all the year. They, of course, do not know me, but I know them. I know them intimately, I have almost made a study of their faces, and am delighted when they are cheerful, and downcast when they are under a cloud.[18]

Netochka Nezvanova, who narrates the story of the same name, also proves herself an attentive physiognomist: she can 'perceive [her father's] least wish at a glance'.[19] In the 1850s and 1860s Dostoevskii begins almost every description of a character by referring to the physiognomical study of his/her *lik*. The narrator of *The Village of Stepanchikovo* recalls that when granted his first sighting of the villainous Foma Fomich, he 'studied this gentleman with intense curiosity'.[20] In *Crime and Punishment*, Raskol'nikov tries to regain his mental equilibrium after the murders by focusing all his attention on a face he sees in an office: 'The clerk, on the other hand, he found intensely interesting; he wanted to guess everything by his features, penetrate the very heart of his being.'[21]

We find here a characteristic principle of the 'literary portrait' in Dostoevskii's works of the 1850s and 1860s. In the 1870s, however, the period of his greatest artistic maturity, Dostoevksii tends less and less to provide such direct indications of his characters' showing particular interest in physiognomical details. This process goes hand in hand with the development of Dostoevskii's distinctive style and is accompanied by fundamental changes in the composition and content of the 'literary portraits' of his characters in his works of this period: the forms he gives them become more varied and more extended; consequently, Dostoevskii's portraits of the 1870s, as seen in *A Raw Youth* and *The Brothers Karamazov*, are fundamentally different from the portraits in *Crime and Punishment*, *The Insulted and the Humiliated*, *The Idiot*, and *The Possessed*.

The quest to uncover the meaning and the moral profile of a specific *human face* was at the heart of Dostoevskii's life and writing. This was what guided his response to great paintings and it was in this vein that he created his own works, which were seen by his contemporaries as 'portrait galleries'. Any attempts to find proto-types for Dostoevskii's heroes only in his actual biography and the literature that preceded him are totally misguided. The point is that the writer also drew the basic physiognomic types for his literary heroes from painting. Dostoevskii's experience of the great artists –

in particular Raphael, Rubens, Cranach, Titian, Van Dyck, Holbein the Younger and many Russian painters – has been very little studied, but it provided the constant and, one might say, fundamental context in which he formed the 'physiognomical definitions', the 'faces of ideas' for his heroes. Every trip Dostoevskii made to Europe turned into a trawl round the museums which provided a foundation for his creative activity in a given period. *The Idiot* and *The Possessed* cannot be understood without the Dresden gallery, the Uffizi and the Sistine Chapel, just as *A Raw Youth* and *The Brothers Karamazov* cannot be understood without a number of paintings by the Russian masters and exhibitions in the Academy of Arts, which the writer could not live without. Constant reflection on the great works of painting provided a foundation for Dostoevskii's own creative work.

Aesthetically and spiritually Dostoevskii lived in medieval Europe, perhaps in a 'medieval Europe' that he himself invented. This explains his intense interest in European art of the Middle Ages and early Renaissance and in the Gothic style of architecture; it also accounts for the polar oppositions between good and evil that he saw in man's nature, and for the open conflict in his works between the 'corporeal' and the 'spiritual'. The art of the Middle Ages, which revealed the human soul in a face, was seen by Dostoevskii as a counterweight to the 'corporeal' theme, which gave expression to the organic and physiological sphere of life: he regarded it as the last kind of art that had remained Christian in spirit, an art whose decline had set in during the 'clumsy historical process' of modern European history. The face versus the physiognomy, the presence versus the absence of the face, and also the possiblity versus the impossiblity of seeing a person's face: these are the main oppositions that structure the writer's inner world and define the characteristics of the works he created. Dostoevskii demonstrates his unusual 'medieval' anthropology in his article 'Regarding an exhibition', written after he had visited the latest exhibition in the Academy of the Arts. In his comments on Repin's famous painting *Burlaki na Volge* (*The Barge-Haulers*) (ill. 1.1), Dostoevskii describes in detail a number of the characters in the painting and picks out as one of the best the figure of a 'wretched, drooping little peasant who is trudging along on his own and whose face isn't even visible'.[22] This characteristic reading of the painting shows clearly to us the hidden reason for the attention the writer paid to great paintings. 'A man trailing

1.1. Il'ia Repin, *Barsuki na Volge* (*The Volga Barge-Haulers*, 1873). Oil on canvas, 131.5 × 281 cm. Russian Museum, St Petersburg.

behind on his own', whose face is difficult to see but absolutely must be 'made out': this is an important, not to say the fundamental, characteristic 'Dostoevskii hero', beginning with Makar Devushkin and ending with Aleksandr Pushkin, the hero of Dostoevskii's last work, which he wrote a few months before he died.

From the great painters Dostoevskii drew his main symbols of beauty. These symbols are clear to see: they provided a moral underpinning for his aesthetic activities and sometimes he marked the moral state of his heroes by the attitude they took to paintings. We find a characteristic example in the novel *The Possessed*. The 'father' of the Russian nihilists, Stepan Trofimovich Verkhovenskii, says of Raphael's *Madonna* in the Sistine Chapel: '*Chère* Varvara Petrovna, I spent two hours sitting in front of that painting and went away disillusioned. [. . .] All this fuss was made by a bunch of old men.'[23] Here Dostoevskii makes fun of the materialist aesthetics propounded by Nikolai Chernyshevskii, who believed the popularity of great works of art was some kind of 'fashion' caused by the herd instinct of the crowd. In his dissertation, *Esteticheskie otnosheniia iskusstva k deistvitel'nosti* (The Aesthetic Relations of Art to Reality), he wrote: 'The phenomena of reality are gold ingots without a hallmark [. . .] A work of art is a bank note which has little intrinsic value, but the nominal value of which is guaranteed by the whole of society.'[24] Chernyshevskii failed to see any moral significance in beauty and reduced the enjoyment of beauty to a variant of purely physiological pleasure, which is incidental and temporary. 'It is well known that our senses soon tire and become satiated, i.e. satisfied [. . .] A man cannot look at a picture, even by Raphael, every day for a month without wearying of it.'[25] Dostoevskii had the opportunity to test out this assertion by his intellectual opponent using his own experience: Anna Grigor'evna Dostoevskaia recalls that in autumn 1867 in Dresden he visited the gallery every day for a month and spent many hours standing in front of Raphael's 'Sistine Madonna'.

When Dostoevskii sought to depict the abasement of beauty, he often did so by showing characters aggressively 'pouncing' on masterpieces of the visual arts. There are many examples of this, one of the best-known being Svidrigailov's intention to rape a girl who is the physiognomical double of Raphael's 'Sistine Madonna'. When he was working on *Crime and Punishment* Dostoevskii searched for the physiognomical type of Sonia Marmeladova, a righteous Christian woman who is forced to become a prostitute in order to save her

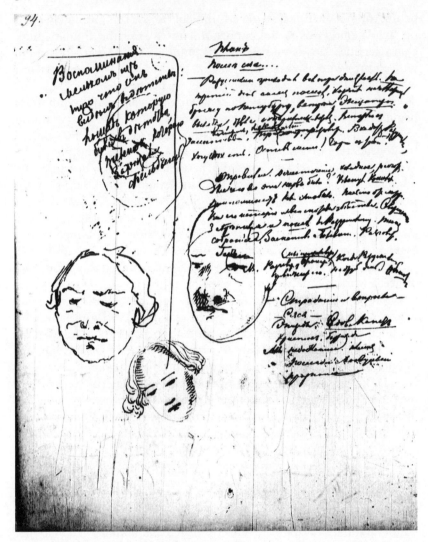

1.2. 'Sistinskaia Madonna' (The Sistine Madonna), with two male characters in the background, from preliminary notes for *The Crocodile*. Russian State Archive of Literature and Art, Moscow.

sisters and mother. Several portraits sketched in the manuscripts of the novel clearly hint at the connection between the type Dostoevskii sought and the face of the Virgin Mary in Raphael's picture (ill. 1.2, lowest portrait). In Dostoevskii's works the idea of the greatest possible evil and the death of the human element in man (man's loss of 'the image and likeness of God') is marked by the obvious destruction of man's face (which is turned into a 'physiognomy'), his *lik* or even – more directly – God's *lik*. We can see here the significance of the violations of icons which occur so very frequently in Dostoevskii and which are not so much blasphemous as anti-human in their import. Examples include Versilov in *A Raw Youth*, a 'Russian gentilhomme' who in a fit of rage breaks a Russian icon made of wood on the corner of a stove, and the revolutionaries in *The Possessed*, who remove the image of the Virgin Mother from an icon case and replace it with a live mouse. The heroine of the story 'A Meek One' pawns an icon when driven to despair by poverty and then clutches the very same icon as she throws herself out of the window to commit suicide. The idea of the superfluity and/or the 'usefulness' of art drew a protest from Dostoevskii, who always formulated his objections by referring to the value of the 'human *lik*'.

This point is developed at some length in 'Mr -bov and the Question of Art' (1861), which is one of Dostoevskii's most important and characteristic statements on aesthetics. In this article Dostoevskii asserts that images of ideal Beauty have come to provide an aesthetic and ethical foundation for man throughout history, taking as his central example the divine features of the goddess in Fet's poem 'Diana'. The striving for beauty was for him a kind of 'symbol of faith', while art was a prayer that fixed man's reverential attitude to Truth and Beauty.[26]

Yet, when he made refined fun of Chernyshevskii's notion of the 'usefulness of beauty', Dostoevskii was in no way hemmed in by the Parnassian conception of 'art for art's sake'. He too had given this question a lot of thought and was convinced, just like Chernyshevskii, of the exceptional usefulness or, more precisely, salutary power of beauty in a modern world that was dying from its growing 'dis-figurement' (the gap opening up between man and the image and likeness of God). This is the foundation of Dostoevskii's aesthetic utopia: the writer believed that when man has contact with Beauty, as formulated by great artists, he 'experiences some kind of internal transformation, his particles are somehow redistributed. . .' (here Dostoevskii makes a concession to the scientistic orientation of the prevailing discourse in the 1860s). Dostoevskii's striving to pay loving attention to the 'I of the other' is underpinned by his conviction that Beauty can save man from evil.

THE VISUAL WORD: DOSTOEVSKII'S NOTEBOOKS

Dostoevskii made many thousands of calligraphical jottings while he was writing his works, and we find an explanation of their meaning in *The Idiot* and the notebooks to that novel. On almost every page of these initial attempts to define the traits of his hero's personality, Dostoevskii mentions his calligraphical abilities as a principal feature of his character that is important for the novel's plot development: 'Shortly before this the fiancée had found a post for the Idiot in an office. For three days the Idiot went there, then he got into an argument and left; descriptions of how they were quarreling, and how the Idiot sat there a long time just copying (*his fine penmanship*) . . .'; 'The uncle turned his attention to the Idiot, for they were already hastening to explain about him. He listened absently. (His handwriting. The clerk had already told him [about the Idiot].'); 'The Idiot takes up work as a copyist in the uncle's house. The uncle had almost forgotten him. His handwriting. A week goes by, they meet . . . The Idiot stares at him derisively. The office correspondence. This he wrote. The uncle is struck by this and invites the Idiot to dinner.'[27]

It should be noted that this is the only detail that was preserved in the character of the hero from the first to the very last, definitive version of the novel. Dostoevskii clearly attached enormous importance to it, and the novel begins just as it was originally conceived by the writer: with a handwriting test imposed on the hero by General Epanchin (the 'uncle' of the initial plan of the work). In this unusual way the writer immediately establishes the depth and genius of the 'universal soul' of his hero Myshkin, who is a talented artistic calligrapher and also a highly distinctive theoretician and critic of calligraphy. Myshkin possesses to the highest degree the qualities that Dostoevskii considered a manifestation of human genius: he is able to understand completely other people's thoughts, ideas and souls. Being a genuine 'artist' (i.e. painter) Dostoevskii's hero can use his unusual skills to bring together the characters of various peoples and epochs – through the study of this graphic art he is able both to identify and to depict a Russian medieval abbot, a French street scribe and an English aristocrat.

'This,' elucidated the prince, highly elated, 'is the personal signature of the Abbot Paphnutius copied from a manuscript of the fourteenth century.

They had splendid signatures, all our old abbots and metropolitans, such exquisite style sometimes and such care! Surely you have Pogodin's edition at least, General? After that I've written using different lettering: this is a large, rounded, French script of the last century, some characters were written in different ways even, it's a script of the market-place, used by public scribes and taken from their specimens (I used to have one) – you'll agree it has its virtues. Look at these rounded d's and a's. I've written the Russian letters in the French style, which is very difficult, but it's come out well.'[28]

The General is impressed enough by Myshkin's demonstration of his skills to offer him a 'not too demanding' office job with a monthly salary of 35 roubles.

It seems that while he was working on this description, Dostoevskii was leafing though pages of his 'notebooks nos 3 and 4' – not only to recall particular details of the composition and plot of the novel he had mapped out there, but also to take another look at the hundreds of calligraphical notes made in them. These notes are always strongly characterised. Some may be classified as 'chancellery scribe's exercises' (phrases such as 'His Excellency', 'Your Worship'). In these words the short tails of the letters convey the stiff military soul of the bureaucrat. In addition, we find a 'round French script' ('Napoleon', 'Napoleon Buonaparte'), a pure, refined 'English hand' with its thin but well-defined lines ('Richard', 'Raphael Sanzio d'Urbino'), and the 'black handwriting' of a French wandering commis, which is in many respects similar to the English hand. The task of 'adapting French characters to Russian lettering' is reflected in many of Dostoevskii's jottings, where he would write either French names in Russian or else Russian names in the Latin alphabet (ill. 1.3). Dostoevskii also employed a similar technique as he was defining the course of his creative work: he would single out calligraphically phrases such as 'Notes for the main plan', 'Final plan', 'Notes for the second plan of the novel', 'Second plan of the novel *The Idiot*. Chronological structure', 'New and final plan' and so on.

The first scholar to draw attention to the special significance of these 'handwriting exercises' was A. L. Volynskii, who made the perceptive point that the hero's character is here revealed in great depth: 'Myshkin writes like a calligrapher – a marvellous quality, which provides further evidence of a soul that transcends the personal. [. . .] This unexpected linear symbol comes as an astonish-

1.3. Exercises in calligraphy from preliminary notes for *The Idiot*, framing a male portrait. Russian State Archive of Literature and Art, Moscow.

ingly simple yet touching and profound hint of the universal qualities of Myshkin's personality.'[29] Of course, if Volynskii had seen Dostoevskii's manuscripts he would have removed the word 'unexpected' from his exceptionally precise observation.

Like his hero Dostoevskii, when he looks at different people's handwriting, treats it as an indication of their spiritual and moral qualities. With an ease and a precision that are testament to the ancient and highly professional occupation of calligraphy, Myshkin, with brilliant, portrait-like vividness, characterises various types of 'script' and the personalities that correspond to them. He draws together various samples of handwriting and human character traits from all kinds of scattered sources, from his conversations with people and from special facsimile editions, and he lovingly stores them away in his collection. But there is nothing in Myshkin's skills and knowledge that Dostoevskii did not possess himself. The writer is surely smiling to himself as he makes Myshkin come across the 'military-clerk script' of the Russian chancelleries in Switzerland. Probably the only place in this country where an example of this script could be found was Dostoevskii's own notebook: here he played about with various types of handwriting, and he certainly used this Russian official script, which he knew well from personal experience.

Prince Myshkin is not only a wonderful calligrapher, he is also, like Dostoevskii himself, a brilliant portrait-painter. In conversation with the Epanchin sisters he imagines a subject for a painting:

Draw the scaffold so that the very last rung only can be seen clearly and close to; the felon has placed his foot on it, the head and face as white as a sheet, the priest is holding out the cross, while the other greedily protrudes his blue lips, and stares, and *knows everything*. The cross and the head – that's the picture; the faces of the priest, the executioner, his two assistants and several heads and eyes from below, all that can be drawn in as distant background, indistinct, subordinate.[30]

This was precisely the graphic form taken by Dostoevskii's original idea for the novel: the portrait of a hero moving with great difficulty towards Truth through the circles of hell ('The cross and the head'). This description is perhaps the most important piece of evidence of Dostoevskii's creative process that is provided by the writer himself. At the same time, it also bears witness to the crisis that Dostoevskii perceived in Christianity: the kissing of the cross, that symbol of Christ's public execution, just before the execution of a man, is a terrible paradox which points to the official Church's abandonment of the Truth of the Gospels.

As an example of a drawing that launched a great artistic conception we may take Dostoevskii's sketch of Miguel Cervantes, which was the first note in preparation for *The Idiot* (ill. 1.4). After

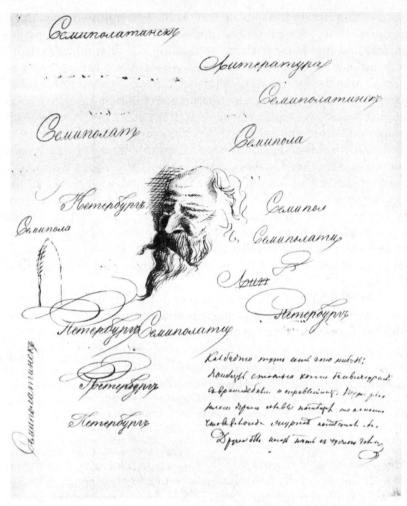

1.4. Portrait of Cervantes, framed by calligraphic exercises, from a draft of *The Idiot*. Russian State Archive of Literature and Art, Moscow.

finishing *Crime and Punishment*, as he was on the verge of beginning a new work, he wrote to his niece, Sof'ia Ivanova:

I destroyed a lot of what I had written . . . The idea of the novel is one that I have treasured for a long time, but it is so difficult that for a long time I couldn't bring myself to tackle it, and if I am tackling it now, then this is simply because I was near desperation. The main idea of the novel is to depict a positively beautiful man. There is nothing more difficult than this, and especially now. All writers who have attempted to depict the positively beautiful have always given up, because this task is limitless . . . But I should just say that of all the beautiful faces in Christian literature Don Quixote is the most complete of all.[31]

This book, which Dostoevskii acknowledged as a model depiction of the character of a man ethically ideal in Christian terms, always accompanied Dostoevskii on his travels, along with the Bible that wives of the Decembrists had given him in Siberia. He was constantly rereading it and looking at the lithographic 'portrait of Cervantes' that is found in many editions of Don Quixote, and often mentioned it in his works and letters.

As early as the 1850s Dostoevskii became preoccupied with the idea of a novel about a new 'Don Quixote'. This drawing, however, gives us good reason to suppose that the novel *The Idiot* was seriously occupying his thoughts even before he finished *Crime and Punishment*. The 'old and beloved' idea of this novel was tightly connected not only with the novel *Don Quixote* but also with the life of its author. The drawing makes a strong impression on the viewer: this is one of the best works of Dostoevskii the visual artist, and it shows his true potential as a sketch-artist. With care and great thoughtfulness Dostoevskii here reconstructs the symbolic features of 'the face of the idea' of 'the greatest book of all time', as he called *Don Quixote*. He depicts Cervantes' hero in the usual style: the eyes are closed, the features are sensitive and exalted; this is the face of a man who seems to have retreated into the world of his own thoughts. We see here the face of the 'Knight of Sad Countenance' (rytsar' pechal'-nogo obraza) who had so much in common with his creator. And with Dostoevskii too, for that matter. On the adjoining page, responding to the critical attacks the nihilists directed against *Crime and Punishment*, which they called 'a slander against students' and 'stupid', Dostoevskii writes: 'Don't worry, it isn't remotely as stupid as all that. *I know that I am writing truthfully and to the point*.' Many years after this drawing, in his *Diary of a Writer* Dostoevskii once again emphasised the importance of the image that he singled out in his earlier reflective sketch on *Don Quixote*: 'Here the great poet and seer of the human heart perceived one of the most profound and most mysterious aspects of the human spirit. Oh, this is a great book, not the sort that are written now; only one such book is sent to humanity in several hundred years.'[32]

When he draws sketches on the pages of his notebook, the writer is essentially a sketch-artist working on the creation of a particular visual image. The first stages of the creative process for a painter and for a writer who draws have a great deal in common: an initial sketch drawing, intended for 'private consumption', creates a starting-point for the further development of artistic form (for a writer that form is literary, for a painter it is visual and iconic). The writer and the sketch-artist use the same 'tools of the trade': paper, pen, ink. Dostoevskii, like all his contemporaries, used oak-gall ink, which, as specialists testify, remains to this day 'the best material for drawing with the pen'.[33] His contemporaries attest that while he was exceptionally modest in his requirements and generally unfussy, Dostoevskii nonetheless insisted on writing materials of the very highest quality. 'Fedor Mikhailovich,' as his wife, Anna Grigor'evna Dostoevskaia, recalled, 'liked good-quality writing materials and always wrote his works on thick, good-quality paper with only very faint lines. He also required me to copy out what he dictated on thick paper of a very particular format. He liked his pen to be sharp and firm. He only very rarely used pencils.'[34]

The notebooks that the writer bought over the years do indeed have by and large the same dimensions of 21 × 17 cm. One might think that for a writer the format of sheets of paper would be a matter of complete indifference, and that their quantity would be more important. The artist, however, is another matter: for him this factor has decisive significance; the form and dimensions of the paper are important, as they have a significant influence on the artistic form of the future work. Dostoevskii's habitual use of paper of a particular format betrays the techniques of a sketch-artist. In his drawings Dostoevskii used paper of a warm, beige-yellow tone: the psychology of visual reception dictates that the space inside the faces, figures and 'cruciferae' seems opaque. For this reason, in the verbal and visual compositions that the writer created on the pages of his notebooks, the lines of text surrounding a drawing do not encroach on drawings that are already on the page, but rather neatly avoid them (ill. 1.3). On the rare occasions when 'superimposition' does take place (ill. 1.1), there are artistic reasons for it: it signals a synthesis of the meanings of the sketch and the verbal note on top of it, and suggests that verbal and visual expressions of the idea coincide. On the whole, however, cursive script, drawings and 'calligraphy' coexist harmoniously within a single common space – the page, where they interact with one another and form a composition. Sometimes drawings that are created while the text is being written or afterwards frame the words, as they occupy free space in the margin, at top or bottom. In some cases the text is written around the drawings and forms a special 'surrounding space', almost a living environment – both in terms of meaning (by providing a verbal commentary on the drawing) and in a compositional sense (by forming a sometimes very striking 'frame' (ill. 4)). Just as the subject of an Old Russian miniature or *lubok* is 'clothed' in the written word, which is either 'dissolved' in the air or 'breathed out' by him in the form of a little cloud of steam, so the hero of Dostoevskii's drawings is generally enveloped by dense thickets of cursive script which provide both a sense-generating and a visual context. On the pages of the writer's notebooks, the written word and the graphic depiction live in close interaction: verbal and visual elements influence each other and together form a single unit of meaning. Both when he was filling up the pages of his notebook and when he was later looking back through them, Dostoevskii was acutely aware of both modes of expression – the content of the idea and the visual image; this is testified by hundreds of pages of his manuscripts. A rectangular sheet of his notebook was for Dostoevskii a model of the four-dimensional 'chronotope' of his future work: here his new idea was born, and he set up the semantic field which would provide the scene of action for the idea-saturated literary hero, the bearer of the plot.

A special feature of a piece of paper with a depiction on it is that both the sketcher and the viewer perceive all that is above the head of the subject as 'air' and all that is below as 'ground' or 'earth'. If we look at the artistic space of Dostoevskii's drawings from this point of view and compare them with the particular sense of space in his works, then we discover a number of interesting points of resemblance.

Within the dynamic space of a page in Dostoevskii's manuscripts the concepts of 'top' and 'bottom' acquired a particular significance. In literal terms they coincide with the upper and lower parts of the sheet, but they also signify two poles of the writer's artistic ideology, at opposite ends of which are located 'earth' and 'heavens', 'evil' and 'good', the concepts of spiritual loftiness and everyday rootedness. This adoption of a system of co-ordinates based on the simple opposition 'above–below' is characteristic of all areas of Dostoevskii's creative activity – from the ideological/philosophical conceptions presented in his works to the visual representations on the pages of his manuscripts. Dostoevskii's creative activity, both as an artist and as a thinker, was directed from 'down below' to 'up above': the Svidrigailov, Stavrogin and Karamazov principles in man were overcome by ideas borne by Sonia Marmeladova, Shatov, Alesha and Zosima. This sense of a manuscript page as a live space inhabited by real characters made Dostoevskii cross out not only words, but drawings as well, and furnish his hero with a halo or even, on several occasions, write the sign of the cross over a page (as during work on *The Possessed*, when he was constructing the image of Petr Verkhovenskii).

Dostoevskii considered a person's face to be the true expression of the spiritual significance of its owner, a genuine reflection of the image and likeness of the Creator of the universe. The Gothic arches drawn by Dostoevskii, for all their fantastic appearance and amazing diversity, are united by the fact that they all express the idea of striving upwards – an idea that is embedded in the aesthetic conception of the Gothic style. Oakleaves and cruciferae appear to be self-sufficient: there is not even a hint of a branch or stem, there is not even the graft of a leaf – there is nothing that might hint at a connection with the soil 'down below'. Not only are these details not included, the very idea of them is excluded: the leaves fuse into a single complete and self-sufficient plastic image. Similarly, 'calligraphy' is a perfect style of writing, one taken to the aesthetic absolute; the 'calligraphic word' therefore presents the word with its maximum aesthetic and semantic significance. Words written in this manner usually crown a layer of associations which unites a large group of facts or phenomena. It emerges that the three types of Dostoevskii's graphic art have two points in common: first, they depict the most characteristic element, the part that symbolises and personifies something whole (face – man, leaf – tree, a lancet arch – Gothic, a calligrapher's word – an ideal and artistically perfect 'word'); second, they embody the literal and symbolic 'heights' of each of the subjects depicted.

It is not only the meanings of isolated drawings that strictly and logically correspond to the ethical and philosophical system of the writer. The basic categories of these drawings match a creative credo which identifies 'above' with the positive ethical ideal and 'below' with the opposing image of 'immorality' and death. The arrangement of graphic elements on a page of Dostoevskii's manuscripts has the same importance as the position of an element of Gothic architecture in the overall compositional structure of a particular building. For this reason a reading of Dostoevskii's visual art, if it takes into account its particular 'grammar' and the interaction between the writer's drawings and the surrounding words, can help us to penetrate more deeply into the essence of the writer's creative process, and will reveal new facts concerning the history of his works' creation.

If we analyse the writer's visual *œuvre* in its three main categories with this in mind, then we find that Dostoevskii drew:

(1) portraits of people: almost always faces, very rarely busts, and only a few full-length figures (in these cases there is generally no connection with the creative process);

(2) Gothic windows and arches; 'cruciferae', pointed towers crowning the roofs of Gothic buildings;

(3) calligraphical compositions which most often comprise proper names.

In all this diversity there is only one detail that all areas of Dostoevskii's graphic art have in common. This characteristic shared feature is the idea of the 'above'.

In the apparent disorder and chaos of a page of Dostoevskii's manuscripts there is in fact nothing random. Here is one example. It might seem that the division of a notebook into pages should not have any real significance for a writer's work: when he finishes writing on one and turns over to the next page, he carries out a purely technical operation which has no direct relationship to the creative process. It is true that when Dostoevskii is writing down a text that is almost final – for example the first version of *Crime and Punishment*, 'The Confession of a Criminal' – Dostoevskii writes the text in a single stream, one line after the other, turning the pages over in sequence as they are filled. These are almost fair copies, and so there are no drawings – just the characteristic 'cruciferae' at the ends of chapters; as Dostoevskii moves closer to creating verbally his 'chronotope', so the borders between the spaces of adjoining pages are erased. The situation is quite different when the writer is just beginning to realise his artistic conception and is outlining his 'plan'. It is precisely at these moments that we find abundant and very diverse drawings; at the same time the sheet itself acquires particular significance, as a page becomes a special kind of 'field' for arranging the points of the 'plan' in whatever form – notes, 'calligraphy' or portraits – these points may take.

The sequential movement of the notes and drawings within a notebook reveals a set of unusual spatial relationships. Movement 'along the time axis', according to the European book tradition, is movement from left to right and from top to bottom. This is precisely how Dostoevskii's notes and drawings are set out in the notebooks. On the other hand, the two-page spread obtained when you open up the notebook was regarded by Dostoevskii as a space clearly divided by a vertical line into a right and a left side, odd- and even-numbered pages; these he saw as two distinct, and sometimes opposed, fields. For this reason the plans for one work would be systematically written out on the left side of the notebook, while the right side would be reserved for another. For example, the notes for *Crime and Punishment* in *Notebook no. 2* are located on the left-hand, even-numbered side, that is, on pages 1, 2, 4, 6, 8, 10 and so on, while notes for the story *The Crocodile* in the very same notebook are to be found on the right-hand, odd-numbered side, on pages 3, 5, 7, 11, 13, and so on. The artistic spaces of the two works each occupied their 'half' of the notebook, and this surely did not happen by chance. Two chronotopes that Dostoevskii created at the same time were neighbours on either side of a distinct boundary within the creative cosmos that they both inhabited.

In a similar way, the 'left' and 'right' sides of a notebook were reserved not for two separate works, but for two separate 'planes' of a single artistic idea. As is almost always the case, the movement from one page to another indicated the movement from one stage of the task to another, from one outcome of the idea to another, which would often be distinct from the previous one, or even opposite to it. We therefore find many pages filled with notes and drawings tightly packed together, at the same time as a page near by remains half-empty with one or two notes or with a single drawing in the middle. There are many such examples. They show that for Dostoevskii the page had a particular, independent significance: the purely literary significance of the text written on it was set off by the visual aspect of the whole page, taken as a single verbal and visual composition. Each one of Dostoevskii's notebooks has its own visual and stylistic atmosphere; each one formulates particular features of the chronotope being created on its pages.

As Dostoevskii consistently used notebooks of the same format and dimensions, there naturally emerged over the years particular aspects of his style of writing and sketching that all his notebooks have in common. It is therefore clear that sketches executed in a particular hand, in one and the same artistic style, and on pages of identical format, ought to be approximately the same size. This is indeed the case. The strict order that reigned in Dostoevskii's graphic art is also apparent in the fact that all drawings with depictions of people's faces can be divided into two formats. If Dostoevskii began drawing on a completely clean sheet of paper, then his drawing generally had the dimensions 7×6 cm, was located on an upright axis of co-ordinates and occupied a position right in the centre of the page (ill. 1.3). In these cases the graphic sketch, sometimes accompanied by 'calligraphy', made up the whole of Dostoevskii's 'entry' on that page. Sometimes it gradually 'sprouted' rough notes which occupied all the space remaining around the drawing (ill. 1.5). However crowded the page became, a 'large-scale' drawing was left untouched.

If a sheet of his notebook was already taken up with some notes or sketches, no matter what their size and type, then the page was not regarded by Dostoevskii as his usual space for entries, and any drawing that was added to the page was executed according to a second, 'lesser' format, whose dimensions were approximately 3×2 cm (ill. 1.2). Almost all of Dostoevskii's sketches match one of these two formats. It is interesting that Dostoevskii's 'Gothic' art comes in the same two sizes: the size of a 'Gothic sketch' varies between the limits of the two portrait formats, with only insignificant increases and decreases within these boundaries; the same thing can be said of Dostoevskii's 'calligraphy'. The sizes of all Dostoevskii's drawings have a corresponding sense-value which recalls the spatial and visual correspondence between the letters of a single alphabet or the signs of pictograms.

This constant relationship helps us to establish, in each separate case, the chronological sequence of entries on a particular page: to resolve, for example, the question, which came first – the sketch or the written entry? In general, if we find a large-format sketch in the centre of a page, we can say with certainty that all the other drawings and entries came afterwards and that this central drawing was the first to appear on the page. Usually this conclusion is confirmed by the arrangement of the text itself, by the continuities of the words that encircle or 'skirt round' the drawing. Small-format drawings are usually located in the margins – to the left, above or below, but never in the middle of the sheet: this shows that they were

1.5. Architectural motifs from a plan for *The Possessed*, showing text encroaching on the drawing. Russian State Library, Moscow.

added after the text was written. If a page contains a central large-scale drawing and one or several small ones, and some rough notes as well, then the sequence of entries is generally as follows:

(1) the central, large-format portrait

(2) cursive texts
(3) small-format sketched portraits (in the free areas, usually below or to the left, in the free margin)
(4) cursive texts (in the unoccupied margins, usually at an angle of 90 or 180 degrees to the preceding texts).

'Gothic' drawings and 'calligraphy' behave in the space of the page in a way analogous to sketched portraits. The only important difference is that they can be repeated many times with different graphic intonations. With portrait sketches this kind of 'repetition' is rare.

'Gothic' appeared as the writer's thoughts moved forwards, while 'cruciferae' tended to mark the end of a big section or chapter. 'Calligraphy', on the other hand, had no fixed place – it might appear at any moment: either at the beginning or at the end of Dostoevskii's reflections, together with cursive text or separate from it. For Dostoevskii to turn to drawing was, as we can see, both a frequent and a significant occurrence in his creative process. In fact, this was a deeply logical phenomenon that was determined by the very course of the writer's artistic development. We may well ask: why did graphic art in particular, and not some other kind of art, take such an important position in the writer's creative arsenal?

The 'material' similarity of writing and drawing – the fact that they both require a pen – and the thorough training that Dostoevskii received at the Engineering Academy were no more than two important prerequisites for this phenomenon. The main reasons are bound up with the character of Dostoevskii's creative process and with the specific role that it accorded pen-drawing.

Several of Dostoevskii's notes and drawings relate either to works that were never written, or else to more than one work at the same time. Confusion is bound to result if we take the erroneous view of Dostoevskii at work as a kind of craftsman manufacturing a particular object from a clearly defined set of materials. Dostoevskii actually created in his 'writing books' an atmosphere of philosophical and aesthetic enquiry which assisted the development of artistic form. Particular notes or drawings could, as we have seen, relate simultaneously to several works fused into one. Dostoevskii's creative style is remarkable for the importance it attaches to the initial period, when there emerges a 'word-symbol' which preserves the features both of the word and of the visual depiction. As A. G. Dostoevskaia explained, the writer had particular trouble at the very earliest stage of work on a novel. Recounting the history of *The Idiot*'s creation, during which Dostoevskii went through about ten different versions of the work over a period of two years, she writes:

Fedor Mikhailovich was faced by the most crucial phase of his work, and one that caused him particular problems: the thinking through and creation of a plan for the novel. Writing itself came relatively easily to him, but creating the plan presented him with great difficulties. The problem was the richness of the author's imagination and his dissatisfaction with the form in which he wanted to express the idea that formed the basis of the novel. Dozens of plans of the novel appeared (were created), each with sketches of the main characters, with plots, sometimes even with short scenes. From the 'notebooks' that have remained we can see how a particular idea of his came into being, in what forms it was expressed (and developed), and what it was that F. M. wanted to express through each of the characters in his novel. In other words, in the notebooks we see all the workings of Dostoevskii's creative processes.[35]

In this period Dostoevskii filled up his notebooks with ideographical signs which seem to occupy a neutral zone in between word and depiction, referential and non-referential sign. The creative imagination works intensely to form a 'full image' (Dostoevskii's own expression), which in turn helps to construct a plot where this initial image is fleshed out in word and action. But these 'word-symbols' by no means represent a finished literary form. They are no more than 'mental notes' which present a 'sketch of the hero' accessible only to the author. The main difficulty was to create a verbal embodiment of an artistic idea which emerges in the writer's consciousness in a whole, undivided form.

Dostoevskii was forced to find a solution to this problem, and he found an effective technique: by using special drawings, 'signs', verbal–visual compositions in which he was able to combine the word and the image, he helped to free the word from 'alien meaning', thus creating new artistic meanings: this was a poetic language arching over the language of literature. In other words, while Dostoevskii was operating with the 'embryos of artistic ideas', he had no problems and created 'plans' by the dozen. However, as soon as the writer moved on to the next stage – the transfer of this whole 'face [*lik*] of the idea' into literary form – he began to experience amazing difficulties; this is confirmed both by the writer himself in his letters and by the notebooks. The language of the sketch, Dostoevskii's 'internal speech', came into conflict with, and sharply diverged from, normal transparent form and 'literary norms'. But there was no way of doing without the notebook. There is no known example in the history of literature of a novel being written without preliminary rough notes. The writer is forced to search for a way of fixing the artistic idea which would, first, adequately perform the function of 'sign' and 'full image' of the idea and, second, offer a non-verbal form which, in order not to break up the literary form as it took shape, could be used at the same time and in the same location as verbal notes. All these conditions are met by drawings, pen sketches and calligraphy, which both fix an idea in its entirety in a single 'sign' and can be used on a manuscript page together with, and as a supplement to, any kind of written entry. Dostoevskii's drawings emerged at the very start of the first stage of his thought processes and they quickly and precisely capture the images that flash through his consciousness. Later on, literary form seizes upon the visual image and takes it as a point of departure for entering the 'second stage' of the creative process. The visual image, whose reflection in Dostoevskii's manuscripts is the sketch-drawing, is a kind of chrysalis from which a 'butterfly' breaks out and flies away – the new artistic word sought by the novelist.

Iconic signs were used by Dostoevskii not only as an initial means of forming the chronotope of a future novel, but also as conventional signs. Once they had exhausted their official function of sketched thought, images presented in the writer's drawings would wander into the novel, where they preserved their function of providing information about a person (the most reliable information possible, as we have seen), but also performed a new, conventional function of binding together the *siuzhet* (plot-ordering elements). Ideographical writing, which was born in the ancient world as a means of recording rituals, proved itself to be an amazing, almost universal instrument in Dostoevskii's creative laboratory as the writer sought to find his style.

For this reason, Dostoevskii's drawings are infinitely removed from figurative art: they are never an end in themselves, but rather the means of 'substituting' a word for a visual image. Calligraphy is a particular way of 'purifying' the word from the alien meanings it has accumulated in other people's usage.

Iurii Tynianov touched on this question many years ago. In an article on the poetics of illustration, he wrote:

There is a case when a drawing can play a more independent role, but on the *verbal plane*: drawings can be used as elements of expression in verbal art. Poetry operates not only and not so much by the *word* as by the *expression*. The concept of expression comprises all *equivalents* of the word: equivalents of this kind can include omitted sections of text (remember the enormous role played by omitted lines in *Evgenii Onegin*), or even drawings. This kind of word-equivalent might be a bottle in Rabelais, or a drawing of a broken line in Sterne [. . .] They have a very particular role, but exclusively on the verbal plane: they are equivalents of the word in the sense that, due to their location in the midst of word-masses, they themselves carry certain functions (and act as visual 'words').[36]

The difference between the pictorial 'word' of Dostoevskii – his portraits, 'Gothic' sketches and 'calligraphy' – and the examples mentioned by Tynianov is that the writer's verbal–visual compositions are not 'equivalents' of the artistic word (and thus are not in any sense 'illustrations'), but only its temporary 'replacements' at a moment when the true artistic word has not yet ripened. Dostoevskii's visual art does not stand alongside his artistic word, but rather comes before it in the chronological sequence of his creative process. The 'visual word' of the novelist's notebooks represents the beginning of work on the literary image.

CONCLUSION

In this essay the interaction of the visual and the verbal in Dostoevskii has been shown to have several aspects. We have seen that Dostoevskii, like many other nineteenth-century European novelists, placed great emphasis on descriptions of faces, facial expressions and reactions. Such descriptions formed an important convention of realist aesthetics, as they helped both to define the individuality of each face and to suggest its typicality.

But Dostoevskii was no mere realist. The meaning of visual description in his works was amplified, first, by his fervent adherence to a romantic aesthetics that insisted on the unity of Beauty, Truth and Goodness, and, second, by the Orthodox tradition of visual representation, where the facial image (*lik*) had enormous metaphysical resonance. The visual image in Dostoevskii can thus be linked to his broad project, as defined notably by Bakhtin, of bringing ideas (and ideals) to life. This confluence of aesthetics – Romanticism, realism and Orthodox iconography – carried Dostoevskii towards Modernism before Modernism even existed; for this reason it is fitting that Dostoevskii should open the present volume's section on the arts in Russian modernist literature.

There is, as we have seen, still another dimension to Dostoevskii's treatment of the visual. A careful examination of the notebooks shows that the visual imagining of characters and ideas was an essential stage in the gestation of Dostoevskii's works. It was in this pre-verbal medium that Dostoevskii tested the depth and idea-bearing capacity of his main characters; at the same time he was able to bypass the semantic field of clichés and to free himself from the alien meanings that take over words. The drawings in any of Dostoevskii's manuscripts encode the future artistic work; they serve as its embryo. They are directly imbued with the content of the artistic idea: by relying on a signifier that is devoid of non-essential connections, the writer has every chance of creating the chronotope of his future work, for the time being doing without words. To adopt Bakhtinian terminology, Dostoevskii created drawings that were 'laden with the word'. The search – with the help of visual art – for the 'potential word', which then establishes a semantic link to the Word, is the main focus of Dostoevskii's creative life, and it was this that led him to create an ideographical means of writing in his 'writing books', as he himself persisted in calling his notebooks.

NOTES

1 'Neizdannyi Dostoevskii', *Literaturnoe nasledstvo* 83 (1971), 436.
2 E. Markov, 'Kriticheskaia beseda', *Russkaia rech'*, 1879. Quoted from the commentary in F. M. Dostoevskii, *Polnoe sobranie sochinenii v tridtsati tomakh* (Leningrad, 1972–90) (hereafter *PSS*), v, p. 492.
3 *A Writer's Diary*, trans. K. Lantz, vol. 1 (London, 1994), p. 216; *PSS*, xxi, p. 77.
4 *A Writer's Diary*, p. 260; *PSS*, xxi, p. 111.
5 The relationship of self and other was made the centrepiece of Mikhail Bakhtin's aesthetics: see especially his early essay, 'Author and Hero in Aesthetic Activity', in *Art and Answerability: Early Philosophical Essays by M. M. Bakhtin*, ed. by M. Holquist and V. Liapunov (Austin, Tex., 1990).
6 *PSS*, xv, p. 337.
7 For example, Stepan Trofimovich in *The Possessed* hangs a portrait of a 12-year-old Liza on his wall between two Turkish curved daggers and, underneath them, a Circassian sabre, thus provoking Liza's enquiry: 'Why has my portrait been hanging under those daggers?' (*Devils* [i.e.

The Possessed], trans. Michael R. Katz, (Oxford and New York, 1992), p. 115; *PSS*, 10, p. 89).

8 Like the author himself, the hero of *The Insulted and the Humiliated*, Nikolai Sergeevich Ikhmenev, even as he curses Natasha aloud, secretly keeps a locket with her portrait: 'in solitude, unseen by all, he had gazed at the face of his adored child with infinite love, had gazed and could not gaze enough' (*The Insulted and the Humiliated*, 2nd impression (Moscow, 1976), p. 92; *PSS*, III, p. 223).

9 *An Accidental Family*, trans. R. Freeborn (Oxford and London, 1994), p. 486 (slightly modified); *PSS*, XIII, p. 371.

10 *The Insulted and the Humiliated*, p. 92; *PSS*, III, p. 223.

11 *The Insulted and the Humiliated*, p. 93, *PSS*, III, p. 224.

12 *The Insulted and the Humiliated*, p. 340; *PSS*, III, p. 397.

13 *An Accidental Family*, pp. 265–6; *PSS*, XIII, pp. 202–3.

14 *A Writer's Diary*, p. 352; *PSS*, XXII, p. 47.

15 *An Accidental Family*, p. 485; *PSS*, XIII, p. 370.

16 *The Brothers Karamazov*, trans. Ignat Avsey (Oxford and New York, 1994), pp. 355–6; *PSS*, XIV, p. 259.

17 *The Brothers Karamazov*, p. 356; *PSS*, XIV, p. 259.

18 *White Nights and Other Stories*, trans. C. Garnett, new impression (London, 1950), p. 1 (translation slightly modified); *PSS*, II, p. 102.

19 *Netochka Nezvanova*, trans. A. Dunnigan (Eaglewood Cliffs, NJ, 1970), p. 45; *PSS*, II, p. 169.

20 *The Village of Stepanchikovo and Its Inhabitants*, trans. Ignat Avsey (London, 1995), p. 72; *PSS*, III, p. 65.

21 *Crime and Punishment*, trans. D. McDuff (London, 1991), p. 136; *PSS*, VI, p. 76.

22 *A Writer's Diary*, p. 212; *PSS*, XXI, p. 74.

23 *Devils*, p. 317; *PSS*, X, p. 235.

24 N. Chernyshevskii, *Selected Philosophical Essays* (Moscow, 1953), p. 362 (translation slightly modified); *Izbrannye esteticheskie proizvedeniia* (Moscow, 1974), p. 152.

25 *Selected Philosophical Essays*, p. 318 (slightly modified); *Izbrannye esteticheskie proizvedeniia*, p. 105.

26 See especially *PSS*, XVIII, pp. 96–7.

27 *The Notebooks for The Idiot*, ed. E. Wasiolek, trans. K. Strelsky (Chicago, 1967), pp. 31–4; *PSS*, IX, pp. 141–3.

28 *The Idiot*, trans. Alan Myers (Oxford and New York, 1992), p. 34; *PSS*, VIII, pp. 28–9.

29 A. L. Volynskii, *Dostoevskii* (St Petersburg, 1906), pp. 56–8.

30 *The Idiot*, p. 69; *PSS*, VIII, pp. 55–6.

31 F. M. Dostoevskii, *Pis'ma v 4-kh tt.* (Moscow and Leningrad, 1928–56), vol. II, pp. 71–2.

32 *A Writer's Diary*, vol. II, p. 1128; *PSS*, XXVI, p. 25.

33 N. S. Samokish, *Risunok perom* (Moscow, 1959), p. 14.

34 L. P. Grossman, *Seminarii po Dostoevskomu* (Moscow and Petrograd, 1922), p. 58.
35 *PSS*, ix, p. 339.
36 Iu. N. Tynianov, *Poetika. Literatura. Kino* (Moscow, 1977), p. 316.

CHAPTER 2

Painting and autobiography: Anna Prismanova's 'Pesok' and Anna Akhmatova's 'Epicheskie motivy'

Catriona Kelly

The revolt against realism that was a primary motivating factor in the Russian modernist movement was often also a revolt against the visual. Like Eliot's *The Waste Land* or Ezra Pound's *Cantos*, Blok's *Dvenadtsat'* (The Twelve), Tsvetaeva's *Poema Gory* (Poem of the Mountain) and *Poema kontsa* (Poem of the End), Akhmatova's *Poema bez geroia* (Poem Without a Hero), or Mandelstam's 'Nashedshii podkovu' (The Horse-Shoe Ode) are poems of the ear rather than the eye.[1] They do not seek to counterfeit an alternative tangible world, but rather to evoke voices; they are (to employ the categorisation invented by a famous Russian modernist theorist, Mikhail Bakhtin) polyphonic rather than referential texts. Objects, landscapes and the human body are represented allegorically or emblematically, and the presence of hidden or 'marked' citations turns the poem into an echo-chamber of previous utterances. Marina Tsvetaeva's cycle 'Sivilla' (The Sibyl, 1922) is at once a manifestation of, and a manifesto for, this process of poetic composition. It invokes in its first section the legend, narrated by Ovid in *Metamorphoses*, Book 14, of the Cumaean Sibyl, who had been granted by Apollo her wish of living as many years as she could hold grains of sand in her hands, but who had forgotten to ask for eternal life. Tsvetaeva represents a woman whose body has all but ceased to exist, which has been reabsorbed into the mineral and vegetable world, as though her death had already occurred, becoming a cave for her miraculous voice:

> И вдруг, отчаявшись искать извне:
> Сердцем и голосом упав: во мне!
>
> Сивилла: вещая! Сивилла: свод!
> Так Благовещенье свершилось в тот
>
> Час не стареющий, так в седость трав
> Бренная девственность, пещерой став

Дивиому голосу . . .
                    – так в звездный вихрь
Сивилла: выбывшая из живых.

[And then, despairing of the search outside,
With sinking heart, with sinking voice: 'In me!'

Sibyl: a prophetess! Sibyl: a vault!
So was the Annunciation achieved in that

Unaging hour, so in the grey-haired grass
Fragile virginity became a cave

For a miracle, that voice . . .
                    so in a whirl of stars
Sibyl is vanished, into death.][2]

The poem cannot immediately be decoded from visual cues: for example the phrase *sedost' trav* (grey-haired grass) is comprehensible as a metaphor for the hair of an old woman only if the reader is familiar with the legend as narrated by Ovid, and is in any case as significant for its integration into one of the poem's governing paradoxes, *brennaia devstvennost'* (virginity that is fragile, i.e. on the point of physical disintegration)[3] as for its evocation of the Sibyl's physical appearance.

The post-Symbolist generation of Russian modernists, such as Tsvetaeva, attuned their ears to dissonance rather than to the magical music that had absorbed their Symbolist predecessors, for example Belyi or the early Blok, but they were equally concerned with sound. Yet there was also a strongly visual impulse behind some Russian modernist poetry, which expressed itself in several different ways. The first and simplest way was through a revival of the traditional device of ekphrasis. This was especially characteristic of Acmeist poets, for whom architecture, sculpture and painting (in that order) were all favourite subjects of lyric, and among whom the term *vaian'e*, 'hewing', was employed as a metaphor for poetic craft. More loosely, the aestheticisation of everyday objects that was characteristic of Acmeist writers, and which is also to be found in the work of Mikhail Kuzmin, an important inspiration for the movement, allies their work with the paintings of the *Mir iskusstva* (World of Art) painters, in particular Konstantin Somov (there is a striking affinity, for example, between Somov's portraits of refined, elegant and nervous women and the heroines of Akhmatova's early poetry). And this was a generation in which the physical appearance of the poet, while not necessarily directly evoked in poetry itself, was often read 'into' or 'alongside' the poetic text, a process of which Acmeist writers such as Akhmatova were just as conscious as their avant-garde opponents, such as Maiakovskii.

But other, and more dynamic, appropriations of the visual arts were also possible. For some modernist poets (as for modernist writers generally), painting, and most particularly semi-figurative painting such as that of the Cubists, provided a way out of the customary conventions of verbal representation, a means of escaping the stereotypes or clichés that so horrified modernist writers all over Europe, and of 'making the world strange'. Evoking the visual could also be a way of displacing sensibility, of confecting the evasive autobiographical discourse that was more attractive to modernist writers than the purported sincerity or candour of their realist predecessors.

The autobiographical writings of Anna Prismanova (1892–1960), a poet of the 'first wave' Paris emigration, show both these tendencies at work simultaneously. Her cycle 'Pesok' (Sand), an evocation of her birthplace in Latvia, Libau (known in Russian as Libava and now renamed Liepaja) addresses the autobiographical predicament of a woman writer who did not have the canonical physical appearance required of a modernist poet, and whose home town did not have a history in the verbal arts, a place in literary tradition. For Prismanova, the more permissive aesthetic of Russian painting was attractive, since it made it possible to write about a place that was not 'poetogenic' in the ordinary sense, while at the same time the obvious formality and non-referentiality of Cubist portraits and landscapes, to which her work gestured, established the distance from life that was so important to Russian modernist artists. Not primarily intended as a general introduction to Prismanova's work,[4] my essay is, rather, an exploration of the relationship between poetry and the visual arts in the work of a characteristic Russian modernist writer, whose 'Pesok' is compared with a better-known, but in some ways less inventive poetic autobiography by a famous twentieth-century Russian poet, Anna Akhmatova's *Epicheskie motivy* (Epic Motifs).

POETS AS ICONS: PORTRAITS AS SUB-TEXTS IN RUSSIAN
MODERNIST POETRY

An aspect of interaction between the verbal and the visual which has
so far attracted little attention among Russian specialists is the
question of how far construction and consumption of literary texts
(and most particularly, of quasi-confessional poetry) is affected by the
reader's, or expected reader's, familiarity with the physical appearance of those texts' biographical authors. Since Orest Kiprenskii
produced his famous image of Pushkin the romantic genius, eyes
fixed on further horizons, in 1828, portraits of writers have been a
vital form of non-verbal intertext, and an important influence on
reading, an influence whose sphere of impact increased in the
second half of the nineteenth century, as photomechanical forms of
reproduction developed, making cheap portraits, such as the picture
postcard, available to a far wider audience than would have had
access to paintings or even engravings.[5] The presentation of texts in
performance, via public readings, was another means of trans-
mission that reached its apogee in the modernist era; both portraits
and readings played their part in establishing the cults of such
important Symbolist and post-Symbolist poets as Aleksandr Blok,
Vladimir Maiakovskii and Anna Akhmatova.

An intriguing account of the interaction between expectations of a
poet's physical appearance and reception is given in Iurii Olesha's
memoir of Maiakovskii. Olesha describes attending a public reading
by the poet in the early 1920s:

I was certain that the man who was about to come on stage would be
theatrical, red-haired, a clown, pretty well . . . After all, how else were we
likely to imagine him; we'd heard all about his yellow jacket and the literary
scandals of former days.

But the man who actually stepped out from the wings was someone quite
different.

To be sure, he was strikingly tall, and his immensely powerful and
beautiful eyes were also striking.

But otherwise he looked very much the ordinary Soviet citizen: rather
tired, in a three-quarter-length overcoat with a sheepskin collar and a
sheepskin hat pushed slightly back off his forehead. And it was immediately
clear that for all his fame as a poet, this man had not come on stage to
garner laurels, but to do a serious job of work. Later I was to see
Maiakovskii during his performances in Moscow at the Polytechnic
Institute, and the impression of a man who was hard-working above all else

would be still further strengthened; he would take off his jacket and roll up his sleeves.[6]

The passage shows with great clarity how a firm expectation of Maiakovskii's likely appearance (an expectation based as much on gossip as on Maiakovskii's poetry, in this particular case) was unsettled by a confrontation with the poet himself; the alternative impression resulting from the confrontation then (by implication) laid the foundation for the reception of Maiakovskii's post-revolutionary poetry, and in particular the diligent promulgation of civic virtues in this. Pondering Maiakovskii's 'legendary fame' (a fame shared with Esenin, Shaliapin and Gorky), Olesha continues: 'This quality of being legendary is part of the personality. Maybe it derives from someone's personal appearance?'[7] Though he considers the question no further, quickly moving on to the more appropriate (in a Soviet context) suggestion that fame derives from the fact that 'in the past the hero achieved something that caught people's imaginations', his brief note illustrates that, on the contrary, Maiakovskii's unusual height, burning eyes and yellow waistcoat (or in later days, rolled-up shirt-sleeves) did more to establish his heroic poetic identity in the popular imagination than any notable 'achievement'.

In the case of Anna Akhmatova, the poet herself, while a young woman, made every effort to stress the centrality of personal appearance to poetic persona, costuming herself in a manner that recalled the heroine of her lyric poetry (shawl, mantilla, beads), and alluding, directly or obliquely, to such physical features as her height, slender build and heavy fringe of dark hair.[8] A more complex intersection between the verbal and the visual, body and voice, is evident, however, in the second section of the mini-cycle *Epicheskie motivy*, where Akhmatova recollects visiting the studio of the painter Natan Al'tman in 1913, in order that he might paint her portrait. The poem expresses a desire on Akhmatova's part to control representations of her physical person. Rather than Al'tman's delineation being seen as the exercise of sexual power (as feminist critics have argued to be the general case when a male artist portrays a female subject),[9] Akhmatova emphasises the harmlessness of the portrait-painter by feminising him. A reference to the girlish friendship of Akhmatova and Al'tman's different 'muses' at once turns Al'tman into one of Akhmatova's many female doubles, and in doing so extends to painting the literary convention of the muse. Turning

Al'tman into a 'poet in paint', Akhmatova also diminishes him by referring to him as a 'siskin' (*chizhik*), a warbling caged bird (semantically equivalent to a canary), whose repetitive song (by implication) lacks the true creativity of Akhmatova's own singing, just as Al'tman's slightly banal cheerfulness contrasts with Akhmatova's own prophetic and uncanny encounter with her portrait-in-progress:

Я подходила к старому мосту.
Там комната, похожая на клетку,
Под самой крышей в грязном, шумном доме,
Где он, как чиж, свистал перед мольбертом,
И жаловался весело и грустно
О радости небывшей говорил.
Как в зеркало глядела я тревожно
На серый холст, и с каждою неделей
Всё горше и страннее было сходство
Мое с моим изображеньем новым.
Теперь не знаю, где художник милый,
С которым я из голубой мансарды
Через окно на крышу выходила
И по карнизу шла над смертной бездной,
Чтоб видеть снег, Неву и облака, –
Но чувствую, что Музы наши дружны
Беспечной и пленительною дружбой,
Как девушки, не знавшие любовь.

[I would go to the old bridge.
There is a room there like a cage,
Right under the roof in an old and dirty house,
Where he would whistle before the easel like a siskin,
And complain merrily, and sadly
Speak of impossible joy.
As into a mirror I gazed anxiously
At the grey canvas, and with every week that passed
The clearer and more striking was the resemblance
Between me and my new image.
I do not know now where that dear artist is
With whom I would step out of the sky-blue garret
And walk round the cornice above the deadly abyss
To look at the snow, the Neva, and the clouds, –
But I feel that our Muses are close to each other
In carefree and captivating friendship
As two girls who have never known love.]   (SP, p. 325)

Al'tman's representation of Akhmatova is not created, according to this poetic evocation, but simply emerges, as does a reflection in a mirror; painting is valued not as an autonomous art form, but because it is the occasion of poetry's prophetic art. Ostensibly about a twinning between the 'Muses' of poetry and painting, the poem in fact makes Al'tman's very well-known and much-loved portrait seem no more than an illustration to Akhmatova's own recollections.

Yet at the same time *Epicheskie motivy* II reveals an awareness of how important the visual image had become to modern poetry; Akhmatova's authority is exercised not only despite the existence of the portrait, but because of this. If a reader lacked familiarity with Al'tman's painting (whose blues and greys are mnemonically cited by Akhmatova), Akhmatova's attempt to wrest control by turning portrait into self-portrait would lose its impact. The authority that *Epicheskie motivy* II expresses, then, depends on a reader's acceptance of painterly representation as a supplement to, if not a substitute for, the poet's own depiction of herself.

A second factor in the interaction between painted image and verbal text is the degree of correspondence between a poet's appearance and customary appreciations of physical beauty, its conformity to contemporary aesthetics of the body. Both Akhmatova and Tsvetaeva were recalled by contemporaries as possessing a stark and unconventional beauty of feature that was repeatedly compared to that of the *liki*, faces, appearing in Russian icons. Tsvetaeva herself played up the resemblance in a famous, and much-reproduced, image of 1916, in which the poet is represented standing against a background that recalls the *oklad*, the jewelled casing that covers the background of a painted icon, leaving face and hands bare.[10] What, though, of writers less favoured than Akhmatova, Tsvetaeva, Blok, Pasternak, the burly and imposing Maiakovskii with his glittering eyes, or for that matter Sergei Esenin and Ol'ga Berggol'ts, all of whom were widely portrayed and whose appearances were widely admired? Here one can witness a different and more subtly allusive process of recognising and naming physical realia. If Maiakovskii's *Vo ves'golos* (At the Top of My Voice) is a performative piece that depends for its full effect upon a reader's knowledge of Maiakovskii's own dominating public readings, a subtler role is played, in the work of other poets, by characteristics that are less readily associated with authority. One thinks here perhaps of the influence upon Mandelstam's symbolic system of the poet's history of asthma, or (to think more laterally) of the possible link between Gumilev's strenuous emphasis on valorous action as a touchstone of masculine identity and the poet's notorious lack of conventional good looks.

For women poets, the effect of appearance on reception and self-construction has been still more important, given the prevalence of the opinion that female beauty is the crucial signifier of identity. Akhmatova's unique success in presenting herself as a poet of masculine intellectual weight and feminine charm cannot be detached from the poet's status as a recognised beauty, and therefore unalienably 'feminine'. To imitate Akhmatova lays a woman poet open to charges of imitativeness (*epigonstvo*), but offers her a chance to pretend to her predecessor's immense authority.[11] The risks are less significant than those which beset those who choose a different path, since to spurn Akhmatova's guidance threatens that one may be seen as a phenomenon not only beyond the bounds of decent literature, but of decency more generally: as an unsuccessful woman as well as an unsuccessful artist. Yet, for those lacking Akhmatova's physical advantages, the risks of the second path are hard to avoid, as can be seen if one considers the career of Anna Prismanova, a poet of Akhmatova's generation, but with an utterly different creative biography.

THE PREDICAMENT OF 'UGLINESS': PRISMANOVA PORTRAYED AND SELF-PORTRAYED

When she began publishing in the mid-1920s, Prismanova had, from some points of view (including Akhmatova's own) already set herself outside the mainstream; as her famous contemporary put it in a poem of 1922, she was one of those who had 'cast their homeland / to be torn apart by the foes' ('brosil zemliu / Na rasterzanie vragam'). Rather than remaining in Russia, Prismanova emigrated to Paris at some point in the early 1920s (the exact date is unknown), where she had a respectable, but by no means 'brilliant', literary career, publishing four books of verse, as well as a number of other poems and two stories in literary magazines.

The most significant indication of the price that Prismanova paid for her failure to be like Akhmatova was not literary neglect (which should not be overestimated: her work was published and received generally respectful, if rather uneasy, reviews – of which more in a moment). Rather, it is the character of those few memoirs of her that exist (their scarcity already tells a tale), which represent her as the antipode to the persona expertly created by Akhmatova for her contemporaries. One small, but in the present context significant, point is that Prismanova's looks were almost always the subject of unfavourable comment. Zinaida Shakhovskaia, for example, describes Prismanova and Aleksandr Ginger, her husband, as looking like 'gargoyles'.[12] Iurii Terapiano, in any case the most hostile of the memoirists to Prismanova, narrates a rather catty story about how Prismanova and Ginger, offended by Merezhkovskii's comments about how a person's looks undoubtedly reflected his or her character, left a gathering precipitately and shunned the society of Merezhkovskii and Gippius thereafter.[13] The considerably more sympathetic Vadim Perel'muter still cannot resist a humorous observation on the striking contrast between Prismanova and her husband Aleksandr Ginger, 'she tiny and plain, he huge and broad-shouldered'.[14]

Not only 'ugly', Anna Prismanova was also, according to the chroniclers of the emigration, withdrawn and aloof (contrast Akhmatova's urgent need, recorded by Lidiia Chukovskaia among others, for company at all hours, including ones inconvenient to those who supplied it: that is, her need for an audience before which she might perform). One relatively sympathetic memoirist, A. Bakhrakh, described Prismanova in words taken from Moréas as characterised by 'the bitter sweetness of solitude', while Perel'muter said that 'she worked unhurriedly, modestly, wrapped up in herself' (again, contrast accounts of Akhmatova as fired up with very public creative intensity.)[15] Even Prismanova's friendship with Tsvetaeva was cited in order to belittle her: Slonim described Prismanova as 'looking up to Tsvetaeva' ('otnoshenie [bylo] snizu vverkh'), while Irina Odoevtseva, recollecting that Tsvetaeva spent her last evening in Paris with Prismanova and Ginger, managed to make Prismanova's action in inviting Tsvetaeva (then ostracised by most of the Paris emigration) less the product of defiance or courage than of absent-mindedness: 'I doubt whether she knows anything about how their friends and acquaintances get on with each other.'[16] (On the other hand, Odoevtseva and Ivanov's own agreement to attend the gathering comes across as an act of pre-meditated and disinterested bravery.)

Disinterring this decades-old gossip might seem pointless were it not for the fact that representations of Prismanova's appearance and behaviour, of her *oblik*, or image, are in harmony with interpretations of her poetry. Here too awkwardness, lack of sociability and gaucherie are the leitmotifs. Interpreters perpetually raise the question of whether Prismanova was actually in control of the effects that she created. Bakhrakh spoke of her as 'always going her own, unhurried path, tormentedly searching for her own personal theme, and, in the end, not finding it'.[17] He also stated that she was a writer whose 'whole poetic biography, in essence, was a duel with words, to which she addressed demands that could not be fulfilled and accusations that had no foundation' – language that recalls the ineffectual claims made by a woman spurned on her departing lover.[18] Again, Terepiano took the accusation further, and Prismanova, in his account, comes across as a ridiculous, slightly spinsterish figure, whose determination to state things in her own way led her to stick (against his and Aleksandr Ginger's advice) to such 'absurd' coinages as 'the swan is unrecognisable on the water / raising his ear like Beethoven' – (Neuznavaem lebed' na vode; / on, kak Betgoven, podnimaet ukho).[19] In refusing to take such advice, Prismanova flew in the face of a long cultural tradition, originating in France in the late seventeenth century, which has set women up on a pedestal as arbiters of taste (a position which Akhmatova, again, exercised to the full), yet denied them the more significant authority of creating, rather than policing, aesthetic norms (what seems admirable daring in a male writer seems unpardonable ignorance in a female).[20]

Though Terapiano spoke at one point of 'intentionally absurd phrasing', his wording elsewhere betrayed his doubt that Prismanova in fact achieved her affects deliberately: 'Some fateful temptation forced her to issue a feeble challenge to common sense, logic and aesthetics.'[21] Yet Prismanova's behaviour could have been just as self-conscious an act of self-definition as Akhmatova's determination to place herself in the Russian literary (and social) elite. It is possible, and indeed I would argue, likely, that Prismanova made a deliberate decision to opt for cultural marginalisation, to make her work, and by extension life, an act of self-scrutiny rather than a ritual of self-affirmation.[22] For Prismanova, as for Akhmatova, the self was a construct, rather than a given; but Prismanova took a less conventional attitude to the dichotomy between masculine and feminine than Akhmatova, not seeing it in terms of intellect, creativity, reason versus innate beauty and capacity for solace. Prismanova accordingly did not use sub-texts as legitimation (employing Dante or Pushkin as a sort of aesthetic gold standard), but explored them as possible perspectives, and women writers are cited by her alongside men (for example, Karolina Pavlova, the Brontë sisters and of course Tsvetaeva, who is by no means seen 'from below' in Prismanova's poetry, whatever the case was in life). Similarly, painting and poetry are seen by her as mutually enriching art forms, which can borrow from each other, rather than contesting legitimacy. If Prismanova's voice is immediately recognisable, her intonation by turns ironical and plangent, so too is her eye for grotesque detail and her sensitivity to painterly composition.

'Pesok', a cycle placed in her second book of poems, *Bliznetsy* (Twins, 1946), displays all these qualities; it also combines confessional autobiography with, or to be more exact displaces it by, a re-vision or revision of her childhood. Self-representation is inextricable from representation of Prismanova's 'fatherland' (*otchizna* – I will discuss the resonance of this term later), Libau/Liepaja, a place without the beauty or the inherited glamour of Akhmatova's St Petersburg, indeed a place outside the historic boundaries of Russia altogether, 'beyond the pale' in the sense of the colloquial British phrase, though well within another sort of pale: the Jewish pale of settlement.

The link between ungainly personal appearance and birth in a place that cannot be classified in the terms of Russian literature's standard myths is emphasised in the title poem of *Pesok*, an exploration of the symbolism of Prismanova's given name, 'Anna', which proceeds from a silent reworking of Anna Akhmatova's own comparison of herself with St Anne in part I of *Epicheskie motivy* (a comparison that both *Epicheskie motivy*'s dedication, to the mosaic artist Boris Anrep, and the juxtaposition to the Al'tman study in Part II, suggest has an iconographical resonance, though the poem itself concentrates on the liturgical role of St Anne, alluding in its opening lines to the saint's many festivals in the church calendar):

> В то время я гостила на земле,
> Мне дали имя при крещенье – Анна,
> Сладчайшее для губ людских и слуха.
> Так дивно знала я земную радость
> И праздников считала не двенадцать,
> А столько, сколько было дней в году.

> [At that time I was a guest on the earth,
> And I was given at my christening the name of Anna,
> The sweetest name for people's lips and ears.
> Thus miraculously did I know earthly joy;

Far from having only twelve festivals,
I had as many as there are days in the year.] (SP, p. 323)

Prismanova, on the other hand, recalls her own ill-favoured appearance as a child, ironically commenting on the unsuitability of a name
derived from the Hebrew word for 'grace' (in the theological sense,
Russian *blagodat'*) to the scrawny infant that she once was:

Я знаю, Анна значит благодать,
я помню якорь на морском солдате . . .
Но что могу я отчей почве дать?
лишь слово *помню* вместо благодати.

Летала с криком птица над водой,
и паровод в туман вдвигался с криком,
и слышен был крик девочки худой,
родившейся с почти-что мертвым ликом.

[I know that Anna means [in Hebrew] grace,
I remember anchors stitched to a sailor's collar . . .
But what can I give back to my father's earth?
No kind of grace, only the word *remember.*

The ships let booming cries out as they crawled
through fog, and gulls cried, shrill above the water:
a fainter cry came from a baby girl
born bony, with a face still as a corpse's.] (SS, p. 75)

Other poems in the cycle *Pesok* provide Prismanova's lack of physical
appeal with a mythic aetiology. In 'Gorlo' (The Throat), the poet
reproduces a childhood vision of her mother, represented with
unsettling clarity in the days before her death from throat cancer:

Искусственному горлу подражать
Не пробуйте: оно страшней кинжала.
Ах, с этим горлом надобно лежать!
Так, умирая, мать моя лежала.

[Do not attempt to imitate
the artificial throat: it is more terrible than a Caucasian dagger.
Ah, with such a throat one must lie down;
so, dying, my mother lay.] (SS, p. 72)

And in 'List'ia' (Leaves), Prismanova recalls her father after his
death, not as a spiritual presence, but as a body subject to physical
decay, to dissolution into the anonymity of the Baltic shoreline's
sandy soil:

Но сам отец навек ушел в песок,
не ощутив минуты погруженья,

оставив нам высокий свой висок,
страсть к странствию, и к «Ниве» приложенья.

[My father has passed into the sand forever,
not sensing the moment when he plunged,
and leaving to us his high cheekbones,
his passion for travelling, and supplements to *Niva*.]   (SS, p. 76)

Akhmatova had customarily represented herself in the company of a beautiful 'double', and in *Northern Elegies*, in an elaboration of this tradition, the writer's mother becomes the prefiguration of her daughter:

. . . женщина с прозрачными глазами
(Такой глубокой синевы, что море
Нельзя не вспомнить, поглядевши в них)

[. . . a woman with transparent eyes
(Of such deep blue, that one could not help remembering
The sea, when looking into them)]   (SP, p. 329)

In contrast to Akhmatova's autobiographical self, Prismanova's is said to have inherited from her father gaunt masculine cheekbones; the emphasis on male lineage is as much as anything a reference to the absence of 'feminine' beauty.

The hidden metaphor of the father's death as drowning (a 'plunge into sand') draws a parallel with *The Tempest*, a text with which *Pesok* shares not only coastal setting and stormy weather, but also the presence of unloved and ugly creatures. In her important essay, 'Difficult Joys', Hélène Cixous has named *The Tempest* as a crucial text in the woman writer's coming to terms with her own marginalisation, a marginalisation which she sees as making every woman 'an exile':

There is something of a foreignness, a feeling of not being accepted or of being unacceptable, which is particularly insistent when as a woman you suddenly get into that strange country of writing where most inhabitants are men and where the fate of women is still not settled. [. . .] Sometimes you are even a double exile, but I'm not going to be tragic about it because I think it is a source of creation and of symbolic wealth.[23]

Similar in the facts of their biography (both Jews transplanted from one alien culture into another), Cixous and Prismanova also have affinities as readers (among joint sources are not only *The Tempest*, but Marina Tsvetaeva's essays on Pushkin, with their central metaphor of the unstable text as letters on a rock effaced by the sea).

It is, though, less the employment of the trope of exile as an expression for the woman writer's marginality within her culture that concerns me here than another project of Prismanova's: to name the unnameable, to use the trope of ekphrasis in order to represent what is visually unalluring. Cixous has spoken of the transfiguration of mortality as a fundamental moment in the history of the writing subject: 'It's one of those keys to writing, writing as the key to death – with father or mother, with the sea, and transfiguration, with the transposition of dead parent into beautiful metaphor.'[24] The link between writing and death is made very forcefully in *Pesok*: the nine poems all represent Prismanova's birthplace seen retrospectively; the act of review in many cases also being a ritual in commemoration of the dead. Apart from Prismanova's mother and father (commemorated in 'Gorlo' and 'List'ia), these dead include Prismanova's cousin, who perished during the Second World War, the dedicatee of the first poem, 'Vospominanie' (Remembrance); her grandfather, in 'Glaza' (Eyes); and her stepmother, in 'Sof'ia'. These five pieces are interspersed with a further four poems, 'Treugol'nik' (Triangles), 'Gavan'' (Harbour), 'Anna' and 'Pesok', which contain different representations of the poet's younger self: as a child riding a cardboard horse through the streets; as a girl in an 'ash-coloured shirt' terrified by a storm at sea; as a child, and later an adult, haunted by graceless visions. Various versions of Prismanova also appear in the other poems, from the child 'on all fours' watching her mother die to the adolescent in her hammock waiting for teenage male visitors, to the adult painfully aware that the memories she has are dreams, illusions comparable in their insubstantiality to the 'monument of sand' she desires in the title poem of the cycle.

But if the deaths of close relations are indeed the *alpha et omega* of 'Pesok', the point in Cixous's formulation that certainly does not help in glossing Prismanova is the reference to 'transformation of dead parent into beautiful metaphor'. Cixous's own exemplary text is Ariel's song from *The Tempest* ('Full fathom five my father lies / Of his bones are coral made / Those are pearls that were his eyes. . .'). Though Prismanova's reference to her father's 'plunge into sand' invokes this text too, her response to it is negative – in 'List'ia' she seems determined not to 'make beautiful' her father's remains in any ordinary sense. This is logical, given her repudiation of beautifying powers in 'Pesok', where she refers to the etymology of Anna from *blagodat'* (grace), but only in order to negate her own connection with the word (which comes from a very rich semantic field, being linked not only with the 'gifts' of the Holy Spirit, but with usefulness, strength of will and energy, happiness, abundance, various dialect terms for grain and food, a healing herb called Gratiole (*Gratiola officinalis*), and finally with *blagodarnost'*, gratitude. Prismanova denies to herself, then, the accepted powers of inspired art (art filled with grace, *grateful* art, in one sense of the English word) to glorify or to offer comfort, whether ethical or aesthetic; just so her face, in an oxymoron as powerful as Gogol's 'dead souls', is described as *mertvyi lik* (*lik* signifying the spiritual 'face' of a person or icon, in other words, something that by definition cannot be 'dead').

APPEARANCE INTO SETTING: THE BALTIC COAST IN 'PESOK'

There is a clear parallel between Prismanova's evocation of this aspect of identity, physical appearance, and her evocation of another: setting. The bony face of the child that Prismanova once was matches the appearance of the bleak and unspectacular landscape in which she grew up:

> Над солью волн шли пресные дожди,
> за рыбою шел парус, ветром полный,
> и важные, седые как вожди,
> над мелкими – девятые шли волны.

> [Fresh-water rains poured down on salty waves,
> a sail swollen with wind ran after fish;
> and pompous as rulers, waves with great white heads
> towered over littler ones, ninth to their eighth.]
>
> ('Treugol'nik', SS, p. 68)

Prismanova's emphasis on her own anti-artistic and untraditional appearance was equalled by her insistence on representing a childhood which was external to Russian literary norms because it had taken place outside Russia, and in a city that did not give her access to the grandiose metonyms available to Petersburg and Moscow writers, 'granite embankments' and 'forty times forty churches', or, more imaginatively, the 'rzhavye perila' (rusted balustrade) of the river bridge to which Akhmatova refers in *Epicheskie motivy* III, or the 'the island low as a raft' *(nizkii ostrov . . . slovno plot)* that she recalls in Part II of the same poem.

'Pesok' is structured round one dominant, but hidden, motif: the hourglass, which apart from its obvious foregrounding of time symbolism (and a time measured inexactly, organically), unifies various images obsessively, but apparently randomly, repeated through the cycle: sand, glass and above all the triangle (suggested by the cone of descending sand in the bottom globe). Despite its preoccupation with time in a metaphysical sense, the frequency of concepts such as *bytie* (heavenly, otherworldly existence), and the fairly widespread use of neo-classical formulae and of periphrasis (most fancifully, rats described as 'long-tailed prophetesses' [*khvostatye vestnitsy*, SS, p. 69 – the prophecy meant is of shipwreck]), the effect of the cycle, as one reads, is neither insubstantial nor abstract. The sense of place that is generated is so vivid, and so foreign to the inherited tradition of the Russian elegy, that a productive dislocation between elegaic sensibility and tangibility of observed phenomena is generated: what results is one of the most unusual pieces of poetic autobiography since Anna Bunina's 'Khot.' bednost' ne porok' (Though Poverty's No Stain) or 'Moi portret' (My Portrait), written in the 1810s. Prismanova was helped here by the nature of the setting that she recalled – provincial, untouched by Russian tradition.

Libau/Libava/Liepaja is a small city, roughly midway between Riga and Königsberg (150 or so miles from each), which, partly because of its almost ice-free harbour, was, by the late nineteenth century, the third most important Baltic port in the Russian Empire, handling traffic to a variety of European countries, above all Britain. Apart from shipping activities, the city had a range of other industries in its modern quarter, 'New Libau'. It also had a certain reputation as a seaside resort: as *Baedeker's Russia* put it in 1914, 'Libau has a good sandy beach and well laid out pleasure grounds, and is frequented to some small extent for sea bathing.'[25]

The resort had, in fact, been well established for at least fifty years when Prismanova was a child around 1900. The Russian writer and censor Aleksandr Nikitenko, who spent a few weeks there in the summer of 1861, recorded excellent beaches, clean and pleasant (if overpriced) lodgings and food, and attractively quaint low houses. With the unselfconscious prejudice all too typical of the pre-revolutionary Russian service class, he majestically concluded: 'even the presence of Jews in the town does not spoil it' ('dazhe prisutstvie v nei zhidov ne portit ee').[26] Anna Prismanova, the daughter of a local doctor, Semen Prisman (her mother's name is not recorded), was, of course, herself one of the 'Jews' so cavalierly referred to by Nikitenko (by the late nineteenth century there were more than 10,000 Jews in Libau, or just under a quarter of the population, a number that slightly exceeded the number of Russian Orthodox, but which was only just over half the number of registered Lutherans).

No doubt partly because of attitudes like Nikitenko's, Prismanova took the assimilationist path that was followed by so many Russian Jews of her generation, including her own husband Aleksandr Ginger and her near-contemporary Sofiya Parnok, and deserted Judaism.[27] The date of her conversion is unknown, but the evidence of her poetry, in which Christian motifs play a considerable role from the first, suggests that it happened in early adulthood. She felt no stronger sense of 'Latvian' than of 'Jewish' identity, stating, in a line of 'Treugol'nik', a poem from the *Pesok* cycle, 'Pochty zabyty mnoiu latyshi' (Latvians are almost forgotten by me, SS, p. 67]). And in several of her works, such as her late cycles dedicated to the poet Nikolai Nekrasov and the revolutionary heroine Vera Figner, she constructed herself an alternative childhood, Northern but specifically Russian in character, and properly idyllic in the manner of the classic gentry memoir, with 'broad shining meadows' ('Chernoles'e', SS, p. 151), and game-shooting expeditions ('Dich'', SS, pp. 180–2).[28]

Prismanova's evocations of her own childhood are considerably less idyllic than her fictions about others' childhoods. Unlike many emigré writers, for example Nabokov in his *Speak, Memory*, she concentrates on grotesque visions of her past, which is often seen refracted through dream (or nightmare). In 'List'ia', for instance, she moves from an ordinary and reassuring image of 'my father's linen hanging on a line' to a glimpse of her father lying in his grave, his corpse 'keeping his bones inside his shoes' (SS, pp. 70–1). If 'Gorlo' uses an apparently lushly Romantic reference to the 'silver throats' of nightingales to introduce a reminiscence of Prismanova's dying mother fitted with a metal tube to aid her swallowing (SS, p. 70), in 'Glaza' (SS, pp. 69–70), it is her grandfather's glass eye that triggers memories of him. Even the landscape is recalled in images suggesting violence: the beach 'splayed' (*rasplastan*) between dunes and water (SS, p. 67), the wind 'tearing the sails from [a ship's] boards with its fists' ('Svirepyi veter kulakami / sryvaet s palok parusa', SS, p. 68). In no sense are the memories invoked in these poems the natural material of art (though there is one charming conceit in 'Pesok' when Prismanova describes her childhood self as 'reading my first syllable on board / a fishing smack'). Though it was Russian Acmeism, the aetheticisation of the everyday, that was the dominant literary orientation in the Paris emigration, though the visually saturated world of early Acmeism should have seemed attractive to her, and though her metrical preferences (a taste for quatrains, iambs and trochees) and elegaic intonations evoke pre-revolutionary Acmeism, the brutality of Prismanova's vision breaks radically with the Acmeist aesthetic. It is, to state the obvious, less significant that she fails to mention the new industries of Libau (for instance, linoleum manufacture) than that she altogether fails to eulogise the town's fourteenth-century cathedral. Indeed, the visual affinities of her work are not to the Gothic vaults eulogised by Akhmatova and Mandel'shtam in their poetry of the 1910s, but to the frescoes representing 'dances of death' found in many Baltic cathedrals. Almost every object can take on the lineaments of a memento mori. One of Prismanova's repeated images is the diver, who plunges with flashlit head into the deep to recover – what is not specified, and though 'the past' is obviously one answer, the recovery of dead bodies is suggested too, besides, of course, the sinister image of an early twentieth-century diver in leaded boots shambling along the seabed like the waking dead.

Above all, though, Prismanova's grotesque imagination is expressed in her remarkably original representation of the father–daughter relation, which is structured round the concepts of *otchizna* (father's country) and *otch'ia pochva* (father's soil). One reason for choosing these terms lay in the fact that Prismanova wished to avoid the terms *otechestvo* and *rodina*, with their heavy political freighting (*otechestvo*, 'fatherland' being the preferred denomination for the Russian state of the Tsarist regime, while *rodina*, 'motherland', had, by the time *Pesok* was published in 1946, become contaminated by Stalinist propaganda). The resonance of *otchizna*, a much more unusual term, is by contrast archaic or folk-poetic: it is unsullied by any official connotations (or recent ones, at any rate). But a more important reason for the choice of lexis lay in Prismanova's associations of her remembered origins above all with her father. Her mother is recalled only at the moment of her death agony, while her stepmother, evoked in life, represents a rather conventional kind of symbolic maternity as intellectual and moral nurture (she is shown, in 'Sof'ia' (SS, p. 70) teaching the young Anna to read). The portrait of Prismanova's father, on the other hand, is linked with imagery on the one hand extraordinary, and on the other profoundly alienating. The key poem here, 'List'ia', begins by reversing the famous image of autumn as a beautiful, but consumptive, young woman that is used by Pushkin in his 1830 'Autumn' ode fragment:

> Мне нравится она,
> Как, вероятно, вам чахоточная дева
> Порою нравится . . .
>
> [She pleases me,
> As, no doubt, a consumptive girl
> Sometimes will please you . . .][29]

This Prismanova transmutes into:

> Явился мне осенний день во сне.
> Он догорал, как юноша в чахотке.
> Цвета его готовились к весне,
> но смерть уже была в его походке.
>
> [An autumn day appeared before me in my dream.
> It was burning to its close, like a youth with consumption.
> Its colours were preparing for spring,
> but death was already in its gait.]   (SS, p. 75)

Then, following an ironic re-vision of the tranquil pastoral sight of a field sloping down to the water (it turns out to be a graveyard), Prismanova turns to the extraordinary image of her dead father 'keeping his bones inside his shoes'. The effect of the poem is defamiliarising in two senses: first, this is a peculiar, almost an obscene, manner of evoking a dead parent and, second, Prismanova reverses the customary tradition of regarding the feminine as 'other'. Here it is not Prismanova's (largely absent and unthreatening) mother so much as her father who represents the uncanny, *das Unheimliche*, an element suggested in the grating half-rhyme *otch'ia pochva*, evoking less the soil of the fatherland than the soil made from Prismanova's father's bones.

Whatever link there is with her father, it is not one based on communication: in Prismanova's world, the dead do not rise from their graves or speak, and it is even left unclear which of the 'three languages' of Libau/Libava/Liepaja in fact was Prismanova's mother- or father-tongue, on what side of the linguistic triangle her family was located. Whether her *otchii iazyk* was Russian, Latvian or German, or indeed a member of a further possible linguistic triangle left unmentioned (Russian, Yiddish and Hebrew), is left (deliber-

ately?) unclear. The exactitude of iconic memory offsets the disturbing absence of aural recollection.

Commemorating Prismanova's own dead relations, *Pesok* may well
also commemorate, at a subliminal level, the fates of the 20,000
Libauers who died during the Second World War, whether in the
conflict itself or in extermination camps. Yet the effects of the cycle
are not primarily grim, gloomy or morbid; indeed, consciousness of
the approaching end seems more an indication of Prismanova's
peculiar sense of humour (death as the ultimate punchline) than of
neurotic brooding on personal destruction. And one of Prismanova's
main strengths is her sense of her home town's physical substance.
Though some other texts she wrote (the short story *O gorode i ogorode*
(On Guard and on Town Gardens, SS, pp. 191–4), the poem 'Zhizn'
Frideriki Forst' (The Life of Friederike Forst, SS, pp. 19–20), dwell
on Libau's Germanic interiors – shiny black pianos, goose in
lingonberry sauce, rhubarb cooling in dishes, photographs of be-
whiskered naval officers – Prismanova's close contemplation was
most often directed at the sea and shoreline. The former is generally
seen with an outsider's eye: the maritime disasters feared in any
harbour town are remembered in 'Gavan'' (Harbour, SS, p. 68), the
sight of passing fishing-boats is frequently mentioned. The latter,
however, is very much the poet's own habitat, in the recording of
which she had the advantages, as well as the disadvantages, of being
a literary pioneer.

SOUTHERN SEAS: THE OCEAN IN NINETEENTH- AND
TWENTIETH-CENTURY RUSSIAN LITERATURE AND PAINTING

The phrase 'from Libau to Vladivostok' has a proverbial ring, 'from
Land's End to John O'Groats', though the distance is more like
'from Rejkjavik to Warsaw', or 'from Miami to Seattle'. Libau, then,
lies at one extreme of the Russian Empire's vast territory. Moreover,
as a town where 'street signs were uttered in three tongues', as
Prismanova herself puts it in 'Pesok' (SS, p. 76), and Russians formed
only a quarter of the population, its identity as a 'Russian city', in
anything other than strict political and legal terms, is highly
questionable. But more important than these two aspects in cultural
terms (after all, Siberia, despite its distance from the centre and its
large Inuit population, has always seemed quintessentially Russian
in terms of national mythology), is the fact that the Baltic coast has

no history as an Ultima Thule, or indeed a favoured place of any kind, in Russian literature or painting.

This is partly to do with the history of representing the sea and shore in Russian culture. Though Russia (even at its historical smallest) has never been landlocked, thinking, painting and writing have all tended to function as though it were. There are few seafaring classics (a rare exception being the fifteenth-century *Khozhdenie za tri moria* [Voyage beyond Three Seas] by Afanasii Nikitin, who got as far as India). Even when Russian literature did turn to the ocean, in the early nineteenth century, though, the Northern seas were spurned in favour of the Southern coasts – the Black Sea, and particularly the Crimea. Apart from the appeal of the South to residents of a Northern capital where the summers were, as Pushkin said, 'like poor imitations of Southern winters', another factor was the emblematic character of Romantic nature poetry. Close observation was of much less importance than portraying scenes that allowed space for sententious or philosophical reflection: so in Pushkin's famous poem to the sea as the epitome of freedom, or Tiutchev's visions of it as the medium of dreams, chaos and Romantic creativity. The Northern seas, seasonally fettered in ice, were less easily evoked as metaphors of free thought or the free imagination, What is more, the Baltic coast did not suit the Russian Romantics' expectations of the picturesque: there were no mountains, no crags, no rocky shores here. The German Baltic might have Caspar David Friedrich, but the most prominent Russian marine painter, Aivazovskii, all too flatteringly known as 'The Russian Turner', preferred the more scenic Black Sea for his facile seascapes.

As Alain Corbin writes in his fascinating history of the seaside resort, *The Lure of the Sea*, the Northern seas had been enthusiastically discovered by Western European Romantics of the early nineteenth century:

The Northern coasts, whose innocence had not yet been undermined by holiday making or tourism, provided travellers with an accessible stage on which the imagination's games could be played out. With growing intensity, a quest was underway along the Baltic, Scottish and Breton coasts for anything that could bestow meaning on the worn rocks, the mysterious ruins, and the curious beings who dwelled among them [. . .] the resonance of Celtism and the Ossianic mode swelled.[30]

For Russians, though, it was the Northern interior, not the coast (flat, windswept and bleak, rather than set about with picturesque rocky pinnacles) that was to be absorbing. Baratynskii's sentimental 1824 narrative poem *Eda* was the harbinger of a tradition that was later to draw twentieth-century painters and writers (Leonid Andreev, Il'ia Repin) to build dachas (summer homes) in woodland resorts such as Kuokkala and Vallenkoski (whose waterfall was the resort of nature pilgrims in the early twentieth century). Since Russian folklore is rich in river-maidens and forest demons, rather than mermaids and talking seals, there was some nationalist rationale in this. But more to the point was the fact that Russian sensibilities towards nature never went through the vast shift described in Corbin, in which the sea ceased, during the nineteenth century, to be the terrifyingly empty haunt of monsters, the image of vacuity before the First Day of God's creation, and became a space for restful contemplation, rambles along the shore and rock-pool naturalism. A whole historical phase seems to have been missed out of Russian culture: from being the embodiment of threatening otherness, the sea has become (as all over the world) the picturesque backdrop to holidays spent lying on the beach, swimming and paddling desultorily, and above all acquiring a tan (holidays poetically evoked, for example, in Akhmatova's *U samogo moria* (By the Very Edge of the Sea, 1914), as well as in *Epicheskie motivy* I).

To be sure, there are tangential points of literary reference for Prismanova's work. In the 1920s and 1930s, Nikolai Kliuev set a number of elegaic nature poems in his Pomor'e homeland in the far North, for example 'Zadvorki Rusi – matiugi na zabore' (The backyards of Russia are foul language on fences, 1924). But here close observation is woven into a fabric of dense symbolism:

Задворки Руси – матюги на заборе,
С пропящей сумой красноносый кабак,
А ветер поет о родимом поморье,
Где плещется солнце – тюленый вожак.

Где заячья свадьба, гагарьи крестины,
И ос новоселье в зобатом дупле ...
О, если б в страницах златились долины,
И строфы плясали на звонкой земле.

[The backyards of Rus are foul language on fences,
A red-nosed drunkard whose satchel's been snatched,
But the wind sings aloud of the shore we were born in
Where the sun and the stars, like bull seals, splash,

Where the loons hold their christenings, the hares their weddings,
And the wasps warm their house in an oak's hollow trunk:
O, if only the valleys were golden on pages,
And strophes might dance on the musical ground!][31]

And the only predecessor Prismanova had for her interest in the
Baltic as a seaside resort minutely observed was Mandelstam, and
then in a prose text, *The Noise of Time*, in which memories of a visit to
relations in Riga provoke the following lyrical reflections on the
coast:

The Riga coast is a whole country. It's famous for its sticky, amazingly fine
and pure yellow sand (so fine it's like hour-glass sand!) and the holey
bridges a plank or so wide flung across the thirty-mile long dacha Sahara.
    There are more dachas on the Riga coast than at any other resort.
Bridges, flowerbeds, fences, glass balls stretch on and on in an endless city,
all set out on that yellow sand, like something out of a sand-pit, canary-
yellow, ground as fine as bird-seed.[32]

The passage comes from Mandelstam's 'Judaic chaos' chapter, and it
is possible that Prismanova's interweaving of family reminiscence
and coast landscape in *Pesok* was directly inspired by it. Certainly,
there is some overlap of imagery – though in Prismanova it is pieces
of Baltic amber, rather than the sand itself, which is compared to
'grain' (something that speaks for her more accustomed eye, probably). The hourglass image is also, as mentioned earlier, used as a
buried metaphor in *Pesok*, while 'Glaza' transmutes the reference to
'glass balls' in a light-hearted reference to the legendary invention of
glass by the Phoenicians, a humorous aetiological myth asserting the
importance of family history over world history:

> Открыли финикийские купцы
> в песке стеклянный шарик ненароком,
> чтоб русские отцовские отцы
> могли нас занимать стеклянным оком.

> [Not in vain did Phoenician merchants
> discover balls of glass in sand:
> the Russian fathers of our fathers
> can amuse us children with their glass eyeballs.]   (SS, p. 69)

But Prismanova's use of detail is much richer than Mandelstam's.
Apart from sand, she also notes shoreline plants – moss, algae,
seaweed (generically), the *aniutiny glazki*, 'Annie's eyes', pansies, that
grow on the sand-dunes. And some of these realia are taken not
from contemporary literature, but from painting. In the 1900s

2.1. Nicholas Roerich (Nikolai Rerikh), *Drevniaia zhizn'* (*Ancient Life*, 1904). Tempera on cardboard, 42.5 × 52 cm. Radishchev Art Museum, Saratov.

Nikolai Roerich (Rerikh), a Symbolist painter and mystic (collaborator of Stravinsky on the ballet *The Rite of Spring*) had turned to the Baltic shores as the site of primal pagan cults, a place where pre-Christian belief lay close to the surface (ill. 2.1).[33] To be sure, the cultic side of her *otchizna* appears not to have interested Prismanova at all: it is the child's-eye view, in which beach treasures (amber, pansies) bulk larger than the frieze of sails on the horizon that concerns her, rather than stone circles or primitive rites. But the colours of Roerich's painting (not only yellow sand, but dark-grey sky) and incidental features, above all the bony pines (described by her in 'O gorode i ogorode' as 'one-armed') are certainly absorbed into her work.

What is more, the poetry is not just visual in the sense of being highly detailed. It is also close to contemporary painting in its compositional principles. Prismanova, whose circle of Paris friends included painters, takes visual punning to an extent which would be

2.2 Vladimir Tatlin, *Portret moriaka* (*Portrait of a Sailor*, 1911). Tempera on canvas, 71.5 × 71.5 cm. Russian Museum, St Petersburg. © DACS.

more characteristic of Cubist painting than poetry. There is an irresistible resemblance between 'Treugol'nik' and Tatlin's portrait of a sailor in St Petersburg (ill. 2.2): both are held together by the iteration of geometrical motifs, in Tatlin's case the parallelogram, and in Prismanova's (not unexpectedly) the triangle. 'Triangulation' in the poem is not simply seen as series of abstractions – the triangle of desire and loss that links the poet with her childhood home, the point of origin and the destination of her dreams; the three languages spoken in her home city; the triangle of experience, experience reviewed and experience recreated in the literary text; Prismanova's own triple identity (Russian, Jewish, Latvian). Triangulation also becomes a compositional dominant. A whole chain of triangle-based visual puns assorts standard elements of sea-shore scenes – houndstooth sails, the sword's blade of a lighthouse beacon, seagulls folding their wings, a child in a sailor suit foreshortened to a triangle – with less predictable visions – a herring's head, a fisherman's smoking kiln, the triangulation of three spires, the triangular pile of sand in the governing hourglass image. It is above all the schematisation of objects and people in a way that emphasises the two-dimensionality of the scene (since in ordinary space the resemblance betwen a sail and a child's body in a sailor-suit is tenuous, to say the least) that recalls Cubist painting.[34]

Not only visual puns, but tactile and verbal paronomasia run through the cycle. Salt water suggests on the one hand tears, on the other the briny sea; when combined with sand, it makes glass, the material from which Prismanova's grandfather's eye is constructed; white-headed waves suggest the white-headed rulers who have swept over the Baltic shore in century after century. Among examples of verbal puns are the play on *Aniutiny glazki* and the poet's own name (an especially resonant instance since the 'child's eye view' is so important in this cycle); the dual interpretation of *nastroen* to mean a mood and a musical key (the idea of Libau as a 'musical town' occurs repeatedly in Prismanova's evocations of her birthplace); and especially, the elaborate sound- and sense-play on *rubl'* (rouble), *rublenyi* (hewn, chopped) and *rebr* (rib) in 'Gorlo', Prismanova's description of her mother dying of cancer. The cycle is also densely alliterative; the *p* and *s* sounds of *pesok* run through all the poems, each of which, however, also has its own sound-world (*r* in 'Gorlo', the *b* of *blagodat'* in 'Pesok', for example). If composition and subject of the cycle are 'painterly', its facture (*faktura*) is eminently literary, alliteration taking the place of the impasto so highly favoured by post-Impressionist painters.

Anna Prismanova's *Pesok*, unlike Akhmatova's *Epicheskie motivy* II, does not attempt to assimilate the visual into the verbal, or assert the hegemony of literature over art. Instead, visual elements dominate the composition of the cycle, most particularly through references to triangulation. And the cycle depends not only on verbal intertexts (Mandelstam, Pushkin, Akhmatova) but also on visual intertexts (Roerich, Tatlin); what is more, no process of subordinating the latter to the former is evident. But perhaps the most significant insight derived by Prismanova from contemporary painting is the fact that it might be possible to create beauty from what lacked allure in a conventional sense; that it might, indeed, be preferable to derive visual stimuli from scenes outside the established representational canon. As modernist painters elevated everyday objects (kitchen chairs, shop signs, boots, sailor suits) to the subject of close and loving scrutiny, so Prismanova switched her gaze from gothic vaults to rhubarb and herring heads in her poetry. Prismanova's work can also be seen as drawing on contemporary painting in the sense that the human subject (even when this is a dead parent) inspires neither more nor less emotion than inanimate subjects such as sails and shirts; sentiment is evoked by elegaic intonation, yet displaced by the disinterested scrutiny of the eye. *Pesok*, then, is an important work of art not only because it is an exceptionally creative instance of how an émigrée writer survived the 'difficult joys' of exile, and because it illustrates how a poet not fitted by the governing aesthetics of the body could never the less evoke her own body, but also because it is a signal demonstration of modern poetry's ability to learn from contemporary painting.

NOTES

1 Cf. the climactic scene of Conrad's *The Heart of Darkness* (1902): 'Of all his gifts the one that stood out pre-eminently, that carried with it a sense of real presence, was his ability to talk, his words – the gift of expression, the bewildering, the illuminating, the most exalted and the most contemptible, the pulsating stream of light, or the deceitful flow from the heart of an impenetrable darkness' (*The Heart of Darkness* (London, 1995), p. 79).
2 Marina Tsvetaeva, *Stikhotvoreniia i poemy* (Leningrad, 1990), p. 293.
3 The Russian word *brennaia* signifies transience, physical fragility and sexual frailty all in one: 'fragile' is not an ideal solution, but no one English word would capture the full range of meanings of the original.
4 For such an introduction, see e.g. Catriona Kelly, 'Grandfather's glass eye: the poetry of Anna Prismanova', *New Poetry Quarterly* 2 (1994), 61–4, and Petra Couvée's preface to her edition of Prismanova's work, *Sobranie sochinenii* (Leyden, 1990), xi–xxxi. (References to this latter edition henceforth in given text as SS and page number.)
5 The part played by appearance in dictating the reception of Russian writers is in need of exhaustive treatment. Some interesting preliminary observations, based on a single source, the catalogues of the Vul'f publishing house, and limited to the case of women writers, are to be found in Beth Holmgren, 'Gendering the icon: marketing women

writers in fin de siècle Russia', in Helena Goscilo and Beth Holmgren (eds.), *Russia: Women: Culture* (Bloomington, Indiana, 1997), pp. 321–46. From the late nineteenth century, editions of Russian writers and poets commonly had an author portrait as frontispiece. See for example *Sochineniia K. D. Batiushkova* (Moscow, 1905); Leonid Andreev, *Polnoe sobranie sochinenii* (St Petersburg, 1913), frontispiece to vol. 1; idem, *Sochineniia* (St Petersburg, c. 1901). The tradition continued after the Revolution: see for example M. Gor'kii, *Stikhi i legendy* (Moscow and Leningrad, 1932), which has a portrait of a proudly windswept young Gorky as frontispiece; A. Blok, *Stikhotvoreniia* (Berlin, 1922); Andrei Belyi, *Pepel': stikhi* (Moscow, 1929). In the case of the post-revolutionary Maiakovskii, the photographic portraits of Aleksandr Rodchenko were fundamental in establishing the poet's physical authority.

6 Iurii Olesha, 'Vospominaniia o Maiakovskom', *Izbrannye sochineniia* (Moscow, 1956), p. 457. On Maiakovskii's appearance as a *leitmotiv* in the poet's work, especially the notorious 'yellow jacket' (alternatively 'waist-coat'), see Svetlana Boym, *Death in Quotation Marks* (Cambridge, Mass., 1991), pp. 59–67.

7 Olesha, 'Vospominaniia', p. 458.

8 See, for example, 'Vse my brazhniki zdes', bludnitsy' (We are all wanderers here, and harlots, 1913), in which the poet refers to the 'narrow skirt' that she has put on to appear 'even more slender', and 'Uedinenie' (Solitude, 1914), in which a symbolic parallel is drawn between the 'tower' to which the poet retreats and her own tall and slender body. (Anna Akhmatova, *Stikhotvoreniia i poemy*, Leningrad, 1977, p. 57, p. 85: future references to this edition in-text, as SP.) On Akhmatova's self-presentation generally, see Alexander Zholkovsky, 'Anna Akhmatova – piat'desiat let spustia', *Zvezda* 9 (1996), 211–27; idem, 'Strakh, tiazhest', mramor: iz materialov k zhiznetvorcheskoi biografii Akhmatovoi', *Wiener Slawistischer Almanach* 26 (1995), 119–54; idem, 'The Obverse of Stalinism: Akhmatova's Self-serving Charisma of Selflessness', in Laura Engelstein and Stephanie Sandler (eds.), *Self and Story in Russian History* (Ithaca, 2000).

9 The pioneer of such interpretations was John Berger in *Ways of Seeing* (London, 1972). See also E. Ann Kaplan, 'Is the Gaze Male?' in A. Snitow, C. Stansell and S. Thompson (eds.), *Powers of Desire: The Politics of Sexuality* (New York, 1983), pp. 309–27.

10 This photograph is used, for example, as the front cover to V. Schweitzer, *Marina Tsvetaeva* (London, 1992). In her study of Tsvetaeva in *Death in Quotation Marks* (pp. 192–240) Boym argues that Tsvetaeva's self-presentation was deliberately 'unfeminine', but in this, as in so much else, the poet's behaviour was unpredictable and contradictory.

11 A case in point would be Bella Akhmadulina, whom Alexander Zholk-ovsky has described as 'an idiosyncratic 1960s reincarnation of Akhma-

tova' (see his 'V minus pervom i minus vtorom zerkale: Tat'iana Tolstaia, Viktor Erofeev – akhmatoviana i arkhetipy', *Literaturnoe obozrenie* 6 (1995), 28.

12 Z. Shakhovskaia, *Otrazheniia* (Paris, 1975), p. 49.

13 Iurii Terapiano, *Literaturnaia zhizn' russkogo Parizha za polveka (1924–1974): esse, vospominaniia, stat'i* (Paris, 1987), p. 133.

14 Vadim Perel'muter, 'Anna Prismanova – neuslyshannyi golos', *Ogonek*, 31 (1990), 31.

15 A. Bakhrakh, 'Pamiati Anny Prismanovoi', *Mosty* 6 (1961), 365; Perel'muter, 'Anna Prismanova – neuslyshannyi golos', 31.

16 Mark Slonim is quoted in V. Losskaia (comp), *Marina Tsvetaeva v zhizni: neizdannye vospominaniia sovremennikov* (Tenafly, NJ, 1989), pp. 199–200; Irina Odoevtseva, *Na beregakh Seny* (Paris, 1983), pp 125–9.

17 Bakhrakh, 'Pamiati Anny Prismanovoi', 365.

18 Ibid.

19 Terapiano, *Literaturnaia zhizn'*, p. 233: the poem concerned is SS, p. 29.

20 On taste see e.g. Madame de Lambert's essay 'Réflexions sur le goût', *Œuvres* (Paris, 1990), 239–41. For an analysis of the historical background to such views, see Kelly's chapter 'Educating Tatiana' in Linda Edmondson (ed.), *Gender and Russian History* (forthcoming, London, 2000).

21 Terapiano, *Literaturnaia zhizn'*, p. 234.

22 For evidence of a conscious process of self-fashioning in Prismanova's biography, compare the account given in Couvee's introduction to SS, p. xix, of her destroying her own pictures and recreating her biography, including subtracting six years from her own age.

23 Hélène Cixous, 'Difficult Joys', in Helen Wilcox, Keith McWalters, Ann Thompson and Linda R. Williams (eds.), *The Body and the Text: Hélène Cixous, Reading and Teaching* (London, 1990), pp. 12–13.

24 Cixous, 'Difficult Joys', p. 19.

25 *Baedeker's Russia* (London, 1914), p. 50.

26 Aleksandr Nikitenko, *Dnevnik*, 3 vols. (Leningrad 1955–6): entry for 10 July 1861, vol. II, p. 195.

27 Like Parnok, Prismanova converted to Russian Orthodoxy (Ginger's inclinations were apparently more towards Buddhism); however, Prismanova went further than these two by also Russifying her name. See the obituary by A. Gorskaia in *Vozrozhdenie*, 108 (1960), pp. 113–14.

28 On the stereotypes of Russian childhood memoirs, see esp. Andrew Wachtel, *The Battle for Childhood: The Creation of a Russian Myth* (Stanford, 1990). Prismanova's most conventionally idyllic representation of the Baltic is perhaps in her interesting, but not wholly successful, 1936 poem 'Lish' tol'ko v glubine usnula ryba' (SS, p. 32), where the North is recollected as a 'sapphire-eyed' woman crowned with rowan (*riabina*), and as free-flowing water, compared with the artificial 'fish-tank' atmosphere of Paris. But this is not specifically named as

Prismanova's childhood, rather as that of all émigrés – the North is more than anything a Russian north, cf. the displaced autobiography of Prismanova's poem to Lomonosov, 'Na kante mira muza Kantemira' (SS, p. 171).

29 Pushkin, 'Osen'', *Polnoe sobranie sochinenii v 17 tomakh* (Lenigrad, 1937–49), vol. III, p. 319.

30 Alain Corbin, *The Lure of the Sea* [Le terretoire du vide, 1988], trans. Jocelyn Phelps (Cambridge, 1994), p. 217.

31 N. Kliuev, 'Zadvorki Rusi', in *Sochineniia* (2 vols, Munich 1969), vol. II, p. 179.

32 O. Mandel'shtam, *Sobranie sochinenii v 3 tomakh*, vol. II (New York, 1971), p. 69.

33 This is not to suggest that Rerikh's interest in the Baltic was unique among visual artists. Other Russian painters who had evoked scenes in the Gulf of Finland included Ivan Shishkin and Valentin Serov, while the film director Sergei Eistenstein's *Battleship Potemkin* (1925), ostensibly set on the Black Sea, clearly owes much to the writer's sea-side childhood in Riga, Latvia.

34 Prismanova carried triangulation into the verbal texture of *Pesok* as well, through such techniques as the use of triads (poems with six or nine stanzas, progressions of three stanzas, and triple repetition: note, for example, the stanzas beginning with 'To byl/o ...' in 'Vospominan'e' (SS, p. 66).

CHAPTER 3

Picture windows and the art of Andrei Siniavskii

Jane Grayson

Квадратик бумаги – как решетка, сквозь которую я выглядываю.

[A little square of lined paper is the barred window from behind which I peep out.][1]

The times would indeed need to be out of joint to claim Siniavskii for a modernist. Born in 1925, he self-evidently belongs, child and man, not to the era of Modernism but to the epoch of 'high Stalinism'. Yet many Soviet writers of Siniavskii's background and education who had close knowledge of the literature and art of the pre-Soviet and immediate post-revolutionary period developed an acute awareness of cultural disjunction and discontinuity. They witnessed the severing of links with Russia's literary past and with the Western European literary tradition. They saw history rewritten to legitimise the politicisation of literature and marginalise or suppress alternative artistic trends in Russia's past. The Russian modernist movement was one of the most conspicuous casualties of the Soviet re-rewriting of history and much of Siniavskii's energies in his academic career as university lecturer and literary critic were devoted to setting the record straight and reforging some of the vital missing links with Russia's recent past. However, Siniavskii was an imaginative writer as well as an academic and his engagement with Modernism was not just of the mind, but of the heart. For him the art of Modernism had a freshness and truth he found lacking in the official art of Socialist Realism and in his own rebellion against jaded art forms he adopted and adapted much of the modernist idiom. Modernism thus became for him the language of dissidence, his stance that of a modernist not *avant* but *après la lettre*.

Yet whilst it is certainly possible to give a fairly plausible represen-

tation of Siniavskii as a latter-day modernist, that would be to ignore
his main article of faith as writer and critic – his belief in the organic
unity of art. The account below is devoted to an examination of the
two main manifestations of this belief in his writing: first, the interest
he demonstrates in the continuity of art through time and, second,
the points of connection he draws across different art forms, between
literature and the visual arts. It will become clear immediately that
this approach runs counter to much of that represented elsewhere in
this volume, but no apology is needed for this. While Siniavskii is
well aware of the discrete differences between artistic periods and
forms as well as of the technical demands of distinct artistic media,
and while he is thoroughly familiar with the language of literary
theory and art criticism that, to borrow Iurii Olesha's phrase from
his speech at the First Writers' Congress, 'was not his theme',
Siniavskii saw himself fighting a holy war, a war between politics and
literature, between art and non-art, and with the stakes set so high,
distinctions between successive '-isms' and between different art
forms figured as mere skirmishes, matters of minor moment.
Indicative of his belief in the permanently contemporary quality of
art was a remark he was fond of quoting in his account of the
dissident movement. It was Pavel Litvinov's disconcerting response
at his trial to the question of who had influenced him in his dissident
beliefs: 'The Russian classics'.[2] Over the years Siniavskii develops an
artistic method which not only escapes the confines of chronology,
but blurs the boundaries between criticism and creative writing,
favours meditation over polemic and substitutes demonstration for
argument. In his later writing he chooses to show rather than say.
Here the word picture and visual art are placed at key points in his
texts where language can go no further. They go beyond words to
express the silence of revelation.

Siniavskii's prison camp memoir, *Golos iz khora* (A Voice from the
Chorus, 1973), being the richest source of his reflections on the
visual arts, is the best vantage-point from which to begin to survey
the interrelation of visual art with his thinking about literature. Part
Five of the memoir opens with this reminiscence from his childhood:

I was lucky that we lived near the Museum of Decorative Arts, and that it
was thus a part of my childhood – as a boy I used to run off there simply to
sit in the company of the statues, and dream, all by myself, in some little
Italian courtyard, always so deserted and plunged in semi-darkness; that

courtyard and the antique portico, particularly in the winter when everything outside was covered in glittering hoarfrost, have remained with me ever since, all my life. Works of art, unlike books, provide an environment in which you can live – they surround you like the trees in a forest and gradually permeate your being in the same way as any other habitat. Forests and museums – these are what I should like to go to; they are somehow intertwined in my memory, and are what I miss most.[3]

    Golos iz khora is made up of moments such as this: vignettes of observation, recollection and reflection composed during snatched periods of calm and sent out to the author's future self in the form of letters to his wife. The narrator of an earlier story, 'Gololeditsa' (The Icicle, 1961), had done something similar, composing a narrative to send 'do vostrebovaniia' (*poste restante*), to re-establish links with himself and his lost love Natasha. But Siniavskii then was writing fiction. Here, in the letters he sent out from the camps between 1966 and 1971, it was for real. His principal addressee, his wife Mariia Vasil'evna Rozanova whom he had known since university days, is an art historian by training. And appropriately, in communicating with her, he drew readily upon a shared familiarity with the visual arts. Thus, describing the luminous texture of the forest close to the forbidden zone, he writes: 'Apart from Claude Lorrain I can think of nothing to compare it with' ('Krome Kloda Lorrena, nichego ne podberu') (*GK*, p. 127; *VC*, p. 123). Again, imagining the interior of a smithy in a popular religious song ('dukhovnyi stikh'), he has: 'I see the scene rather in Rembrandt-esque style' (*GK*, p. 100; *VC*, p. 96). Rozanova helped support herself and their young son during Siniavskii's imprisonment by making jewellery, and it is very probably in recognition of this that he introduces a comparison to the jeweller's craft when commenting on book illustration: 'It is closer to the work of a jeweller than to drawing or painting' (*GK*, p. 21; *VC*, p. 17).

    The frequent allusions to pictures and paintings in these prison letters are testimony not only to a cultivated mind and a tender heart, but to a sensibility heightened by sensory deprivation. Some years ago Sir David Piper, the former Director of the Ashmolean Museum in Oxford, recalled most movingly on radio the haunting memory of listening to the andante from Mozart's 21st Piano Concerto played on a wind-up gramophone in a Japanese prisoner-of-war camp. Siniavskii's associations are visual rather than auditory: *Golos iz khora* is pervaded by light and colour. He recalls spending one New Year's Eve turning over pictures cut out of old magazines: Giorgione's *Sleeping Venus*, a glass decoration from a Christmas tree, a trinket. These bright images appear to him to be more real than 'all the dreary greyness which leaves no memories' (*GK*, pp. 161–2; *VC*, p. 159). Colour in art, he muses, may be a manifestation of nature's property of attracting and retaining the attention. And, perhaps, the fact that it is works of art which survive from past ages is also linked with nature's use of colour to propagate itself and overcome death:

The colours of a flower, a peacock's tail, the rays of the setting sun – anything that singles out the species or the individual in defiance of the levelling action of death belongs to the realm of art. Is this perhaps what links art to sex and the continuation of the race? If so, is it possible that art is the bright mating plumage in which life decks itself out with a view to its self-propagation?' (*GK*, p. 37; *VC*, pp. 33–4)

He has, he says, no time to read books, but thinks of them constantly 'with wonder and gratitude' (*GK*, p. 19; *VC*, p. 15). And, despite the disclaimer in the passage quoted above (pp. 89–90) that books do not create an environment in which the reader can live, here he likens them to windows opening on to welcoming interiors:

Books resemble windows when the lights come on in the evening and begin to glow in the surrounding darkness, forming little golden pictures from the window panes, the curtains, the wall-paper, and creating the impression of a cosy existence known only to those who dwell within, a secret life invisible to the outside world. This happens particularly when it is cold or snowing (most of all when it is snowing) and looking up from the street at the light cast by patterned lamp shades you imagine that sweet music must be playing and glamorous, cultivated people walking about there inside. (*GK*, pp. 20–1; *VC*, p. 17)

He remembers fondly the pictorial appeal and magical properties of children's books: the glittering promise of shining titles such as *Treasure Island* and A. K. Tolstoi's *Kniaz′ Serebrianyi* (The Silver Prince) (*GK*, p. 156; *VC*, p. 152); the large letters which encouraged him as a child to read with such intensity of feeling (*GK*, p. 36; *VC*, p. 33); the pictures which would suddenly pop out from behind drab grey covers (*GK*, p. 19; *VC*, p. 15). Makers of old books understood the importance of the look and feel of a book. They understood the art of creating pleasurable anticipation, of enticing the reader to delve deeper, of launching him on an expedition into a 'wonderland of letters' ('puteshestvie po chudnym bukvam') (*GK*, p. 21; *VC*, p. 17). Illustration he sees as, ideally, having the joyous function of illuminating rather than explaining the text; it should 'proclaim the festival which a book brings into our life' ('illiustratsiia prizvana vozvestit' o prazdnike, s kotorym iavliaetsia kniga v nashu zhizn'') (*GK*, p. 21, *VC*, p. 17). And he felt medieval scribes understood this when they illuminated their manuscripts, allowing words to flower and transform themselves, and delay the process of reading the text by delicious pauses (*GK*, p. 19; *VC*, p. 15).

Siniavskii's emphasis in *Golos iz khora* on art's function being essentially to entertain and to bring joy into people's lives is also no doubt influenced by the contrast with his cheerless physical surroundings. When he deplores Chekhov's indifference to the visual arts and his understanding of culture as education, when he bemoans the conception of writing as 'toil' and 'labour' which he sees as deriving from writers like Chekhov and Flaubert who in their earnestness forgot that the end product of their labours is an entertainment, he speaks with the authority of someone who knows from personal experience what 'toil' and 'labour' really are:

Even if the writer's work is the most thankless of occupations, exhausting and desiccating, the product of it is still – in principle – an entertainment, a way of pleasantly passing the time by the light of a lamp, akin to the theatre or a carnival. Flaubert and Chekhov, agonizing over their literary work, forgot this and ever since it has been customary to talk about the 'toil' or 'labour' of writing. Well, what if it is labour? Hard work it may be, but no less sweet for that. Writing *Salammbô* or *Kashtanka* was not the same as loading timber. And they forgot that a book should always have pretty pictures . . . (*GK*, pp. 21–2; *VC*, pp. 17–18)

However, this anti-utilitarian view of art and the prominence Siniavskii gives in *Golos iz khora* to the visual arts, though affected by his prison environment, are not a product of it. These are not new elements in his thinking, nor should the anecdotal, discursive manner beguile the reader into deeming them to be views that are lightly held and merely the whimsical musings of a captive but freewheeling intelligence. Siniavskii is among the most consistent and consistently serious of thinkers. His aesthetic and philosophical positions remain in all essentials unchanged from the 1950s right through to the 1990s. The difference is of tone and of focus. *Golos iz khora* is presented as a collation of personal reflections set against a background 'chorus' of prison camp life. Most of his early fiction and literary essays of the late 1950s and early 1960s is sharply polemical, his target the artistic method of Socialist Realism and behind that the Marxist-Leninist philosophy of history. However, the central preoccupation of all his writing, both before and after his arrest, is a defence of 'pure art'. He does not shun the bogey-word 'pure'; he wears the badge of art for art's sake with pride, yet he makes clear that his understanding of the term is very different from the common conception of the artist ensconced in his ivory-tower, indifferent to surrounding reality. He conceives of art as a free play of the imagination which is at one and the same time a powerful instrument of intellectual and spiritual enquiry.

When Siniavskii in *Golos iz khora* turns from considering manifestations of art to formulating his views on art's essence, his mode of thinking takes on a historical dimension and assumes an ethical charge. He has a perception of the organic wholeness of all creation which is his touchstone for artistic authenticity. Art's ability to grasp this interconnectedness of all things is what he understands by 'real realism'. In his imagination he reaches back to a Golden Age when the world was but recently formed, when 'vse bylo vsem', when 'all was everything' (*GK*, p. 197; *VC*, p. 195). He finds himself drawn to primitive art forms for their reminiscences of this innocent state of harmony, for the identifiable connections they retain with the matter from which they were formed. True art in his understanding of it is art which is organically linked with its people and its time. The responsibility of the artist is to seek out the links and connections that bind the diversity of nature. At the deepest level this accounts for the vital importance in his writing of the interplay between the visual dimension and the verbal. It is a demonstration of the artist's perception of connections and contact with the core of things. Visual art's interaction with the verbal medium is essential to the generation of meaning in his texts – visual art and its verbal equivalent, that is, metaphor.

Metaphor, the word picture, is of crucial importance in his aesthetic system. He speaks of it as a memory of the Golden Age, 'a fragment of metamorphosis'.[4] And in a later passage, discussing the riddles in the medieval 'Discourse between Pepin and Alcuin', he elaborates on its importance in early art:

We are here present, as it were, at the act of the birth of art, when
metaphors sprouted profusely in the still hot and steaming soil of folklore
and when language, mindful of the miracle of its origin, still showed off the
tricks – as well as the riddles, knavishness, deceit, invention and cunning
which fill our fairy-tales and make them so effervescent. Here it becomes
clear that a poet, even in the new, modern sense of the word, is a failed
magician or miracle-worker who has substituted metaphor for metamorphosis, word-play for deeds. (*GK*, p. 202; *VC*, p. 200)

Siniavskii's ideas on the organic connections between art and
reality are amply illustrated in *Golos iz khora* by his reflections on the
different characteristics of art of different peoples and different
countries, and on the links between early art forms and the
landscape, flora and fauna whence they originated. His reading of
an old Indian tale in which a maiden dances before Brahma
prompts the observations that in India sculpture seems to have
grown out of the dance into a forest of many-armed and many-faced
gods, and that elephants are to be found there because their trunks
are in the style of the country.[5] In another passage he ponders the
kinship between the 'wooden' quality of the art and architecture of
Ancient Russia and its history and people. He sees the relative
perishability and formlessness of wood as corresponding to the
shapelessness and precariousness of Russian history and the mix of
its races and genes. This he contrasts, on the one hand, with the
landscape and physiognomy of the Caucasus and its people: the
starkly etched mountains, and their men to match, with their hooked
noses and spiked moustaches; and, on the other, with the geometric
starkness of Gothic architecture of Western Europe, all sinews and
bones, fan vaulting, flying buttresses and lead tracery.[6]

He observes no hierarchy of lower or higher art forms, and, whilst
he attends closely to the evolution of art, he refuses to accept any
crude notion of progress. Primitive art is not treated in any way as
inferior. On the contrary, as indicated above, he is continually
expressing his admiration for the freshness and directness of simple
forms; he describes anecdotes, proverbs and fairy-tales with the
same interest he gives to classics of world literature, and examines
tattoos with as much attention as portrait-painting.[7]

Golos iz khora does in fact provide an excellent retrospective
commentary on his earlier writings. There we find the elaboration
and positive formulation of ideas which previously were expressed
negatively and satirically. In the novella *Sud idet* (The Trial Begins,

1960), for example, he makes use of the visual arts to satirise the utilitarian view of art and the belief in historical progress. He juxtaposes two visits to the Pushkin Museum of Fine Arts, one in the reality of the narrative, the other in dream. The utilitarian view is mocked through the actions of the cynical art connoisseur Karlinskii who takes the woman he is planning to seduce on a carefully selected tour of the gallery's erotic pictures and sculptures. And the folly of a blinkered belief in historical progress is exposed in the nightmare of the Stalinist Public Prosecutor Globov. Globov finds himself first in his dream in the Egyptian hall of the Pushkin Museum where he comments with ignorant distaste on the crude barbarity of the art:

The hall was like a zoo. Ancient peoples were so downtrodden and superstitious that they worshipped lions and rams. But their drawing was no good, so they fitted human heads to beasts and vice versa.[8]

He is then led on a journey through time, through successive halls of the museum, past the Christian art of the Middle Ages to the art of the Renaissance, where, vividly recorded in paintings and sculptures, he is confronted with images of the unending butchery and harrowing tortures inflicted throughout the ages in the name of ideology and progress.

In his well-known attack on Socialist Realism, 'Chto takoe sotsialisticheskii realizm?' (On Socialist Realism, 1960) Siniavskii challenges the teleological principle of Soviet art and ridicules its vaunted progressiveness by first identifying it as a religious not a socialist art and as didactic classicism not realism, and then pointing out the glaring inappropriateness of holding up nineteenth-century realist authors, with their uncertainties, complexities and superfluous heroes, as models to be imitated. Chekhov, together with Tolstoi, figures prominently in his indictment of what he calls the 'loathsome literary salad' ('samaia bezobraznaia meshanina') of contemporary Soviet fiction.[9] Reread in the light of *Golos iz khora*, Siniavskii's call for a 'phantasmagoric art' to replace Socialist Realism appears as more than just a gesture of dissident iconoclasm. He means precisely what he says: he wants an art which will correspond to the spirit of the age, and, because the times themselves have a weird surreal quality, it is the fantastic and the grotesque rather than the realism of the nineteenth century which he deems the appropriate artistic forms.

However, the insistence on an art's appropriateness to its time does not, in Siniavskii's thinking, require a never-ending search for novelty, nor preclude identification with models from other times and places. It was in the Russian and Western European art of the avant-garde in the early years of the century that Siniavskii found his most congenial companions and allies in his attack on Soviet art and ideology. In his fictional autobiography *Spokoinoi nochi* (*Goodnight!*, 1984) he writes at length of his early passion for the modernist painters, Gauguin, Matisse, Van Gogh and Picasso. He remembers seeing their pictures hanging in Moscow galleries before they were taken down and consigned to storehouses after the war. He recalls the exquisite joy at being given a book of Cézanne by his French friend Hélène Pelletier in the late 1940s: forbidden fruit from a far-off land. He records, too, his debt to Maiakovskii for his unquench-able revolutionary spirit, and for the access he provided, as an officially recognised Soviet poet, to the forbidden world of the Russian avant-garde, to writers and artists of Russia's Silver Age who had long since disappeared from view. And he writes that he was not alone in this. Many young people of his generation arrived at dissidence via Maiakovskii. Maiakovskii's poetry spoke to the times.[10]

Siniavskii's early fiction abounds in reminiscences and adapta-tions of avant-garde techniques, themes and motifs, and the 'common reader' needs little or no guidance to identify the echoes of his favourite modernist prose writers, Babel', Zamiatin, Olesha and Bulgakov. There are the circuses (Olesha), zoos (Khlebnikov) and football matches (Olesha); the 'making strange', the developed use of visual metaphor (*passim*); the cinematic freezing of shots and acceleration of action (e.g. Bulgakov in *D'iavoliada*); the shifts from black and white to technicolour (Zamiatin in his story, 'Peshchera'), and from dream to reality (*passim*). And, looking ahead to his later writing, it is easy to trace the influence of the Futurists and Andrei Belyi in the interest he shows in the visual impact of a book: its cover, illustrations and typography. Rozanova's setting up of a printing press in their home outside Paris allowed for a modest realisation of the richness of decoration he had seen in his mind's eye in labour camp. These home-produced books form a delightful contrast to the drab uniformity of the standard Soviet product. *Spokoinoi nochi* has a cover made up of a collage of fragments of the book's text. Two colours of print are used: black for 'fact', red for 'fiction', and the five chapters are prefaced and ended with Rozanova's red and black ink drawings. Nor is this idle decoration. The book's design collaborates with the meaning of the text and its central themes of writing and love. The fragments of closely written text on the cover introduce the motif of Siniavskii in prison using up every scrap of paper. The red and black and the white of the paper are the colours of the hands in the cave paintings he encounters near the climax of his story. The drawings by his wife are tacit yet eloquent reminders that the writer, though solitary, is not alone.

Apart from this excursion into typography it must be said that comparison with the writers of the avant-garde in general does Siniavskii no favours. It is hard not to read much of his early fiction without a slightly jaded sense of *déjà lu*, and the reminder of being in the presence of a lesser talent than a Zamiatin, or a Babel'. Nowhere, for instance, is there anything, even in his later work, to match the concision and power of the unveiling of the statue of Christ at the climax of Babel''s story 'U sviatogo Valenta' (St Valentine's Church) in *Konarmiia* (Red Cavalry, 1926). Yet it needs to be emphasised that Siniavskii's engagement with the avant-garde was vital and real, and not simply a literary critic's conscientious work of archeological reconstruction, reforging severed links in Russia's cultural history. In his struggle with the grey monolith of Soviet power and the consoling lie of Socialist Realism Siniavskii felt a deep affinity with Zamiatin's fight against entropy, with Maiakovskii's battle with *byt*, with Zoshchenko's and Bulgakov's tireless exposure of philistinism and *poshlost'*. And the plea for an art of sunshine and joy which he makes in *Golos iz khora* is as passionate and heartfelt as that which he wrote of Babel' making nearly sixty years earlier in 1916.[11]

Whilst Siniavskii in his dissident rebellion made common cause with the modernists' repudiation of what Babel' termed gloomy 'Petersburg' realism, he always, even in his earliest writing, maintained the literary historian's wider perspective. He never sympathised with the extreme avant-garde position, entertained by early Futurists, that the culture of the past was cumbersome baggage which must be jettisoned. He could see beyond the quarrel between the avant-garde and materialist positivism to older quarrels between Romanticism and Classicism, between the ancients and the moderns. It is not hard to see 'Chto takoe sotsialisticheskii realizm?'

as his version of Victor Hugo's manifesto of Romanticism in the preface to the play *Cromwell* ('Préface de Cromwell', 1827), with its famous definition of the spirit of modernity as 'la féconde union du type grotesque au type sublime'. Siniavskii champions the 'romanticism' of Maiakovskii against the 'classicism' of Soviet art and calls upon the fantasy of Hoffmann, the fantastic realism of Dostoevskii and the grotesque creations of Goya to join with the modernists Maiakovskii and Chagall in teaching his contemporary writers how to be truthful with the aid of the grotesque. If his early writing is cast in the modernist mould, it also owes a debt to earlier models, and especially to Dostoevskii and Gogol and the Western European Romantics. His excellent short story 'Pkhentz', for example, exploits, within a science fiction framework, the old romantic tension between the ugly and the beautiful, the grotesque and the sublime. The relationship between the alien Pkhentz and his lonely neighbour Veronica provides the opportunity for a neat parody of the pillory scene in Hugo's novel, *Notre Dame de Paris*, where the young gypsy dancer Esmeralda offers water to the thirsty hunchback Quasimodo. In Siniavskii's narrative the thirsty hunchback also cries out for water and the woman ministers to the tormented sufferer. But she misunderstands: Pkhentz is not a deformed human, he is a creature from another planet, and he does not need the water to drink, but to pour over his parched body.[12]

This awareness of the broader historical perspective is in evidence even where the subject is strictly circumscribed, as in the two books written in collaboration with close friends, one with poetry as its subject, the other with an artist: *Poeziia pervykh let revoliutsii* (Poetry of the First Years of the Revolution, 1964), written in collaboration with a fellow literary historian, Andrei Men'shutin, and *Pikasso* (Picasso, 1960), written together with the art historian Igor Golomstock.[13]

Both books are products of the post-Stalin 'thaw' and have a clearly educative role in their treatment of politically sensitive material. The chief achievement of *Poeziia pervykh let revoliutsii* is to restore three long-disgraced and neglected poets, Tsvetaeva, Mandelstam and Pasternak, to their rightful places in the Russian literary process alongside the declared supporter of the Bolshevik Revolution, Maiakovskii. What is noteworthy in connection with the argument of this essay is that the case for the rehabilitation of these poets rests on the same principle of all three being acutely sensitive to the movement and spirit of the times. This link is shown to operate on a deeper level than class affiliation or political sympathies and involves a renewal, not an artificial break with cultural tradition. The authors emphasise that none of the three poets retreats from an alien reality into the past and aestheticism, as did, in their view, a poet such as Khodasevich. All are innovators, who have revitalised and extended the range of the poetic language, and who spoke of their times to their times.

Pikasso is a slighter and less sophisticated work. It was commissioned in connection with the award to Picasso of the Nobel Peace Prize, and appeared shortly after the first Russian exhibition of the painter's work at the Pushkin State Museum of Fine Arts in Moscow. As a member of the Communist Party Picasso was ideologically beyond reproach, but ordinary Russians, schooled to regard avant-garde art as a product of decadent capitalism, needed some re-educating in the language of his art. Notwithstanding these simple aims, the booklet puts forward ideas of fundamental importance to Siniavskii and Golomstock's aesthetic outlook. This is the portrait of a quintessential modern, but Picasso is also shown to be an artist very much in touch with the culture of the past. It is the portrait of an artist preoccupied with formal considerations (the actual term 'formalist' is used with caution, in deference to the sensibilities of the times), but one who is shown responding directly and forcefully to social and political events of his day. And the driving force behind all his work, giving a unity to all the experimentation and variety of styles, is seen as a search for the inner essence of his subjects. It is this, not any attraction for the exotic, nor any warped desire to destroy the harmony of nature's forms, which the author sees as prompting his interest in the primitive forms of negro sculpture and the dislocations and deformations of Cubism.

Analysis of individual paintings, with the text accompanying black and white reproductions, brings out Picasso's masterly ability to concentrate an image. One example is 'Weeping Woman' (1937), where the distortion of the facial features focuses on the essence of the woman's distress: swollen eyes, runnels of tears, twisted mouth chewing a kneaded handkerchief.[14] Another example is 'Woman with a Fan' (1905), where the description expertly shows how the woman's whole stance and set of face, reserved and withdrawn, yet hinting at the possibility of her opening out and revealing her inner

spiritual strength, are summed up in the object she is holding in her
left hand, a folded fan:

This is not a woman with a fan, rather the woman is a fan, ready to fly up
and open out, yet at the same time closed and inaccessible . . . [15]

Golomstock and Siniavskii also examine the series of three portraits
of the art collector and dealer Ambroise Vollard, two done in the
representational manner (1915, 1937), one in the Cubist style
(1908–9).[16] The Cubist portrait is shown to be more rather than less
revealing than the two more conventional works: by accentuating
the head and massive forehead Picasso brings out the dominant
rational character of his sitter. This permits Golomstock and
Siniavskii to draw the following important – and, in the context of its
time, daring – conclusion:

Picasso is not interested in conveying external verisimilitude, details of
dress, surroundings, or a portrait likeness (although he does succeed in
capturing a likeness), but in revealing the spiritual world, the inner essence
of a person. In this he follows the traditions of Rembrandt, Velazquez and
other great portrait-painters of the past.[17]

Siniavskii's arrest and the years in prison camp did not, then,
bring about any dramatic Damascene transformation in his outlook.
The sense of history was with him before that, and so was the
understanding of genuine realism as something lying beneath
surface appearances. The statement made in 1960 that Picasso's
artistic achievement is the capturing of reality and not an escape
from it can be set comfortably alongside the comment in *Golos iz
khora à propos* of Javanese shadow theatre that the artist 'is concerned
not with appearance, but with reality' ('Ne vidimost', no real'nost'
zanimaet khudozhnika').[18] However, the years spent in the camps
did bring a significant shift in Siniavskii's position. They allowed
him, removed from the battleground of polemic, to ponder more
deeply questions of art, religion and metaphysics. There the revolutionary romanticism of his early hero Maiakovskii gave place to
concerns of the ageing Pasternak to reach 'do samoi suti', to 'the
heart of the matter'.[19] This transference of allegiance from one poet
to another of the same generation may seem but a short distance to
travel, and yet the distance between the two points is all of Stalinist
Russia.

Time and accumulated life experience come to play an increasing
part in Siniavskii's writing. Like the older Pasternak, the older

Siniavskii perceives the significance of things which hitherto he had only imperfectly noticed. In prison, and cast ashore in the 'gulag archipelago' of the labour camps, he notes how Defoe's *Robinson Crusoe* and Swift's *Gulliver's Travels* acquired for him a sharp immediacy entirely lacking when he had first read them as a child.[20] And in common with Pasternak he begins to discern patterns of meaning and of destiny not only as he had always done, in history and in art, but in his own biography.[21] He becomes increasingly struck by the sometimes uncanny way that fiction or the world of his imagination turns into reality. In this he finds confirmation of his belief that imagination and art are not an escape from reality or a substitute for it, but give access to it, and define and help to understand experience. A new departure in the later writing is, then, the incorporation of the actuality of his own life experience into his literary criticism and into his imaginative writing. This process is especially marked in two of his last works, the autobiography *Spokoinoi nochi* (Goodnight!, 1984) and his article on Pushkin's historical novel *Kapitanskaia dochka* (The Captain's Daughter), 'Puteshestvie na Chernuiu rechku' (Journey to Chernaia rechka, 1994).

Much of Siniavskii's later writing, whether consciously or unconsciously, bears out the truth of Pasternak's proposition from *Doctor Zhivago* that 'life is symbolic because it has meaning' ('zhizn' simvolichna, potomu chto ona znachitel'na').[22] And it is visual art and visual art's nearest literary equivalent, metaphor, which have a key role to play in communicating Siniavskii's apprehension of meaning. Images show rather than say; they can convey moments of epiphany, reaching beyond words to silence. Siniavskii does not arrive at a sense of the significance of experience just through intellectual enquiry or rational argument. For him meaning is often revealed quite fortuitously in moments when 'fiction' becomes fact and he experiences something that he has hitherto imagined or read about, or when he sees something transformed in a new context which he has seen before without really noticing. In *Golos iz khora*, as has been suggested by examples cited above, Siniavskii has a good deal to say about metaphor and the different uses to which it can be put in a piece of narrative prose. He tells of its valuable cohesive properties and of how he will often have recourse to an image to bind his narrative together when he feels his thoughts straying in all directions.[23] He appreciates too that metaphors are based not only on the likeness of things compared, but on their remoteness from each other, and delights in the way that they can have the very opposite function of interrupting the narrative and distracting it with extraneous fantastical associations.[24] However, in a significant central passage when he is trying to put into words what he means by a true image, Siniavskii accords to metaphor a function of the utmost importance – as an instrument of revelation. He describes the true image as 'akin to Transfiguration'. This passage merits quoting in full:

It is just like a tree growing and bearing fruit in the form of eyes. At the sight of it you understand that art or poetry consist above all in the opening of eyes in the raw material and thereby endowing it with their own vision, and that an image, a true image, is akin to Transfiguration. (*GK*, p. 213; *VC*, p. 211)

This function of the verbal image to reveal the essence of things is demonstrated tellingly in Siniavskii's later writing in conjunction with images of visual art. And again it is *Golos i khora* that provides a model for his later creative use of the visual medium. This is an arresting description of Rembrandt's *Return of the Prodigal Son*. Siniavskii's 'reading' of the painting absorbs and holds the attention and draws his reader into the experience of viewing the canvas. Nothing in Rembrandt's picture, he points out, is directed towards the spectator. Like the main characters in it, it is turned in upon itself, yet it draws the spectator into its darkness. He lets his fancy play upon the picture bringing it to life:

All is submerged in that munificent cathedral darkness more deeply than Sadko sitting on the bottom of the sea. And it is a good thing that the paint has become so dark over the years. When it becomes so dark that we can no longer see it at all, then the Prodigal Son will rise from his knees and reveal his face. (*GK*, p. 103; *VC*, p. 99)[25]

Though Rembrandt's subject is biblical, this is a history painting, not an icon. It has too much complication and psychological realism to function as an icon functions, that is, as a pure channel to an otherworldly reality, but it can give intimations of another dimension, a hint of revelation. Siniavskii in *Golos iz khora* and elsewhere in his book on Russian folk beliefs, *Ivan-Durak* (Ivan the Fool, 1991), writes expertly and lovingly of the icon's function as a window or a door onto the other world.[26] But this, like his fondness for fairy-tales, is the love for the immediacy and naiveté of earlier art forms. His own art, the product of a more complex and confused age, does not seek to recreate that simplicity or that certainty of belief. But it can, like the Rembrandt, offer a window on to understanding.

'Puteshestvie na Chernuiu rechku' (Journey to Chernaia rechka) is Siniavskii's last substantial published work of literary criticism. It is typical of his later period in being a hybrid work, part literary criticism, part autobiography, part imaginative fiction, but it offers the most striking instance of epiphany in all his writing through the climactic placement of some paintings by Goya. Siniavskii is examining the connections between Pushkin's difficult last years, leading up to the duel and his death, and the themes of love, honour and betrayal played out in his novel about the Pugachev rebellion, *Kapitanskaia dochka* (1836). Into this narrative Siniavskii weaves an autobiographical sub-text which refers to the trial of his own honour, when he was wrongfully accused of working for the KGB. He draws all these threads together when he describes his return with his wife to St Petersburg after a gap of some thirty years and their visit to Chernaia rechka, the scene of Pushkin's duel. Suddenly they find themselves halted at a barrier, confronted by people dressed in costume from another age. There is a peasant carrying a club, a coachman finding difficulty in restraining his panicked horses. Hordes of people have materialised from nowhere. It appears that Siniavskii and his wife have stumbled on a film set.[27] Already in this description there is a blurring of time and place, fact and fiction, as the world of Pugachev intrudes into the St Petersburg of the early 1990s. But the image of the film-shoot triggers the recall of an earlier jarring confrontation of time and place when Siniavskii and Mariia Vasil'evna witnessed the sight of a party of Soviet tourists from Central Asia being shown round the Prado in Madrid. East meets West as these outlandishly dressed descendants of Tamburlaine process through the galleries while the attendants, the guardians of these halls of culture and civilisation, snigger behind their hands. East meets West when suddenly the party confront Goya – not the elegant portraits of Goya, painter to the Spanish court, but the ghouls and monsters and hallucinatory hordes of Goya's disturbed imagination (ill. 3.1). The two cultures meet, recognising, but not knowing themselves in each other. They come together, then they part, like giant black waves from a ship:

3.1. Goya, *El Ritual de las Brujas* (*The Witches' Sabbath*). Museo del Prado, Madrid.

3.2. Goya, *La Romaria de San Isidro* (*The Pilgrimage of St Ididore*). Museo del Prado, Madrid.

What a meeting this was. I froze. Ugly black faces, crowding and clambering over each other, with a guitar at the ready, with the black Goat-Prophet presiding over the witches' sabbath, and further off, distorted mouths, necks craning forward to meet the tourist group, with flattened noses, no lips, and splayed bat-like ears. They stared at each other as though looking in a mirror, rams not recognizing or sensing the dark affinity and secret change of form. They met, heedless of the explanations of the Spanish witch who intruded into their midst. Like black waves from a ship they parted, like two herds of beasts who, by their horns and their eyes, each identified the other as their own kind.[28]

This is a moment of drama after which there is little need for words. All the dark forces of evil which lurk beneath the veneer of civilisation and beneath the surface of Pushkin's and Siniavskii's lives are here revealed in all their brutish ugliness (ill. 3.2). His attention shifts back to St Petersburg, and the narrative draws to a close. He and his wife move on: 'It was but a step . . . to Chernaia rechka' ('Do Chernoi rechki . . . bylo rukoi podat'').[29]

Siniavskii's presentation of visual art, of which this use of Goya provides one of the clearest illustrations, is always situational. He never lets a work of art stand in isolation, but always presents it as 'seen' by someone. This focus on art's reception is an indication that for him art has an ethics as well as an aesthetics. It reflects his belief that art lives in history and is continually being changed and renewed by the succession of individuals who come into contact with it and who are in their turn altered and enriched by the contact. This view of art as a shared experience accounts for the seeming paradox of Siniavskii readily bringing his own skill with words into service to evoke examples of visual art. Not for him the photographic reproductions such as are available in this volume! It explains, too, why he does not shy away from selecting and modifying details in a description to fit in with his own perception (as in the above example).

All Siniavskii's thinking about art – art's relation to ethics, to history and to reality – is distilled in *Spokoinoi nochi*. In this his major work he demonstrates the truth of his proposition set out in the opening pages of *Golos iz khora* that the activity of an artist is as natural as breathing and that all art is but the stuff of everyday reality filtered through an individual's consciousness:

A man enters into art in rather the same way as he comes into the world at his birth [. . .] People say of someone: 'He has a good eye' (because he is an artist). But what does he see with his 'good eye'? Only this: that the world is filled with art. (*GK*, p. 15; *VC*, p. 11)

Siniavskii's central theme is the vital importance of art, and he demonstrates the truth of his main idea in the most striking way by allocating to art the chief role of structuring and giving meaning to his narrative. He discards conventional structuring devices of chronology and location and instead employs metaphor as the binding agent and visual art as the agent of revelation. An intricate web of imagery connects the different stories which make up the whole, and the reader is allowed to apprehend these links as Siniavskii discloses his growing awareness of the patterns of his own destiny. One group of images is made up of things which Siniavskii actually experienced: a prison wall, stalagmites and stalactites in a prehistoric cave, and hands painted on the walls of that cave. Another group is of images which are invented or recounted, chief among these being the apparition of the dead Stalin in the shape of a cylinder of frozen air. A third group which forms the climax and 'reveals' the meaning of the work consists of a triptych of works of art – an icon, a bas-relief, a tapestry – their very placement, like the placement of the Goya in *Puteshestvie*, demonstrating Siniavskii's most cherished belief in the enduring power of art.

Siniavskii's theme in *Spokoinoi nochi* is art; his subject is his becoming a writer, the story of how the literary critic and lecturer Andrei Siniavskii turned into Abram Tertz. The point is made simply and directly. There is nothing here about the apprenticeship of the young writer, the discovery of a latent talent. These matters are remote from his concern. He presents the decision to write as the recognition of a compulsion, the acceptance of a necessity. But what modesty and a lifelong habit of self-deprecation make nothing of is the burden of moral responsibility he assumed when he took up his pen. Siniavskii's autobiographical novel is filled with self-irony and has nothing of the portentous solemnity of Pasternak's *Doctor Zhivago*, yet essentially it tells the same story. It is the spiritual journey of a writer who accepts his part as one of 'the children of Russia's terrible years' ('deti strashnykh let Rossii') and elects to bear witness to his times.[30] And Siniavskii quietly acknowledges the identity of the role in the many small reminiscences and quotations from Pasternak's novel which he inserts into his text.

The subject of writing generates clusters of images which, when brought into contact with images of constraint and confinement, demonstrate the power of the word to create inner space and windows on to other dimensions. In the first chapter Siniavskii meets his 'Room 101' in a solitary confinement cell in Potma transit prison. For him it is not Winston Smith's rats that constitute his idea of hell, nor Svidrigailov's room full of spiders, it is four walls on which it is impossible to write. The cell walls have been coated with a hard ridged surface which renders it impossible to scratch any mark on them. His response is to take out a pencil and a copy of *Izvestiia* that he had managed to keep hidden from the duty sergeant – and write. He writes all over the newspaper, in the margins, between the headings, wherever he can find space. and as he does so the unyielding walls miraculously become 'ephemeral cardboard'; he discovers he can hear clearly through them, and he finds himself recording all the sounds of prison life going on beyond their confines.[31]

In the final chapter Siniavskii re-encounters this image of the harsh stone wall. Years have passed. Siniavskii is by now an émigré, resident in France. This time he enters a confined space as a free man, together with a group of tourists. It is a palaeolithic cave in the Pyrenees. Inside he confronts not just the past of Stone Age man, but his own inner self and his own earlier imaginings. He enters a cavern filled with stalactites and stalagmites – huge unmoving water-falls of stone, great stone towers of Babel. The cave is some 170 metres below ground. Bearing down on it is the weight of thousands of tons of solid rock and dripping through its ceiling is the stone rain, seeping through from the heavens above. Here is the reality of the icicles imagined in his fantastic story 'Gololeditsa': the treacher-ous icicle that kills the narrator's beloved Natasha, and the gigantic icicle, the pure image of absolute power, which, with his gift of second sight, the narrator sees as the future incarnation of the KGB's Colonel Tarasov. Here, too, is the reality of the supernatural experience recounted to Siniavskii by his friend Alla which he records earlier in *Spokoinoi nochi*. On the night of his death, Stalin had appeared to Alla as she lay in bed in the form of a transparent column of pure coldness, a colossal cylinder of a gas so concentrated that, if touched, it would freeze a person's hand off.[32] Siniavskii crawls through more passages beyond the calcium formations and there encounters the chief revelation of this cave popularly known as the 'Cave of the Maimed', or the 'Cave of the Cut-Off Hands' (ill. 3.3):[33] stencilled prints, red, black and white, of human hands with joints of the fingers missing:

Then, in the flashlight's flickering beam, I see them – fingerprints. I realize I don't have my camera with me. But taking pictures isn't allowed anyway. Fingerprints, red, white, black, the phalanges of fingers chopped in half, which appear with increasing frequency on the walls as we begin to get our bearings.[34]

Siniavskii does not comment upon this description. It is left to the reader to make the connection with the Potma cell and recognise the hands, as Siniavskii does, as the hands of suffering humanity like himself, worn and broken but struggling to make their mark on intractable matter. There is, however, a significant difference from the Potma image. The cave, though a place of confinement, appears as a place of refuge, not a prison. Siniavskii reflects how good it would be to stay there in its protection, to be buried there and saved, but he crawls up and out into the open air to face the bombardment of 'stone rain' from the implacable gods who have presided over his century and his destiny: 'stalin', 'lenin', 'hitler', 'zhdanov'.[35]

Siniavskii returns to the image and the worn fingers of the writer at the very end of the book when he has decided upon his future path as a writer. He is travelling back to the Soviet Union from Austria, where he has not co-operated with the KGB in the entrapment of Hélène Pelletier. The spiritual journey has been so great that it seems he has been on a trip round the world:

It wasn't life that I wanted during those soporific hours while returning to Russia from a trip round the world, but only to write, to write, until there was nothing left of me but fingers.[36]

Again he leaves it to the reader to make the connection, just as he leaves the reader to see how the red, black and white of the typesetting and illustrations represent the two 'hands' of the writer and his art historian wife.

The strength of *Spokoinoi nochi* derives from the successful combination of the three narrative strands of autobiography, artist as

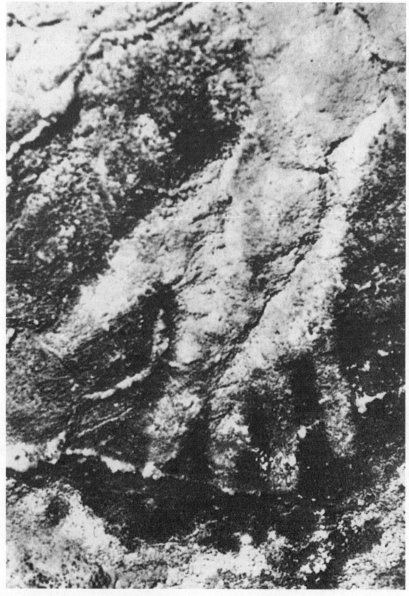

3.3. Gargas Hand. Wall-painting from the Caves of Lascaux, France, from
Abbé H. Breuil, *Four Hundred Centuries of Cave Art*, trans. Mary E. Boyle
(New York, 1979) © Hacker Art Books, New York, 1979.

witness, and writing about writing, and the avoidance of the pitfalls that attend over-indulgence in each one of them: sentimentality, hagiography and aestheticism. This delicate balance is boldly and triumphantly demonstrated in the three pieces of visual art which Siniavskii places at the climax of *Spokoinoi nochi*. They are images of death and resurrection: two of them religious and Christian in subject, the third secular and pagan. The first is a grotesque fantastic invention which grows out of Siniavskii's reading about the Time of Troubles and the image of the grief-stricken mother of the dead Tsarevich Dmitrii calling upon Christ, the Virgin Mary and the saints for mercy. It is a talking icon and an unconventional treatment of a traditional subject of Russian iconography. Christ Pantocrator, ruler of the universe, sits on his purple throne, flanked on the one side by the Virgin Mary the Intercessor, holding a flower, and on the other by John the Baptist, holding out his severed head on its tray. The icon presides as sorrowful witness over the repeated tyrannies and brutalities of Russian history. The Virgin Mary intercedes for forgiveness; the head of John the Baptist fulminates from his tray; and Christ is merciful, yet, looking into the future, he can see no end to the bloodshed and suffering: 'Bad weather's coming' ('Vidat', k nepogode'). The tableau freezes in irresolution; the three figures remain still for years, perhaps for centuries ('Zamerli za mnogie gody, esli ne veka'), and John the Baptist's eye covers over with a dull film like a lizard falling asleep.[37]

Despite the grotesque treatment, this passage reads as another reminiscence of *Doctor Zhivago* and the poem 'Skazka' (A Fairy-Tale) which Pasternak places at the centre of the cycle of poems which form the last chapter and the climax of the novel. The poem recounts the legend of George and the Dragon, but suspends the action at the point when the knight holds his spear raised over the beast. Eyelids are closed; years and centuries pass: 'Somknutye veki. / Vysi. / Oblaka. / Vody. Brody. Reki. / Gody i veka.' When the poet returns from the dimension of eternity to history, the dragon is dead, but George and the maiden lie suspended between life, sleep and death, their fates in the balance. And the years and the centuries flow past.[38]

Pasternak's poetic cycle does have a resolution. The last poems describe the the Passion and death of Christ and end with the assurance of the resurrection. Siniavskii, too, rejoins Pasternak at his journey's end in his Epilogue with an image of Christ carrying his cross on the way to Calvary. Before leaving Vienna he decides to visit the art gallery. There he comes upon this tapestry which in the magic of its playful embroidery transfigures its grim subject of Christ's Passion, and affirms the power of art to see past suffering and death to the resurrection that comes after:

Doesn't the hope of resurrection work its way into all art, no matter what its subject? [. . .] Art is stronger and more enduring, and, if you will, more alive, than destructive life.[39]

Between these two images of icon and tapestry, with their Christian message of forgiveness and resurrection, Siniavskii places the violence and drama of a pagan masterpiece from Nineveh: the magnificent Assyrian stone reliefs depicting the royal lion hunt, battles and triumphs of the reign of King Ashurbanipal (668–627 BC). The description opens his final chapter and dominates the entire novel, gathering its images and focusing its energy. Here are walls of stone, walls which do not frustrate the pencil of the prisoner or break the fingers of the cave-dweller, but demonstrate the triumph of the stonemason's art over unyielding matter. They are very old, carved some 645 years BC, the civilisation they record so vividly has long since disappeared, but they speak to the present out of the continuum of history through the permanence of art. As well as being a fragment of world history, they are a fragment of Siniavskii's biography. He has known these friezes practically all his life. He first met them as a boy in picture reproductions in the 1930s. Some forty years later, after he had already settled into a life in emigration, he encountered the originals in the British Museum and greeted them joyfully as long-lost relatives.[40] Here he was seeing them for the first time 'for real', yet their essential reality for him lay not in London, but in what they had come to mean for him through the persecution and terror of the intervening Stalinist years. His fascination with them as a child had been naive, untouched by experience. They were pictures from another world. Time made them part of his world: the implacable Assyrian rulers and foot-soldiers turned into Stalin and his henchman; the cruelly tortured lions turned into all the régime's innocent victims who, like Pasternak, could cry out 'I have fallen like a beast into a trap' (ill. 3.4).[41] So, accordingly, in *Spokoinoi nochi* Siniavskii positions the

3.4. The Dying Lioness. Detail from Ashurbanipal's lion-hunt scene of stone
bas-reliefs, Ninevah, *c.* 645 BC © British Museum, London.

carvings at just the point when he is summing up the meaning of
those years. He plunges *in medias res*: 'On the jagged Assyrian
friezes, the lions growled with all the veracity of human speech, as
they breathed their last.'[42] The hunted lions are dying; the serried
ranks of implacable Assyrian warriors are marching triumphantly
on; butchered bodies float in the Euphrates. And Siniavskii enters
inside the carving. He feels the pain of the butchered beasts; it is
they alone he feels compassion for, individualised in their suffering
and death. Yet he identifies with their Stalinist tormentors too, as
he sees their bodies, lower down and later in the narrative sequence
of the carving, floating downriver in the disfigurement of death.
Here is a demonstration of the cathartic power of art. Pity and
terror, and acceptance of a part both in universal suffering and
universal guilt.

    Purely in the manner of its telling, this description of the Assyrian
friezes provides the answer to the questions which preoccupy
Siniavskii in this concluding section of his book. Does art carry a

moral charge? Is there a connection between aesthetics and ethics? How could his childhood friend Khmel'nitskii (who is referred to in the novel as 'S'), with all his love and expert knowledge of art, endowed with the gift of perfect aesthetic 'pitch', decide with Dostoevskii's Ivan Karamazov that 'all is permitted' ('vse dozvoleno') and become a KGB agent and a traitor? The question is posed urgently here with the Assyrian friezes, because the memory of Khmel'nitskii is inextricably tied up with them. It was a shared childhood enthusiasm. Yet a Khmel'nitskii could not have written this passage; an aesthetic sense does not bestow the negative capability to enter into and absorb experience. Nor could a Khmel'-nitskii have reached Siniavskii's simple yet difficult conclusion: 'There is no art without love':

Art is stronger and more enduring, and, if you will, more alive, than destructive life. That is why it is both healing and always moral, but independent of foolish morality... There is no art without love.[43]

NOTES

This essay is dedicated to the memory of Andrei Siniavskii who died shortly after it was written, 25 February 1997. An urn filled with earth from Pasternak's grave outside Moscow was buried with him in Fontenay-aux-Roses.

1 Siniavskii as 'Abram Tertz', *Golos iz khora* (London, 1973), p. 36. *A Voice from the Chorus*, English translation by Kyril Fitzlyon and Max Hayward (London, 1976), p. 33. Quotations are from this translation.
2 See Andrei Sinyavsky, *Soviet Civilization: A Cultural History* (New York, 1990), p. 232.
3 Tertz, *Golos iz khora*, p. 225. *A Voice from the Chorus*, p. 225. Future references to these editions in-text as '*GK; VC*'.
4 *A Voice from the Chorus*: 'A metaphor is a memory of that Golden Age when all was everything. A fragment of metamorphosis.'
5 *GK*, pp. 212–13; *VC*, p. 210.
6 *GK*, pp. 141–2, pp. 262–4; *VC*, pp. 137–8, pp. 262–4.
7 For more on the association between primitivism and Russian Modernism, see Pamela Chester's chapter in the present volume.
8 Abram Tertz, *Sud idet*, in *Sobranie sochinenii v dvukh tomakh*, 1 (Moscow, 1992), p. 283. English translation, *The Trial Begins*, by Max Hayward in *The Trial Begins and Socialist Realism* (Berkeley and Los Angeles, 1982), p. 67.
9 'Chto takoe sotsialisticheskii realizm?', in *Fantasticheskii mir Abrama Tertsa*

(New York, 1967), pp. 401–46 (443). English translation, 'On Socialist Realism', by George Dennis in *The Trial Begins and Socialist Realism* (Berkeley and Los Angeles, 1982), pp. 127–219 (215).

10 Abram Tertz, *Spokoinoi nochi* (Paris, 1984), pp. 395–9. *Goodnight!*, English translation by Richard Lourie (Harmondsworth, 1989), pp. 325–7. Quotations are from this translation unless otherwise stated. See also Andrei Sinyavsky, *Soviet Civilization: A Cultural History*, pp. 232–3.

11 See Isaak Babel', 'Moi listki: Odessa', in *Konarmiia, Odesskie rasskazy, P'esy* (Letchworth, 1965), pp. 155–8. See also Andrei Siniavskii, 'Isaac Babel'', *Œuvres et Opinions*, 8 (1964), 157–63. English translation in *Major Soviet Writers: Essays in Criticism*, ed. Edward J. Brown (New York, 1973), pp. 301–9 (306).

12 Abram Tertz, 'Pkhents', in *Fantasticheskii mir Abrama Tertsa*, pp. 175–96 (192–3). English translation, 'Pkhentz', by Manya Harari, in *Fantastic Stories* (Evanston, Ill. 1987). *Golos iz khora* contains further reference to Hugo when Siniavskii comments on how much richer and more rewarding than realism Romanticism proved to be in the history of culture, and names, a trifle surprisingly, Quasimodo as a forerunner of Platon Karataev. A few pages before this passage, *à propos* of his reading of Irish sagas, he virtually restates Hugo's Cromwellian credo when he identifies the power of armed combat as deriving from a sharply defined sense of the beautiful combined with the grotesque:

Not only because of its dramatic potential, but also by reason of the sharply defined sense it gives of the beautiful merging into the grotesque, the description of combat and war [. . .] has always held the centre of the stage in world art. (*GK*, p. 206; *VC*, p. 204)

13 I. Golomstock and A. Siniavskii, *Pikasso* (Moscow, 1960). A. Men'shutin and A. Siniavskii, *Poeziia pervykh let revoliutsii: 1917–1920* (Moscow, 1964). In both these collaborations the views of the authors are so consonant as to make it unnecessary, and, indeed, impossible to apportion responsibility for different sections. Golomstock himself remembers *Pikasso* as an evenly shared labour, but has no recollection of who wrote which parts.

14 Golomstock and Siniavskii, *Pikasso*, pp. 51–2. This painting is in the Tate Gallery, London.

15 Ibid., pp. 42, 44. This painting is in the National Gallery of Art, Washington, DC. It provides an excellent example of Picasso's inter-action with art of the past. His idealised image of the Montmartre girl, Juliette, who was the model for the painting, has its origins in two pictures: Velazquez's *Woman with a Fan* (1638–9), and the figure of Augustus in Ingres's fragment *Tu Marcellus Eris*. See John Richardson, *A Life of Picasso. Volume 1: 1881–1906* (London, 1992), pp. 422–3, p. 420.

16 This cubist painting is in the Pushkin State Museum of Fine Arts, Moscow. It is dated 1910 in other catalogues of Picasso's works.

17 Golomstock and Siniavskii, *Pikasso*, pp. 24–8.
18 *GK*, p. 213; *VC*, p. 211.
19 The first poem of Pasternak's last poetic cycle *Kogda razguliaetsia* (When the Weather Clears), begins: 'Vo vsem mne khochetsia doiti / Do samoi suti' ('I want in everything to reach to the heart of the matter', 1956). Boris Pasternak, *Sochineniia*, ed. G. P. Struve and B. A. Filippov, 3 vols (Ann Arbor, 1961), vol. III, pp. 61–2.
20 *GK*, pp. 24–8; *VC*, pp. 21–4.
21 Pasternak uses the phrase 'crossings of fate' ('sudeb skreshchen'ia') in the poem from the Zhivago cycle, 'Zimniaia noch'' (Winter Night). Boris Pasternak, *Doktor Zhivago* (Ann Arbor, 1967), p. 550. English translation, *Doctor Zhivago*, by Max Hayward and Manya Harari (London, 1958), p. 288.
22 Pasternak, *Doctor Zhivago*, p. 48. *Doktor Zhivago*, p. 42.
23 'Density of style appears in my writing when I have nothing but a sheet of paper – a tiny raft on which I must clamber, trying to settlethere while all the time my thoughts are palpitating and thrashing around. It is then that I have to keep myself afloat on my little ark by binding it together with a superfluity of metaphor.' (*GK*, p. 208; *VC*, p. 206)
24 'Metaphors and similes are based not only on the likeness or closeness of the things compared, but even on their remoteness from each other. It is this that makes it possible for us to indulge our fantasies by means of language – stare hard enough into the obscure depths of some object or other and it will grow a funny little face. It is such little faces, claws, wings, tails, tongues, fleetingly glimpsed in things, that probably attract me most about metaphors – they can turn the drab page of an exercise book into a flowing, ornamental pattern, full of wild beasts.' (*GK*, pp. 85–6; *VC*, pp. 80–1)
25 This painting is in the Hermitage, St Petersburg. Painted in about 1666–9, it was the last of Rembrandt's history paintings and, though completed by another artist, is rated by some art historians among his finest works.
26 See A. Siniavskii, *Ivan-Durak: ocherk russkoi narodnoi very* (Ivan-The Fool: a Study of Russian Popular Beliefs) (Paris, 1991), pp. 233–41 (233–4).
27 This crowd and this film set are, it turns out, entirely fictional (personal conversation with Mariia Rozanova, 1995). But then, as Siniavskii tells us in a discussion of Hogarth's ostensibly autobiographical *Anecdotes*, art has nothing to do with real life. His account of Hogarth's method gives a good lesson in his own practice:

The viewer is delighted to see that everything fits together so neatly – which it does, not because it has anything to do with real life, but because this is how the painter has programmed it. [. . .] The art of imitating reality ('realism') boils down to an ability to excite curiosity, to devise a puzzle with a key to its solution.

As in real life? Not at all – as in art, where everything is always pre-conceived and invented. (*GK*, pp. 137–8; *VC*, pp. 133–4)

28 Abram Tertz, 'Puteshestvie na Chernuiu rechku', *Sintaksis* 34 (1994), 39. Siniavskii's description can be identified as a reference to pictures belonging to the series of huge murals, popularly known as 'las pinturas negras' (the Black Paintings), which Goya painted in his suburban villa, the Quinta des sordo (Country house of the deaf-man), and which now hang, transferred to canvas, in the Prado. Yet it is a composite description. Siniavskii would appear to be combining an allusion to the *Witches' Sabbath* (*El Ritual de las Brujas*, c. 1821–3), which shows a he-goat addressing a grotesque gaggle of witches, with the painting known as *The Pilgrimage of St Isidore* (*La Romaria de San Isidro*), which originally complemented it, on the opposite wall of the villa. There another huddle of distorted faces are grouped in a dark landscape behind a man playing a guitar. As commentators have pointed out, the subject of both these paintings is the psychology of the masses, with the grotesque packed faces showing the primitive emotions of the crowd displacing rational thought. See, for example, Janis Tomlinson, *Francisco Goya y Lucientes: 1746–1828* (London, 1994), pp. 240–4. Siniavskii, we note, here exercises the same freedom as with any other 'raw' material, actual or historical, which he incorporates into his art. He selects, recombines, concentrates the images, fashioning them so as best to convey his meaning.

29 Tertz, 'Puteshestvie na Chernuiu rechku', 3–51 (40).

30 'My, deti strashnykh let Rossii'. This line of Aleksandr Blok's is quoted by Gordon in the Epilogue of *Doctor Zhivago* and applied to Stalin's times. Pasternak, *Doktor Zhivago*, p. 530. Siniavskii paraphrases the quotation in the fourth chapter of *Spokoinoi nochi*: 'I am not ashamed to say that I am the child of those grim years' (*Spokoinoi nochi* (Paris, 1984), p. 323; *Goodnight!*, p. 266). Siniavskii was deeply impressed by Pasternak's novel, which he first read in 1956 before it was sent abroad for publication. He and Iulii Daniel' were pall-bearers at Pasternak's funeral in 1960.

31 Tertz, *Spokoinoi nochi*, pp. 39–40. *Goodnight!*, pp. 26–7.

32 Tertz, *Spokoinoi nochi*, pp. 277–8. *Goodnight!*, pp. 226–35.

33 Lourie's translation misleadingly has 'The Cave of the Cut-Off Arms', p. 288.

34 Tertz, *Spokoinoi nochi*, p. 352. *Goodnight!*, pp. 289–90. Paintings of the type Siniavskii describes are found in several locations in France, including the regions of the Dordogne, Lot and Gard. The cave at Gargas in the Hautes Pyrénées is the most famous site, containing a striking collection of more than 150 negative and positive images of these mutilated hands, nearly all painted in red and black, with a few white and one yellow. Archeologists and art historians to this day are intrigued by the unsolved mystery of how and why they were made. It

seems evident that the stencilled images were done by paint being applied (most likely by blowing powder paste or liquid, with hollow tubes of long bone used as blow pipes) round the outline of hands pressed against the rock. But were these images made simply by the fingers being bent back, or do they represent genuine mutilations? If so, how were these deformities caused? Were they inflicted in connection with ancient magic or initiation rituals, or were the causes natural: severe frostbite or some form of disease? The more recent research tends to support the natural causes hypothesis. It has been established that the same outlines of hands are repeated many times and the likelihood is that the paintings were made by a small group of fewer than twenty men, women and children. This, however, still does not explain what reason or purpose the painters had in making them. There is an extensive literature on the subject. See Abbé H. Breuil, *Four Hundred Centuries of Cave Art*, translated by Mary E. Boyle (Paris, 1952); André Leroi-Gourhan, *Les Religions de la Préhistoire (Paléolithique)* (Paris, 1964); André Leroi-Gourhan, *Préhistoire de l'Art Occidental* (Paris, 1965); Peter J. Ucko and Andrée Rosenfeld, *Paleolithic Cave Art* (London, 1967); André Clot, *L'Art Graphique préhistorique des Hautes-Pyrénées: Essai de synthèse et catalogue à l'occasion d'une exposition* (Morlaas, 1973); *L'Art des Cavernes: Atlas des grottes ornées paléolithiques françaises*, preface by André Leroi-Gourhan (Paris, 1984).

These scientific descriptions of the cave provide further indication of Siniavskii's selectivity in the treatment of his source material, since the cave at Gargas is not just renowned for these paintings of hands, but for its ossuary of bear bones and its many fine drawings of animals: horses, bison, bulls, mammoths, deer, and ibex. Siniavskii, however, is interested only in those objects which symbolise his theme of the individual crushed under the weight of Stalinist oppression, that is, the hands, the calcium formations and the weight of rock.

35 Tertz, *Spokoinoi nochi*, p. 352. *Goodnight!*, p. 290.

36 Tertz, *Spokoinoi nochi*, p. 437. *Goodnight!*, p. 358. The theme of hands and writing is developed further in the novella *Kroshka Tsores* (Paris, 1980): *Little Jinx*, trans. Larry P. Joseph and Rachel May (Evanston, Illinois, 1992), which was originally conceived as a part of *Spokoinoi nochi* and which Siniavskii also published under the signature of Abram Tertz.

37 Tertz, *Spokoinoi nochi*, pp. 332–9; *Goodnight!*, pp. 273–8.

38 Pasternak, *Doktor Zhivago*, pp. 545–58.

39 Tertz, *Spokoinoi nochi*, p. 428. *Goodnight!*, p. 350.

40 Tertz, *Spokoinoi nochi*, p. 341. *Goodnight!*, p. 280. The British Museum's collection of Assyrian art also includes earlier reliefs dating from the ninth century BC from the royal palace at Nimrud.

41 Boris Pasternak, 'Nobelevskaia premiia' (The Nobel Prize), in *Sochineniia*, vol. III, pp. 107–8.

42 Tertz, *Spokoinoi nochi*, p. 339. *Goodnight!*, p. 279.
43 Tertz, *Spokoinoi nochi*, p. 428. *Goodnight!*, p. 350. The character of the amoral aesthete Karlinskii in *Sud idet* is recognisable as a first artistic representation of Khmel'nitskii.

CHAPTER 4

Mikhail Zoshchenko's shadow operas

Alexander Zholkovsky

In Zoshchenko criticism, the two major components of the writer's *œuvre* tend to be treated separately. While his comic corpus is interpreted in a 'cultural–sociological' vein – as an Aesopian satire of the 'new, i.e. Soviet, Man',[1] the studies of his 'serious' works (especially, *Pered voskhodom solntsa* (Before Sunrise), 1943, henceforth abbreviated as *PVS*), following his own lead, focus more or less psychoanalytically on his morbid self.[2] Elsewhere I have argued for a 'single Zoshchenko', claiming that all of his works revolve around one obsessive theme: 'fear of environment'; that the notorious 'Zoshchenkovian characters' are the author's own alter egos, defensively demoted by him to a comic status (according to the formula first developed by Gogol); that his unreliable *skaz* narrative represents his and his characters' unreliable responses to an unreliable world; that Zoshchenko's 'mask' is existential rather than Aesopian; in sum, that he is a classic of the Soviet era not so much as a satirist of communal apartment mores but rather as a poet of a mistrustful and hopeless quest for calm, protection, law and order.[3]

Not surprisingly, given this general philosophical orientation, the problems of the self's fluid boundaries, author's/characters' masks and role-playing take centre-stage, and this is perhaps why Zoshchenko devotes so much attention to various theatrical motifs. Theatre ranks equally with the other 'other art' that is so conspicuous in his texts: painting, whose prominence may be in part due to his having been the son of a professional artist.[4] Zoshchenko wrote for the theatre (mostly comedies of errors),[5] and many of his comic texts involve theatre in one way or another.

Indeed, more than a dozen stories, some of them among his best, beginning with the famous 'Aristokratka' (Lady Aristocrat, 1922), unfold at the theatre.[6] Still others, including his other signature piece of the 1920s, 'Bania' (The Bathhouse, 1925), promote the characteristically Zoshchenkovian commandment: 'Ne v teatre!' (This is not a theatre!).[7] Viewed through the 'cultural–sociological' lens, these texts display with perfect clarity the cultural predicament of the Zoshchenkovian character – primitive, uncouth, under-dressed, ill-mannered, pathetically helpless in his 'inability to meet culture's challenge',[8] yet posing as a 'new man,' arbiter of new tastes and morals, and thus a threat to all things refined, including the gentlemanly and sophisticated M. M. Zoshchenko himself. The opposition is thus construed as an indictment of the new man's barbarity. The ambiguity of the 'cultured/uncultured' dichotomy, which becomes inescapably evident when its 'cultured' pole takes the form of oppressive Soviet officialdom, is duly reflected in some of the analyses – as a further extension of the same 'unculturedness' now parading as 'culture.' From this perspective the theatre, with its emphasis on dress and other codes, demarcations, and conventiona-lised roles, both on stage and in the arrangement of the entire theatrical chronotope, is an ideal *objet trouvé* for enhancing and playing out the 'culture/unculture' opposition.[9]

What passes unnoticed when such constructions are made is the existential, rather than merely Soviet, nature of the human condition as perceived and inhabited by the 'Zoshchenkovian character,' be this the ridiculous *meshchanin* (petit bourgeois), the writer's auto-biographical persona (in *PVS*), or the real author himself (who increasingly emerges, now that a growing mass of documentary evidence becomes available, as a coherent identity).[10] In the overall pattern of 'desperate attempts to cope with fear', a major role is reserved for 'feigning'. The Zoshchenkovian character tries to pretend (be it to his superiors, society at large, himself or the reader) that the threatening object is not to be feared, that he himself is not what he seems, and, eventually, that the text is not about his real concern – namely, his deep-seated fear of his environment (whether represented by the Soviet regime, parents or quasi-parental figures, thieves, guests, relatives, threatening women, ageing or death).[11] To be sure, he knows all along that this tactic is wrong and doomed to failure. In the stories, this is manifested through the pathetic incompetence of the comic characters, in the 'serious' works, through the characters' (including the autobiographical persona's) case histories and direct authorial comments.

An ambiguous interplay of such critical (self-)awareness and a defensive need for cover underlies Zoshchenko's impervious narrative posture in general and his obsession with masks, roles and theatre in particular. Of special interest, however, are the cases where the recourse to 'theatre' is almost completely written out of the picture. I will dwell on two such instances, one from Zoshchenko's comic period, the other from *PVS*, with their different techniques of dissimulation.

'MONTER'

'Monter' (The Electrician, 1926)[12] is one of those among Zoshchenko's openly theatrical stories which make a point of distorting or even completely ignoring (as does 'Aristokratka') what is happening on the stage.

'When the entire theatre . . . was having its picture taken . . . they shoved the electrician . . . somewhere on the side, as if to say, technical staff. And in the middle . . . they put the tenor. The electrician . . . never said a word to this loutishness, but in his soul he harboured a certain rudeness . . .

'Now this here comes up . . . Two young lady-friends turn up at his booth. Either he had invited them before, or else they just barged in – nobody knows . . . [They] basically ask to be seated with everyone in the hall,' but the administrator refuses, saying that 'every chair has been accounted for.' Then the electrician, in his turn, refuses 'to play': he 'turns off the lights in the entire goddamn theatre . . . and sits there flirting desperately' with his dames.

A 'total filibuster' [obstruktsiia] arises. 'The cashier screams, afraid they'll filch his money in the darkness . . . [T]he chancer, the opera's principal tenor . . . goes right to the management and says in his tenor voice: "I refuse to sing tenor in the dark. . . Let that son-of-a-bitch electrician sing." The electrician says: ". . . Since he . . . gets photographed in the middle, let him sing with one hand and switch the light on with the other . . . We're through with tenors!"'

Relenting, the administrator seats 'the young girls in prominent positions.' Now that the electrician's claims have been satisfied ('"[T]he ruin is not via them, the ruin is via me . . . I am not in principle stingy about the current . . ."'), he 'gives light', and the show begins.[13]

A cultural–sociological interpretation of the story easily suggests itself, with such 'typically Zoshchenkovian' issues as egalitarianism, new technology, embezzlement, uncivilised attitudes and so on, echoed, on the formal level, by his inimitable combination of quasi-illiterate use of language, representing 'unculture', with thematic and rhythmical repetitions of a kind close to those found in poetry and to be understood as projections of 'culture'. Yet such an approach takes one only so far. The question, with a slight variation, that frames the story – 'Who is more important in the theatre: the actor, the director, or perhaps the stage carpenter?' – seems to remain unresolved and, moreover, to be a false dilemma, intended, as is often the case in Zoshchenko, to throw the reader off the track. One hesitates to side either with the electrician against the tenor, thus espousing the 'anti-cultural' stance of a vulgar womaniser, or with the tenor-cum-management against the 'monter', thus defending 'culture' at the cost of the human dignity of the 'little man'. The only recourse left, short of dismissing the story as a mere sketch about the goings-on in a provincial company, would be to invoke the general Zoshchenkovian 'ambivalence', blanketing the cultural failures of all parties involved. It is only natural, therefore, to focus, in search of more specific answers, on the story's existential aspects.

The main conflict takes place if not 'via' (cherez) the young ladies, then certainly in connection with them, as the hero is publicly humiliated in the most acutely existential – amorous – quarter and responds in kind by demonstratively preferring the girls' company to his immediate professional duties. Public humiliation is a recurrent theme in Zoshchenko's stories (see, for example, 'Aristokratka'). In 'Monter' it is first foreshadowed in the episode of collective and artistic photograph-taking, during which the electrician is pointedly marginalised, and then taken to its limit, dramatic in every sense, as the electrician's ego is further injured by the neglect shown towards his lady guests, and the ensuing row involves the on-stage tenor, off-stage personnel (the electrician, the cashier, the administrator, the management), and the entire theatre hall ('The audience is shouting').

The playhouse dimension is highlighted by the consistent recurrence in the narrative of two leitmotifs pertaining to theatre. One is the motif of 'seating', directly associated in the story with the theme of 'human dignity':

'But in the centre, on the chair with a back, they *seated* [the italics henceforth are mine – AZ] the tenor' – '[T]he young ladies . . . asked *to be seated* with everyone in the hall' – ' "I'll whip up a pair of tickets for you right away. Just *sit down* here, by the booth" ' – ' "Then we"ll see . . . who to photograph on the side and who *to seat* in the middle" ' – '[H]e has locked the booth with all the keys – and *sits* flirting desperately. . .' – ' "I'll *seat* them somewhere right away" ' – 'So they *seat* his young ladies in outstanding *seats* and begin the performance.'

Indeed, as the 'monter' sits flirting with the women in his darkened booth, he assumes the position, as it were, of a privileged theatregoer entertaining his ladyguests in a box of his own.

The other is the motif of 'acting', set in additional relief by the ungrammaticalities that accompany its mentions and culminate in the electrician's representation of his sit-down strike in thespian terms:

'They *acted* an opera in this municipal theatre' – 'Besides the outstanding acting by the actors [igry artistov], this theatre . . . had an electrician' – 'Today, for example, they are *acting* [the opera] *Ruslan i Liudmila* [Ruslan and Ludmilla] . . .' – ' "Well, in that case, I refuse to *act*. I refuse, in short, to illuminate your production. *Act* it without me." '

The theatricalisation of the plot does not stop there, as it taps the most natural of available resources: the staged performance proper, despite the usual Zoshchenkovian lack of any narrative fore-grounding of this theatricality. Indeed, although the actual opera performed that night, Mikhail Glinka's *Ruslan*,[14] is mentioned only in passing, it is highly relevant to the story – compare the single most pronounced case of such 'mousetrap' interaction in Zoshchenko: the story 'Akter' (Actor, 1925), in which an amateur replacement actor is actually robbed by his fellow performers, thus enacting the play's fictional plot, while the audience, taking the victim's screams for hyper-realistic action, cheer their lungs out.[15] On close inspection the two plots, of 'Monter' and of its intertext – Zoshchenko's frame narrative story, on the one hand, and Glinka's 'play within a play,' on the other – exhibit telling parallels.

Both plots feature a conflict over women (the two young ladies; Liudmila), pitting the hero (the electrician; Ruslan) against over-whelming opposition (the administrator, the tenor; Prince Svetozar, Golova [the Head], Chernomor, Farlaf), which is unexpectedly overcome so that the stories end happily (ignoring the tenor, the administrator eventually accedes to the electrician's demands; seeing that the rivals have been removed, Svetozar gives Liudmila away to Ruslan, although, in earlier stages of the plot, he had promised her to any successful rescuer). Compared to the evil wizard Chernomor and the Grand Prince Svetozar, Ruslan is, if not a 'little man', certainly a personage of lesser rank, whose victory is made possible thanks only to the help of the good magician Finn (and a magic donor, hostile to Ruslan, Golova). In the story, this aid motif is paralleled, on a reduced scale, by the final intervention of the administrator, who combines the roles of Svetozar and Finn. These rather generic similarities are bolstered by one quite specific resonance. The turning-off of the lights, naturalised by the nature of the electrician's job, forms an unexpected parallel to the spectacular episode at the end of the opera's first act when Ruslan and Liudmila's wedding feast is interrupted by a 'loud stroke of thunder . . . the stage is in a complete darkness . . . all the characters are stunned, dumbfounded, frozen', and it turns out that Liudmila has been abducted.[16] Thus the electrician suddenly switches from the role of a Ruslan to that of a Chernomor, rendering the archetypal underpinnings of his action even more intriguing.

The 'light/dark' opposition is central to Glinka's opera (even the name of the grand prince is a tell-tale one: Svetozar (literally Light-Dawn), contrasted to Chernomor (literally Black-Sea, or even Black-Plague). Moreover, in the original Pushkin poem (which, instead of Svetozar, a character straight out of a 'magic tale' (volshebnaia skazka), has a fictionalised historical Kievan Prince: Vladimir-solnyshko (Vladimir-the-Sun)), Zoshchenko's 'light/dark' motif has a counterpart in the 'invisibility' bestowed by Chernomor's magic cap, which conceals the abductor and victim from Ruslan. In its turn, the 'darkness' caused by the electrician spawns multiple variations: the cashier fears that 'in the dark' the proceeds will be stolen; the tenor refuses 'to sing tenor in the dark'; and the culprit himself, having plunged the entire theatre into darkness 'to the devil's grandmother' (literally, 'k chertovoi babushke'), tries to reap, Chernomor-style, the sexual fruits of his black magic. The 'diabolical' motif reappears in the words of both the administrator and the 'monter' about 'the devil's girls' (chertovy devitsy). Moreover, in the story's closure, the motif of 'supernatural power over light' returns in a positive, 'divine', quasi-biblical key: 'Right away, he says, I'll give you light . . . He gave them light that minute. Begin, he says.'[17]

Even the inimitably Zoshchenkovian phrase, 'Let him sing with one hand and switch on the light with the other', follows a venerable poetic formula – even as it pushes it to a paradoxical extreme. In Pushkin's poem, the same verbal pattern appears at a decisive moment in Ruslan's combat with Chernomor:

'Togda Ruslan odnoi rukoiu / Vzial mech srazhennoi golovy / I, borodu skhvativ drugoiu, / Otsek ee, kak gorst'travy.' 'Then Ruslan with one hand took the sword of the vanquished Golova and, seizing [Chernomor's magical] beard with the other, severed it, like a grassy tuft' (Canto Five).[18]

The dualism of the electrician's mapping on to both Ruslan and Chernomor is aggravated by yet another intertextual incongruity. While the story features the tenor as the main performer in the opera, Glinka's *Ruslan* is rather poorly suited to such a casting. The opera's main protagonist, Ruslan, is a baritone; his magic adversary Chernomor is an extra without a singing role; Ruslan's earthly antagonist, Farlaf, is a bass; the ambivalent father-figure, Svetozar, is a bass, too; and Ruslan's effeminate ally Ratmir is a contralto. Only more-or-less episodic characters are tenors: the epic singer Baian, who is only on hand in the first act; the magic helper Finn, who appears in the second and, briefly, the fifth acts; and the hostile donor Golova, whose part is sung by a chorus of tenors (Act 2). This subtle incongruity is, of course, noticeable – and appreciable – only by connoisseurs, like Zoshchenko himself, who was a man of refined culture, a friend of the composer Dmitrii Shostakovich, and an eager concert- and theatre-goer, often in the company of the women he courted.

The blurring of the correspondences between the two casts is actually in accord with the general 'alternativeness' characteristic of Zoshchenko's narrative.[19] The events take place 'in Saratov or Simbirsk, in a word, somewhere not far from Turkestan'. Similarly, appearing modestly as a 'monter' is someone whose job would be officially described as 'zaveduiushchii osvetitel'noi chast'u' (lighting director). By the same token, the word 'tenor' does not so much denote here a specific type of operatic voice as refer – with semi-literate vagueness – to the show's 'star', premier lover, and thus Ruslan, after all.[20] As a result, both the electrician and the tenor emerge as counterparts of Ruslan, complicating – rendering alter-native – the intertextual correspondences even further.

Be that as it may, in seeking to locate the likely projection of the authorial self, one naturally looks to the main protagonist. Moreover, the electrician's interest in the young ladies, his thin skin and his marginal position in the theatre all speak in favour of such an identification. Zoshchenko had the reputation of a womaniser, was quick to take offence (among the Serapions, his sensitivity was proverbial), and deliberately worked in a 'disreputable' literary genre. Add to this his neurotic obsession with such 'pathogenic objects,' painstakingly analysed in *PVS*, as 'ruka' (hand/arm) and 'udar groma' (thunderclap), and the opposition 'light/darkness'.

To begin with the last-named, this appears even in the title of Zoshchenko's autobiographical narrative, which persistently deploys the 'light of reason' metaphor.

'What could have *illuminated* these scenes [of infancy]? Fear, perhaps? . . . Now these stories are cast in an entirely *different light*. Now you *can see* almost everything in them . . . *The light of logic* expels . . . these [basest of] forces . . . *The light of my reason lit up* the horrible thickets where the fears were lurking. . . I had . . . suffered defeat *in the darkness* . . . But now, as *the sun lit up* the duelling place, I *spied* my enemy's pathetic and barbaric mug . . . The old fears said farewell to my person . . . only because *the light of my reason illuminated* the illogic of their existence.'[21]

The same 'enlightenment' motifs, only in a more ambiguous vein, befitting Zoshchenko's comic style, appear in 'Elektrifikatsiia' (Electrification, 1924):

'This business . . . to *illuminate* Soviet Russia with *light* . . . And they started *bringing in light* here . . . [T]he little landlady . . . suggested they *illuminate* the apartment . . . They did, and goodness gracious [batiushki-*svety*, lit. fathers-lights], the *lights* did *illuminate* it! Mould and filth all around us . . . You *couldn't see* any of it when we had the oil lamps . . . Batiushki-*svety*! A nauseating *spectacle to see* . . .

'I *lit* the electricity – batiushki-*svety*! . . . "It's disgusting to *look* at it all." And all this is *filled with bright light*, and everything *leapt into the eye* . . . I started coming home bored. I arrived, *didn't light the light*, and burrowed into my cot . . .

'The landlady cut the line. "It hurts," she said. "It all looks so poor *in that light*. Why *illuminate* that kind of poverty with *light* for the bedbugs' amusement . . .? I don't want to live *with light*", she said.

Hey, lads, *light* is fine, but *lighting it up* is bad! . . . Everything that's good *in the dark* is bad *in the light*.'[22]

The motifs of 'hand/arm' and 'thunderclap' in *PVS* have been discussed at length in Zoshchenko criticism in connection with *PVS*.[23] Here I will only point out their uncanny relevance to the Glinkian sub-text of 'Monter'.

In *Ruslan*, the scene of thunder, darkness, freeze action, and abduction of the bride right before the consummation of the marriage is accompanied by the words of the chorus: 'What happened? The wrath of Perun?' and those of Ruslan: 'What a wondrous moment! What does this marvellous dream mean? This numbness of feeling? And the mysterious dark/gloom

all around? Where's Liudmila?' – Chorus: 'Where's our princess?' –
Ruslan: 'She was speaking to me here with a quiet tenderness.'[24]

Compare in *PVS*:

'I recalled a dream from long ago . . . From out of the wall, toward me,
there stretched a huge hand . . . I scream. Awake in terror . . . Evidently in
the daytime a hand took, seized, removed something from the infant . . .
But what? . . .The mother's breast? . . . Perhaps the father's hand, placed
on the mother's breast . . . frightened the baby . . .
   'Lightning struck in the yard of our dacha . . . Horrible thunder shook
our whole dacha. This coincided with the very moment when mother had
begun to breast-feed me. The clap of thunder was so strong and unexpected
that mother lost consciousness for a minute and dropped me. I fell on the
bed . . . Hurt my hand . . .
   'In the future the mother's breast came to personify woman, love, and
sexuality . . . Yes, without a doubt – I avoided woman . . . and at the same
time yearned for her . . . in order to flee from her in fear of the expected
retribution . . . Did there not follow on her heels – a shot, a clap [of
thunder], a knife? . . . The chastising [karaiushchaia] hand – of a husband,
a brother, father – accompanied this [woman's] image.'[25]

The traumatic cluster and its auto-interpretation comprise a
dream, a clap of thunder and lighting (= Perun's wrath), frozen
senselessness and loss of woman. One could safely assume Glinka's
opera to be a favourite of Zoshchenko's – if not a direct, then a
subliminal, source of the cited episode from *PVS*.
   In 'Monter', the 'hand/arm' motif is not as pervasive. The initial
switching on of the lights is presumed but never described; in the
scene of the demonstrative extinguishing of the light and locking up
of the booth, the hand is implied but not mentioned; and the same is
true for the final giving of light. But these omissions are more than
made up for by the mocking retort about the tenor's putative help-
yourself performance, with its close-ups of the two hands: first the
'singing' and then the 'lighting' one.
   Unlike the neurotic persona of *PVS*, the authorial mask of the
electrician comes out a clear winner, proving that power over light,
dark and women is 'in his hands'. The 'hand/arm anxiety' is
presented as overcome. This may help to explain the electrician's
metamorphosis from a Ruslan into a Chernomor, which would
otherwise be enigmatic, given the relative empowerment of these
two characters in the intertexts.
   Pondering the moral dilemma posed by his one-time alleged

victory over, but by the same token, fusion with, the baser forces of his soul, the author–narrator of *PVS* writes:

'I got up from my bed no longer the man I had been. Unusually healthy, strong . . . I arose from my bed . . . I nearly ran in circles, not knowing how to direct my barbaric forces . . . Like a tank, I moved through the fields of my life, overcoming all obstacles, all barriers with ease . . . I seemed to have started to bring people more grief than before, when I was fettered, feeble.'[26]

The solution to this problem of Nietzschean amoralism[27] Zoshchenko finds in channelling his newly found strength into the sphere of art: 'Now my reason was free. I was at liberty to do what I wanted. Once again I took up what my hands had once held – art. But now I took it up without trembling hands, with no despair in my heart . . .'[28] This sensation of creative omnipotence is akin to the 'divine giving of light' at the close of our story.

To resume the theme of Zoshchenko's 'touchiness', in *PVS* there are quite a few episodes from the persona's childhood and youth that exhibit his repressed or defiant reaction to humiliation by authority figures, in particular in matters connected with 'cultural' activities: his visit to the arrogant artist-bureaucrat on whom depended the size of the pension for his late father; his threat to 'spit on' the school-teacher who had treated him with mockery; his attempted suicide over a failing grade for a composition on a Turgenevian topic; the dismissal, by the editor of a thick journal, of his short stories as 'drivel'.[29] In some of these cases, the autobiographical young Zoshchenko, like the electrician, 'harboured a certain rudeness', while in others, he gave it a desperate vent and was even ready, to use the electrician's phrase, 'to spit in the gob' of his mighty opponent the teacher. In a further characteristic link to 'Monter', the persona's (over)reaction was misinterpreted by the authority figures (e.g., ascribed to the low grade – cf. the lack of seats for the 'dames'), while what was at issue was human and professional dignity (of the little boy Zoshchenko and the electrician).

The problem of professional standing was close to Zoshchenko's heart. In February 1927, that is, soon after writing 'Monter', he publicly opted for 'petty literature', 'the disreputable form of the . . . very short story', 'bad literary traditions' and so on, thereby defiantly depriving himself of 'criticism's enlightened [!] attention'.[30] In the context of Zoshchenko's obstinate pleading of his aesthetic case, the defence of the peripheral 'technical staff' in 'Monter' finally acquires programmatic significance. From behind the figure of the tenor, then, peeks the emblematic representative of 'major literature': Lev Tolstoi or, rather, a literary official who 'places an order for a red Lev Tolstoi', or a thick-journal editor like Voronskii. By publicly facing down his powerful opponents (the tenor, the administrator, the management) the electrician fulfils Zoshchenko's authorial dream of recognition on his own – 'marginalistic' – creative terms.[31]

The figure of the lighting man suits this role all the better as it combines 'marginality' with a resemblance to the director who, too, acts from behind the scenes, after all. Remarkably, Glinka's Chernomor, in his turn, is an extra, yet one responsible for powerful stage effects: the thunder, darkness etc. (in Act 1) as well as the putting on of a ballet performance intended to seduce Liudmila (Act 4).[32]

The plausibility of Zoshchenko's self-identification with the electrician is also buttressed by the following passage in *Golubaia kniga* (The Sky-Blue Book, 1934; henceforth abbreviated as *GK*), which is rich in 'enlightening', 'inflammatory', 'marginal' and 'theatrical' motifs:

'In his day. . . Voltaire with his laughter *extinguished the bonfires* that *burned* [szhigali] people up. But we, with our *weak and insignificant powers*, take on a much more *modest task*. We hope with our laughter to *light* [*zazhech'*] at least a small *splinter-candle by the light* of which some people might notice what is good for them . . . If this happens, then in the overall *show of life* [*spektakle zhizni*] we would consider our *modest role* of a laboratory assistant and *lighting man* [*osvetitelia*] of the performance fulfilled.'[33]

The 'modesty' of this 'lighting role' is, of course, self-consciously exaggerated, in the spirit of pride-aping humility. Zoshchenko's narrator picks up here on a motif from an earlier discussion (with a 'bourgeois philosopher') of the meaning of life's spectacle – one strikingly, perhaps deliberately, similar to the situation in 'Monter':

'Yes,' said the philosopher. 'In essence, life is unreal . . . So let peoples amuse themselves, arrange for operettas with all those kings and soldiers and merchants of theirs . . .' And we say to him . . . '. . . Even if your amusing definition of life as operetta stands . . . you are in favour of an operetta in which one actor sings and the rest raise the curtain for him. Whereas we . . .' – 'Whereas you,' he breaks in, 'are in favour of an operetta in which all the actors are extras . . . and want to be tenors.' 'By no means. We are in favour of a spectacle in which the roles are all correctly distributed among the actors – according to their talents.'[34]

The proposed view of the electrician as a stand-in for his author's 'creative ego' finds a further corroboration in the rebuff given by

Zoshchenko to his accusers at the Writers' Union meeting in Leningrad in June 1954 – after he had refused (in an interview with visiting British students) to accept Zhdanov's 1946 denunciation of (Akhmatova and) himself. As a witness remembered:

'It suddenly turned out that Zoshchenko was not defending himself . . . he was on the offensive. One man against the entire organization with its secretaries of administration, sections, editors-in-chief . . . He had been invited to the podium in order to bow his head and repent . . .

   '[He declared:] "I can say that . . . my literary life and fate are over . . . A satirist must be a morally pure man, and I have been humiliated like the worst son of a bitch . . . I have no intention of asking for anything. I don't need your leniency" – he looked at the presidium – "or your Druzin, or your abuse and shouts . . ."

   This was a victory . . . [T]he price did not concern him. There was nothing stopping him any more.'[35]

This dates from a much later stage of Zoshchenko's life than 'Monter', but in archetypal matters chronology is not overly important. Zoshchenko's defiant behaviour at the close of his career was of a piece with his anti-authoritarian outbursts as a child, at school, and in the early 1920s. Reminiscing about the times of the Serapion Brothers, V. A. Kaverin wrote:

'There were no crummy guests ["gostishek"] and I especially liked such gatherings – I was a proponent of our "order" being closed . . . something knightly, requiring rituals and "initiations" . . . Then Zoshchenko came, dressed up like a dandy. His first book had just come out . . . [U]nfortunately he had invited three actresses from some theatre . . .

   'The girls were quite pretty . . . especially one . . . who . . . while her girlfriends were reciting their poetry . . . was making eyes at me . . . Did I think that the unceremonious invasion . . . was an insult to our "order"? . . . I listened with revulsion to our guests' trite poems and . . . attacked them scornfully and sharply . . . [T]he girls took offence and left. Zoshchenko saw them home.

   'The Serapions all fell upon me like one man . . . [W]hen he returned [,] [e]veryone fell silent . . . [No one] had ever seen him like that before . . . He was enraged . . . [H]e said I had behaved like a sanctimonious hypocrite . . . and demanded that my comrades condemn my behaviour.'[36]

Kaverin then challenged Zoshchenko to a duel, but at the next meeting of the 'order' they were reconciled.

   The many parallels with 'Monter' are obvious: the ladies' semi-legitimate intrusion; the theatrical element (actresses); the main opponent's insistence on prescribed artistic exclusivity ('knightly order'); the furiously taken offence almost resulting in extreme consequences (duel; compare the electrician's strike and, even more appropriately, Ruslan's knightly combats); and the ultimate appeal to authority (the Serapions). One cannot exclude at least some influence of this incident, which occurred in January 1922, on the writing of 'Monter', which first appeared in 1926 and begins 'when the entire theatre was photographed in 1923'.

As for the story's take on theatre, it is summed up aptly in the closing words about the 'complex theatrical mechanism' (used also in the story's early titles[37]). This time around Zoshchenko focused precisely on the inner workings of an artistic institution by involving on-stage as well as off-stage personnel, the management, the audience (including the 'devitsy') and the actual work of art performed. And, last but not least, by donning, to covertly express his existential and artistic ambitions and frustrations, the unlikely mask of a stage-hand, whom he then let steal the show from the usual star through the appropriation – in an intertextual *tour de force* – of two roles and a central theatrical effect of the opera in question.

'EL'VIRA'

This ultra-short vignette places the autobiographical persona of *PVS* in the vicinity of Kislovodsk, where a 20-year-old historical Zoshchenko worked as a railway ticket-collector.

The narrator was enjoying his quiet room, but then El'vira, a formidably strong but practically illiterate circus performer, moved in next door. Back in Penza, she had a brief affair with a married general, whom (and whose spouse) she now followed to the spa. Showing her powerful 'ruki' [hands/ arms], she said she could kill the general – unless he 'out of decency' reimbursed her at least for the round-trip. She wanted to write to him but, because of her illiteracy, this task fell to the narrator, inspired by the hope that, with the money, she would leave for home. His composition, hailed by El'vira as a genuine 'cry of a woman's soul . . . turned over the general's innards', and he sent her five hundred roubles. Flush with the sudden wealth – and gratitude to the letter-writer, she stayed at the spa and 'almost never left my room. It's a good thing the world war began soon after – so I could leave.'[38]

The similarities with 'Monter' – and Glinka's *Ruslan* – are rather slight: El'vira's profession ('aktrisa tsirka'), her 'ruki', and the motif of a victorious confrontation with an authority figure (the general).

The differences, on the other hand, are considerable: from the prominence of the sexual theme to the undisguised involvement of the autobiographical persona to the text's consummate stylistic simplicity (characteristic of *PVS*) and the absence of any specific theatrical reference. As for the place of the two stories in Zoshchenko's life-and-works, it is less simple than the mere fact of their belonging to different creative periods might suggest. Completed in 1943, 'El'vira' refers to and quite probably reflects a personal experience of 1914, thus, in a sense, both post- and predating 'Monter'. In fact, Zoshchenko had kept planning and working on what was to become *PVS* ever since 1922.[39] Incidentally, in the same year, Zoshchenko published the story 'Veselaia zhizn'' ('Merry Life', 1922), which reads as a remote, yet recognisable version of 'El'vira'.

An ageing general, tired of his wife, starts an affair with a circus performer, 'mamzel'' [Mlle] Ziuzil''. He takes her to Kislovodsk but, realising that she lacks class, decides, on the advice of his valet, to let her go. She threatens to 'tear his head clean out' [golovu vyrvu], and, fearing for his military honour, he determines to stay in his room. He is then visited by a certain Lezghian, who, over some soup, demands, on Ziuzil''s behalf, that the general settle the matter with an influx of 'capital' [udovletvorite kapitalom] – or else she will 'insult him physically in public'. Stressing that he 'will always intervene on behalf of a lady's honour', the Lezghian adds that he 'can press three poods with his left hand/arm' and that because of his 'heavy hand' there have occurred 'terminal outcomes'.

The general sends Ziuzil' three hundred roubles [tri katen'ki], but the valet spends the money on drink. Not aware of this, the general ventures out to a cafe, is slapped in the face by Ziuzil', and falls to the ground. He contemplates shooting himself but decides against it, since he was insulted by a woman, not a man, after all. He leaves town, but soon dies of overeating and dysentery.[40]

The elements that later went, in the same or altered guise, into the *PVS* vignette are many and obvious (the general–spouse–'actress' triangle; Kislovodsk; abandonment; blackmail; threatening hands/arms; several-hundred-rouble ransom), including the presence of mediators (valet, Lezghian; author–narrator). Even the 'honour' leitmotif has a counterpart in El'vira's appeal to the general's 'decency' (and the electrician's hypersensitivity). The only major motif of 'Veselaia zhizn'' absent from 'El'vira' is Zoshchenko's 'food anxiety' (note the soup, the cafe, the dysentery) – unless one counts the spa's gastroenterological specialisation and the impact of the letter on the general's insides.

The transformation of 'Veselaia zhizn'' into 'El'vira' involves several operations: a drastic abridgement; the introduction (or restoration – if such happened to be the real-life scenario) of a first-person perspective on the events (in the person of the author acting as a mediator between the general and the 'actress'); and the renaming of the woman – with interesting intertextual implications.

The name 'El'vira' is presented as fictitious – invented by its bearer, who, 'according to her passport, is Nastia Gorokhova'. In this, the heroine seems to do the bidding of the author, who changes the name from the earlier 'Ziuzil'' and, by choosing this stagey alias,[41] highlights her resemblance to her namesake in Mozart's *Don Giovanni*:[42]

Seduced and abandoned by the Don, Donna Elvira pursues him, torn between love, forgiveness, and care, on the one hand, and vengeance, on the other [Nastia-El'vira hesitates, too – between murder, blackmail, and insistence on 'decency'], and keeps interfering in his actions at every step [just as Nastia invades the narrator's room].

Unlike the meretricious circus performer, however, the operatic Donna does not ask even for emotional 'favours' (*mercè*), measuring the 'price' of her loss only in terms of the tears she has shed; yet, the very motif of 'damages and compensation' is there.

More resemblances emerge if we allow for multiple correlations among the characters. Thus, Donna Elvira threatens to 'tear out the heart' of her seducer ('Gli vo' cavar il cor'!), while in the story the letter 'turned over the general's innards' – to say nothing of Ziuzil''s intention to 'tear out his head'. In fact, all of Don Giovanni's opponents want to kill him in one way or another (Masetto, for one, 'want[s] to cut him into a hundred pieces') and to watch how 'the scoundrel draws the noose around his neck', that is, gets metaphorically strangled, which is precisely the end that awaits the general at the hands of Nastia-El'vira.

If Donna Elvira does not try to blackmail the Don for money, he himself keeps paying off his peasant victims and, while feasting, proclaims openly his desire to have fun for his money. The 'reimbursement' motif appears also in the relationship between Donna Anna and Don Ottavio, who offers his 'heart and hand' as a 'sweet compensation' for the bitter loss of her father. The clearest case of successful extortion is, of course, the four-pistoles raise that Leporello gets out of Don Giovanni by moral strictures and threats to leave his employ.

The figure of Leporello provides more material for story–opera parallels. In Act 1, trying to get rid of Donna Elvira, Don Giovanni leaves it to Leporello to do the explaining (Leporello obliges with the famous 'catalogo' of the Don's conquests). In Act 2, in order to make love to Elvira's maid, Don Giovanni exchanges clothes with Leporello, who is to divert Elvira's attention by impersonating his master. To start things off, the Don talks to Elvira from behind the disguised Leporello's back and, proud with the show he has put on, praises his own talent ('Più fertile talento / Del mio, no, no si da'). Donna Elvira duly takes Leporello for her 'adored husband'; having enjoyed this for a while, he, too, soon gets bored with her and eventually finds 'the moment to escape,' but then falls into the hands of Don Giovanni's three pursuers (Elvira, Anna, Ottavio), in a farcical foreshadowing of his master's fate.

Almost all of this is to be found in Zoshchenko's 'El'vira' – with interesting shifts in role distribution. The authorial narrator combines some of Leporello's features (replacing the general as El'vira's involuntary lover and casting about for ways to get rid of her) with those of Don Giovanni (acting as a verbal artist and the author of a substitution). Although the motif of 'writing love letters on behalf of another' points to other intertexts (*Les Liaisons dangereuses*, *Cyrano de Bergerac* – or Maxim Gorky's 'Boles''[43]), the theme of 'proud, if ambiguous, authorship' clearly links the story to *Don Giovanni*, all the more so thanks to the mediation of Pushkin. In *Kamennyi gost'* (The Stone Guest, 1830), Don Guan is a variously gifted artistic personality – protean, Pushkin-like, the author of a lyric sung by one of his mistresses, Laura (compare the 'cry of a woman's soul' penned by the author-narrator in 'El'vira').

Thus, Zoshchenko's narrative reads like a rewrite of a classical libretto, which, of course, was itself a product of a long tradition of transformations, beginning with Tirso de Molina's play (1630) and including Molière's (1665). Moreover, almost all of the opera's characters keep donning masks and play-acting, even when they purport to act 'natural'. On hearing Donna Elvira complain about her seduction by the Don, Leporello makes a pithy aside: 'Pare un libro stampato!' (She sounds like a book.) The Don Juan list, which follows soon after this, is, too, a textual object, which Leporello invites Donna Elvira to read together with him ('Osservate, leggete con me') and which Don Giovanni is busy completing in the course of the action ('Ah, to my list / Tomorrow morning / You will have to add / At least ten names!'). To crown these metatextual activities, during his last dinner Don Giovanni enjoys the performance of three musical pieces, among them – in a virtuoso auto-quotation by Mozart – a fragment from *The Marriage of Figaro*![44]

Among the motifs that 'El'vira' shares with 'Veselaia zhizn'' (and 'Monter'/*Ruslan*) are the potentially murderous 'ruki', in this case spectacularly shown off by the heroine. The second occurrence of the motif, however, is elaborately hidden: the punitive task is carried out by the 'hand' of another character – the litterateur-narrator, and on a different – verbal, albeit figuratively physical, plane: 'My hand is guided by the hope . . . My letter turned over the general's innards . . .' Now, if there is an obsessively hand-fetishist opera in the world repertoire, it is *Don Giovanni*. The two key manifestations of this leitmotif are, of course, the seduction of Zerlina ('La ci darem la mano . . .' [There you will give me your hand . . .]) and Don Giovanni's fatal handshake with the Statue ('Dammi la mano . . .' [Give me your hand . . .]), but they are echoed by a dozen others.

Don Giovanni, together with Zerlina, tells a jealous Masetto that she is 'in the hands of a gentleman' (*in man d'un cavalier*) and then praises her 'perfumed fingers' (*dituccie . . . odorose*).[45] Later, he brazenly offers Donna Anna 'this arm' (*questa man*) to fight against her offender, i.e. himself. Having finally identified Don Giovanni, Donna Anna tells her fiancé Don Ottavio about the way Don Giovanni tried to possess her: 'with one hand he stops me from screaming, and with the other he sqeezes me so hard, that I already believed myself conquered' ('Con una mano cerca d'impedire la voce, e coll'altra m'afferra stretta cosi, che gia mi credo vinta').[46] A guilty Zerlina asks Masetto to beat her, promising masochistically to kiss his hands ('E le care tue mane / Lieta poi sapro baciar').

In Act 2, Leporello, disguised as Don Giovanni, kisses Donna Elvira's hand; Masetto, beaten up by the Don, complains to Zerlina about hurting everywhere including *questa mano*, and she offers him, as a cure, to put it on her beating heart; Don Giovanni tells Leporello how in his clothes he went about seducing his girlfriend: first he took her hand, then she his; and Don Ottavio offers Donna Anna his heart and hand as a compensation.

Pushkin in *Kamennyi gost'* settles, like Zoshchenko, for two main displays of 'ruka', one being the inevitable final handshake, the other, an original variation, which combines ingeniously the 'hand' motif with that of 'substituted identity':

Inspecting the statue of the Commendatore, Don Guan notes that it represents him as a giant – 'A sam pokoinik mal byl i tschedushen, / Zdes' stav na tsypochki ne mog by ruku / Do svoego on nosu dotianut'' (Whereas the dead man was but short and weedy, / Here, had he stood on tiptoe, he could not with his hand / Have reached his own nose).[47]

In the light of the parallels between the Don Giovanni topos and Zoshchenko's hand anxiety, the character of the general in 'El'vira' acquires new overtones. His military rank makes him a fearsome Commendatore-like figure (in addition to his Don Giovanni role), especially given Zoshchenko's fear of the 'chastising hand of the husband. . . father' and the Pushkin paradigm 'the Commendatore – the Bronze Horseman – Tat'iana's "impressive general" [vazhnyi general] of a husband').[48] In *PVS*, the hand is associated with a woman's breast and desire/fear of a woman, but the punishing extremity itself is that of a man. However, El'vira's 'ruki', which 'have held three men under the big top' and are thus thrice masculine, as it were, stand out as a uniquely androgynous hybrid, akin to the many ambiguous role reversals of the story. In keeping with the tradition, El'vira is a victim harbouring a vengeful attitude that is to be carried out by a man; but the modernist transplantation of the deadly superhuman hands on to her female body is Zoshchenko's own. An intermediate stage of this metamorphosis is attested by 'Veselaia zhizn'', where 'mamzel' Ziuzil'' can slap the general off his feet, but the deadly 'ruki' still remain the privileged distinction of a special male character – her Lezghian sidekick.[49] The pattern is subtly echoed and modified in 'El'vira': the heroine parades her athletic hands/arms, but it is now the author/narrator's writing hand that delivers the decisive blow. The theme of sexual ambiguity is carried further in the product of that writing hand: the letter. This is, androgynously, 'a cry of a woman's soul', but also 'turns over the general's innards', suggesting certain anal, that is, homosexual, connotations.

'Androgyny' finds its parallels elsewhere in Zoshchenko, for instance, in his comic story 'Fotokartochka' (The Photograph, 1945), where the first-person protagonist, ill-served by a professional photographer, buys instead a 'ready-made' photo, which turns out to be a woman's.[50] As for 'homosexuality', Zoshchenko's avowed fear of women can be said to take, in 'El'vira', the form of an attraction to/rejection of the virago-ish El'vira in both of her partners, whose coming together through the letter can then be said to represent a sort of male bonding through a shared woman. It is such hidden homosexual overtones that may underlie the aura of shame that envelopes the story's entire triangle.[51]

Don Giovanni, despite its general atmosphere of play-acting and masquerade, does not offer sex inversion models (unlike, say, *Così fan tutte*), but *Kamennyi gost'* does – to an extent. In seducing Donna Anna, Don Guan uses and discards several disguises, among them the monastic cloth, used to gain access to the pious widow, who, according to a real hermit, 'never converses with a man /. . . / With me it's quite another thing – I'm a monk.'[52]

There seems to be a method to the role redistributions that yield 'El'vira''s cast. While the author–narrator accumulates some or other functions of Don Giovanni/Don Guan (creative author, role-player, lover and deserter [of Elvira], unconventional lover [of the general]), the Statue (avenging hand), Leporello (confidant, substitute lover, role-player), the monk (sex change), the Lezghian (mediator, blackmailer, avenging hand), and even Donna Elvira and Donna Anna (seduced, if not raped, and suffering lover), he does so in a consistently 'weak' – involuntary, passive, cautious, secret, almost cowardly – manner. He is invaded and dominated by El'vira, performs his major feat on her orders and under her name – from behind her back, as it were, and never comes into open contact with his adversary (and obscure object of desire), the general. This mode of behaviour is, of course, a direct opposite of that instanced by the authorial protagonist of the other operatic story analysed in this essay. Or, rather, the two are complementary manifestations of one and the same aggressive–defensive Zoshchenkovian posture.

To conclude, theatrical sub-texts loom rather large behind the explicit plots of some of Zoshchenko's stories. This theatricalisation is called upon to reflect neither a multi-faceted bustle of society mores, as in William Todd's picture of the age of Pushkin,[53] nor merely the cultural and hierarchical problematic of the early Soviet times, as in Cathy Popkin's study of Zoshchenko, but rather the more specific concerns of Zoshchenkovian characters – by providing scripts, roles and masks for their aggressive–defensive dissimulation. The conspiratorial strategies may, indeed, account for the inconspicuous manner itself in which the theatrical plots appear in the stories. Tellingly, the electrician's bold move, appropriating the operatic villain's act, is accompanied by a more direct textual reference to the underlying opera, whereas the covert ways of 'El'vira''s timid author–narrator are reproduced in his total failure to acknowledge his sources.

Accordingly, more 'shadow plays' mentioned in Zoshchenko only in passing may yet prove highly relevant to the respective stories, and still others will be discovered where no pointers seem to exist. Thus, the narrator of 'Dushevnaia prostota' (Simplicity of Soul, 1926), before proceeding to the story's main topic ('we tread on each other's feet'), holds forth about a visiting troupe of black musicians performing a 'negro operetta [negritianskaia negrooperetta]', who, being 'spoilt by European civilisation', are appalled by our rude manners. Theatre, and European theatre at that, is, in the usual Zoshchenkovian manner, held up as a cultural paragon. Research into contemporary press coverage makes it clear that the particular group of black artists which toured Russia in 1926 was remarkable for its elaborate dance acts;[54] knowledge of this factual background allows readers to appreciate Zoshchenko's subtly contrapuntal use of material that is more relevant to a story about a 'leg-and-foot issue' than it seems at first sight. Perhaps one day scholars will be able to identify even the actual opera that is so utterly – and tantalisingly – ignored by the notorious 'aristokratka' and her gentleman friend.[55]

NOTES

1 For more-or-less recent 'cultural–sociological' scholarship, see, for instance, M. O. Chudakova, *Poetika Mikhaila Zoshchenko* (Moscow, 1979); Iu. K. Shcheglov, 'Entsiklopediia nekul'turnosti: rasskazy dvadtsaykh godov i Golubaia kniga', in A. K. Zholkovskii and Iu. K. Shcheglov, *Mir avtora i struktura teksta* (Tenafly, NJ, 1986), pp. 53–84; Tsezar' Vol'pe, *Iskusstvo nepokhozhesti* (Moscow, 1991), pp. 141–316; Cathy Popkin, *The Pragmatics of Insignificance: Chekhov, Zoshchenko, Gogol* (Stanford, 1993), pp. 53–124; Alexander Zholkovsky, *Text Counter Text. Rereadings in Russian Literary History* (Stanford, 1994), pp. 35–87.
2 See Hugh McLean, 'Zoshchenko's Unfinished Novel: *Before Sunrise*', in Edward Brown (ed.), *Major Soviet Writers. Essays in Criticism* (London, 1973), pp. 310–20, and 'Belated Sunrise: A review article', *Slavic and East European Journal* 18:4 (1974), 406–10; Gary Kern, 'After the afterword', in Mikhail Zoshchenko, *Before Sunrise. A Novella*, trans. Gary Kern (Ann Arbor, 1974), pp. 345–66; Irene Masing-Delic, 'Biology, reason and

literature in Zoshchenko's *Pered voskhodom solntsa*, *Russian Literature* 8 (1980), 77–101; Thomas Hodge, 'Freudian elements in Zoshchenko's *Pered voskhodom solntsa*, *The Slavonic and East European Review* 67:1 (1989), 1–28; Krista Hanson, 'Autobiography and conversion: Zoshchenko's *Before Sunrise*', in Jane Harris (ed.), *Autobiographical Statements in Twentieth-Century Russian Literature* (Princeton, 1990), pp. 133–53; Rachel May, 'Superego as literary subtext: story and structure in Mikhail Zoshchenko's *Before Sunrise*', *Slavic Review* 55:1 (1996), 106–24.

3 See Alexander Zholkovsky, '"What is the author trying to say with his artistic work?": Rereading Zoshchenko's œuvre', *Slavic and East European Journal* 40:3 (1996): 458–74, 'Zoshchenko iz XXI veka, ili Poetika nedoveriia', *Zvezda* 5 (1996), 190–204, 'Food, fear, feigning, and flight in Zoshchenko's "Foreigners"', *Russian Literature* 40 (1996), 385–404, and a cumulative monograph in Russian: A. K. Zholkovskii, *Mikhail Zoshchenko: Poetika nedoveriia* (Moscow, 1999). For the integration of both approaches see Vera von Wiren-Garczynski, 'Zoshchenko's psychological interests', *Slavic and East European Journal* 11:1 (1967), 3–22; Krista Hanson, 'Kto vinovat? Guilt and Rebellion in Zoshchenko's Accounts of Childhood', in Daniel Rancour-Laferrière (ed.), *Russian Literature and Psychoanalysis* (Amsterdam and Philadelphia, 1989), pp. 285–302; Linda Scatton, *Mikhail Zoshchenko. Evolution of a Writer* (Cambridge, 1993); Andrei Siniavskii, 'Mify Mikhaila Zoshchenko,' in Iu. V. Tomashevskii (ed.), *Litso i maska Mikhaila Zoshchenko* (Moscow, 1994), pp. 238–53 (trans. in *Russian Studies in Literature. A Journal of Translations* 33:1 (1996–97), 39–58).

4 See, for instance, such stories as 'Ne pushchu' (I Won't Let You) (M. Zoshchenko, *Sobranie sochinenii v trekh tomakh* (Leningrad, 1987), vol. I, pp. 355–6; further references to this edition will be as SS, vol. and p.), which invokes the eponymous picture by the Wanderer artist V. E. Makovskii; or 'Neravnyi brak' (Unequal Marriage) (first appearing in *Golubaia kniga* (A Sky-Blue Book) as 'Rasskaz o starom durake' (The Story of an Old Fool), SS, vol. III, pp. 242–5), which similarly plays with the 1862 eponymous picture by V. V. Pukirev. An intriguing reference to the little boy Zoshchenko's 'collaboration' on one of his father's artistic projects appears in *PVS*, in the episode of the father's burial:

'Ahead, on a little velvet cushion, they bear the decoration which Papa received for his Picture "Suvorov's Departure". This picture hangs on the wall of the Suvorov Museum. It's done in mosaic. In the left corner of the picture there is a little green fir [elochka]. The lowest branch of this fir was done by me. It turned out crooked, but Papa was satisfied with my work.' (SS, vol. III, p. 547)

For a correlation of this detail with the quasi-autobiographical little Min'ka's confrontation with his father against the background of a Christmas fir tree in the story 'Elka' (The Christmas Tree), see A. K. Zholkovskii, '"Aristokastratka"', in Tomashevskii (ed.), *Litso i maska*, pp. 331–9 (p. 337); on the biblical and Oedipal aspects of that children's story, see Hanson, 'Kto vinovat?', p. 295.

5 Zoshchenko's achievement as playwright remains underappreciated. It is practically left out of the extant monographs (Chudakova's, Scatton's) and in general is rarely discussed either as part of Zoshchenko's *œuvre* or as a special topic. For a rare overview, see Aleksandra Filippova, ' "Delo v tom, chto ia – proletarskii pisatel' ": Mikhail Zoshchenko', in E. I. Strel'tsova (ed.), *Paradoks o drame: Perechityvaia p'esy 1920–1930–kh godov* (Moscow, 1993), pp. 401–26; for the vicissitudes in Zoshchenko's writing of plays, radio and film scripts, musical comedy librettos, and sketches, most of them banned, either before or after staging, see Iu. V. Tomashevskii, 'Khronologicheskaia kanva zhizni i tvorchestva Mikhaila Zoshchenko', in his *Litso i maska*, pp. 340–65, and M. Z. Dolinskii, 'Dokumenty. Materialy k biograficheskoi khronike', 'Kommentarii i dopolneniia', in M. Zoshchenko, *Uvazhaemye grazhdane. Parodii. Rasskazy. Fel'etony. Satiricheskie zametki. Pis'ma k pisateliu. Odnoaktnye komedii*, ed. M. Z. Dolinskii (Moscow, 1991), pp. 32–144, 572–655. For the texts of some of the plays see Zoshchenko, *Uvazhaemye grazhdane*, ed. Dolinskii; M. Zoshchenko, *Sobranie sochinenii v 5–ti tomakh* (Moscow, 1993), vol. III; M. Zoshchenko, *Izbrannoe v dvukh tomakh* (Leningrad, 1978), vol. II.
Many of the plays were dramatised versions of comic stories, for example *Uvazhaemyi tovarishch* (Respected Comrade, 1930), *Svad'ba* (Wedding, 1933; staged under Zoshchenko's direction), *Prestuplenie i nakazanie* (Crime and Punishment, 1933), *Neudachnyi den'* (A Bad Day, 1935–36), *Parusinovyi portfel'* (A Canvas Briefcase, 1939). The staging histories of *Uvazhaemyi tovarishch* and *Opasnye sviazi* (Liaisons Dangereuses, 1940) were quite dramatic. Of especial relevance to the topic of the present essay is the metaliterary 'fantastic comedy' *Kul'turnoe nasledstvo* (Cultural Heritage, 1933), featuring as dramatis personae the statues of several Russian tsars and a live Pushkin.
6 On Zoshchenko's 'theatrical' motifs see Popkin, *The Pragmatics of Insignificance*, *passim*; Shcheglov, 'Entsiklopediia nekul'turnosti', pp. 61–3; Zholkovsky, *Text Counter Text*, pp. 36–40; on ' "Aristokratka" ' and its interplay with Natasha Rostova's opera outing, see Zholkovsky, *Text Counter Text*, and ' "Aristokastratka" '.
7 See Popkin, *The Pragmatics of Insignificance*, p. 79; Zholkovsky, *Text Counter Text*, p. 38.
8 On this Zoshchenko motif see Shcheglov, 'Entsiklopediia nekul'turnosti', pp. 61–3.
9 See Popkin, *The Pragmatics of Insignificance*, pp. 29–30, pp. 76–81.
10 For a juxtaposition of Zoshchenko's real life, fictionalised autobiography and comic stories, see A. K. Zholkovskii, 'Zubnoi vrach, korystnaia molochnitsa, intelligentnyi monter i ikh avtor: Krepkovatyi brak v mire Zoshchenko', *Literaturnoe obozrenie* 5/6 (1996): 128–44.
11 See Zholkovsky, ' "What is the author trying to say" ' and 'Food, fear, feigning, and flight'.
12 For more details on the story, see Zholkovsky, 'Zoshchenko's "The

Electrician", or the complex theatrical mechanism', *Russian Studies in Literature* 33:1 (1996–97), 59–79. In what follows, the longer citations are given in small type and in quotation marks, while plot paraphrases are merely given in small type. The translations from the Russian are all mine, with the exception of *PVS*, where I used/emended Gary Kern's version (Zoshchenko, *Before Sunrise*).

13 Similar conflicts around photograph-taking form an episode in Zoshchenko's comedy *Uvazhaemyi tovarishch* (Dear Comrade, 1930): see M. I. Zoshchenko, *Sobranie sochinenii v piati tomakh* (Moscow, 1993), vol. 3, pp. 211–19. A photo-retoucher as a quasi-artist appears in Zoshchenko's sentimental tale 'Siren' tsvetet' (Lilacs in Bloom, 1930).

14 Dated 1842, libretto after Pushkin's eponymous mock-epic poem (1818–20); see M. I. Glinka, *Ruslan i Liudmila. Volshebnaia opera v 5 deistviiakh*, in his *Polnoe sobranie sochinenii*, vol. xv, ed. G. V. Kirkor (Moscow, 1967).

15 See Zoshchenko, SS, vol. III, pp. 268–70. The play is referred to as *Kto vinovat?* (Who Is To Blame?) – misleadingly, it turns out, since no robbery is to be found in the eponymous 1840 Herzen novel (whose famous title is liberally used in *PVS* in connection with the pervasive issue of guilt; cf. the title of Hanson's 1989 article). The episode may have been borrowed from Zoshchenko's favourite Leskov tale 'Grabezh' (Robbery, 1887). In his *Pis'ma k pisateliu* (Letters to a Writer, 1929), Zoshchenko boils down the tale's complicated plot to this one scene ('an excellent story about a merchant by accident robbing a passer-by of his watch'; see M. Zoshchenko, *Uvazhaemye grazhdane*, pp. 363–4) – singled out most likely by virtue of its affinity to his own recurrent motif 'everybody is to blame or, at least, to be suspected' (see, e. g., 'Sobachii niukh' (Dog Scent, 1924) and 'Mokroe delo' (The Bloody Affair, 1925)). Incidentally, this motif underlies the subtle intertextual counterpoint (latent in Zoshchenko's text), of the two robberies: in 'Akter', the amateur is deliberately robbed by professional actors under the cover of acting; in 'Grabezh', one honest person unwittingly robs another, thus 'playing the role' of a thief.

16 Glinka, *Ruslan i Liudmila*, p. 80.

17 Compare Genesis 1:1–3; cf. also Boris Pasternak's poem 'Meier-khol'dam' (To the Meierkhol'ds, 1928), where the stage, the director, the lighting, the star actress and so on are metaphorised in terms of Genesis 1 and 2.

18 A. S. Pushkin, *Ruslan i Liudmila. Poema*, in his *Polnoe sobranie sochinenii* (17 vols; Leningrad, 1937–49), vol. IV, pp. 1–87, see p. 62. The formulaic pattern 'with one hand – with the other hand', parodied by the electrician and his author (and naturalised by the exaggerated gesticulation of certain opera singers who seem to think they are 'singing with their hands'), goes all the way back to Ovid's classical line about the Scythians, who at all times had to be ready to defend themselves: 'Hac

arat infelix, hac tenet arma manu' (With this [one he] is tilling, the unlucky [man], with the other hand [he] is holding weapons) (*Tristia*, v, 10:24). In Glinka's opera, the 'hand' motif becomes prominent in Act 2, as Ruslan wrests the magic sword from Golova: 'I will destroy everything before me – all I need is a sword that would fit my hand . . . Here's the sword I have desired! I can feel its worth in my hand' (Glinka, *Ruslan i Liudmila*, pp. 181, 184).

19 On 'alternativeness' see Shcheglov, 'Entsiklopediia nekul'turnosti', 73–4.

20 The contraposition of the 'monter' and the 'tenor' gains also from the paronomastic interplay of the two Russian nouns, especially when the latter appears in the instrumental case: 'tenorom', e.g.: 'Tut, konechno, monter skhlestnulsia s tenorom.'

21 Zoshchenko, SS, vol. III, p. 558, p. 619, p. 622, pp. 625–8.

22 Zoshchenko, *Uvazhaemye grazhdane* (1991), pp. 220–1, emended according to M. Zoshchenko, *Uvazhaemye grazhdane* (Moscow, 1927), pp. 150–1.

23 See Masing-Delic, 'Biology, reason, and literature . . .'; Hanson, 'Kto vinovat?'; A. K. Zholkovskii, 'Ruka blizhnego i ee mesto v poetike Zoshchenko', *Novoe literaturnoe obozrenie* 15 (1995), 262–86.

24 Glinka, *Ruslan i Liudmila*, pp. 81–5.

25 Zoshchenko, SS, vol. III, pp. 607–15.

26 Zoshchenko, SS, vol. III, pp. 626–7.

27 On Zoshchenko's Nietzschean connection see Tat'iana Kadash, ' "Zver' " i "nezhivoi chelovek" ' v mire rannego Zoshchenko', *Literaturnoe obozrenie*, 1 (1995): 36–8; Richard Grose, 'Zoshchenko and Nietzsche's philosophy: lessons in misogyny, sex and self-overcoming', *The Russian Review* 54:3 (1995), 352–64.

28 Zoshchenko, SS, vol. III, p. 627.

29 See Zoshchenko, SS, vol. III, pp. 590–1, pp. 549–50, p. 467, p. 507. On some of these episodes and Zoshchenko's ambivalent attitude towards authority figures and power in general, see Hanson, 'Kto vinovat?'

30 See Zoshchenko, *Uvazhaemye grazhdane* (1991), p. 585; cf. also Viktor Shklovskii's telling 1928 title and essay, 'O Zoshchenke i bol'shoi literature', in his *Gamburgskii schet (1914–1933)* (Moscow, 1990), pp. 413–19, translated as: 'On Zoshchenko and major literature', in *Russian Literature Triquarterly* 14 (1976), 407–14.

31 This author–character parallel is noted by Popkin (*The Pragmatics of Insignificance*, p. 78). A. K. Voronskii, who published an early critique of Zoshchenko's writing (see his 1922 'Mikhail Zoshchenko. Rasskazy Nazara Il'icha gospodina Sinebriukhova', in Tomashevskii (ed.), *Litso i maska*, pp. 136–7) was a target of Zoshchenko's polemic (see 'O sebe, ob ideologii i eshche koe o chem', in his *Uvazhaemye grazhdane* (1991), pp. 578–80). One possible 'prototype' of the tenor figure could have been the poet Aleksandr Blok, whom Anna Akhmatova later (in her 1960 'Tri stikhotvoreniia') labelled 'the epoch's tragic tenor' – with a nod to their 1913 backstage exchange, in which Blok, to allay her stage fright, had

said: 'Anna Andreevna, we are not tenors' (see her 1965 'Vospominaniia ob Al. Bloke', in her *Sochineniia*, vol. II (Munich, 1968), pp. 191–2). Zoshchenko may have known about this from Akhmatova herself or otherwise; his own ambiguous attitude towards Blok's grandeur and fall as an archetypal representative of the *ancien* culture is on record in his 1919 essay 'Konets rytsaria Pechal'nogo Obraza' (in Tomashevskii (ed.), *Litso i maska*, pp. 78–85), *Mishel' Siniagin* (1930) and *PVS*.

32 'Authorial/directorial' talents promoting the action are a hallmark of negative and ambiguous characters: evil magicians, villains, provocateurs, swindlers, clowns and the like, e.g. Mephistopheles, Chichikov, Petr Verkhovenskii, Ostap Bender.

33 Zoshchenko, SS, vol. III, pp. 441–2. An enlightened electrician appears in 'Rasskaz pro odnu korystnuiu molochnitsu' (A Story About a Greedy Milkwoman) (*Golubaia kniga*, in Zoshchenko, SS, vol. III, pp. 206–9), where his profession is referred to as an 'intellectual' one; about this story, see Zholkovskii, 'Zubnoi vrach . . . '.

34 Zoshchenko, SS, vol. III, p. 396.

35 D. Granin, 'Mimoletnoe iavlenie', in Iu. V. Tomashevskii (ed.), *Vospominaniia o Mikhaile Zoshchenko* (St Petersburg, 1995), pp. 483–505.

36 V. Kaverin, 'Molodoi Zoshchenko', in Tomashevskii (ed.), *Vospominaniia o Mikhaile Zoshchenko*, pp. 120–38, see pp. 127–8.

37 It has appeared as 'Slozhnyi mekhanizm' and 'Teatral'nyi mekhanizm'; see commentaries in Zoshchenko, SS, vol. I, p. 548.

38 Zoshchenko, SS, vol. III, pp. 471–2. For a detailed analysis, see A. K. Zholkovskii, *Inventsii* (Moscow, 1995), pp. 57–71.

39 See Chudakova, *Poetika Mikhaila Zoshchenko*, p. 179.

40 Zoshchenko, SS, vol. I, pp. 74–81.

41 A circus-rider, Miss Elvira (devitsa El'vira) appears in the chapter 'Tsirk' (Circus) of K. S. Stanislavskii's *Moia zhizn' v iskusstve* (see vol. I of his *Sobranie sochinenii v vos'mi tomakh* (Moscow, 1954)), pp. 13–20 (absent in the 1924 English-language edition). As a teenager (c. 1875), the future famous actor-director relishes his personal acquaintance with a friend-of-the-family ballerina, prefers circus to ballet, opera, and drama, admires El'vira appearing in a 'Pas de châle', kisses the hem of her dress, is kidded as her presumed fiancé, plays at becoming the manager (direktor) of a home circus, and so on. Along with the parallels to Zoshchenko's 'El'vira', the chapter also contains an unexpected one to 'Monter' – the performances of the home circus are often undermined by the actions of the brother of the 'manager':

'My brother, who alone could replace the orchestra, is . . . careless and undisciplined. He did not take our business seriously and could, therefore, do God knows what. He would play for a while, and then, suddenly, in front of all the "public", he would lie down on the floor in the middle of the hall, feet up, and start screaming: "I won't play any more!" In the long run, for a bar of chocolate, he would of course, resume playing. But the . . . "for-realness" [vsamdelishnost'] of the performance would be ruined' (p. 17).

Zoshchenko's heroine's 'real' name, Nastia Gorokhova, may, in its turn, be of fictitious origin, going back to that of the 'charming Wanda', who, according to her passport, was Nastas'ia Kanavkina, in Chekhov's 1886 story 'Znakomyi muzhchina' (A Male Acquaintance): both street-walkers' names come from those of St Petersburg streets (Gorokhovaia, [Zimniaia] Kanavka). (Pers. comm. from Professor Omry Ronen.)

42 Dated 1787; libretto by Lorenzo Da Ponte. The subsequent quotes are from the multi-language libretto: Wolfgang Amadeus Mozart, *Don Giovanni. Drama giocoso in due atti* (Vienna, 1986), an attachment to a cassette recording by EMI Records Ltd. Zoshchenko may have been exposed to one or other of the two Russian versions: *Don Zhuan. Komicheskaia opera v dvukh aktakh. Muzyka V.-A. Motsarta* (Moscow, 1882 [libretto]); *Don Zhuan. Opera V.-A. Motsarta* (Moscow, 1899 [piano reduction]).

43 That 1897 story is narrated by a student who writes, for his neighbour the muscular and vulgar prostitute, letters from her imaginary lover Boles' and her responses to him; she repays the student by mending his clothes.

44 On Mozart's self-quoting and Pushkin's play with it, see B. M. Gasparov, ' "Ty, Motsart, nedostoin sam sebia" ', in *Vremennik pushkinskoi komissii. 1974* (Leningrad, 1977), pp. 115–22; B. A. Kats, ' "Iz Motsarta nam chto-nibud!" ', in *Vremennik pushkinskoi komissii. 1979* (Leningrad, 1982), pp. 120–4.

45 In the Russian versions of the libretto, the 'fingers' become 'ruchki' [little hands]. An interesting Zoshchenko-like effect can be found in Molière's rendition of the same motif, which focuses on the dirtiness of the hands of one of the peasant girls wooed by Dom Juan (Dom Juan, ou le Festin de Pierre [1665], Act 2, scene 2).

46 A comparison suggests itself with the tenor's (imaginary) hand job in 'Monter', bringing out in it, given the sexual overtones of the conflict over the 'dames', certain hidden erotic connotations. Note also the 'vocal' seme common to both situations: Don Giovanni's one hand is used to impede Donna Anna's voice, the tenor's, to sing; moreover, the action of the other hand is in both cases the more 'electrifying': physically arousing in Don Giovanni, illuminating in 'Monter'.

47 A. S. Pushkin, *Kamennyi gost'*, Act III, in his 16-volume *Polnoe sobranie sochinenii*, vol. VII, *Dramaticheskie proizvedeniia* (Moscow, 1948), p. 153.

48 On this Pushkin invariant see Roman Jakobson's 1937 article, 'The statue in Pushkin's poetic mythology', in his *Selected Writings*, vol. V (The Hague–Paris, 1979), pp. 237–80; and also A. K. Zholkovskii, 'Materialy k opisaniiu poeticheskogo mira Pushkina', in Nils Åke Nilsson (ed.), *Russian Romanticism: Studies in Poetic Codes* (Stockholm, 1979), pp. 45–93, see pp. 46–52.

Zoshchenko's attraction to the 'Don Juan' (donzhuanskii) topos, in its predominantly Pushkinian Russian version, is interestingly manifested in the story 'Lichnaia zhizn'' (Personal Life, 1933), later included in *Golubaia kniga* as 'Melkii sluchai iz lichnoi zhizni' (A Trifling Incident from Private Life) in the 'Love' section (SS, vol. III, pp. 255–9), where the first-person narrator's womanising is dealt a major blow in front of the Pushkin statue (in Moscow's Pushkin Square), thus casting Pushkin in the role of an avenging Commendatore (see Zholkovskii, *Bluzhdaiushchie sny i drugie raboty* (Moscow, 1994), pp. 228–9).

49 Both in *Don Giovanni* and in *Kamennyi gost'*, women speak of avenging themselves on him in physical terms, but the actual violence is reserved for the Statue to perform.

50 About this story and its problematics, see A. K. Zholkovskii, *Bluzhdaiushchie sny*, pp. 228–31.

51 For a Freudian reading of such situations, with special reference to Pushkin, see Daniel [Rancour-]Laferrière, *Five Russian Poems* (Englewood, NJ, 1977), pp. 48–79; for an alternative, 'Girardian' interpretation, see Rene Girard, ' "Triangular desire" ', in his *Deceit, Desire, and the Novel* (Baltimore, 1965), pp. 1–52. On 'homosexual shame', with special reference to Lev Tolstoi's 'Posle bala' (After the Ball), see Stephanie Sandler, 'Pleasure, Danger, and the Dance: Nineteenth-Century Russian Variations', in Helena Goscilo and Beth Holmgren (eds.), *Russia, Women, Culture* (Bloomington, Indiana, 1996), pp. 247–72, esp. pp. 260–3.

52 Pushkin, *Kamennyi gost'*, I, p. 142.

53 See William Mills Todd III, *Fiction and Society in the Age of Pushkin* (Cambridge, Mass., 1986), *passim*.

54 See M. A. Kuzmin, 'Negry', in *Krasnaia gazeta* 108 (10 May 1926), 4; V. S. Poliakov, *Tovarishch smekh* (Moscow, 1976), p. 82; A. K. Zholkovskii, 'K reinterpretatsii poetiki Mikhaila Zoshchenko ("Entsiklopediia strakha" i ideinaia struktura rasskaza "Dushevnaia prosota")', *Izvestiia Akademii Nauk. Seriia literatury i iazyka* 54:5 (1995), 50–60.

55 Among the literary sub-texts of 'Aristokratka' are two Chekhov stories with theatre settings: 'Anna na shee' (Anna on the Neck, 1895), where the stingy husband picks up a pear from the concessions stand, squashes it and puts it back (see Zholkovskii, ' "Aristokastratka" ', p. 334), and 'Dama s sobachkoi' (The Lady with the Little Dog, 1899), whose separate seating arrangements are reproduced in Zoshchenko's story (see Popkin, *The Pragmatics of Insignificance*, p. 77). As for virtual operatic sub-texts, one might consider several nineteenth-century French operas sharing the theme of man's public humiliation by his indomitable, sometimes 'alien', mistress: Georges Bizet's *Carmen* (1875), Camille Saint-Saens' *Samson et Dalila* (1877) and Jules Massenet's *Herodiade* (1881) and *Manon [Lescaut]* (1884). *Samson et Dalila* and *Hérodiade* would be additionally suitable because the humiliation takes place at a feast, and

Carmen, because it was singled out for praise by one of Zoshchenko's favourite writers – Friedrich Nietzsche (see his 'The Case of Wagner', where he also accuses Wagner's operas of a lack of 'aristocraticism' and 'nourishment' ('not enough to bite')). To be sure, other operas, similar to the story in other respects, deserve to be considered as well.

PART 2

Adaptations, collaborations, disputes, rapprochements: Russian literature, visual arts, and performance

CHAPTER 5

Theatricality, anti-theatricality and cabaret in Russian Modernism

Barbara Henry

As the nineteenth century drew to a close, an ancient prejudice against the theatre, which once fuelled the relentless persecution of actors, the closings of theatres, the creation of special censorship laws for plays and prompted torrents of condemnation from pulpit and parliament, began to erode at last.[1] In Russia, the comparatively late development of a formal theatrical culture meant that some of the more extreme anti-theatrical sentiments, as voiced in countries such as England or France, were effectively bypassed. However, the peculiarities of the Tsarist government, and the intelligentsia's mixed expectations regarding the theatre's functions placed the theatre in a unique and contradictory position among Russia's arts. The Tsarist government was both the principal patron of the theatre and its chief censor: the tsars brought the theatre to court and country, established imperial theatres in Moscow and St Petersburg, fired the passion for serf theatre on noble estates, and even, in the case of Catherine II, put the official seal of approval on the theatre by the monarch's own dabblings in playwriting. At the same time, however, the imperial government exhibited considerable anxiety regarding the theatre, particularly with respect to the theatre's association with public disorder. To safeguard official control over theatrical form and content, the government operated a strict monopoly on all plays, reserving the best works for its own theatres, and, in doing so, ensuring that little in the way of quality drama developed outside Russia's two major cities. A rigorous censorship was imposed, and was applied with particular vigour in the case of theatres catering for the underclass.[2] The conservatism of the imperial theatres and the dearth of good plays outside Moscow and St Petersburg, in conjunction with the Russian repertoire's over-reliance on foreign adaptations, did little to endear the art to the intelligentsia. While the value of the theatre as a tool for educating a largely illiterate populace could hardly be doubted, the reality of the popular Russian theatre, with its melodramas, virtuoso performers and effects-driven extravaganzas, fell far short of the intelligentsia's idealised imaginings. For every champion of the theatre, such as Vissarion Belinskii (1811–48), there were antagonists such as Aleksandr Griboedov (1795–1829), who recalled centuries of anti-theatrical disgust in his remarks on his own play, *Gore ot uma* (*Woe from Wit*, 1824): 'The puerile satisfaction of hearing my verse in the theatre, and a desire for their success, has forced me to spoil my creation greatly. Such is the destiny of those who write for the stage: Racine and Shakespeare were subject to such a fate, so how am I to demur?'[3] The apparent contradiction of writing for a stage that one despises was echoed by another occasional playwright, Lev Tolstoi (1828–1910). Tolstoi's palpable revulsion for what he took to be the elaborate fakery of the stage and its shameless performers makes an appearance in *War and Peace* (1869) and is fully articulated in *Chto takoe iskusstvo?* (*What is Art?* 1898). Although Tolstoi reserves his most acerbic commentary for the operatic stage, the 'unnatural' conventions of which he felt disqualified it from the category of 'true' art, the belief that the theatre's 'unreal' conventions (be they monologues or musical interludes) were at odds with its patently 'real' form was widely held.

Stage realism, heralded by the Moscow première of Aleksandr Ostrovskii's (1823–86) *Ne v svoi sani ne sadis'* (Stay in Your Own Lane, 1853), initially appeared to be the aesthetic and ethical force necessary to combat the more ludicrous excesses of the romantic nineteenth-century theatre. Under the influence of realism, life portrayed on the stage would no longer diverge so fantastically from the one around it; the drama would, rather, acquiesce in the rational laws of 'real' life and attempt to mirror that life. Russian theatre, more so than any other in the latter half of the nineteenth century, was to become associated with the most sophisticated refinements in the use of realism on stage, due principally to the work of the Moscow Art Theatre (MKhAT), established in 1898 by Konstantin Stanislavskii (1863–1938) and Vladimir Nemirovich-Danchenko (1858–1943). The triumph of realism, however, proved brief, and soon threatened to harden into a dogmatic denial of the theatre as anything but a vehicle for eloquent language and superficial scenic verisimilitude. The crabbed submissiveness to order, logic and transparent meaning that realism dictated on the stage prompted severe criticism of its limitations by directors of modernist inclination such as Vsevolod Meierkhol'd (1874–1940) in Russia, Edward Gordon Craig (1872–1966) in England and Max Reinhardt (1873–1943) in Germany. Their disenchantment with traditional, 'rational' means of expression, which they felt to be essentially anti-theatrical, and their doubts about the role of language in artistic representation, led to a radical re-examination of the very nature and practice of performance itself.

For anti-theatricalists, live performance had long suffered by comparison with the literary drama, and the live element of the theatrical experience, with its inherently volatile tendencies, was carefully subordinated to the playwright's text and to the logical strictures of the realist form. In order to develop a modern, non-realist theatre, therefore, Meierkhol'd looked outside Russia to the plays of European Symbolists such as Maurice Maeterlinck (1862–1949) and Stanislaw Przybyszewski (1868–1927).[4] Although Meierkhol'd's and others' productions of symbolist plays foundered repeatedly on the contradiction of trying to evoke a metaphysical, other-worldly atmosphere by means of tangible theatrical realities,[5] the minimalist aesthetic of the symbolist play prompted the idea that the theatrical performance might be pared down still further, indeed returned to its original form as a religious ritual, as suggested by Wagner, Nietzsche and Russian writers such as Viacheslav Ivanov (1866–1949). Yet Russian symbolist writers could not be considered united in their approval of the theatre, as the important collection of essays, *Teatr. Kniga o novom teatre* (Theatre. A Book on the New Theatre, St Petersburg, 1908), makes clear. Here Fedor Sologub (1863–1927), in one of the most famous essays of the era, 'Teatr odnoi voli' (The Theatre of One Will), echoed the words of centuries of 'closet drama' enthusiasts when he advocated the replacement of theatrical performance with a 'theatricalised' reading of a play, so that the subtleties of the author's words might be better appreciated, and any distortions introduced to the interpretation of the work by the actor were precluded. Predictably, Sologub did not extend his argument to the other performing arts, and refrained from pro-claiming that the music-lover should likewise content himself with reading sheet music, rather than suffer the shortcomings of musi-cians: for Sologub, dramatic literature alone suffered from the attentions of performers. In 'Teatr i sovremennaia dramaturgiia' (The Theatre and Modern Drama), however, Andrei Belyi (1880–1934) distanced himself from the anti-theatricality of Sologub

as well as the more ecstatic, Dionysian excesses urged by Viacheslav
Ivanov by reiterating the absolute necessity of seeing a play in
performance rather than in textual form.

Still another permutation of symbolist anti-theatricality can be
found in Aleksandr Blok's (1880–1921) own express authorial disclaimer of theatrical intent in his introduction to *Liricheskie dramy*
(Lyric Dramas, 1907). Blok claims, 'The sheer technical imperfec-
tions of my initial experiments with the dramatic form attest to the
fact that not one of these three plays was intended for the stage.'[6]
Intellectual condemnation of the stage reached an apex in 1914 in
the literary critic Iulii Aikhenval'd's (1872–1928) *Otritsanie teatra* ('A
Rejection of the Theatre'), in which the author questioned the
theatre's claim to being even a legitimate art form, as its physical
nature rendered it incapable of communicating the abstractions that
were more properly the sphere of literature.[7]

Meanwhile, Meierkhol'd's continuing experiments in non-realistic
theatre involved changes to stage architecture, the use of music as a
narrative element and the incorporation of dance, rhythmic gesture
and chanting, in order to pre-empt both his actors' and audiences'
inclinations to interpret the live production according to naturalistic
criteria. Along with Meierkhol'd other Russian directors, such as
Nikolai Evreinov (1879–1953), Fedor Komissarzhevskii (1882–1954)
and the young Aleksandr Tairov (1885–1950), also rejected the view
that the live theatre was an inevitably degraded form of the literary
drama, and emphasised that the theatrical performance was the only
true means for realising a dramatic work's full artistic potential.
Their defence of the autonomy and integrity of theatrical performance was only natural, given their place within the theatrical
hierarchy itself, which was gradually seeing the discretionary powers
that were once the province of the playwright ceded to the increasingly indispensable director. Across the European and Russian
theatre this shift in favour of the director, who now possessed the
power to orchestrate a complete production according to his own
vision, precipitated a rebellion against the authority of the dramatic
text, which was accused of subjugating the live theatre to the
immobilising, dictatorial properties of 'literature'.

The conventions of stage realism were continually cited as the
most egregious example of theatrical subservience to 'literature'.[8]
What was under attack was not literature *per se*, but the continuing
prevalence of the realist idiom.[9] An ideological rift had opened

between those who favoured the superficial coherence of 'literary', realist theatre, and those who looked to the stage for meaning imbued in the fusion of language with gesture and movement. This rift was essentially rooted in the same pragmatic and philosophical conflict that had once fuelled the anti-theatrical bias itself. As Jonas Barish has argued, loathing and love for the theatre arise from two distinctly different world views. One prizes a 'conservative ethical emphasis in which the key terms are those of order, stability, constancy, and integrity'.[10] The other derives from 'a more existential emphasis that prizes growth, process, exploration, flexibility, variety, and versatility of response. In one case we have an ideal of stasis, in the other an ideal of movement, in one case an ideal of rectitude, in the other an ideal of plenitude.'[11] This conflict of kinetic and static impulses underlies much of the rhetoric of the early twentieth-century Russian theatre, when modernist, avant-garde 'theatricality' assumed the status of an aesthetic and ethical alternative to conservative, realist 'literature'.

One of the theories to emerge from the search for alternatives to realism and symbolism was the director and playwright Nikolai Evreinov's concept of *teatral'nost'*.[12] Evreinov ascribed the ills of the Russian theatre to its loss of *teatral'nost'*: the active, instinctual inclination towards self-transformation that both propelled the art of the theatre and formed a necessary component in human life.[13] In *Vvedenie v monodramu* (An Introduction to Monodrama, 1909), Evreinov described a means of overcoming the growing alienation of actor and audience by blurring the emotional as well as physical distinctions between them. According to his plan, an audience member could be made to empathise so intensely with a character on stage that he or she would actually experience the play through the consciousness of that character. In order to effect this transformation, a play should be performed as if seen solely through the eyes of its hero: lighting, scenery and costumes should change to reflect the impressions of the leading character, lights would grow dark to express boredom or forgetfulness, characters might alter in appearance according to the protagonist's opinion of them and so on. In theory, an audience would see the action as the hero does and lose awareness of their individual identities; empathy would transfigure consciousness.

Evreinov's monodrama is a deliberate attempt to manipulate the same hypnotic power of the stage that had once so disturbed anti-theatricalists, who regarded this power as so beguiling that merely watching a play could lead to doing what was depicted in it. Evreinov, however, replaces 'doing' with 'being', so that the viewer is supposed to actually *become* the performer. A believer in what Laura Levine calls the 'magical' ability of the theatre to transform one person into another, Evreinov had a contradictory notion of human nature as both fixed and mutable.[14] It is mutable because the theatre can render it so – to the point of self-abnegation – but it is also fixed, because once the play has finished, the observer returns to her own, individual state. Evreinov extrapolates from this contradictory model of the self to the world around it, finding mutability in 'theatricality', and its opposite value, fixity, in the static properties of 'literature'.

The desire to render the self permanently mutable and permanently theatrical guides Evreinov's concept of 'teatr dlia sebia' (theatre for oneself), a programme which exhorts the individual to engage in elaborate game-playing and fantasy in order to supersede, or even replace, the collective, commercial theatre. By becoming the 'hero' of one's own life, reasoned Evreinov, the distinctions between performer and observer, theatre and reality would be eradicated. This passion for the aestheticisation of real life is hardly unique; as Iuri Lotman has demonstrated, it was characteristic also of Russian Romanticism.[15] But Evreinov, whose ideas cohered with the self-dramatising tendencies of the modernist avant-garde in literature and painting, as well as theatre, had ample practical opportunity to see his ideas made flesh.

Evreinov's most consistent venue for putting his theories into action was St Petersburg's Crooked Mirror (Krivoe zerkalo), a highly regarded cabaret theatre where Evreinov was employed as principal director from 1910 until 1918. Established and run by the actress Zinaida Kholmskaia (1866–1936) and her partner, the critic and journalist Aleksandr Kugel' (1864–1928), the Crooked Mirror's comic and satiric repertoire featured short plays, parodies, pantomimes, mock-operas and dance numbers in a series of short, rapidly changing acts of varied mood and character.[16] Unlike the other leading cabaret theatre of the time, the MKhAT's Bat (Letuchaia mysh'), which drew largely on literary adaptations for its repertoire, the Crooked Mirror reflected Evreinov and Kugel''s shared hostility towards 'literary' theatre in general and the Moscow Art Theatre in particular. Evreinov and Kugel''s professed 'anti-literary' preferences determined the company's focus on theatrical parodies, a form whose scepticism tends to subvert the dramatic work under scrutiny and treat it as a vehicle for contradictory discourses. The 'anti-literary' bias also guided the company's tendency to exaggerate spatial and temporal characteristics unique to the performing arts. As a way of flaunting the mobile theatre's freedom from static literature, the Crooked Mirror's plays and parodies transgressed spatial and temporal logic, unity and conventional boundaries. Distinctions between performers and observers were customarily abrogated by the crossing of physical barriers, as actors left the stage to play in the house, and 'audience members' and backstage personnel appeared to become involved in the action onstage. Plays also frequently dwelt on themes pertaining to the nature and experience of time, and rendered its inexorable progress arbitrary in dramatic devices such as flashbacks, reiteration, reversals and elisions, while the company's shadow-plays, mime and dance re-nounced expository dialogue and linear narrative in a revolt against logic, cause and effect.[17]

In the Crooked Mirror's early years (1908–10), prior to Evreinov's engagement, the company staged a number of what might be called 'theatricalised' literary parodies, most of which elicited only mid-dling enthusiasm from audiences and critics, and the Crooked Mirror soon turned directly to theatrical subjects for inspiration. Evreinov's engagement initiated the company's most fertile creative period, when the Crooked Mirror's satirical inclinations were honed and refined by their combination with Evreinov's more existentialist pursuit of the many incarnations of 'theatricality'. As a consequence of this examination of the meanings and modes of 'theatricality', a contradictory picture of its presumed opposite, 'literature', emerges from the Crooked Mirror's repertoire.

On a superficial level, 'anti-literary' elements occur in several variations in many of the Crooked Mirror's plays; the most basic and enduring of these was the caricature of the idea of the writer's privileged moral status and superior aesthetic sensibilities.

One such parody is *Torzhestvennoe publichnoe zasedanie, posviashchennoe pamiati Koz'my Prutkova* (A Gala Public Ceremony in Memory of Koz'ma Prutkov, 1913) written by two Moscow university students, Nikolai Smirnov (1890–1933) and Sergei Shcherbakov (*c.* 1890–?), who contributed more than a dozen co-authored and individually written plays for the Crooked Mirror. In this work, Smirnov and

Shcherbakov indulged their penchant for deflating the pretensions of authors, and in particular academics, in a tribute to a writer who never existed at all. 'Born' in 1852, Prutkov was the brainchild of Alexei Konstantinovich Tolstoi (1817–75) and his cousins, the Zhemchuzhnikov brothers, Alexei Mikhailovich (1821–1908), Vladimir (1830–84) (and, to a lesser degree, Aleksandr (1826–96)). Prutkov combined the traits of an inept rhymster with those of a vainglorious government official, and dabbled without prejudice or merit in prose, poetry, epigrams and drama of a surpassingly banal character. Would-be romantic poets in particular are sent up brilliantly in Prutkov, who sees no contradiction between his desire to embody the romantic poet's *Weltschmerz* and his own position as a pencil-pushing bureaucrat.[18] Of eight dramatic parodies written by Prutkov, few were actually staged; the largest number of these were produced and directed in the twentieth century by Nikolai Evreinov, who was a tireless advocate of Prutkov's satiric genius. Evreinov's decision to stage the unfinished play *Oprometchivyi turka, ili, Priiatno li byt' vnukom?* (The Hasty Turk, or Is it Pleasant to Be a Grandson?, 1863),[19] as part of Prutkov's jubilee, probably provided the impetus for Smirnov and Shcherbakov's introductory piece, *Torzhestvennoe zasedanie*, an amiable lampoon that leaves no doubt that Prutkov's legacy is alive and thriving.

On a stage set with a table and a bust of Prutkov, the Chairman of the Koz'ma Prutkov Society introduces the first speaker, Professor Vladimir Nekudykin-Netudykin,[20] who is supposed to read a lecture examining the role of Prutkov in Russian literature. But the pompous Professor spends so much time talking about what he will not be talking about that he runs out of time to read his paper. Several people applaud this development. Next, the breathlessly sincere poet Merezhevius,[21] a wicked parody of the symbolist writers Dmitrii Merezhkovskii (1865–1941) and Zinaida Gippius (1869–1945), proves to be a more stimulating speaker as he recites a meandering elaboration of Prutkov's eight-line poem *Iunker Shmidt* (Cadet Schmidt) entitled *Prutkov i Antikhrist* (Prutkov and the Anti-Christ) It begins:

> Вянет лист, проходит лето,
> Иней серебрится . . .
> Вянет лист, иней серебрится . . .
> Серебрится . . . Сере-брится . . .
> Брится-сере . . . Это иней серебрится . . .

Он серебрится, а лист вянет . . .
Лист зеленый . . . Клейкий листочек . . .
Иней и лист . . . Лист и иней . . .
Лист с одной стороны, иней с другой . . .
Антиподы! Полярности!

(The leaf withers, the summer passes,
The hoar-frost silvers
The leaf withers, the hoar-frost silvers. . .
Silvers . . . sil-vers . . .
Silvers . . . it is the hoar frost that silvers . . .
It silvers, but the leaf withers . . .
The leaf is green . . . a sticky little leaf . . .
Hoar-frost and leaf . . . leaf and hoar-frost . . .
The leaf on one side, the hoar-frost the other . . .
Antipodes! Polarities!)[22]

The poem winds on and on, giving new meaning to the phrase 'strong misreading' as Merezhevius extrapolates a symbolist ethos from his highly selective study of Prutkov's plays and aphorisms. The parody finally concludes with Merezhevius sobbing ecstatically, after which the Chairman smoothly introduces the next speaker, the 100-year-old Privy Councillor Ivan Korachovskii, who, it turns out, thought that he had been invited to talk about his service under a Brigadier 'Kirill Prytkov'. Semion Derimidontych Erundo-Erundo-vich, the world's worst post-graduate student, gives the final address.[23] Drawing from his meagre dissertation on 'Prutkov's major themes', Erundo-Erundovich (from 'erunda', or nonsense) pads out his miserable observations with vague allusions, bizarre conclusions and pre-emptive defensive remarks. The speeches conclude, and the second portion of the jubilee celebration – musical adaptations of Prutkov's epigrams – gets under way, followed directly by a perform-ance of Prutkov's unfinished play, *Oprometchivyi turka*.

The 'author' figure returned in Sergei Shcherbakov's solo effort, *Kolbasa iz babochek* (Butterfly Sausage, 1914), which affectionately parodies the futurist movement.[24] The Futurists' 'slap in the face of public taste' and assault on the Russian literary canon is rendered here as a physical assault on the person of 'the Explainer', who enters, head mysteriously bandaged, to offer an introductory history of modern art, and of Futurism's place therein. He describes the rise of Futurism in terms of coups, counter-attacks and resistance move-ments; futurist rebels proliferate, using ever-more far-fetched mon-ikers: 'narodniki-primitivisty, lubochnye chistye, vyvesochniki podnosniki, prianichniki, svistul'shchiki, kafel'shchiki, gorodushniki, i gruppa oslinokhvostnikov'. (Populist-Primitivists, Popular Purists, Signboardists, Salverists, Spice-Cakers, Tin-Whistlers, Tilists, Skittlerists, and a group of Ass-Tailers [or Asinine-Tailers].)[25] In attempting to elucidate for the audience the bizarre events about to take place on stage, the Explainer garbles the convoluted history of the movement. The Author enters and testily corrects him. Chided, the Explainer exits, but returns not long after with a fresh injury and another bandage. The action of *Kolbasa iz babochek* is abstruse and confounds any attempts to tease a narrative from it. The play is set in an unspecified urban location, there is an engineer hero, a scene in a restaurant where an orchestra plays a dyspeptic, Schoenbergian 'Digestion Symphony' and a character called Catarrh, who is cut in two by an automobile. The play is supposed to end in a conflagration that consumes the entire theatre, but this is cancelled by the disillusioned Author, who falls to droning incoherent syllables as the stage blacks out. Apparently, Shcherbakov's work exhibited some of the same unsettling power of Maiakovskii's own *Tragediia*, for Evreinov recalled that even as the audience laughed, something strangely akin to fear spread through the house.[26] In attempting to 'out-future the Futurists',[27] Shcherbakov shows not only a keen grasp of the movement's 'transrational' language and confrontational theatricality, but a genuine sense of the grotesque.[28]

Kolbasa iz babochek relies as much on the audience's knowledge of futurist poetry and painting and the group's outrageous social poses as on the particulars of *Pobeda nad solntsem* and *Vladimir Maiakovskii. Tragediia*. This apparent consonance with 'literature' underlines the essentially ironic nature of the Crooked Mirror's 'anti-literary' position, for the theatre's work often shows a high degree of correspondence with techniques and themes associated with other modernist-influenced arts, including literature. In part this is true of much modernist art, which increasingly required that the observer make connections between art works of different media in order to grasp the significance of a single work.[29]

This 'holistic' approach embraces a stylistic and philosophical multiplicity which is central to the Crooked Mirror's signature 'kaleidoscopic' plays. These works embody a perspectival relativism that offers an 'affront' to the ontological certainties of realism by implying that 'no one version can claim to be adequate to the complexity of the objects it purports to represent'.[30] Boris Geier

(1876–1916), a writer and journalist who contributed sixteen independent and collaborative plays to the Crooked Mirror's repertoire, was the acknowledged master of the form. Typically, the kaleidoscopic play presented an initial, apparently straightforward scene – such as men drinking in a tavern, as in Geier's *Voda zhizni* (*Aqua Vita*, 1911) – and then repeated the scene several times in variation, as it was seen through the different characters' eyes.[31]

The best of the Crooked Mirror's kaleidoscopic plays is Boris Geier's *Vospominaniia* (Memories, 1911), which tells the story of a marriage proposal and the engagement party which follows it from the discordant perspectives of four of the party-goers. *Vospominaniia*'s literary influence is underlined in Geier's subtitle to the play, which calls it 'an illustrated tale in five chapters'.[32] The play is introduced by a character called the Reader, who takes a seat on stage and opens a book as if to read out the action of the play – possibly an ironic reference to Sologub's 'Teatr odnoi voli'. As he reads aloud, the curtain rises on an engagement party organised by the impoverished widow Krynkina for her gauche daughter, Neonila. The two hope to ply Neonila's painfully shy admirer, the *chinovnik* Spichkin, with enough alcohol so that he summons the courage to propose. Neonila succeeds in choking the proposal out of Spichkin, and the engagement is announced to the guests, who include two of Spichkin's co-workers, the lugubrious Tabachinskii and the dipsomaniac poetaster Lakeev. During the meal that follows, Lakeev offers increasingly suggestive toasts to Neonila, until he is finally frogmarched from the flat by Tabachinskii. The scene closes with the guests' departure and Neonila's bitter complaints to her mother about Spichkin's inadequacies. The stage blacks out, and in scene two, the audience see Spichkin's version of events, in which the coarse Neonila is transformed into a lovely shrinking violet, and Spichkin into a man of smouldering intensity, who dazzles the guests with his fiery gaze and noble bearing. Another blackout segues to the acutely hungover Lakeev's version of events. Where the party in scene one was a subdued affair in a flat of Dostoevskian squalor, Lakeev remembers it as blazing with lights and riotous with madly dancing guests. Lakeev sees himself an urbane man of literature, who charms the party with impromptu verse and stirring toasts. The scene ends with Lakeev hoisted upon everyone's shoulders to shouts of 'hurrah!' Following this, the gloomy Tabachinskii recalls the party as something like a wake, all hushed tones, low light, mourning clothes and dire predictions for the future. The final scene depicts Krynkina's senile recollections of the party fifteen years on. The elderly woman sits behind a scrim, rocking and knitting an endless stocking. In the wings, the cast whisper incoherently, lights flare briefly like camera flashes; the scene grows lively and noisy for a second. Just as suddenly, the stage blacks out and silence falls. As the curtain drops, the Reader looks up and enigmatically asks the audience if, after they have gone home and are preparing to sleep, they could themselves really remember what they had just seen. He shrugs, '. . . do not believe that all was as it seemed, for none can know what reality is, and there is nothing so deceptive in this world as impressions and memories'.[33]

Vospominaniia's themes and structure attest to a number of disparate contemporary influences, among them Evreinov's theory of monodrama and the techniques and reception of the early cinema, but in particular the question of whether time and memory are experienced as discrete elements which are strung together, or as a stream of consciousness – an issue that preoccupied the minds of many writers at the turn of the century, most famously James Joyce and Marcel Proust. The idea finds a natural application in the cabaret theatre, which is also composed of separate elements or acts that can be read either as forming a differentiated but loosely cohesive programme, or as a fragmented and discontinuous narrative. The advantage in conveying this message through a performing medium is that the live theatre reinforces the inescapable 'presentness' of the action, a strength which comes with the melancholy knowledge that its destiny is to survive only in textual form once the play itself has concluded.

Of all the conflicts between 'literary' and 'theatrical' values, none is so contentious as the question of whose will – that of the playwright or the director – should prevail in the production of a dramatic work. Nothing angers connoisseurs of the written word more than a theatrical production that is 'not as the author wrote it'. Similarly, nothing is guaranteed to make theatrical practitioners despair of their audiences more than a remark such as this, which supremely ignores the collaborative, improvisatory nature of the theatre. The ineradicable tension between the dramatic ideal as conceived by the writer and the theatrical reality produced by the director had been exacerbated in the early twentieth century by the increasing importance attached to the director as the cohesive force behind a stage production. This new prestige elevated the director to the position of a co-creator with the playwright which, unless the playwright were conveniently deceased, frequently pitted the two in an adversarial relationship. As early as 1908, Sologub's 'Teatr odnoi voli' identified the frustration experienced by the playwright as this balance of power shifted, and the struggle to assert authority, in every sense of the word, began. The question of whose will should predominate in a production was more than a theoretical issue for Nikolai Evreinov, who was both author and *auteur*. In his *Revizor* (*The Government Inspector*, 1912) one of the Crooked Mirror's most famous works, Evreinov manages the near-impossible: he defends the sanctity of the dramatic text while submitting it to merciless theatrical parody.

Taking the opening and closing scenes from the first act of Gogol's *Revizor*, Evreinov presents these in five different productions, three of which are directed by fictitious acolytes of Stanislavskii, Reinhardt and Edward Gordon Craig. Each vignette shows the director in question using the play as an excuse to demonstrate his own virtuosity, with little regard for the integrity of the text. The directors justify their manipulations of *Revizor* by pedantically citing Gogol's own defences and explications of the play in *Teatral'nyi raz"ezd posle predstavleniia novoi komedii* (The Audience Departs the Theatre After the Performance of a New Comedy, 1836), and *Razviazka Revizora* (The Dénouement of *The Government Inspector*, 1846).

The play opens with a Lecturer announcing that this production of *Revizor* is the result of a competition sponsored by the Crooked Mirror. In an attempt to remedy the grievous lack of great Russian plays, the administrators hit upon an unusual solution: simply quintuple the number of classics by presenting one play in five different productions. The only aspect common to the five productions is that *'each method renders the author's work utterly unrecognisable'*.[34]

The first production is one that might be played by a provincial or a touring company. It is not bad, but neither is it very good, and comic relief is inadvertently supplied by the actors' painstaking efforts not to knock over the flimsy set. The actors playing the Mayor, Anna Andreevna, Liapkin-Tiapkin *et al.* are to perform the same roles in each of the ensuing versions of *Revizor*.

While the actors change their costumes and the stage is set for the next scene, the Lecturer returns to introduce the second production, which is the work of a student of Stanislavskii. Like his mentor, this director has diligently researched the play, establishing which town might have been used by Gogol as a model for the town in *Revizor*, what time of year the action took place, and even, supposedly, what the local Ukrainian-inflected accent would have sounded like. In keeping with the Art Theatre's obsessively detailed stage directions, Evreinov's stage directions significantly outnumber the lines of spoken dialogue. Before a single word is spoken, a serving-girl hurries across the yard, gingerly holding a chamberpot, the caco-phonous singing of birds and the lowing of a herd of cattle are heard offstage, the Mayor pads about in his underwear, scratching his backside, and Liapkin-Tiapkin enters carrying live puppies.[35] Each line of dialogue is accompanied by irrelevant stage 'business' that lengthens interminably the time between exchanges. The Mayor's first line is delivered with no particular urgency, and is interrupted by Anna Andreevna, who strolls across the stage noisily jangling a bunch of keys. The Mayor remarks in cod-Ukrainian, 'S″ogodnia usiu nich′ meni snilis′ iakis′ dve zvychainye krysy' (all night I dreamed of two extraordinary rats) '. . . Priishli, poniukhali – tai pishli get'. Os′, poslukhaite pis′mo, shcho poluchiv ia vid Andreia Ivanovicha' ('They stopped, sniffed – and were off. Here, listen to the letter I received from Andrei Ivanovich.')[36] In the second half of the parody the mood turns 'Chekhovian', and the scene is punctu-ated by mournful clock chimes and tormented gazing out of windows. The pathetic mood proves difficult to sustain, though, as Anna Andreevna shouts her lines to be heard over a dog barking furiously backstage.

The third version of *Revizor*, scripted by one of the Crooked Mirror's leading actors, Sergei Antimonov,[37] is in the style of Max Reinhardt, whose work Russian audiences had seen as recently as 1911, when the director toured to St Petersburg with his production of *Oedipus Rex*. The parody makes specific reference to the Austrian poet and dramatist Hugo von Hofmannsthal (1874–1929) as the 'adapter' of Gogol's text, and reflects as well elements of Frank Wedekind's (1864–1918) verse Prologue to the first of his 'Lulu' plays, *Erdgeist* (*Earthspirit*, 1895). Both writers shared Reinhardt's enthusiasm for the variety stage and the circus, and this is reflected in Evreinov's lampoon, which turns *Revizor* into a vaudeville populated by hyperki-netic *kupletisty* and comely dancing girls.[38] The pretext for the changes made to Gogol's play is to be found in Gogol's own *Teatral′nyi raz″ezd*, wherein the author remarks: 'I am disappointed that no one noticed the honourable character in my play. . . That honourable, noble character was *laughter*.'[39] The director of this third scene, a German from Königsberg, takes the liberty of actually casting an actress as Laughter. Dressed in a clown's costume festooned with little bells, Laughter leads the cast through the house to the accompaniment of a brisk march. She is joined by her 'sisters', Satire and Humour, who lead the company in a 'symbolic dance in the Russian spirit'. The *chinovniki*, clad in outlandish tricorne hats and military uniform, also enter through the house to the stage, where the Mayor, in a Prussian helmet and Wilhelmine walrus-whiskers, greets them in verse: 'Ia sobral vas gospoda / Na ser'eznyi razgovor / Edet k nam seichas siuda / Na pochtovykh revizor.' ('I have called you here today / For a serious discussion / Heading right here our way / On the post-coach, is an inspector.')[40] Anna Andreevna and Mar'ia Antonovna, tricked out in Gilbert-and-Sullivan-meet-Taras-Bul'ba costumes, join in and the whole enterprise concludes with another merry round dance by Laughter and her cohorts.

The fourth scene purports to be the work of a follower of the English director Edward Gordon Craig, who directed a famously ill-starred production of *Hamlet* with Stanislavskii at the Moscow Art Theatre in 1911. Preliminary work on *Hamlet* began as early as April 1909, but the vastly different temperaments and artistic credos of the two directors did not bode well for the production, and was not aided by their decision to use *Hamlet* as a testing-ground for their respective theses. Craig wished to fuse his personal obsession with Shakespeare's play to his ideal of theatre as ritual and rhythmic, luminous movement. Central to Craig's concept of the production were a complex series of lighting and scene changes, undertaken in full view of the audience, which were to reflect the different moods of Hamlet himself. Very high screens on casters were arranged and mobilised to suggest an other-worldly geometric space. After many months of postponements and a disastrous technical rehearsal that meant scrapping Craig's original scenic concept, *Hamlet* finally opened to mixed reviews on 23 December 1911.[41] The production's troubles were common knowledge among theatregoers, an asset that Evreinov exploits in the fourth *Revizor* parody. Billed as a 'mystery play', the scene looks to Gogol's *Razviazka Revizora* for its justification: 'The inspector is our awakening conscience, which forces us suddenly, and at once, to look intensely at our very selves.'[42] The

action, relates the Lecturer with ersatz gravitas, is set in interplanetary space. The masked and black-robed *chinovniki* enter as the
Mayor intones the news of the inspector's visit. A bell sounds a grim
contrapuntal note to each of his pronouncements. To the music of a
requiem mass, the *chinovniki* exit in a 'stylised' panic. Anna Andreevna and Mar'ia Antonovna enter, dressed in white, weeping and
beseeching the Mayor in tones of existential anguish, 'Where, oh
where are they? Oh, my God, husband! Antosha! Anton . . . To
where? To where? They have gone . . .'[43] The scene concludes with
the actors freezing into poses of melancholy and ennui, while a bell
rings and an organ reverberates with a penitential chorus.

The last scene presents *Revizor* as a silent film, a medium that adds
insult to injury by eradicating Gogol's text entirely. The text that
does survive – the letter received by the Mayor that tells of the
inspector's visit – is projected on stage as an intertitle, full of spelling
and grammatical errors. 'Glupyshkin', the Russian name for the
French comedian André Deed (1884–1931), has top billing in the
role of the Mayor.[44] The action consists entirely of wild gesticulations, pratfalls and an extended chase sequence, seen through a
flickering light that approximates the jumpy quality of early, hand-
cranked films.

Evreinov's treatment of his fellow directors in *Revizor* is revealing
less for what it discloses about Stanislavskii, Reinhardt or Craig,
than for what it says about Evreinov himself.[45] Of the three directors
lampooned, Stanislavskii's fussy naturalism is the only artistic
method to which Evreinov had serious objections.[46] Max Reinhardt
was far closer to Evreinov's own ideology, as was apparent from an
enthusiastic review of the Austrian's 1911 touring production of
Oedipus Rex, written by Evreinov for Aleksandr Kugel'''s journal, *Teatr
i Iskusstvo* (Theatre and Art).[47] An interesting feature of Reinhardt's
production that received little attention was that it was not strictly a
translation of Sophocles's tragedy but a modernised adaptation of it
by Hugo von Hofmannsthal, *König Ödipus* (1907). This is, ostensibly,
the very practice against which Evreinov's *Revizor* campaigns, leaving
the observer to wonder if there is a statute of limitations within
which the writer's work is inviolable, and without which the play is
fair game. Craig, too, was a director with whom Evreinov felt such
sympathy that one critic even called him the 'Gordon Craig of
Russia'.[48] In terms of the aim and scope of his ideas and ambitions,
Evreinov was strikingly like Craig, and their similarities include a

parallel interest in monodrama. Craig knew no Russian, and could not have been familiar with Evreinov's *Vvedenie v monodramu*, but the English director's *Hamlet* at the MKhAT is regarded as 'the most striking and completely realised example of monodrama' of the period.[49] As with Evreinov's proposal to focus audience sympathies on a single character, and submit all elements of performance and design to conveying the protagonist's mental state, Craig's *Hamlet* was to be played as if it 'took place in Hamlet's soul', with the other characters acting as 'psychic emanations of his loves and hates'.[50] As was also the case with Evreinov, Craig's reach exceeded his grasp, and many of his suggestions for playing *Hamlet* as a monodrama proved impossible to realise due to the technical limitations of the time and, indeed, of the theatrical medium itself.[51]

Against this backdrop of ambition and failure, Evreinov's *Revizor* offers no solution to the conflict of writer and director, theory and practice. Rather, Evreinov's agile satire highlights an essential attribute of any great play, in whose interstitial silence and italicised actions an enduring strangeness exists to accommodate an endless variety of theatrical interpretations.[52] The very flux in which the dramatic text exists, as an always-unfinished and yet apparently complete work of art is the paradox that fuels the tug-of-war between writer and director, 'literature' and 'theatre', and it is a conflict which cannot, by its very nature, be resolved. The theatre's 'anti-literary' rebellion was ever doomed to failure on these terms alone, but the experiment itself, engendered by the tumultuous energies of the early modernist movement, was crucial in asserting and legitimising a much-maligned art's claim to poetic integrity, if not autonomy.

NOTES

1 See Jonas Barish, *The Antitheatrical Prejudice* (Berkeley, 1980), which traces the origins and development of this bias from Plato to the 1970s. For discussion of traditional academic disdain for the theatre see also Robert Brustein, 'The Humanist and the Artist', in *Who Needs Theatre: Dramatic Opinions* (London, 1987), pp. 223–34; Robertson Davies, 'Oblivion's Balm', in *The Mirror of Nature* (Toronto, 1996), pp. 3–42.

2 For accounts of theatrical censorship in Russia see E. Anthony Swift, 'Fighting the germs of disorder: the censorship of Russian popular theatre, 1888–1917', *Russian History/Histoire Russe* 18: 1 (1991), 1–49; M. Frame, 'Censorship and control in the Russian imperial theatres

during the 1905 revolution and its aftermath', *Revolutionary Russia* 7:2 (1994), 164–91.

3 A. S. Griboedov, *Sochineniia v stikhakh* (Leningrad, 1951), p. 277.

4 For accounts of these experiments, see Konstantin Rudnitskii's *Rezhisser Meierkhol'd* (Moscow, 1969), and *Russkoe rezhisserskoe iskusstvo, 1898–1907* (Moscow, 1989). Meierkhol'd's own writings are published in *Meierkhol'-dovskii sbornik: Vypusk pervyi*, in two vols., ed. A. Sherel (Moscow, 1993); these are translated by Edward Braun in *Meyerhold on Theatre* (London, 1969). See also Braun's and Robert Leach's critical biographies: respectively, *Meyerhold: A Revolution in Theatre*, 2nd ed. (London, 1995), and *Vsevolod Meyerhold* (Cambridge, 1993). See also Braun's *The Director and the Stage* (London, 1990), pp. 109–29, Leach's *Directors in Perspective: Vsevolod Meyerhold* (Cambridge, 1989), and *Revolutionary Theatre* (London, 1994).

5 The difficulty of integrating the actor with abstract text and stylised production design complicated most attempts to devise alternatives to realist theatre. This state of affairs led Meierkhol'd and theorists such as Sologub to ponder, as had Heinrich von Kleist (1777–1811) and Edward Gordon Craig, the suitability of replacing the actor with the marionette. Sologub's 'Teatr odnoi voli' appears to have been influenced in part by von Kleist's 'Über das Marionettentheater' (1810), which suggests the marionette as the perfect union of human operator and mechanical performer. See also Craig's 'The actor and the Über-marionette', *Mask* 1:2 (1908). J. Woodward's 'From Brjusov to Aikhenvald: attitudes to the Russian theatre, 1902–1914', *Canadian Slavonic Papers* 1 (1965), 173–88, is an excellent overview of the many theories of the theatre circulating at this time.

6 A. Blok, *Lirika, teatr* (Moscow, 1982), p. 332.

7 Aikhenval'd's article generated a great deal of controversy; his article, and responses to it, are published in *V sporakh o teatre* (Moscow, 1914).

8 See Valerii Briusov's seminal article, 'Nenuzhnaia pravda (Po povodu Moskovskogo khudozhestvennogo teatra)' (The Unnecessary Truth (On the Moscow Art Theatre)), *Mir iskusstva* (The World of Art) 4 (1902), 67–74, in which he argues that intrinsic theatrical conventions, regardless of how cleverly they were concealed by theatrical illusion, always emerged to thwart attempts to present the stage as a 'slice of life'.

9 Indeed, Meierkhol'd explicitly stated, 'I read somewhere that "the stage inspires literature". This is not true. If the stage is influencing literature, then it is in one respect only: it is tending to arrest the progress of literature by creating a group of writers who are influenced by the prevailing tendency (Chekhov and his imitators). The growth of the New Theatre is rooted in literature. Literature has always taken the initiative in the breaking down of dramatic forms . . .' 'The New Theatre Foreshadowed in Literature', originally published in *Teatr. Kniga o novom teatre*, trans. by E. Braun, in *Meyerhold on Theatre*, p. 34.

10 Barish, *The Antitheatrical Prejudice*, p. 117.

11 Ibid.

12 The principle of *teatral'nost'* was first put forward by Evreinov in 'Apologiia teatral'nosti', published in the journal *Utro* (8 September 1908), and re-issued in a collection of his essays, *Teatr kak takovoi* (Berlin, 1923).

13 For analyses and biographical information on Evreinov, see Sharon Marie Carnicke, *The Theatrical Instinct: Nikolai Evreinov and the Russian Theatre of the Early Twentieth Century* (New York, 1989); Anna Kashina-Evreinova, *N. N. Evreinov v mirovom teatre XX veka* (Paris, 1964); Spencer Golub, *Evreinov: The Theatre of Paradox and Transformation* (Ann Arbor, 1984) and 'Mortal Masks: Yevreinov's Drama in Two Acts', in R. Russell and A. Barratt (eds.), *Russian Theatre in the Age of Modernism* (Houndmills, Basingstoke, Hampshire and London, 1990), pp. 123–47; Vasilii Kamenskii, *Kniga ob Evreinove* (St Petersburg, 1917). Articles in scholarly journals include a special edition of *Revue des études slaves* 53:1 (1981), Gérard Absensour (ed.), *Evreinov: L'apôtre russe de la théâtricalité*; Christopher Moody, 'Nikolai Nikolaevich Evreinov: 1879–1953', *Russian Literature Triquarterly* 13 (1975), 659–95; Anthony Pearson, 'Evreinov and Pirandello: twin apostles of theatricality', *Theatre Research International* 12: 2 (1987), 147–67; Pearson, 'Meyerhold and Evreinov: "Originals" at each other's expense', *New Theatre Quarterly* 8 (1992), 321–33.

14 Laura Levine, *Men in Women's Clothing: Anti-theatricality and Effeminization, 1579–1642* (Cambridge, 1994), p. 15.

15 See Iurii Lotman, 'The Theater and Theatricality as Components of Early Nineteenth-Century Culture', trans. by G. S. Smith; and 'The Stage and Painting as Code Mechanism for Cultural Behaviour in the Early Nineteenth Century', trans. by J. Armstrong, both in Ann Shukman (ed.), *The Semiotics of Russian Culture* (Ann Arbor, 1984), pp. 141–64, and pp. 165–76, respectively. See also Priscilla Roosevelt, 'Emerald thrones and living statues: theater and theatricality on the Russian estate', *Russian Review* 50:1 (1991), 1–24; Richard Wortman, 'Comment: theatricality, myth, and authority', *Russian Review* 50:1 (1991), 48–53.

16 There are numerous, if scattered, Russian accounts of the Crooked Mirror. Liudmila Tikhvinskaia's *Kabare i teatry miniatiur v Rossii. 1908–1917* (Moscow, 1995) is the first monograph on the subject of Russian cabaret, and devotes several chapters to the Crooked Mirror. See also the following articles and chapters in books: Z. Kholmskaia, 'Krivoe zerkalo', *Rabochii i Teatr* 9 (1937), 52–6, and 'Teatr "Krivoe zerkalo" (iz memuarov)', *Peterburgskii teatral'nyi zhurnal* 5 (1994), 5–11; G. Kryzhitskii, 'Laboratoriia smekha', *Teatr* 8 (1967), 110–20; A. Kugel', *List'ia s dereva. Vospominaniia* (Leningrad, 1926), pp. 190–209; I. Petrovskaia and V. Somina, *Teatral'nyi Peterburg. Nachalo XVIII veka–oktiabr' 1917 goda* (St Petersburg, 1994), pp. 314–23. For a complete bibliography, see B. Henry, 'Theatrical parody at the Krivoe zerkalo: Russian "Teatr

Miniatyur", 1908–1931', D. Phil. dissertation, Oxford University, 1997, forthcoming as *Parody and the Russian Theatre: The Crooked Mirror, 1908–1930*, 2000. See also Harold Segel, *Turn-of-the-Century Cabaret* (New York, 1987) and 'Russian Cabaret in the European Context: Preliminary Considerations', in Lars Kleberg and Nils Åke Nilsson (eds.), *Theatre and Literature in Russia 1900–1930* (Stockholm, 1984), pp. 83–100; Anthony Pearson, 'The cabaret comes to Russia: "Theatre of Small Forms" as cultural catalyst', *Theatre Quarterly* 9 (Winter, 1980), 31–44; Laurence Senelick, 'Boris Geyer and Cabaretic Playwriting', in *Russian Theatre in the Age of Modernism*, pp. 33–65, and, in the same volume, Michael Green, 'Boris Pronin, Meyerhold and Cabaret', pp. 66–86.

17 The majority of the Crooked Mirror's plays are unpublished. The St Petersburg Theatrical Library has the largest collection of the pre-revolutionary plays, in the form of Tsarist censors' typescripts. The Library also has a smaller number of unpublished post-Revolutionary plays. In Moscow, RGALI and the All-Russian Theatrical Union (VTO) also have small collections of Crooked Mirror plays, as well as those of other contemporary cabaret theatres.

18 See B. Bukhshtab's essay 'Koz'ma Prutkov' in *Koz'ma Prutkov, Polnoe sobranie sochinenii* (Moscow, Leningrad, 1965); Barbara Heldt Monter, *Koz'ma Prutkov, the Art of Parody* (Paris, 1972); Nikolai Evreinov's 'Koz'ma Prutkov: Pochitaemyi ottsom "Krivogo zerkala"', *Vozrozhdenie* 50 (1956), 101–20.

19 The apparently ungrammatical 'turka' is an archaic folk form of the noun, in keeping with the subtitle to Prutkov's Ostrovsky parody, which proclaims it a 'naturally conversational presentation'. See *Sochineniia Koz'my Prutkova* (Moscow, 1976), pp. 236–43.

20 The censor's copy lists this character both as 'Netudykin-Pole' and 'Nekudykin-Pole', while some reviews and accounts of the production give the name as 'Netudykin-Nekudykin'. I have used a version of the name that appears most often, and coincides with the one listed in Evreinov's and the actors' Mariia Iarotskaia and Sergei Antimonov's first-person accounts. See Iarotskaia and Antimonov, *'Letopis' teatra "Krivogo zerkala"'. Sbornik vyskazyvanii pressy, teatral'nykh deiatelei o teatre, programm spektaklei teatra, sostav truppy i dr. za period 1908 g.–1918 g.*, RGALI, f. 2353, op. 1, ed. khr. 59, 61, 62.

21 Most contemporary sources list this character as Mezherepius, although the censor's text gives the name as Merezhevius.

22 N. Smirnov and S. Shcherbakov, *Torzhestvennoe publichnoe zasedanie, posviashchennoe pamiati Koz'my Prutkova*, St Petersburg Theatrical Library, Fond no. 34793 [passed for performance 9 January 1913], p. 7.

23 In performance, this character was merged with that of another long-winded lecturer, Dr Ivan Karlovich Adol'f, who gives a biographical sketch of Prutkov, to create a 'famous' literary man, Fedor Fomich Voskresenskii. There are considerable variances with the censor's text

and the acting version, a partial copy of which is appended to Iarotskaia and Antimonov's *Letopis'*. The version quoted here is the censor's text.

24 The play was apparently prompted by the performances of Aleksei Kruchenykh's (1886–1969) *Pobeda nad solntsem* and Vladimir Maiakovskii's (1893–1930) *Vladimir Maiakovskii, Tragediia*, in St Petersburg, 2–3 December 1913. The play gained added publicity by the fortuitously timed visit to Russia of Filippo Marinetti in January 1914.

25 S. Shcherbakov, *Kolbasa iz babochek – Zapendiu. Gliadelishche v odnom deistvii s interfeozom*, St Petersburg Theatrical Library, Fond. no. 40217 [passed for performance: 10 January 1914], p. ii. The only real-life name included here is 'Ass-Tailers' or 'Donkey-Tailers', from 'Oslinyi khvost' (The Donkey's Tail), an avant-garde painters' group led by Mikhail Larionov and Nataliia Goncharova.

26 N. Evreinov, *V shkole ostroumiia. O teatre "Krivoe zerkalo" i moei mnogoletnei rabote v nem, kak dramaturga i glavnogo rezhissera*, RGALI, Fond. no. 982, opis'. 1, ed. khr. nos. 4, 5, 6, 7, 8, 9, 10, 12, 13. Glava 15-ia. 'O smekhe s prepiatstviiami. . .', p. 63.

27 'B., Ars', 'Khronika', *Teatr i Iskusstvo* 4 (1914), 78.

28 See Michel Aucouturier's 'Theatricality as a Category of Early Twentieth-Century Russian Culture', and Håken Lövgren's 'Sergei Radlov's Electric Baton: The Futurization of Russian Theater', both in Kleberg and Nilsson (eds.) *Theatre and Literature in Russia 1900–1930*, pp. 9–21 and 101–12 respectively, for subtle analyses of the 'anti-literary' bias, 'theatricality' and their relation to Futurism.

29 In *Early Modernism: Literature, Music and Painting in Europe, 1900–1916* (Oxford, 1994), Christopher Butler gives an example of this tendency to connect the arts in the associations that Gustave Moreau's *Salomé* makes with the biblical story, with J. K. Huysmans's *À Rebours*, Oscar Wilde's *Salomé*, and Richard Strauss's *Salomé* (p. 19). Appropriately, the Crooked Mirror's first performance in December 1908 featured a parody of *Salomé* entitled *Tantsy* or *Pokhorony Salomei*.

30 Butler, *Early Modernism*, p. 14.

31 This technique, sometimes called the 'Rashomon' perspective, after Akira Kurosawa's 1950 film of the same title, probably originated at Max Reinhardt's Berlin cabaret Schall und Rauch in 1901. See Laurence Senelick's 'Boris Geyer and Cabaretic Playwriting', and Peter Jelavich, *Berlin Cabaret* (Cambridge, Mass., 1993), pp. 62–84.

32 B. Geier, *Vospominaniia, illiustrirovannaia povest' v 5 glavakh*, 1911, p. 13. Photocopy of a text belonging to Zinaida Kholmskaia's grand-daughter, Svetlana Sergeevna Timofeeva-Tomskaia, p. 1.

33 Ibid., p. 13.

34 N. Evreinov, *Revizor*, in M. Poliakov (ed.), *Russkaia teatral'naia parodiia XIX-nachala XX veka* (Moscow, 1976), p. 614.

35 As to the question of how close Evreinov's spoof came to Stanislavskii's

style, one Moscow journalist commented, 'Is not the Crooked Mirror's *Government Inspector* "à la Stanislavskii" a bullet in the heart of the Art Theatre? Is it not what goes on at the Art Theatre in reality? It is practically photographic.' (E. Beskin, 'Moskovskie pis'ma', *Teatr i Iskusstvo* 17 (1913), 380).

36 Z. Kholmskaia, 'Teatr "Krivoe zerkalo" (iz memuarov)', *Peterburgskii teatral'nyi zhurnal*, 11 (1996).

37 The text of *Revizor* was the subject of considerable controversy in later years, with Evreinov claiming sole credit for everything but the Reinhardt sketch, and Kugel' and Kholmskaia insisting that the play was a collective effort. Kholmskaia maintained that the idea for the parody was hers, while acknowledging her debt to Boris Geier's earlier *Evoliutsiia teatra* for the kaleidoscopic structure.

38 See N. Evreinov's review of Reinhardt's *Oedipus*; *Teatr i Iskusstvo* 14 (1911), 291–2, in which he discusses Wedekind and Reinhardt.

39 N. Evreinov, *Revizor*, p. 624.

40 Ibid., p. 626.

41 On the *Hamlet* affair, see L. Senelick, 'Moscow and monodrama: the meaning of the Craig–Stanislavsky Hamlet', *Theatre Research International*, 6:2 (1981), 109–24.

42 N. Evreinov, *Revizor*, p. 629.

43 Ibid., p. 631. Compare this excerpt from one of Gogol's letters to Shchepkin: 'Pay particular attention to the final scene. It is absolutely essential that it work as a tableau, and a striking one. The Mayor must be completely dazed and not funny in the least. His wife and daughter are in utter fright and must fix their eyes upon him alone' (*Gogol' i teatr*, 'Perepiski N. V. Gogolia s M. S. Shchepkinym', from a letter dated October 1846, p. 412).

44 The *International Encyclopedia of Film* (London, 1972) notes that Deed's 'only constant characteristic was a pure and insuperable idiocy which generally resulted in a fine chaos of destruction' (p. 155). Evreinov may have been inspired by a 1910 cartoon by M. Mikhailov of a cinema advertisement that promises a double bill of Tolstoi and the adventures of Glupyshkin. (Reproduced in Iurii Tsivian's *Early Cinema in Russia and its Cultural Reception* (London and New York, 1994) pp. 140–1.) Ironically, Evreinov was not far off the mark in this last scene, for in 1914 Aleksandr Drankov's studio released the first film version of *Revizor*.

45 Anthony Pearson suggests that Evreinov's neglect of Meierkhol'd in the Crooked Mirror parody was a deliberate snub. See Pearson's 'Meyerhold and Evreinov: "Originals" at Each Other's Expense'.

46 Evreinov claimed that after *Revizor* Stanislavskii was obliged to make alterations to the MKhAT's own production of Gogol's play, because it reminded audiences overmuch of the Crooked Mirror parody. See Evreinov, 'Krivoe zerkalo v Tsarskom Sele', *Vozrozhdenie* 13 (1951), 117. See also Evreinov's exasperated article on stage realism, 'K voprosu o

predelakh teatral'noi illiuzii', *Teatr i Iskusstvo* 36 (1912), 680–3, written a
few months prior to the première of *Revizor.*

47 'Reingardtiada: Nepostizhimyi volshebnik. (Panegirik Maksu Rein-
gardtu)', *Teatr i Iskusstvo* 14 (1911), 291–2. As further evidence of his
regard, Evreinov staged a work at the Crooked Mirror in early 1912,
Sumurun, which had originated at Reinhardt's Berlin theatre.

48 B. Kazanskii, *Metod teatra: Analiz sistemy N. N. Evreinova* (Leningrad,
1925), pp. 7–8, cited by Pearson, 'Evreinov and Pirandello: Twin
Apostles of Theatricality', 154–5. Evreinov, fluent in French, German
and, apparently, English, would have been familiar with Craig's work
early on. Moreover, Craig's early writings were pirated and published
in Russian in 1906; a German translation was also available. See
Senelick, 'Moscow and monodrama', 112.

49 Pearson, 'Evreinov and Pirandello', p. 161. See also Senelick, 'Moscow
and monodrama'; Golub, *Evreinov*, p. 163.

50 Senelick, 'Moscow and Monodrama', 119.

51 Laurence Senelick concludes that 'the true medium for monodrama is
the cinema, Sologub's "single will" and Evreinov's "protagonist"
incorporated as the camera's eye' (ibid., 123). Liudmila Tikhvinskaia
comes to the same conclusion in *Kabare i teatry miniatiur*, pp. 279–80.

52 Curiously, the conflation of Gogol's plays, articles and letters, as
practised by the fictitious directors whom Evreinov satirises, is the very
technique used by Meierkhol'd in 1926, for his celebrated production of
Revizor.

CHAPTER 6

Design on drama: V. A. Simov and Chekhov

Cynthia Marsh

The turn-of-the-century Russian theatre is an outstanding example of the creative force generated by collaborations between the arts in the era of Modernism. It is above all in the relationship between dramatist and designer – the latter a relatively new concept at the beginning of the twentieth century – that the possibilities of collaboration and fusion have been realised. In a manner similar to other literary forms, the play text creates a fictional world. Simultaneously, however, the play text as a performance text contains another potential chronotope, that of the stage set.[1] Sometimes these two chronotopes are distanced, sometimes entirely interactive. The designer has the responsibility for responding to the visual and spatial aspects of a play text, and creating the chronotope of the stage set. Theatrical collaborations are, as A. Ia. Zis' has argued, 'synthetic', in that each art form obeys its own sovereign laws, but the process of combination may highlight characteristics obscured when the arts in question are considered in isolation, or indeed allow new artistic techniques to emerge.[2]

V. A. Simov's and Anton Chekhov's joint work in the Moscow Arts Theatre (MAT) provides a telling example of the kind of revelations produced when different arts are brought into proximity. In the process of their unwritten dialogue, or 'synthetic intertextuality', Chekhov responded critically to Simov's designs. Chekhov's gradual rebuttal of Simov's agenda, principally through parody, displays his increasing awareness of the specificities of the stage chronotope; this awareness determined what will be termed here his 'pre-absurdist' approach to the stage set. His developing sense of the theatre in his mature plays more and more exposed the artificiality implied by the realist/naturalist staging which marked Simov's and the MAT house style. Chekhov's response was to, as the Formalists would have termed it, 'lay bare the device': to expose the mechanics of theatre as an art form, and to incorporate this insight into the writing of the drama itself.

The heart of the synthesis between literature and performance in Chekhov's later plays lies in the way that the writer's sensitivity to the spectacle of theatre – and especially to its spatial and visual impact as expressed in the design – became part of his verbal text. In his expression of this sensitivity, he opened the way not only to Modernism in the Russian theatre, but also to the engagement with the absurd that has marked the European theatre in the first half of the twentieth century.[3]

Before I begin to examine closely the relationship between these two artists, some background information about Simov, the play texts and their collaboration at MAT needs to be provided. (Chekhov's biographical details, I shall assume, are already familiar to the reader.) I shall discuss the innovative aspects of Simov's designs and how they contributed to the formidable reputation of MAT. The relationship between the two artists itself then becomes my focus, as I analyse Chekhov's responses to Simov's designs in his play texts.

CHEKHOV AND SIMOV'S ARTISTIC CONTACTS: AN OUTLINE

Viktor Andreevich Simov was born in 1858. His father was a surveyor, but he died when Simov was only four. Simov's mother supported him through school and then art college by giving piano lessons. He completed his training in 1882: he had been taught by the painter Perov and was close friends with a number of the younger *Peredvizhniki* (Wanderers) including Levitan and Kasatkin. He began his career as a portrait-painter. In the mid-1880s he worked with Levitan, scene painting in Mamontov's private opera company, which gave performances at Mamontov's country house in Abramtsevo, near Moscow. Chekhov's brother Nikolai, a painter, shared their studio, and Simov met Chekhov on a number of occasions. Stanislavskii was also involved in the Mamontov productions, but his first acquaintance was made with Simov when he needed help with a production for the Society of Art and Literature, Stanislavskii's amateur training ground for his career as actor and director. Subsequently, Simov was invited to work in MAT at its foundation in 1898 and became its major designer. He worked in very close collaboration with Stanislavskii. Often the inspiration behind the various research trips undertaken to play locations,

Simov was instrumental in creating the house style for which MAT became world-famous: thorough research, authenticity, rigorous planning and execution of the *mise-en-scène*, careful attention to detail and designs which responded to the thematic structure of the plays. Apart from one or two excursions into work for the cinema and the odd commission in other theatres Simov stayed with MAT until a couple of years before his death in 1935, his last production being Gogol's *Mertvye dushi* (*Dead Souls*) in 1932.[4]

The plays by Chekhov which are crucial to this partnership are his four major ones: *Chaika* (*The Seagull*), *Diadia Vania* (*Uncle Vania*), *Tri sestry* (*Three Sisters*), and *Vishnevyi sad* (*The Cherry Orchard*). (The MAT production of *Ivanov* in 1904, also designed by Simov, is excluded from discussion here, since it took place after Chekhov's death.) I should sketch here some brief details of the stage history of these plays, since they are important to this essay. Written in 1896, *Chaika* was given a disastrous performance at the Aleksandrinskii Theatre that year; the MAT production, of 1898, was designed by Simov and was the second play in the opening season. *Diadia Vania* (1895/6: refashioned by Chekhov from his earlier play *Leshii* [*The Wood Demon*, 1889]), was performed at MAT in 1899 to Simov's design. *Tri sestry* was written for MAT; the première took place in 1901 and was designed by Simov. *Vishnevyi sad* was also written for MAT, and given its première, designed by Simov, in January 1904, just six months before Chekhov's death. These four productions in the six years from 1898 to 1904 form the nucleus of this chapter. Not only was this period an extremely intense one for Simov (he designed no fewer than ten of the major productions in MAT's repertoire in these years), but it also coincides with the brilliant culmination of Chekhov's dramatic work.

Konstantin Stanislavskii and Vladimir Nemirovich-Danchenko, the founders of MAT, assembled a formidable array of talent for the opening in 1898. High on their agenda stood the concept of ensemble work. This not only targeted the excessive actorly domination of the theatrical process inherent in the 'star system' of the Imperial Theatres, but also recognised that play production drew upon the skills of a range of professional artists and creators. At least at the beginning of this theatrical venture, ensemble work was understood as artistic collaboration, and fostered the kind of relationship which was to develop between Chekhov and Simov. Simov was responsible for the designs for Chekhov's four major plays, two of which were premières especially written for MAT, and created the visual style still associated with Chekhov. His contribution to these productions should be better recognised: Simov is occasionally acknowledged as a co-*rezhisser*[5] of MAT in the early years, but his work is usually eclipsed by the adulation accorded to Stanislavskii.

Such a durable working relationship as that between Chekhov and Simov is not only relatively rare in any theatre, but is also unusual in some other respects. There seems to have been very little overt communication between Chekhov and Simov. One letter only appears to have passed between them. Always there is the intermediary figure of Stanislavskii between Chekhov and Simov. This is probably a consequence of the increasing importance given to the director in theatrical productions of the day, as the chief co-ordinator of the stage and backstage processes. And yet Simov's careful exploration, analysis and revelation of Chekhov's text contributed significantly to the power of these mode-setting productions.

There may have been little overt communication but in my view there was, in compensation, much dialogue. Intertextuality among different art forms implies a form of statement, response and reaction quite different from normal verbal interchanges. Dialogue is achieved by interaction between different modes: between text and production, as well as between text and text, and between production and production. And in this case the unwritten debate conducted between Chekhov and his designer went to the heart of Chekhov's dramatic technique, and particularly his understanding of stage space. Synthesis took place between the dramatist's and the designer's skills: what came about was essentially a process by which the textual medium was rendered in visual and spatial terms.

Before proceeding to the details of this synthesis, we should identify one particular condition which determined it. A time-lapse operates in the example of interaction between a verbal text and a visual medium that is represented by the staging of a play: the work of the designer is normally based round a finished literary text, and certainly this is how Simov worked with Chekhov's material. Traditionally, words are considered to be the key element in performance. But analysis of this particular relationship shows how much Chekhov learnt about stage space from his work with Simov, and how he began to anticipate the designer's needs in his dramatic text: text and design combined to produce a new form – the production itself. In collaborative dialogue of this kind, the verbal text acquires an unwritten potency which only developed in the kind of intertextual dialogue under examination here, and which is only realised in performance.

Even a brief perusal of Simov's work shows what an innovative set designer he was. He shared the dedication of MAT to breaking free from the stereotypical and tired production standards to be found in the Imperial Theatres. The removal in 1882 of these theatres' monopoly on dramatic performances in Russia's capitals had given the first impetus to the creation of a 'free' commercial theatre, but progress had been slow. The inception of MAT along the lines of the free theatres of Europe and in the context of the growing demands that naturalism was making on stage production was to be of great significance for design and repertoire in the next decade.

The standard stage design at the end of the nineteenth century focused on the box set, allowing easy redeployment from play to play. Furniture would be provided from the theatre's store and costume was often the property of the actors themselves. There was little or no concept of an overall design to coordinate and harmonise all aspects of the production.[6]

The opening production in the MAT repertoire was ground-breaking in many respects, not least in Simov's designs. A.K. Tolstoi's play *Tsar' Fedor Ioannovich* entailed extensive research into sixteenth-century costume, language, behaviour, and not least architecture. Simov radically altered many conventions of stage perspective. The proportions of the buildings were new: for example, only the lower half of the exterior of the Kremlin was shown, a device that emphasised the imposing grandeur of the building in relation to the figures who inhabit the stage space (ill. 6.1).[7] (A design from 1907 for Pushkin's *Boris Godunov* shows how Simov continued to develop this technique (ill. 6.2).) Thorough attention to architectural detail in the interior scenes is immediately clear: arched ceilings, low doorways add to the sense of authenticity (ill. 6.3). A new principle emerged as well: the stage design was conceived as a major means of enhancing the play's thematic structure (here, the power and grandeur of the institution of autocracy as against the constriction and embattlement experienced by Tsar Fedor himself). Furthermore, in direct contrast to the box set, internal and external walls were used not to enclose

6.1 V. A. Simov, set design for A. K. Tolstoi's historical drama *Tsar' Fedor Ioannovich*. From S. S. Danilov, *Ocherki po istorii russkogo dramaticheskogo teatra* (Moscow and Leningrad, 1948).

6.2 Simov, set design for Pushkin's *Boris Godunov* (1907). From A. Bassekhes, *Khudozhniki na tsene MkhAT* (Moscow, 1960).

6.3 Simov, architectural detail from set design for *Tsar' Fedor Ioannovich*.
From Danilov, *Ocherki po istorii russkogo dramaticheskogo teatra*.

the space but to divide it. The scenic space was conceived in terms
of separate performance areas (ill. 6.4).

Similar innovation marked the designs Simov produced from the
beginning for Chekhov's plays. The first act of *Chaika* is a formidable test of any designer's skill. No pictures of the set from the
original 1896 production at the St Petersburg Aleksandrinskii
theatre have been traced. But we know that Chekhov went
frequently to the theatre. He must have been aware of the
constraints on the technical resources available for staging, particularly when plays were often given only for a single performance.
The fictional world he created in *Chaika* seems entirely at odds with
these limitations. His stage instructions required not only a stage-
within-a-stage but also a lake and trees, and a gradually darkening
scene at sunset. The salient point about the scenic implications of
this first act, apart from the complexity already noted, is that the
actors by forming an audience on stage, are forced to turn their
backs on the audience. Simov's set was clearly structured on this
principle. His response to implications about space in the dramatic
text were powerfully seen both in his exteriors and in his interiors.
Abandoning the box set, he constructed walls at angles whose lines
imply important divisions in the acting space. An example is
provided by Act 4 of *Chaika* (ill. 6.5).[8]

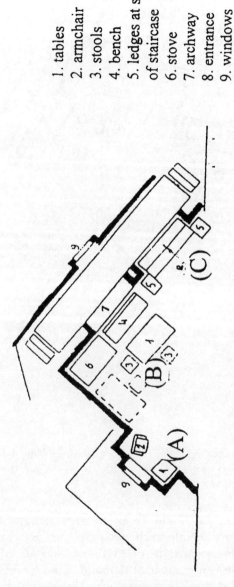

1. tables
2. armchair
3. stools
4. bench
5. ledges at side
   of staircase
6. stove
7. archway
8. entrance
9. windows

6.4 Schema showing division into separate performance areas marked A, B, C in Simov's designs for *Tsar' Fedor Ioannovich*. After L. Ia. Gremislavskii, *Kompozitsiia tsenicheskogo prostranstva v tvorchestve V. A. Simova* (Moscow, 1983).

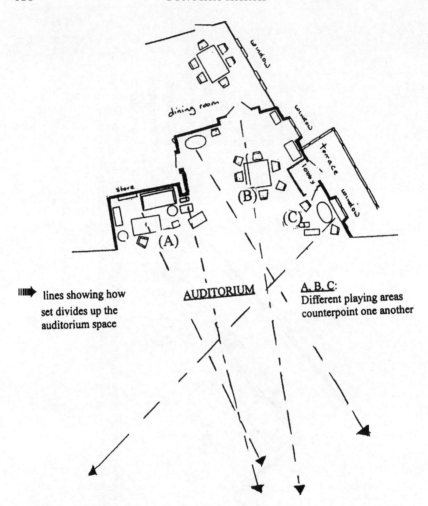

lines showing how
set divides up the
auditorium space

AUDITORIUM

A, B, C:
Different playing areas
counterpoint one another

6.5 Simov's design for Act 4 of *Chaika* (*The Seagull*), showing the divisions of scenic
    space (labelled A, B, C) by angled walls. After Gremislavskii, *Kompozitsiia*.

Similar points can be made about Simov's designs for all of
Chekhov's productions. While in this analysis they are explored for
their innovation, it is important to emphasise that all this innovation takes place within a context of demands for verisimilitude, be
it in the context of realism or naturalism. Along with this innovation went implications that were ultimately to provide a straitjacket

for productions of Chekhov's plays. In *Chaika*, his early masterpiece, Chekhov was writing well within the conventions of a naturalistic style: his trees had to be or look real, the lake had to be convincing. Environment is an important determining factor in the lives and destinies of the characters. But in the case of the later plays, verisimilitude is no longer so important, and undue attention to authenticity, detail and contemporaneity in the staging locks the plays into a particular period, and arguably also into a particular style of playing, which does little justice to the radical changes in dramatic style Chekhov gradually introduced into his last two plays.

Chekhov's innovative concept of a play's theatricality – what might be described as the designer-led or scenic quality of his dramatic writing – meant that as he created his fictional world, he gradually incorporated more and more sense of stage space into his verbal text. An analysis of this aspect of the four major plays will clarify Chekhov's evolution away from naturalism, and also Simov's contribution to this.

CHEKHOV'S AWARENESS OF THEATRICS AND OF THE VISUAL ARTS

Both *Chaika* (1896) and *Diadia Vania* (1895/6) were written before the founding of MAT, and so before the establishment of the synthesis we are investigating. Examining their visual and spatial qualities indicates how engrained this aspect of Chekhov's work already was. One part of the visual and spatial aspect of theatre derives from painting. Lotman has argued that the contemporary painterly view of representation of space is usually appropriated by theatre.[9] Other critics have commented on the closeness, both personal and artistic, between Chekhov and the painter Levitan, among others.[10] Chekhov's representations of the country estate are influenced by his affection for the provincial Russian landscape. The fictional worlds of *Chaika* and *Diadia Vania* incorporate landscape: the lake and park of Act 1, the garden of Act 2, in *Chaika*, and the garden of Act 1 in *Diadia Vania*. This landscape enters deeply into the psyche of the characters. *Chaika* is an exploration of characters in relation to their environment. The seagull itself as a casualty of noxious elements in the environment is a potent symbol of this relationship. In *Diadia Vania* the presence of landscape is extended through Astrov's interest in conservation. Landscape is at the heart of the drama but is fraught with conflict. On the one hand it is a victim of human exploitation, while on the other it victimises Vania, who remains trapped in a hostile environment.

Chekhov wrote in recognition of the traditional proscenium arch stage. In general, dramatists write in the knowledge that the audience will 'read' the production not only at the level of text but also at the level of the utilisation of stage space, or, in other words, in awareness of the proxemics (distribution of characters within the stage space, in relation to other characters or objects or parts of the stage set) used in a production and thus will subconsciously form judgements on the basis of this information. Some aspects of the proxemics are the decision of actors or director, or are dictated by prevailing conditions such as stage size. Some, however, can be prescribed in an authorial text. How much prescription there is varies according to individual dramatists and can be a signature of their style. For example, plays-within-plays create stage audiences which require particular utilisation of space; or the different per- formance styles implied by different theatrical genres such as melodrama or comedy dictate different spatial relationships on stage.

As noted above, the realist and naturalist theatre made large demands on technical ability. This is the period where it was not uncommon for complete shipwrecks or train crashes to be staged, especially within the theatre of popular melodrama. On the other hand, the late nineteenth century also witnessed the beginning of another, quite separate, tradition of the manipulation of scenic space. The plays-within-the-plays of Chekhov have attracted comment.[11] Among the more important of these, in *Chaika*, are Treplev's play and the lotto game; in *Diadia Vania* the play-within-a-play takes a more sophisticated form, involving the juxtaposition of a melodrama (Serebriakovs, Astrov) to a brutally realistic and con- temporary tragedy (Sonia, Vania). In such 'counterpointing', areas of stage space are balanced one against the other as different focal points of action. In the lotto game of Act 4 in *Chaika*, for example, Konstantin and the rest of the family occupy separate scenic spaces, and the inhabitants of each space echo one another in their dialogue and/or bodily reactions.

Simov's designs for the productions of these two plays were a major contribution to their success. Simov's new type of stage set responded to and further enhanced this aspect of Chekhov's work as we have seen earlier. From this we can argue that the divided stage set was already embryonically part of Chekhov's dramatic text in *Chaika* and *Diadia Vania*. We need to examine how this process is taken further in *Tri sestry* and *Vishnevyi sad*.

TRI SESTRY AND VISHNEVYI SAD: CHEKHOV'S PARODIES OF REALISM AND NATURALISM

Those who write about the artistic standards of MAT frequently indicate a divergence between the work of Chekhov on the one hand, and Stanislavskii and Simov on the other, which begins with *Tri sestry*.[12] This distancing has been masked by the compelling theatrical achievements of director and designer. The fact that Chekhov's plays contain much beyond what Stanislavskii and Simov saw, or chose to add, has been sidelined in favour of celebrating what was undoubtedly impressive in the work of Stanislavskii and Simov. Interrogating the play texts for their spatial implications indicates the intimacy and estrangement between dramatist and designer.

In *Tri sestry*, Chekhov created the ultimate counterpointed or 'spaced' play, employing devices such as relocation, interlocking, echoing, juxtaposition and overlay to transcend the verbal dimension of his text. There is a relentless spatial relocation expressed in the different settings for the acts: the slow, uncompromising ejection of the sisters from the house, a motion that reverses the process of the two previous plays. The latter were structured round a slow uncompromising move into the inner sanctum of the main character, encouraging the audience continually to narrow their spatial focus as the various locations disappeared entirely from view. The implied settings of the different acts of *Tri sestry*, on the other hand, encourage the counterpointing of one space against another. The various spaces continue to exist within the house, whose entirety is still implied by the stage set. At the same time we note a new economy of setting, Acts 1 and 2 being set in the same room, albeit at a different time of day and year. We also note that this is true of *Vishnevyi sad*, while *Chaika* and *Diadia Vania* each have four settings. Theatrical technique played some part in this: the advent of electricity facilitated a subtle modulation of atmosphere in one and the same set by its ability to suggest the passing of time over the course of one day, as well as the alternation of the seasons.

Tri sestry is characterised by another kind of counterpointing too: the off-stage world interlocks powerfully with the on-stage world. The interlocking is achieved by means of off-stage characters (Protopopov; the sisters' parents; Vershinin's wife), sound effects (music; troikas; mummers; wind in chimney; street musicians, snatches of song; shots; shouts from the distance) and events (the duel, Masha and Vershinin's love affair, Vershinin's wife's attempted suicide). Internal reference and echoing become spatial concepts when they make a visual impact through costume or props; for example, the echoing reference to ill-chosen belts (Act 1, Ol'ga to Natasha; Act 4, Natasha to Irina) or to clocks and watches with doom-ridden connotations: the clock strikes in Act 1 (anniversary of death), a clock is smashed in Act 3 (lost love) and the striking pocket-watch in Act 4 (signal for the fatal duel). Props are made to utilise scenic space in surprising ways. Juxtaposition of props with assigned significances is particularly important in this play. For example, in Act 1 a cake and a samovar divide the stage space in a potent manner. Both are presented to Irina within a few moments of each other to mark her name-day, the cake sent by Protopopov, a character from the off-stage world whose gift is commented upon as unsuitable, and the samovar, normally a gift to mark a silver wedding, inappropriately presented by Chebutykin more in memory of her mother than as a gift to Irina. United in their inappropriateness, the cake and the samovar exist side by side, colonising the space around them with their electrifying associations. One is quickly despatched to the kitchen for consumption, thereby extending audience perception to the off-stage world.

References to time in Chekhov's play text are also spatially addressed. In the theatre naturalism and realism invite the imaginary construction of the off-stage world. Sometimes, this could be a different time world, whether of the past or the future. Juxtaposition of these different time worlds frequently occurs by means of characters or places: the sisters' father (recent past); their mother or a street in Moscow (the distant past); or through props, the samovar or the mother's clock. The future is given tangible form in the sculptured stillness of the sisters at the end of the play as they grasp for knowledge of the future, their need for physical closeness expressing their uncertainty and fear in the face of the unknown.

A curious sense of the 'spatiality' of time is also created in another way. Time sequences are invited to overlie one another, creating a sense, for the play as a whole, of time as illusory and unstable. The 24-hour cycle provides one level of interpretation: the play begins and ends in the middle of the day, with Act 2 taking place in the evening and Act 3 in the middle of the night. But a second level is provided by the alternating seasons: the play begins in spring; Act 2 takes place in winter, Act 3 in summer and Act 4 in the autumn, suggesting a year's cycle. And the final level is that the time span of the action is, in fact, four or more years. These time dimensions are not immediately obvious: the various layers have to be 'excavated' from the text and from the 2- to 3-hour real time experience of watching the play.[13]

There is much here that Simov was able to capitalise upon in his designs for the play: the importance and symbolic significance of setting, costume and props, and also the need to suggest the different times of day and night as well as the different seasons through subtle lighting changes. The spatial sense is potent. In Act 3 the small room now occupied by Irina and Olga becomes a barricaded refuge against the rest of the house, the town and even the world. It is also spatially offset by the fire raging outside. There are dialogues counterpointed to dialogues, suggesting the manipulation of space, extended, for example, in the use of screens and curtains as the sisters seek refuge from one another. This technique is also used in Act 1 in the division between dining-room and salon. The stage set for the MAT production also suggested the whole house; a verandah in Act 1 clearly looks to the outside of the house. Simov cleverly divides even the auditorium space by this device. The same verandah is repeated in Act 4, which shows the outside of the house (ill. 6.6 and 6.7).[14] However, the verandah now lies on the other side: the orientation of the audience has undergone a complete reversal. It is as if the two sides of the auditorium have changed places.

But if all this may be related to Chekhov's practices in his earlier plays, a new element had also begun to make itself felt, representing a distinct change of tone on his part. If we interrogate the text, we find him beginning to ironise at the expense of MAT house style and of the Moscow audience. A fire threatens the town, the house and perhaps even the set in Act 3. Chekhov knew Simov's designs would be utterly true to life. The fire referred to in the play is near enough for its glow to be seen through the windows. Moreover, the play, set in the remote provinces, constantly invokes a 'Moscow' where the

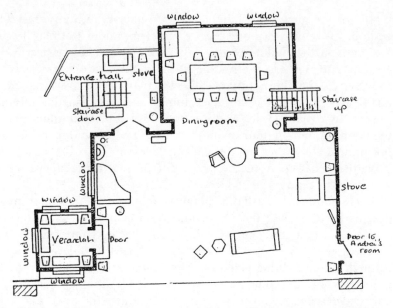

6.6 Schema of Simov's design for Act 1 of *Tri sestry* (*Three Sisters*), showing use of
verandah to divide scenic space. After Gremislavskii, *Kompozitsiia*.

6.7 Simov, set design for *Tri sestry*, Act 4. I. Vinogradskaia, *Zhizn' i tvorchestvo
K. S. Stanislavskogo*, vol. 1 (Moscow, 1971).

audience is sitting. Moscow is a very strong presence in the play: as well as perceiving the thematic significance of the city, members of the Moscow audience were also required to reorient themselves spatially, being in Moscow watching a play set in the provinces in which the characters' main desire is to get to Moscow. Such reorientation upsets the conventionally comfortable experience of play-watching. Is Chekhov also discomforting his audience with an elaborate joke? He wrote the play knowingly for a Moscow audience. Is he not mocking them just a little, by encouraging them to indulge in a little self-satisfaction at the sophisticated desirability of their life style? A self-satisfaction that in the end proves to be all too short-lived, since, in the eventuality, Moscow is not reached, the characters stay where they are and endure. That is their reality: Moscow is not real for them, just as the onstage fire is, though an illusion, more real than the actual bodies of the audience.

We can pursue the argument further. Natasha threatens to cut down the trees in Act 4. Is she also threatening Simov's elaborate set? The reference to a fork left carelessly on a bench, which immediately follows her remark about the trees, by its very incongruity could likewise be seen as a comment on the over-elaborate detail and authenticity sometimes unnecessarily indulged in by Stanislavskii and Simov.

Parody always has an element of contrivance. The deliberate 'sculpting' of the sisters at the end of the play suggests an artificiality unprecedented in Chekhov's approach to actors and set. Is this perhaps a conscious gesture towards proxemics? At this point the counterpointing of characters and their destinies begins to look posed: Kulygin stands holding Masha's coat, signalling her role as his wife; Andrei wheels the pram with Bobik, indicating his role as Natasha's husband and minder of her children; the doctor sits on his *tumba* (incidentally the word also used for the pedestal of a lavatory!) singing his favourite music-hall song, *Ta-ra-ra-boom-di-ay*, displaying his resignation; the music of the military fades into the distance, signalling the sisters' isolation.

Appreciation of the spatial elements of Chekhov's texts also illuminates the function of the street musicians in Act 4 of *Tri sestry*. Local colour, wandering, homelessness, are meanings associated with them which fit the thematic structure. They also have spatial implications in this tightly constructed play. One such implication is to confirm Ol'ga's remark that everyone uses the Prozorovs' garden as a thoroughfare. Not only do the musicians imply the proximity of the public road, but they also function as a visual sign of the intrusion of the public into private space. Simov responded by formalising the border between public and private space in the fence which figures so prominently in his design for Act 4 (fig 6.7[15]). However, the musicians also provide a 'performance-within-a-performance'. Spatial implications are important. The characters' relationship to space around them changes: Ol'ga, Anfisa, Vershinin and latterly Irina form an on-stage audience. The set must allow them to take on this new function, an important one which, for the duration of the music, conjoins stage and auditorium in the same role.[16]

We should also examine the modes of language used in this play in order to heighten the sense of the spatial. Instead of the usual forms of interaction, characters use quotation on several occasions. As well as having significance for the themes of the play, quotation has a number of consequences for performance. Quotation suggests a different gestural language and vocal tone. It is frequently marked by the pose of the actor and is usually accompanied by a special, artificial tone of voice. Both of these also have consequences for stage proxemics. Declamation and recitation demand more space for the speaker. The quotation tone also focuses the attention of the spectator on the actor's body, in expectation of a rhetorical pose. In this way the verbal form is extended to embrace visual impact.

The two characteristics we have observed, parody and extension of the verbal to embrace the visual, draw two theorists of form, Bakhtin and Likhachev, into our argument. Bakhtin saw parody as essential to the working out of new artistic forms. Contrived, and therefore often comic or grotesque, imitation implies a dialogue taking place between various texts. Here the dialogue is not between texts but between text and stage design through the medium of performance. For what he thought were very good reasons Bakhtin dismissed drama from his projections for modern literature. However, the mechanisms he uncovered operate with potent force not only with regard to the number of competing 'voices' within performance, but also with regard to the interaction of the play text with other art forms.[17]

Such mixing of forms towards the extension of one is neither new, nor entirely rational. Likhachev in his article on medieval miniatures has pointed in the direction of the necessity to resort to absurdity to transcend existing boundaries of form.[18] He shows us how the Russian medieval illustrator defied logic in order to develop narrative. These miniaturists transcended the static and visual limitations of their art by incorporating space and time indicators. As a result, one tiny picture could tell a complete narrative that covered an expanse of both distance and time. By so doing, the miniaturist broke through the convention of the period.

Chekhov brought realist and naturalist theatre face to face with the absurd through parody and through the exploitation of the polyphonic potential of performance. My view is that the elements in *Tri sestry*, described above, worked as a prelude to the determination of a new theatrical form in *Vishnevyi sad*. *Tri sestry* projects a closed or contained fictional world, felt in the constraints of provincial life and in the sisters' inability to know what the future holds. The play ends with the refrain: '*Esli by znat'!*' (If only we knew!). Characters remain trapped in unhappy marriages (Andrei, Masha, Vershinin), or in demanding, stressful jobs (Olga); in *meshchanstvo* (philistinism) (Natasha, Andrei), in loneliness (Irina) or unproductive lonely old age (Chebutykin). Alternatively, lives are cut short by untimely death (Tuzenbach). Moreover, the fates of the characters are all static in geographical terms (this applies even to Vershinin and the other officers in the regiment in Poland and arguably even to Tuzenbach), and all are at the mercy of their various environments. In this way, the play not only expresses the pessimism inherent in the contemporary naturalist movement, but also the implied spatial limitations imposed on drama by the ideology of naturalism in which human behaviour is determined by environment. In contrast, *Vishnevyi sad* presents a fictional world which is wide open: all the characters go on to new locations and new destinies. Even Firs is liberated from the slave-like relationship to his master (whether by abandonment or death hardly matters). In fact, the fictional world of the play is systematically destroyed, first by these departures, then by the felling of the orchard at the end of the play and finally by the projected demolition of the house the following spring.

In between *Tri sestry* (1901) and *Vishnevyi sad* (1904), the new productions mounted by MAT were of plays by Ibsen, Hauptmann, Nemirovich-Danchenko, Gorky, Tolstoi and Shakespeare.[19] With the exception of the last, all these writers were united in their espousal of the issues and ideology of naturalism, from its most conventional to its most radical expressions. The naturalistic style, sometimes called authenticity, of these productions became a byword for the MAT house style. All had designs developed for them by Simov. By imposing a similar, environmentally driven design on *Vishnevyi sad* Simov, while exposing to the full the contemporary significance of the play, masked the revolutionary implications of its form.

Chekhov executed a superb parody of the designer's art in a naturalist/realist theatre in *Vishnevyi sad*, and in the process produced a play the techniques of which were markedly new. The gulf between director, designer and author already commented upon supplied Chekhov with a salutary distance. Where previously, in *Tri sestry*, Stanislavskii and Simov had been able to contribute overtly to the collaborative effort, in *Vishnveyi sad* the relationship with the author was stretched to breaking-point. Stanislavskii argued the play was a tragedy, Chekhov subtitled it a comedy. Stanislavskii changed Chekhov's setting for the final act to repeat that of Act 1. Chekhov agreed to this alteration but it allowed Stanislavskii and generations of directors and critics to argue for the poignancy of the piece at the expense of its originality, innovativeness and comic power.[20]

If we examine the text of *Vishnevyi sad* as a parody in the Bakhtinian sense of the word, what do we find? First, some aspects parody the 'blind' acceptance of the illusion of the fictional world. This is exemplified in the physical abandonment of the set by the actors/characters, the 'locking in' of one actor/character (Firs), and then the destruction of the orchard and the house – that is, the destruction not only of the fictional, but also of the stage, world of the play. Secondly, there is Chekhov's 'game' with the cherry orchard itself. Despite its eponymous centrality, and almost despite the conventions of naturalist theatre, the orchard has to be conjured up in the audience's imagination. Chekhov's stage instructions suggest that only the glow, as it were, of the orchard is visible as the sun has not yet risen in Act 1. The windows remain closed until opened by Ranevskaia and Varia two-thirds of the way through the act. The orchard is not seen again in the play: it borders the setting of Act 2; Act 3, the ball, takes place indoors; and in Act 4 the shutters are presumably closed for departure. The orchard is only 'heard', falling to the axe at the end. Yet Simov's response to this calculated allusiveness was to provide no less than six windows through which the orchard might be glimpsed.[21]

Thirdly, there is the character of the landscape for Act 2 – which, incidentally, Chekhov in one of his few reported statements about Simov's work stated was wrongly interpreted.[22] He had wanted a southern Russian landscape with a great sense of distance, *'dal'*.[23] Simov provided a northern landscape as would be found in the Moscow region, a vision that, according to some, was inspired by the work of Levitan. The details are important: the broken-down shrine; the telegraph poles, the railway and the distant town. B. Zingerman writes of the vivid sense of space introduced here,[24] entirely at odds with the theatre building, the box set and the artifice of the scene painter's art. Undoubtedly, such a scene, while emphasising the almost 'cosmic'[25] dimensions of the play and its theme, at the same time underlined the incongruity of trying to capture this space within the confines of a realist/naturalist theatre, or indeed, a naturalistic set by Simov!

Fourthly, there is case of the breaking string. I should like to argue, in the 'absurd' mode of Likhachev, that the sense of space is extended further by the strangeness of this sound, whether this is to be explained as the noise of a mine-shaft cable breaking or not. The transference between sound and space here is the closest we come to synaesthesia in this discussion.[26] By this sound, the audience is invited to contemplate the nature of the off-stage fictional (and perhaps also the backstage, technical) world. The reference to the possible breaking of a mineshaft cable immediately locates the source of the sound at a distance from the estate, vastly extending the audience's spatial perception of the fictional world. However, it is clear the sound should not be confined in import to the noise of a breaking mineshaft cable: there is ample evidence against a simplistic acceptance of this view in the way the sound is treated in the *verbal* text. The various interpretations offered by on-stage characters are not simply indications of the personality of the utterer. Their more complex function is to call into question, for characters and audience alike, the 'meaning' of this sound. Its cosmic (and therefore immensely spatial) significance is underlined by a number of factors. First, Act 2 is the act with the widest range of reference to international geography. The Russia–Europe juxtaposition is most clearly made: Iasha (France) and Charlotta (Germany) are ranged against homely Duniasha and Epikhodov (Russia), comically anticipating the juxtaposition of Europeanised Ranevskaia and localised Lopakhin for the rest of the act. Secondly, by placing a repetition of the sound of breaking string in the closing moments of the play, Chekhov enhances this interpretation of its cosmic role. In terms of strict verisimilitude, it is highly unlikely that two mineshaft cables would break in the same vicinity within two or three months. Thirdly, this mysterious, unreal sound could be seen as a mischievous challenge to the technical resources of MAT. Finally, and most importantly, it stands at the climax of the interrogation of naturalism. It is a bridge between the two chronotopes of the play, identified in the play's fictional and stage worlds. This sound is also deliberately not recognisable, not a contribution to verisimilitude. It is deliberately irrational. It is absurd.

CONCLUSION

Two main points to be drawn from the material presented here suggest how Chekhov engaged with the 'boundaries of the spectacular'. The first relates to the importance of Simov as designer to Chekhov's changing dramatic style, and the second relates to the non-verbal dialogue the two conducted. In response to the accumulated irritation inspired by Simov's design work on his first two plays, Chekhov began to make a parodic riposte in *Tri sestry*. The closed set employed here belongs to naturalism. However, the emphasis placed by naturalism on the relationship between individuals and environments intensifies the need for verisimilitude in the production of the stage set: once space becomes an issue, the narrow focus of the environmentally driven text is seen for all its paradoxical, illusionistic unreality. Chekhov's 'destruction' of his stage set in *Vishnevyi sad* was his final and most telling comment upon this point.

All of this bears out Bakhtin's case that parody, despite its initial and inherent dependence on what it mocks, is in essence a great liberating force and signals new forms. And though Bakhtin neglected the application of his dialogic theory to drama, I would see, in the material analysed here, a compelling illustration of the potency of parody. Through his parody of naturalism in *Vishnevyi sad*, Chekhov set an important agenda for twentieth-century theatre, anticipating, decades in advance, principles employed by Beckett, Ionesco and others who contributed to the Theatre of the Absurd.

In sum, then, the example of Chekhov and Simov demonstrates that interrelation between one artistic medium and another stimulates, not the felicitous harmony we might expect of synthesis, but dissociation and fragmentation, provoking a major change in direction. Collaboration or synthesis, ideas at the heart of Modernism, proffer the opportunity to see aspects of an art which may not necessarily be perceptible when that art is viewed in isolation. The participants assert autonomy as well as reaching out towards alternative practices; contemplating the 'boundaries of the spectacular' is as illuminating an experience as the attempt to work against ordinary convention and across artistic dividing lines.

NOTES

1 The term chronotope is used here, after Bakhtin, to indicate the locations of the fictional world of a play which are moulded by the biographical and crisis time of the characters. They usually form the settings for scenes or acts. Examples of chronotopes in Chekhov's plays are the garden or study of a late-nineteenth-century Russian family estate. In performance, the stage set provides a realisation of the fictional chronotope, but this version of the chronotope is subject to additional laws of space and time quite separate from those of the fictional world. Examples would be the architecture of the individual theatre building, the period in which the production is set or the date of the performance. For discussion of this term see M. Bakhtin, 'Forms of Time and of the Chronotope in the Novel: Notes Toward a Historical Poetics', in *The Dialogic Imagination: Four Essays by M. M. Bakhtin*, ed. M. Holquist, trans. C. Emerson and M. Holquist (Austin, Texas, 1981); M. Holquist, *Dialogism. Bakhtin and His World* (London, 1990), pp. 287ff. See also n. 17 of this essay for reference to Bakhtin's views on drama.

2 A. Ia. Zis', 'Teoreticheskie predposylki sinteza iskusstv', in D. D. Blagoi *et al.* (eds.), *Vzaimodeistvie i sintez iskusstv* (Moscow, 1978), pp. 5–20.

3 For a later stage of Russian 'pre-absurdism', see Barbara Henry's chapter on the work of the Krivoe Zerkalo cabaret in this volume.

4 For fuller accounts of Simov's biography see Iu. I. Nekhoroshev, *Dekorator Khudozhestvennogo Teatra Viktor Andreevich Simov* (Moscow, 1984); O. Nekrasova, *Viktor Andreevich Simov 1858–1935* (Moscow, 1952).

5 See e.g. I. Ia. Gremislavskii, *Kompozitsiia stsenicheskogo prostranstva v tvorchestve V. A. Simova* (Moscow, 1983), p. 12. The word means 'co-director' in the sense of director of a production.

6 One notable exception is A. K.Tolstoi's production of his play *Smert' Ioanna Groznogo* (*The Death of Ivan the Terrible*) at the Aleksandrinskii Theatre in 1867. Tolstoi set new standards of collaboration in the design of a production, seeing the author as the coordinator of the design process. See C. Marsh, 'Realism in the Russian Theatre', R. Leach and V. Borovsky (eds.), *The Cambridge History of Russian Theatre* (forthcoming).

7 Illustrations 6.1 and 6.3 are taken from S. S. Danilov, *Ocherki po istorii russkogo dramaticheskogo teatra* (Moscow-Leningrad, 1948), facing p. 417. Illustration 6.2 is from A. Bassekhes, *Khudozhnik na stsene MKhAT* (Moscow, 1960), p. 8.

8 Fig 6.5 is based on Gremislavskii, *Kompozitsiia*, p. 61

9 Iu. Lotman, 'Teatral'nyi iazyk i zhivopis'' (1979), *Izbrannye stat'i v 3-kh tomakh* (Talinn, 1993), vol. III, pp. 308–15.

10 See, for example, A. Turunov, 'Brat'ia A.P. i N.P. Chekhovy i I.I. Levitan', *Iskusstvo*, 4, 1938; V. Prytkov, *Chekhov i Levitan* (Moscow, 1948); K. Pigarev, *Russkaia literatura i izobrazitel'noe iskusstvo* (Moscow, 1972), pp. 11–114; A. A. Fedorov-Davydov, *Isaak Il'ich Levitan. Zhizn' i tvorchestvo* (Moscow, 1966).

11 W. G. Jones, ' *The Seagull's* second symbolist play-within-the-play', *The Slavonic and East European Review*, 53 (1975), 17–26; C. Marsh, 'Chekhov's "Modernist" Theatre', in C. Marsh, W. Rosslyn (eds), *Russian and Yugoslav Culture in the Age of Modernism* (Nottingham, 1991), pp. 17–29.

12 See, for example, N. Chushkin, 'Simov – rodonachal'nik novogo tipa teatral'nykh khudozhnikov', in *Ezhegodnik Moskovskogo Khudozhestvennogo Teatra, 1953–1958* (Moscow, 1961), p. 396.

13 C. J. G. Turner, in 'Time in Chekhov's *Tri sestry*', *Canadian Slavonic Papers*, 28 (1986), 63–7, and in his monograph, *Time and Temporal Structures in Chekhov*, Birmingham Slavonic Monographs 22 (1994) gives an exhaustive account of time references in this play, but does not follow through entirely their implications for performance. It was not possible, within the space limitations of this paper, to analyse Chekhov's manipulation of time in the two major chronotopes that he creates, the fictional world of the play, and the stage world. It is clear, however, that he was aware of the chronological worlds, both fictional and stage, which parallel the spatial fictional and stage worlds he was creating, and the importance of these chronological dimensions to performance.

14 Fig 6: *Three Sisters*, Act 1, based on Gremislavskii, *Kompozitsiia*, p. 65; fig 7 design for *Three Sisters*, Act 4, K. S. Stanislavskii, *Sobranie sochinenii*, vol. I, facing p. 289.

15 F. Rokem, *Theatrical Space in Ibsen, Chekhov and Strindberg* (Ann Arbor, 1986), pp. 29–47, discusses public and private space in Chekhov's plays.

16 The musicians also have important implications for the manipulation of time. Their music has to be played in performance in 'real' time and has the significant function of determining pace in the final act.

17 Invoking Mikhail Bakhtin in a study relating to modernist collaboration between the arts is not new. K. Hirschkop stressed Bakhtin's relevance to Modernism in his introduction to K. Hirschkop and D. Shepherd (eds.), *Bakhtin and Cultural Theory* (Manchester, 1989), p. 4. For a concise analysis and reassessment of Bakhtin's dismissal of drama, see Hélène Keyssar, 'Drama and the dialogic imagination: The Heidi Chronicles and Fefu and Her Friends', *Modern Drama* 34 (1991), 88–106; Jennifer

Wise, 'Marginalising drama: Bakhtin's theory of genre', *Essays in Theatre* 8: 1 (1989), 15–22.

18 D. S. Likhachev, ' "Povestvovatel'noe prostranstvo" kak vyrazhenie "povestvovatel'nogo vremeni" v drevne-russkikh miniatiurakh', in V. G. Bazanov and A. N. Iezuitov (eds.) *Literatura i zhivopis'* (Leningrad, 1982), pp. 93–111.

19 The MAT repertoire of new productions between 1901 and 1904 was as follows: **1901** Jan.: *Tri sestry*; Sept: Ibsen, *The Wild Duck*; Oct.: Hauptmann, *Michael Kramer*; Dec.: Nemirovich- Danchenko: *V mechtakh* (In Dreams). **1902** March: Gorky, *Meshchane* (Philistines); Nov.: Tolstoi, *Vlast' t'my* (The Power of Darkness); Dec.: Gorky, *Na dne* (*The Lower Depths*). **1903** Feb: Ibsen, *The Pillars of Society*; Oct: Shakespeare, *Julius Caesar*. **1904** Jan: *Vishnevyi sad*. (Details here taken from E. G. Kholodov *et al.* (eds.), *Istoriia russkogo dramaticheskogo teatra*, vol. VII (Moscow, 1987), 546–7). The production of *Julius Caesar* was noted for its naturalistic style, and an expedition to Rome was undertaken to ensure authenticity. The remaining six plays were all regarded as part of the contemporary canon of 'new' drama inspired by naturalism.

20 See Chushkin, 'Simov – Rodonachal'nik', pp. 404–9. On p. 405 he gives support to Stanislavskii's and Simov's independence, but agrees (p. 404) that they neglected the comedy of the piece in favour of their emphasis on mood and nostalgia, of which he approves (p. 409).

21 It is unclear whether this room is on the ground or the first floor. Chekhov refers to a two-story building in his letters. This location was changed by Stanislavskii to a ground-floor room that had at one time been used as a nursery, implying that at first it may have been on the first floor. (Chushkin, 'Simov – rodonachal'nik', p. 408). On 20 November Chekhov wrote that the two-story building would allow little light to reach the garden very close to the house, perhaps implying that the trees would not grow in the kind of courtyard he envisaged. He supplies a little drawing in his text ('sad' means garden or orchard):

(A. P. Chekhov, *Polnoe sobranie sochinenii i pisem* (henceforth PSSP), *Pis'ma*, vol. XI (Moscow, 1982), pp. 297, 309). Earlier, on 9 November, Nemirovich-Danchenko, in a letter to Chekhov, had referred to a meeting in which concessions had apparently been made: he had had to give way over windows so that the orchard could be seen in the room by the spectators. This letter is quoted in the notes to PSSP, *Pis'ma*, XI, p. 627.

22 A. Bassekhes, *Khudozhniki*, p. 34. In writing, Chekhov confined himself

to describing the design for Act 2 as *uzhasnuiu* (dreadful). His real view was reported by his wife Ol'ga Knipper long after his death.

23 Letter from Chekhov to Nemirovich-Danchenko, 22 August 1903, Chekhov, PSSP, *Pis'ma*, vol. XI, p. 243.

24 B. Zingerman, *Teatr Chekhova i ego mirovoe znachenie* (Moscow, 1988), pp. 68–9.

25 J. L. Styan, *Chekhov in Performance* (Cambridge, 1971), p. 337. The word 'cosmic' is, however, used by Styan to imply a sense of unearthliness as well.

26 On synaesthesia, see Catriona Kelly and Stephen Lovell's introduction to the present volume.

CHAPTER 7

Khlebnikov's eye

Robin Milner-Gulland

As everybody knows, the period of the European 'Modern Move-ment' (c. 1880–1930) witnessed close interaction among the various forms of art: a Mallarmé and a Debussy, a Schoenberg and a Kandinskii, a Picasso and an Apollinaire could be linked not only by ties of friendship and co-operation, but by a feeling of common purpose across normal generic boundaries. Practitioners of one art frequently operated at a serious level in other territories: Schoenberg painted, Picasso, Klee, Filonov and Kandinskii all wrote, Maia-kovskii trained as an artist, Pasternak as a musician, Ciurlionis was equally composer and painter, Arp painter and poet and so on. Such a pattern of common activity and purposefulness is particularly apparent in Russia, whose relatively small and compact group of avant-gardists felt (both before and after the Revolution) a sense of cross-arts significance that went beyond the merely aesthetic in their questioning of old high-cultural forms and their explorations of new paths.

Among writers for whom the visual sphere of experience played a key role, Velimir Khlebnikov (1885–1922) has a special and extra-ordinary place. He had, as writers ought to have, a sharp eye for the delineation (verbally or pictorially) of *realia*; beyond that, 'seeing' was a correlative of his verbal creativity and a crucial constituent of his metaphoric system; he sensed that conceptual advances in the modern visual arts opened the way to a new literature and a new perception of the world; he struck up co-operative relationships with several visual artists that were of profound importance to both sides; he subjected the very concept of 'eye', and its verbal signifiers (*glaz, oko*), to a characteristically Khlebnikovian scrutiny with surprising results – that may themselves facilitate our access to his symbolic world. Though studies of Khlebnikov generally mention his contacts with visual art and artists – can hardly help but do so, indeed –

investigations of the topic have been at best fragmentary, its profundities seldom understood.[1] Specialists have been even slower to recognise the impact of Khlebnikov's work and ideas on certain major visual artists. These topics are undoubtedly vast enough to fill a substantial monograph. In this essay, by way of introducing them and sketching out the large territory they cover, I intend to begin by selectively enumerating and briefly discussing, with examples, the main ways in which Khlebnikov's 'eye' affected the configuration of his work, then examining more closely the creative relationship with several artists, notably Vladimir Tatlin, and the use made of the word *oko* (eye) in his writing generally.

First, though, a note is needed on Khlebnikov's poetics – again a large topic that lacks a systematic investigation, though much good work has been published on it in recent years.[2] We can start from the feelings typically experienced by those who encounter Khlebnikov's poetry for the first time. If at all sensitive to the excitements of poetic language and of strange ideas, they may well be intrigued and captivated, yet puzzled. Here, it seems, is something at one and the same time very complex and simple to the point of naïveté, poems (sometimes also prose-pieces or dramas) whose difficulties are of a different order from the arcane, intellectualised or anti-rational obscurity of other modern poetic schools. The many neologisms and occasional use of 'trans-sense language' (*zaum'*) seem not so much flights of absurdism as an effort to pack yet more messages into a poetic texture that we would surely find highly meaningful were we but able to read the clues to these meanings. There is a 'fragmentary' feel to many or most of his works (indeed it is often hard to establish a canonical text of them) that suggests we should analyse them most profitably not as discrete entities, but should somehow contextualise them. What though is their elusive 'context'? Modern scholars have firmly answered this: the context of a given Khlebnikov poem is the totality of his work.[3] It represents a poetic world that in its author's eyes seems to have been contiguous with the phenomenal world or cosmos, yet multidimensional, unconstrained by temporality and attainable through various orders of symbolisation ('trans-sense', myth, the non-literary arts, mathematics etc. as well as 'normal' literary or colloquial language). Khlebnikov's work is full of unexpected transitions, and the most down-to-earth, personal or banal elements melt without warning into macrocosmic considerations.

The direct practical consequences of this remarkable poetic vision for Khlebnikov's idiolect (*idiostil'*, as V. P. Grigor'ev calls it) is an extraordinary interest in, and reliance on, double or multiple verbal and other meanings. Now word-play, phonetic patterning and so on are part of the stock-in-trade of poetry, and are rightly the subject of analysis by those who would understand its workings and savour its aesthetic delights. But for Khlebnikov the whole business of punning, paranomasia, sound-repetition (particularly, but not only, of initial consonants), anagrams, rebuses, palindromes and so on had a particular urgency and significance as symbolising or exemplifying the hidden cosmic interconnectedness, the order and balance of the human and natural world that it was his business to lay bare.

Words, for Khlebnikov, have thus multiple meanings – a 'constellation' of significances (this metaphor is related to his concept of 'starry language'). A word's everyday meaning normally blots out the others, rendering them invisible from the earthbound human standpoint; yet the sun is merely another star, and it is the poet's business to discern, like an astronomer, the word's 'starry intelligence' or range of potential meanings, to realise them and their inter-relationships. This could in practical terms be accomplished in many ways: for example by the placing of the word in 'defamiliarising' contexts, by 'inner declension' (usually a change of one or more of its internal vowels), by substituting new initial consonants (the 'seeds' from which the 'forest of language' could grow), by splitting the word into component syllables, by turning it into an anagram or working it into a palindrome, by transforming it neologistically on the model of other linguistic forms and even by reductive means – through slicing off and discarding part of the word (note the title of his long poem about Persia *Tiran bez Te*), or through the ancient riddling method of designedly *not* mentioning the crucial word. Hidden meaning could also be revealed by counting such features as the recurrence of phonetic units or the internal structural units (parts, maybe letters, lines and syllables) of a literary work. The linguistic material on which Khlebnikov wrought these sidereal transformations was constituted fundamentally by the 'circle of roots', in his phrase, of the Slavonic languages: the roots came from God, while their linguistic elaboration was man-made, and everyday meanings were no more than 'rag dolls' with which mankind played. Clearly the concept of 'meaning' for Khlebnikov was extraordinarily broad – not to be contained within merely 'literary' bounds.

As was suggested above, Khlebnikov's 'eye' operates at various levels in his work and world, playing a key role in establishing his 'polysemy' or 'polysemantics' (Jakobson's term) that we have just outlined. We may categorise the main levels as follows.

THE ARTIST'S EYE

Most straightforwardly, Khlebnikov saw with an artist's eye. He was a good draughtsman, and meticulous drawings and oil paintings survive from the period of his youthful ornithological studies. But he was always sketching – doodles in his manuscripts, self-portraits, portraits of friends (that of Tatlin *c.* 1916 is particularly significant for reasons that will be mentioned on p. 209). Like his colleague Maiakovskii he drew agitational propaganda in the Civil War period. An important sub-category of his drawings are startlingly futuristic architectural plans associated above all with the text *My i doma* (We and Houses) of 1915. Here we should note that the most frequently reproduced fragment of paper carrying such architectural sketches is more likely to date from 1915 to 1916 rather than 1919 or 1920, as editors have normally stated;[4] the difference is significant.

Beyond his drawings and paintings, Khlebnikov brought a strong degree of visualisation into his poetic system of tropes. Normally abstract concepts are startlingly concretised: thus, to take one striking example, the letter M (in the Tenth Plane of *Zangezi*) is concretised as 'humanity's Pole Star, this support-post of all the haystacks of faith', towards which 'sails the boat of the centuries . . . proudly puffing out the sails of governments' and arriving at the 'zamok *Mogu*' ('castle of *I can*').[5] Numbers – the very digits with which he performed his endless calculations – are concretised, more than once as 'towers' but also, for example, as 'number names' (*chisloimena*), as sculptor's clay, even as the old man 'Numbergod' (*Chislobog*), who becomes an *alter ego* of the poet himself. Three more 'towers', to which he must lay siege, are visualisations of the masses, the word and time itself. In a most astonishing metaphor war becomes a fly that lands in the writer's inkwell: 'dying, it crawled some way across the book and these are the traces of the steps it made as it crawled in a sticky lump, all covered in ink'.[6] Time itself is regularly concretised by Khlebnikov, can be painted, can even be torn off in lumps by an artist-warrior crouched in a battlefield trench (in *Ka*; see below, p. 208). More than one scholar has pointed out that 'I have seen . . .' (*Ia videl*), and similar expressions, often serve as introductory formulae to Khlebnikov's poetry, even as a *topos* for poetic inspiration itself[7] – though it should be remembered that Khlebnikov generally, and deliberately, avoided *Ich-Dichtung*: we are dealing with a stylisation rather than a report from personal experience.

An interesting sub-category of Khlebnikov's 'painting with words' is that of concealed portraiture. The classic case of this is the well-known early short poem 'Bobeobi . . .' (1912: see Appendix to this essay): Khlebnikov himself later wrote explanatory notes, mocking a critic's failure to understand it.[8] The striking neologisms that begin each of the poem's first five lines represent the colour pigments through which features of the imagined painting 'are sung', in accordance with guidelines of letter–colour correspondences Khlebnikov more than once laid down (see p. 203). But Vladimir Markov has argued in a conference discussion that the portrait is also evoked and completed through a subtler encoding of the whole *oblik*, the figure portrayed, into the associated neologism *lieeei* in rebus fashion (see section 3 below) through the very forms of its letters: л (l) suggesting tumbling hair, the triple э (è) representing three female curves (!), й (i) a pair of legs. Such a procedure would have been quite characteristic of the poet, as we shall see later, though at the same discussion Mojmir Grygar objected that it would not necessarily have been intentional here.[9] There are other more-or-less disguised 'word-paintings', including portraits, in Khlebnikov. One that deserves attention occurs in the seldom-discussed long poem *Perevorot v Vladivostoke* (Revolution in Vladivostok, 1921), a work to a large extent underpinned by the methods of the Japanese and Russian popular print (*lubok*). One fine passage (see Appendix to this essay), where a soldier's face becomes a whole landscape – over which hovers a blue and gold butterfly, representing the poet himself, as often in Khlebnikov – was well characterised by Markov: 'The picture is like an abstract painting, full of unexpected relationships.'[10] Another class of such portraits are icons, described without being directly mentioned in the riddling periphrastic manner Khlebnikov so often employs. In *Nochnoi obysk* (Night Search, 1921) the unnamed icon of Christ – '*bog v uglu*' (God in the corner) – plays a dramatic role in the plot. In the less-known 'Sayan' (1920–21) the affecting lines invoking an icon as *obraz ubogii* (pitiful image) conclude a poem largely devoted to ancient petroglyphs in the Sayan mountains; the poem, incidentally, is probably a verbal depiction of a picture-postcard or similar view (this happens elsewhere in Khlebnikov). His portraitist's eye is extraordinarily sensitive to colour, as 'Bobeobi . . .' and *Perevorot v Vladivostoke* demonstrate; yet here, as often, these are rather heraldic or iconic than naturalistic colours, above all gold and dark blue, symbolic probably of poetic inspiration. He is capable (e.g. in 'Khadzhi Tarkhan' (Haji Tarkhan, 1913)) of a far more varied set of colour epithets, and in some grotesques (*Vila i leshii* (Vila and the Wood Demon, 1912)) uses deliberately inappropriate coloration: 'Tam nebesa stoiat zelenye' (There stand green skies), 'Moi tovarishch zheltookii' (My yellow-eyed comrade).[11] But in solemn, eighteenth-century mode his colours can be stylised too: e.g. 'Kak osen' izmeniaet sad, / daet bagrets, tsvet sinei medi' (When autumn changes the garden, / giving us crimson, the colour of blue copper) (the opening of 'Poet', 1919 – which, incidentally, portrays yet another icon, of the Mother of God). Sharp as his artist's eye was, Khlebnikov was never in the business of mimesis, his motto would never have been *ut pictura poesis*: his mind's eye was his best creative tool. There is a 'mind's ear', maybe too a 'mind's touch' at work in Khlebnikov as well – but they fall outside the scope of this essay.[12]

TEXT AS VISUAL EXPERIENCE

Russian Futurism is well known for its commitment to the 'self-sufficient word' and to verbal texture generally: a short manifesto of 1913, *Slovo kak takovoe* (The Word as Such) signed by Khlebnikov and Kruchenykh (who describe themselves as 'word-workers' in it) is often cited in this context. Yet 'from the beginning he [Khlebnikov] manifests a certain scepticism' towards the word as 'the complex material of poetry'.[13] A lesser-known manifesto, *Bukva kak takovaia* (The Letter as Such),[14] produced in the same year by the same authors, draws attention to the importance of the visual appearance of written signs; to the autonomous role of handwriting(!) and variegation of typeface in conveying emotion or inspiration; to the early Futurist 'through-designed' books about which 'it is finally possible to say: every letter is perfect'. Thereafter time and again

Khlebnikov suggests the inadequacy of language alone to match the cognitive purposes that underlie his aesthetic: it must be supplemented or replaced by other codes, of which the numerical and the visual are closest to his heart. Sometimes these two codes interact, reinforce each other and are set against that of language: we saw earlier that Khlebnikov envisaged 'towers' of numbers, while in his programmatic statement of 1919 known as 'Svoiasi' ('Self-Statement' in Schmidt's translation) he claims 'Recently I have begun writing with numbers, as Number-Artist of the eternal head of the universe', an art 'developed out of bits and pieces of modern science, just like contemporary painting', and regrets that he can speak of his insights 'only with words, allusive words [*tol'ko namekami slov*]'.[15]

Characteristically, he tackled the problem head on (rather than merely wringing his hands about it) in a conceptually most daring way – with a long manifesto or open letter of universal import addressed to 'The Artists of the World', proposing a 'system of hieroglyphs that the peoples of the planet could hold in common'. Building on his earlier hypotheses (as articulated, e.g. in 'Perechen': Azbuka uma' (Enumeration: An Alphabet of the Mind, 1916)), he presents structural–geometric significances that he intuits for nineteen consonants of the Russian alphabet, implying their cross-cultural validity. Some are quite simple ('ц (ts) means the passage of one body through an empty space in another'), others distinctly complex, indeed hard for the reader to visualise ('п means the increase along a straight line of the empty space between two points, the movement along a straight line of one point away from another and, as in the sum of a point set, the rapid growth in the volume occupied by a certain number of points.')[16] He advances a synaesthetic set of correspondences between certain consonants and colours (see the discussion of 'Bobeobi', above), providing visual hieroglyphs for others. Trusting that 'mute graphic marks will reconcile the cacophony of language', Khlebnikov takes as his starting-point the rather optimistic belief that 'painting has always spoken a language accessible to all', and thus can overcome the misunderstandings and enmities that language in its present fallen state provokes. The proclamation of the primacy of visual art was not new: five years earlier, in a fragment beginning 'My khotim devu slova . . .' (We want a word maiden, 1912) he expressed the rousing wish 'We want the word to follow boldly after painting.'[17] Visual art as the central metaphor for creativity, even for the manipulation of Time, remains characteristic to the end of his life: in the unfinished *Doski sud'by* (Boards of Fate; in Schmidt's version, Tables of Destiny, pub. 1922) he memorably tells us how 'the face of time was painted in words on the old canvases of the Koran, the Vedas, the Gospels and other doctrines. That great face is adumbrated here also in the pure Laws of Time, but this time with the brush of number. . . The canvas contains no words, only precise number, which functions here as a brush-stroke . . . Time-painting has abandoned the indeterminacy of words . . .'[18] Elsewhere, I have argued that among the 'constellation of meanings' evoked for Khlebnikov by *doska*, 'board', was that of 'icon', a concept of self-evident high significance for Russians.[19] Not just painting, but monumental sculpture and visionary architecture remain central in Khlebnikov's visual imagination throughout his mature works. When (in the Introduction to *Zangezi*, 1920–2) he attempts to define the nature of his greatest literary innovation, the *sverkhpovest'* ('Super-tale' or 'Supersaga'), an architectural–sculptural metaphor comes naturally to him: it 'resembles a statue made from blocks of different kinds of stone of varying colours', 'carved from the varicoloured blocks of the Word . . . an architecture composed of narratives', so that 'the artist's building block is no longer the word, but the first order narrative'.[20] For Khlebnikov, at least in his mind's eye, the literary text was not just an auditory and ideological, but equally a visual, experience.

REBUS AND VISUAL PUNNING

There are moments when Khlebnikov treats his text, or elements within it, as a 'rebus' (visual pun or puzzle). This aspect of his method has been little explored by scholars, and Khlebnikov himself does not refer to it directly, but it is closely related to his interest in the text as hieroglyph discussed above. A Cyrillic letter that apparently had inbuilt rebus-type possibilities for the poet was ч (ch), implying by its very shape for him the notion of 'cupping' (*chasha*) or of 'containment'; more esoterically, he related the form of the letter Λ to the irrational number $\sqrt{-1}$, which as early as 1908 he proclaimed a concept of liberation, a contradiction of the past (and which he identified with his own 'stern reason' in a short poem near the end of his life).[21]

Two fairly early works show a range of possibilities within the

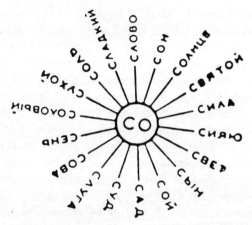

7.1. Diagram from Khlebnikov's 1912–13 essay 'Kakim obrazom v *so* est' oblast' sna' (Here is the way the syllable *so* is a field, 1912–13), showing words radiating out from a central syllable. Russian State Archive of Literature and Art, Moscow.

general area of the self-illustrative, hieroglyphic or rebus-based text. One is a brief theoretical piece beginning 'Kakim obrazom v *so* est' oblast' sna . . .' (in Schmidt's translation 'Here is the way the syllable *so* is a field', 1912–13) (ill. 7.1).[22] Here the interconnections perceived by the poet between a number of words beginning with *c* (s) are explored with the aid of a diagram. The letters *co* (so) inside a circle are surrounded by eighteen lines that lead to words beginning in *c*- (s-). At '12 o'clock' stands *slovo*, the 'word' itself; immediately to its right *son* (sleep, dream) and *soltnse* (sun). All are of particular significance, as of course is the *so* at the centre; it means 'with', and this suggestion of collectivity is reinforced by Khlebnikov's conviction that *s* represents 'the act of multiplication' and 'motion out from a fixed point', while *o* 'increases size'. *Son* is self-referential, as indicating a state of being 'with oneself', reintegrated; but the most dynamic of the concepts linked in this constellation is *solntse*, a word much used in general by Khlebnikov. Its significance is visually signalled by the very fact that the diagram itself is an emblematic 'sun' with the *s*- words positioned as if its rays. It serves as a kind of map of the utopia 'Sunland' (*Solntsestan*).

The second is a lithographed supplement to Khlebnikov's *Izbornik* (Selection, 1914), designed by Pavel Filonov (it contains the poems 'Perunu' (To Perun) and 'Noch' v Galitsii' (Night in Galicia), under

the general title 'From the book *Wooden Idols*'). In his search for a
'primitivistic' manner to match Khlebnikov's vision (Perun was the
pre-Christian Slavs' God of Thunder, and chief of their pantheon),
Filonov not only rejects conventional standards of the beautiful –
preferring, as do other early futurist book designers, intentional
clumsiness, roughness and asymmetry – but abandons normal
typography, in some cases turning the very letters of the text into
hieroglyphs of his own devising, their visual appearance echoing its
verbal associations. Thus the form of the letters of Perun's name
suggests his attributes, spears or thunderbolts, while the word
shipovnik (wild rose) sprouts thorns and the initial letter of *gadiuka*
(viper) writhes. But this 'hieroglyphic' approach should not be
considered a mere exercise in quaint literalism: there is no false
naivety in Filonov's conception, any more than in Khlebnikov's text,
with its avant-garde use of *zaum'* (transrational language). Both
create an idiom in which the modern elements are fused with the
primitivistic: artist and writer equally strive to break through the
bonds of time and human history, seeking the organic links between
past and present, word and object, humanity and nature. It is a
landmark in the history of book design; Khlebnikov was delighted
with it.

Among other possible instances of the rebus type of device in
Khlebnikov are the elucidation proposed by Markov for the 'trans-
sense' word *lieeeo* in the portrait-poem *Bobeobi* . . . discussed above,
and the intriguing possibility that he may have perceived one of his
favourite words, *oko* (eye), in such a way: I devote the last section of
the chapter to this word. In a sense the palindromes that Khlebnikov
particularly relished all have this quality: he perceived them as
'reflected rays of the future cast by a subconscious "I" upon the sky
of the rational mind'.[23] But the final rebus that I wish to mention
here is of a quite different and extraordinary nature. Examining the
manuscript fair copy of the important long poem *Nochnoi obysk* (Night
Search, 1921), the Khlebnikov scholar Raymond Cooke noticed a
passage deleted with horizontal and vertical lines in a 'grid-like'
manner not characteristic of Khlebnikov's usual emendations (ill.
7.2). In a subtle and convincing investigation Cooke relates these to
the typically Khlebnikovian word *reshetka* (grid) and related concepts
that form a 'constellation' of meanings generally, but here have the
specific role of representing the 'barred window' that plays a crucial
role in the poem's dénouement.[24]

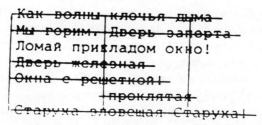

7.2. *Reshetka* (grid)-style deletion in the manuscript of Khlebnikov's narrative poem *Nochnoi obysk* (Night Search, 1921). From R. Cooke, *Velimir Khlebnikov: A Critical Study* (Cambridge, 1987). © Cambridge University Press, 1987.

KHLEBNIKOV AND THE ARTISTS

Khlebnikov knew and worked with the major Russian visual artists of his generation; he also had an interestingly eclectic appreciation of art from a variety of periods and cultures. There are innumerable mentions of individual such figures and works in his writings. That he knew the ambience of artistic life is not in doubt (and not only because his sister Vera was an artist): at any rate two of his works reflect, however distortedly, experiences of *vernissage* parties. The remarkable early drama *Markiza Dezes* (published 1910; the title is probably best rendered The Marquise des S.,[25] though there are other possibilities), a fragmented and in part satirical work, drawing on Griboedov's *Gore ot uma* (Woe from Wit), has such an event as its setting. Less known is a short but haunting prose piece of *c.* 1915, *Son* (Dream),[26] where the terrible real events of the Dardanelles campaign intersect, as a kind of dream-within-a-dream, with the petty concerns of visitors to 'the exhibition $\sqrt{-2}$'. At the centre of the piece Khlebnikov poses what he probably considered the most crucial question any artist or writer could face: 'Is it possible to position oneself between a source of light and a people so that the shadow of one's "I" should coincide with the boundaries of the people?' – a literary or philosophical dilemma characteristically expressed in visual terms.

At one time or another Khlebnikov refers to an unexpectedly heterogeneous selection of visual artists in his letters, diary notes or imaginative works, from Leonardo to Canova, from Murillo to Rops. Often we can do no more than guess what particular quality caught his attention. Sometimes though he reveals more: the neo-classical architect A. Voronikhin appealed to him not only because of his

humble (serf) origins, but because he understood the rule of the
'alternation of the density of stone with the immateriality of air'[27] (a
reference to the great colonnade of the Kazan Cathedral in Petersburg, 1801). The comment comes in *My i doma* (We and Houses; in
Schmidt's translation Ourselves and Our Buildings, 1920–1), his
most detailed, thoughtful and visionary account of a topic that had
always exercised him: the architecture and city planning of the
future.

Khlebnikov was generally scornful of the realist painting of the
later nineteenth century. He knew modernistic French painters and
saw them as operating in similar experimental territory to his own;[28]
but this is not reflected in his writing. Rather, his comments are
directed to Russian moderns from 'the great Vrubel' (i.e. the painter
Mikhail Vrubel', 1856–1910) onwards: they are by turns quirky,
allusive, ironical and penetrating.[29] The Burliuk brothers, Goncharova, Larionov, Lentulov all make appearances; but Khlebnikov
evidently felt closest to the three great conceptual innovators – very
different from each other – Malevich, Filonov and Tatlin. The oldest
of the three, Kazimir Malevich (1878–1935), he perceived as a
'number artist' like himself: 'Proclaiming a free triangle with three
points – the works, the artist and the number – he draws the ear or
the mouth of the universe with the broad brush of numbers', and
concludes from calculating proportions in some of Malevich's drawings that 'Once more in the realm of painting I had observed time
commanding space.'[30] Their fruitful collaboration in the futurist
opera *Pobeda nad solntsem* (Victory over the Sun, 1913) marked a crucial
stage in Malevich's progress towards 'non-objective' Suprematism.

Pavel Filonov (1883–1941) had much in common with Khlebnikov:
both were ascetic visionaries for whom art and life were inseparable
(and both art and life were a battle). Filonov's remarkable work on
Khlebnikov's *Izbornik* (1914) has already been mentioned. For Khlebnikov in 1918 Filonov was 'the beautiful martyr Filonov, who sings
hymns of urban suffering',[31] but the most celebrated description of
him dates from the time of the First World War, when Khlebnikov
writes in his 'Egyptian' tale *Ka* 'I met this one artist and asked him if
he was going to war. "I'm already at war", he answered "only it's a
war to conquer time, not space. I crouch in my trench and grab
scraps of time from the past. It's a tough assignment, just as bad as
you'd have in a battle for space" . . . This painter painted a feast

of corpses, a feast of vengeance. The dead ate vegetables in solemn ceremony, and over them all, like the rays of the moon, shone a grief-stricken madness.' (The reference is to Filonov's 'Feast of the Kings' in the Russian Museum, St Petersburg.) As Alfonsov acutely remarks, such a portrait both 'is and is not' Filonov:[32] it is evident that Khlebnikov subjected his friends and colleagues, just as he did the phenomenal world, to the metamorphic alchemy of his mental processes.

Vladimir Tatlin (1885–1953) was the same age as Khlebnikov, and probably closest of all to him as artist and as thinker.[33] He worked with Khlebnikov on the publication *Mirskontsa* (*Worldbackwards*, 1912), but their affinity seems to date from a chance meeting in the southern city of Tsaritsyn during May 1916. Together with a young futurist poet, D. Petrovskii, they spent a happy if impoverished month there, giving a public performance called *Chugunnye kryl'ia* (Iron Wings); Petrovskii published a memoir of it later.[34] Towards the end of the month Khlebnikov wrote a remarkable short poem about Tatlin, 'Tatlin, tainovidets lopastei . . .' (Tatlin, secret-seer of blades: see Appendix to this essay for the text) and presented it to the artist, who subsequently guarded the manuscript 'religiously, or like a conspirator'.[35] I have analysed this work – only thirty-five words long – in detail elsewhere:[36] it is extraordinarily rich in overt and hidden meaning for both writer and recipient, based as it is on Tatlin's non-figurative sculptural constructions first exhibited in December 1915. It presents Tatlin as a possessor of 'secret vision' (*tainoviden'e*), giving him power to animate 'things' (*veshchi*), a word frequently employed by Khlebnikov for pieces of writing or art objects. During the stay in Tsaritsyn his friends gave Tatlin the nickname *zodchii*, 'The Builder', though he had had no previous connection (so far as we know) with architecture. The fascinating possibility arises that at that juncture Khlebnikov inspired Tatlin with the concept of a vast spirally based project of monumental architecture, one that after the Revolution would become the famous 'Tatlin's Tower' – intended first to commemorate the Revolution, then rededicated to the Third International (if so, art history will have to be rewritten!). There may be an indirect clue in a drawing Khlebnikov made of Tatlin at the time with a spiral motif in the middle of the face (ill. 7.3). I have also argued that Tatlin dedicated at least one non-figurative work of 1916–17 to Khlebnikov.[37]

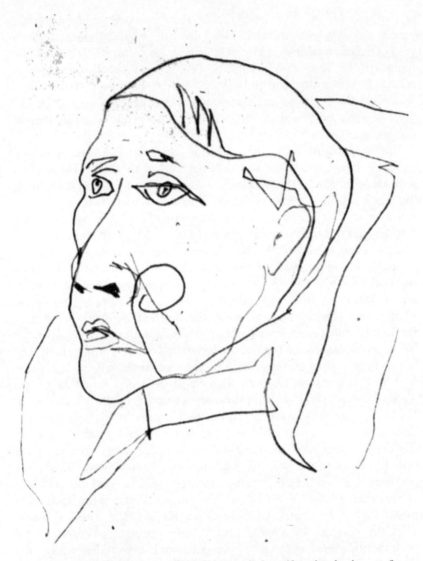

7.3. Sketch by Khlebnikov of Tatlin with a spiral motif on the cheek, *c.* 1916.
Russian State Archive of Literature and Art, Moscow.

Tatlin was shattered by Khlebnikov's early death (1922), and as a posthumous tribute undertook the stage production of his culminating 'supertale' *Zangezi* – a huge task that was a landmark in the Russian theatre of Modernism.

PROPHETIC EYE

At about the time of the fateful meeting in Tsaritsyn, Khlebnikov proposed the creation of a 'detachment of prophetic eyes' (*otriad veshchikh ochei*),[38] in which Tatlin was surely to be counted (maybe the poem to Tatlin marked his initiation into it). What was so significant about *ochi*, 'eyes'? The word *oko* lies at the heart of one of Khlebnikov's most characteristic semantic 'constellations', and it is easily encoded into other words and phrases. Its significances have not yet been explored by scholarship, and it would be appropriate to end a study of 'Khlebnikov's eye' by examining them. I shall not attempt to list or categorise the occurrences of *oko* in Khlebnikov's work, for the simple reason that it is extraordinarily common, doubtless far commoner than in any other twentieth-century poet. Now, as everyone who knows Russian beyond elementary level is aware, the word for 'eye' / 'eyes' in the modern literary and colloquial language is *glaz* / *glaza*, which has displaced *oko* in all save archaic, 'high', self-consciously 'poetic', proverbial and perhaps dialect usages. It is clear though from reading Khlebnikov that he does not always employ *oko* as if it were stylistically 'marked' in such a way – indeed it seems his standard or neutral word for 'eye'. Yet he also frequently uses the word *glaz*: indeed there are some works (e.g. the long poem *Tri sestry*) where it predominates. Research needs to be done into this, with a comprehensive word-count related to context. In any case, 'seeing' is an outstandingly ubiquitous concept in Khlebnikov: I pointed out earlier that many poems begin with 'I saw . . .' or some similar form of words, and it would seem that for him, as for the late-antique or medieval philosophers, sight was king of the senses, the outer symbol of inner knowledge: the eye the link of humanity with the sun and with the cosmos itself.[39]

In its meaning of 'eye' *oko* is straightforward enough, whether or not stylistically 'loaded'. But it also has a second meaning. This emerges from an early prose work retelling part of a myth of the Oroch people of the Amur valley in Siberia. Khlebnikov, who found the Oroch tales in a nineteenth-century Russian-language collection, was delighted by them (considering them the most primitive in the world) and reused them in several works, notably the *sverkhpovest'* ('supertale') *Deti vydry* (Otter's Children). The short piece to which Khlebnikov gave the title *Okó* recounts in dialogue form the first part of a myth relating the incest between a brother and a sister. Not only does Khlebnikov use the word *okó* as the title: he emphasises it by placing it alone as the story's first word. Its meaning has remained obscure, however, to most of the world until a textual note to the recent *Tvoreniia* edition disclosed that for the Orochi *okó* means the female breast. It is scarcely credible that Khlebnikov, of all writers, would not have perceived and relished the remarkable visual coincidence suggested by this fortuitous homonym (a coincidence known colloquially, as it happens, to other Eurasian languages). Since however he did not explain *okó* (though indicating its unexpected stress-accent), the homonym remained a secret between Khlebnikov and those of his readers industrious enough to hunt out an Oroch dictionary.[40] The motif of the bared breast occurs in this story and elsewhere in Khlebnikov: the erotic connotations may come as a surprise to readers who consider him totally otherworldly.

It may be too speculative to suggest this (in the absence of direct evidence), but it seems possible that Khlebnikov perceived *oko*, in both its senses, as a sort of pictogram – given the symmetrical disposition of the two letters *o* that could easily be stylised representations of breasts or eyes. It is of interest that early scribes certainly saw *oko*/eye in this way: many late-medieval Slavonic manuscripts turn *oko* into a rebus or pictogram by placing a 'pupil' in the form of a dot inside each *o* thus: ѺКѺ (the single *o* of the plural *ochi* has two dots placed side by side).[41] This quaint usage, scarcely investigated by scholars, could well have been known to Khlebnikov with his strong medieval interests; but in any case he would have had no difficulty in spotting the pictographic potential of *oko* for himself. Study of the Khlebnikov manuscripts by those specialists fortunate enough to have access to them might reveal further clues (one such will be mentioned below); perhaps we should note the 'breasts' in the form of Ѻ in the highly stylised figure of a water-sprite (*rusalka*) forming a capital cyrillic *P* (R) in Filonov's strange transcription of *Noch' v Galitsii*: see section 3.

It is not worth attempting to list the innumerable words (some of them neologistic) into which the letters *oko* or *ochi* are inscribed in Khlebnikov's work: they are ubiquitous, and include among their number even the people from whom he borrowed the word *okó* ('Orochi'). But it should be remembered that for Khlebnikov palindromes, of which *oko* is of course an example, had particular value. In this role *oko* appears, alone, as the 150th line of the long palindromic poem *Razin*: but it is also incorporated into many other lines of the same work ('Ili venok one vili'; 'Gul rezok, ozer lug'; 'V oko roka okorokov'; 'Pokoi i okop'; 'A kolokol okolo oka'; 'Operiv sokolom moloko svirepo?'; 'Sokol okolo kos', this perhaps the most 'saturated' of all *oko* palindromes!) Space permits mention of only a few other less obvious ramifications of the *oko* nexus. First, there is the evident phonetic connection with the river Oka. This great Central Russian river must be second in importance only to the Volga in Khlebnikov's 'inner geography'. The relationship to *oko* is made explicit in the following small poem, quoted *in toto*: 'Ochi Oki / Bleshchut vdali' (The eyes of the Oka / Shine afar). But another intriguing geographical connection might also have been in Khlebnikov's mind: with Okovskii les (Okov forest), a densely forested region located to the west of Rzhev, at the edge of the Valdai Hills. This is where many of the great rivers of Russia (including the Dnepr and Volga) have their source. Here, according to a remarkable passage near the beginning of the twelfth-century 'Primary Chronicle' (which was brilliantly analysed by Dennis Ward in the 1970s, and with which Khlebnikov would have been familiar) the heart of Russia was located.[42]

Secondly we may observe the use made of (*oko*)/*ochi*/*ochki* in the important poem 'Kamennaia baba' cited earlier. Here *babochki* is made to 'rhyme' homonymically with *bab ochki* (the eyes of women), and the 'eyes' on the wings of the peacock butterfly are suggested without being named. But more remarkable in this poem is the chain of associations that goes *ochi>óko>okó* (a 'missing link')>*moloko>Mlechnyi put'* (eyes-oko-milk-Milky Way). Mere knowledge of the Oroch word *okó*/breast makes 'double sense' of the several references to milk, as in the splendid lines 'Mne mnogo-l' nado? / Kovriga khleba / I kaplia moloka. / Da eto nebo, / Da eti oblaka! / Liubliu ia mlechnykh zhon, i etikh, / Chto ne toropiatsia tsvesti. / I eto ia zabilsia v setiakh / Na setke Mlechnogo Puti. . .' (Do I need much? / A loaf of bread / And a drop of milk / And this sky, / And these clouds! / I love milky women, even those / Who do not hurry to bloom. / And thus I am enmeshed in / The net of the Milky Way); later *oko* (with both associations) is implied without being named in the lines 'Smelo smotri bol'shim motyl'kom / Vidiashchim Mlechnym Putem' (Gaze boldly like a big moth / seeing through the Milky Way).[43] Lastly, the *oko* 'constellation' seems to play a significant role in the long and complex late poem *Sinie okovy* (Blue Fetters) (ill. 7.4). It has always been recognised

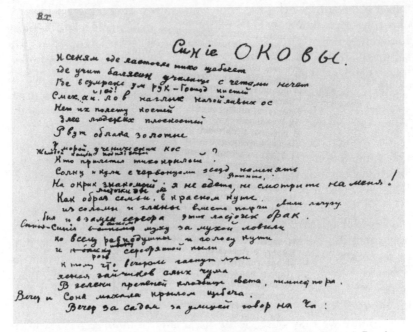

7.4. The manuscript of Khlebnikov's poem 'Sinie okovy' (Blue Fetters). Russian State Archive of Literature and Art, Moscow.

that this title is a lightly encoded reference to *Siniakovy*, the surname of the five remarkable girls with each of whom, according to Lili Brik, Khlebnikov was successively enamoured (and three of whom are portrayed in his *Tri sestry*). The editors of the *Tvoreniia* edition indicate how full of private references and word-play this poem is: but they perform an even greater service by reproducing in facsimile the poem's first manuscript page.[44] Here the three letters *oko* are noticeably detached from, and larger than, the letters before and after them, and the reader is undoubtedly justified in taking the hint to watch for the *óko / okó* 'constellation' in whatever guise it may appear.

For Khlebnikov, the role of the 'seer' or 'painter' was clearly bound up with the 'inner eye', with prophecy and illumination; yet it was not remote from the contemporary world, and the connections could be harrowing. In the same *Kamennaia baba*, the poet describes himself in the aftermath of civil war thus: 'I ia – poslednii zhivopisets /

zemli neslykhannogo strakha' ('I am the last painter / of the earth's unheard-of horror'). Yet only 'eyes' could make the world a better place: one of his best lyric poems ends with the words 'I s uzhasom / ia ponial, chto ia nikem ne vidim, / Chto nuzhno seiat' ochi, / chto dolzhen seiatel' ochei idti!' (and with horror / I understood that I am unseen by all, / That it is necessary to sow eyes, / that a sower of eyes must go forth!).[45] Khlebnikov, ostensibly so esoteric and so sunk in his own preoccupations, turned outward to the world with an urgency that few of his fellow writers could match. He would have counted a harvest of 'perspicacious eyes' his best possible legacy.

NOTES

Abbreviations

CW I & II   *Collected Works of Velimir Khlebnikov*, transl. Paul Schmidt (2 vols.; Cambridge, Massachusetts, 1987, 1989).

MR   W. Weststeijn (ed.), *Velimir Chlebnikov (1885–1922): Myth and Reality* (Amsterdam, 1986).

SP   N. Stepanov and Iu. Tynianov (eds.), *Sobranie proizvedenii Velimira Khlebnikova* (5 vols.; Leningrad, 1928–33).

T   M. Poliakov et al. (eds.) *Tvoreniia* (Moscow, 1986).

Translations are my own, save where I cite CW.

1 There is one good single-volume biographical and critical account in English: R. F. Cooke, *Velimir Khlebnikov: a Critical Study* (Cambridge, 1987). On Khlebnikov and painting, see V. Al'fonsov, ' "Chtoby slovo smelo poshlo za zhivopis' " (V. Khlebnikov i zhivopis')', in A. I. Iezuitov (ed.), *Literatura i zhivopis'* (Leningrad, 1982). In some sections (particularly the last) of this essay I draw on my own article 'Eyes and Icons (Some Verbal-Visual Constellations in the Work of Velimir Khlebnikov)' in M. Falchikov, C. Pike and D. Ward (eds.), *Words and Images* (Letchworth, 1989: a *Festschrift* for Dennis Ward), pp. 85–96.

2 See especially the essays collected in MR.

3 See Hansen-Löve in MR, p. 186.

4 See MR, p. 388; C. Lodder, *Russian Constructivism* (New Haven, CT, 1983), p. 207; V. Khlebnikov, *The King of Time*, trans. P. Schmidt (Cambridge, MA, 1985), p. 115. A pre-revolutionary dating is also likely in view of the use of the old orthography on the sketch.

5 T, pp. 484–5.

6 Cooke, *Velimir Khlebnikov*, p. 160.

7 cf. MR, p. 206, p. 241.

8 SP, vol. v, p. 276; CW, vol. I, p. 404.

9 MR, p. 360.

10 V. Markov, *The Longer Poems of Velimir Khlebnikov* (Berkeley, 1962), p. 193.

11 See ibid., p. 114, p. 109.

12 There is a splendid image of the Futurist as balalaika player with the 'phantom of humanity' trembling on its strings in 'Nasha osnova' (SP, vol. v, p. 243). Elsewhere the poet is 'eternal prisoner of harmony': T, p. 267.

13 V. Dietsch in MR, p. 392.

14 CW, vol. 1, p. 277.

15 CW, vol. 1, pp. 48–9.

16 CW, vol. 1, p. 366, p. 365.

17 CW, vol. 1, p. 246.

18 CW, vol. 1, p. 419.

19 See Milner-Gulland, 'Eyes and Icons', pp. 147–8.

20 CW, vol. 2, p. 331.

21 T, p. 623; CW, vol. 1, p. 314; T, p. 579, p. 177.

22 CW, vol. 1, pp. 272–3.

23 *Ibid.*, p. 147.

24 R. Cooke, 'Chlebnikov's Grid (*Reshetka*): a Missing Key to *Nočnoj obysk*?', in MR, pp. 217–42.

25 So rendered by Schmidt in CW, vol. 11, pp. 218–29.

26 SP, vol. iv, p. 74; CW, vol. 11, pp. 83–4.

27 CW, vol. 1, p. 349.

28 As remembered by Prof. B. Denike; cf. Al'fonsov, *Chtoby slovo*, p. 211.

29 Note his (approving!) comment that 'their work is frequently less a matter of painting than bold attempts to blow up the very foundations of painting' (CW, vol. 1, p. 442).

30 CW, vol. 1, pp. 362–3. Note the recent study by J. Milner, *Kazimir Malevich and the Art of Geometry* (New Haven, 1996), particularly ch. 4 which, among many other relevant points, draws attention to several instances of rebus-type effects in Malevich's paintings of 1913–15.

31 CW, vol. 1, p. 442.

32 Al'fonsov, *Chtoby slovo*, p. 213.

33 Well explored in J. Milner *Vladimir Tatlin and The Russian Avant-Garde* (New Haven, 1983); but scarcely noticed by earlier commentators (e.g. C. Gray; V. Markov).

34 D. Petrovskii, 'Vospominaniia o V. Khlebnikove' in *Lef* 1 (1923), 143–71.

35 D. Danin, 'Uletavl'' in *Druzhba narodov* 2 (1979), 225; Danin had been Tatlin's pupil.

36 R. Milner-Gulland, 'Khlebnikov, Tatlin and Khlebnikov's Poem to Tatlin' in *Essays in Poetics* 2 (1987), 82–102.

37 *Ibid.*, p. 92.

38 See 'Predlozheniia' 1915–16 (Proposals), SP, vol. v, pp. 151–62.

39 Anthropological connections between the sun, the eye and the speaking mouth have been persuasively applied to Khlebnikov by J. Faryno, '*V*

etot den', kogda vianet osennee . . .' in MR, p. 106, pp. 117–18. On medieval optics, see G. Mathew, *Byzantine Aesthetics* (London, 1963), ch. 3 etc.

40 The meaning given in the note in *Tvoreniia* (see above), p. 699, has been kindly confirmed by R. F. Cooke, perhaps the only private owner of an Oroch dictionary in England.

41 I am indebted to Dr W. F. Ryan of the Warburg Institute for an interesting answer to my enquiry about this 'rebus': he mentions the possibility that it derives from the Glagolitic equivalent of the Greek letter omega. The word *okrest* can similarly be found with a cross inscribed in the o. See also D. Worth, *The Origins of Russian Grammar* (Columbus, 1983), pp. 23–4.

42 D. Ward, 'From the Varangians to the Greeks and other matters' in *Gorski Vijenac: Essays Presented to Professor Elizabeth Hill*, ed. R. Auty *et al.* (MHRA Publications vol. II, London, 1970), pp. 303–11. The standard English translation, *The Russian Primary Chronicle*, trans. and ed. S. H. Cross (Cambridge, MA, 1953), pp. 6– 7, somewhat capriciously omits the name of this forest.

43 Had Maiakovskii been reading this passage from his colleague, whom he much admired, when he wrote in one of his last poetic fragments the words 'V nochi Mlechput' serebriannoi Okoiu'? For 'Kamennaia baba', see T, pp. 255–6.

44 T, p. 365.

45 'Odinokii litsedei' ('Solitary Player'), T, pp. 166–7.

Appendices A, B and C

A.   Бобэоби пелись губы,
      Вээоми пелись взоры,
      Пиээо пелись брови,
      Лиэээй – пелся облик,
      Гзи-гзи-гзэо пелась цепь.
      Так на холсте каких-то соответствий
      Вне протяжения жило Лицо.   (1908–9)

      [Bobeobi were sung the lips.
      Veeomi were sung the faces,
      Pieeo were sung the brows,
      Lieeei – was sung the aspect,
      Gzi-gzi-gzeo was sung the chain;
      Thus on the canvas of certain correspondences
      Beyond dimension lived the Face.]

B.   (Extract from *Perevorot v Vladivostoke*)

      В старом городе никого нет, город умер и зачах, –
      Бабочка голубая, в золотых лучах!

Черные сосны в снегу,
Черные сосны над морем, черные птицы на соснах –
Это ресницы,
Белое зарево –
Черного месяца ноша, –
Это глаза.
Золотая бабочка
Присела на гребень высокий
Золотого потопа,
Золотой волны –
Это лицо. Брызгами дерево,
Золотая волна золотого потопа
Сотнями брызг закипела,
Набежала на кручу
Золотой пучины.
Золотая бабочка
Тихо присела на ней отдохнуть,
На гребень морей золотой,
Волны закипевшей.
Это лицо.
Это училось синее море у золотого,
Как подыматься и падать
И закипать и рассыпаться золотыми нитями,
Золотыми брызгами, золотыми кудрями
Золотого моря.
Золотыми брызгами таять
На песке морском,
Около раковин моря.

[In the old town there is no one, the town has died and withered –
A sky-blue butterfly in golden rays!
Black pine trees in snow,
Black pine trees over the sea, black birds on the pines –
Those are eyebrows.
White sun,
White dawn-light –
Burden of a black moon –
Those are eyes.
A golden butterfly
Has perched on the high crest
Of a golden flood,
A gold wave –
That is the face. Wood in shavings,
A gold wave of a golden flood
Seething with hundreds of shavings
Has run up to the edge

Of the golden abyss.
A gold butterfly
Has quietly settled upon it to rest,
On the golden crest of seas,
Of the seething wave.
That is the face.
That is what the dark-blue sea has learnt from that which is gold,
How to rise and to fall
And seethe and dissolve in gold threads
In golden foam, in golden locks,
Of a golden sea.
To melt in golden foam
On the sea's sand
Around the shells of the sea . . .]

1912

C.

Татлин, тайновидец лопастей
И винта певец суровый,
Из отряда солнцеловов.
Паутинный дол снастей
Он железною подковой
Рукой мертвой завязал.
В тайновиденье щипцы
Смотрят, что он показал,
Онемевшие слепцы.
Так неслыханны и вещи
Жестяные кистью вещи.

[Tatlin, secret-seer of blades,
And stern bard of the screw,
From the detachment of suncatchers.
The spidersweb vale of rigging [or tackle]
He into an iron horseshoe
With dead hand has tied.
In secret vision the tongs [or pincers]
Look at what he has shown,
Blind ones made dumb,
Thus unheard-of and prophetic
Are the metal objects of his brush [or hand].]

1916

CHAPTER 8

Cinematic literature and literary cinema: Olesha, Room and the search for a new art form

Milena Michalski

LITERATURE AND FILM: IURII OLESHA IN CONTEXT

The 1920s and early 1930s in the Soviet Union was a period of experimentation and innovation in both literature and cinema. Writers felt that there should be a new Soviet literature, just as filmmakers felt that a new Soviet cinema was needed. The same general issues faced both arts: how to find a balance between elite and mass cultures, between 'proletarian' art and that of non-proletarian writers and filmmakers, whether or not writers and filmmakers should be forced to join organisations and what the Party's role should be.

In the early 1920s filmmakers such as Kuleshov, Pudovkin, Eisenstein and Vertov were keen to find new forms of expression in the cinema which would ensure that film was treated as an art form quite distinct from literature. Formal experimentation with filming and editing techniques to convey meaning was their main concern, rather than questions of plot. However, parallel to the activities of these directors there were also many other filmmakers turning out more conventional films, whose purpose was precisely to tell a story. The great problem these directors faced was the fact that they had to rely on a script as the basis of their narrative films, and there was a serious shortage of these.

Scripts tended to be written, in the early 1920s, by specialist scriptwriters (*stsenaristy*), many of whom were not particularly talented. The authorities attached much importance to the script, and ultimately the scriptwriter was considered to be the person responsible for the failure or success of a film. The script was supposed to convey the ideological message, and it had to be passed by the censorship authorities before the film could be made; the director was then expected to follow it closely. The problem, therefore, was how to produce scripts worth realising as films. For this, there were bodies of scriptwriters and so-called 'script-doctors', working in the 'literary departments' of film studios, who would try to improve other people's scripts. Yet even these writers were often second-rate, or worse. The problem was so bad that in the mid-1920s competitions were held for scenario-writers, but the majority of submissions were rejected, either on ideological grounds, or because they were incompetent in a technical sense.

One solution to the 'script crisis', as it was called, was to try to attract the best writers to the world of film. Although, on the whole, many writers had initially felt the cinema to be unworthy of their contributions, and some, no doubt, had seen it simply as a means of earning money, the number of those who perceived it as a challenge and a chance to try something new grew to include some of the best-known figures of the 1920s and 1930s.[1]

From the early days of cinema in Russia, writers have shown an interest in the medium of film manifested, for instance, in Lev Tolstoi's statement that he wished to write something for the cinema, Andrei Belyi's script for a film of his *Peterburg* and Vladimir Maiakovskii's scripts for and acting roles in the cinema. It is not until the 1920s, however, that one sees a trend amongst writers of using literary techniques which are clearly inspired by film, such as those of the close-up, the fragmented narrative, and 'cinematic' visual metaphors. Several important writers of the period, such as Evgenii Zamiatin, Isaak Babel', Viktor Shklovskii, Iurii Tynianov and Il'f and Petrov, were influenced by techniques of this kind, and became actively involved in film work by writing scenarios.[2] Among the most interesting of these are Shklovskii's *Tret'ia meshchanskaia* (known as *Bed and Sofa* in English) of 1927, Tynianov's *Poruchik Kizhe* (*Lieutenant Kizhe*) of 1927 and 1934 (originally intended as a silent film to be directed by Sergei Iutkevich, but the script was subsequently revised for Aleksandr Faintsimmer's sound film of 1934[3]), and Iurii Olesha's *Strogii iunosha* (*A Strict Youth*) of 1936. The following discussion focuses on *Strogii iunosha*.

The writer of the script *Strogii iunosha*, Iurii Olesha, is best known for his novel *Zavist'* (*Envy*), a book which brought him praise from some quarters and serious condemnation from others, for its unusual style and content. Here, Olesha experimented with fragmentation of narrative, unexpected angles of vision and striking similes, while conveying an ambiguous attitude to the changes wrought by the

Bolshevik Revolution, and the direction in which the Soviet Union was heading. However, Olesha also wrote many short stories, a memoir, plays and film scripts, as well as journalistic pieces and film reviews. Throughout his work there is great emphasis on the visual, lending his work a cinematic quality, which is sometimes explicitly evoked. The culmination of this technique was the decision to try to create a new genre, a hybrid of film script and literary text in its own right, something to be used as the basis for a film, but also to be read for pleasure. The result was *Strogii iunosha*, published in 1934, which was made into a film by Abram Room in 1936. *Strogii iunosha* is of particular interest because it was an experiment in mixing film and literature, an attempt to break down barriers. In a speech to 'scenario writers and writers working in film' in 1936, Olesha expresses his enthusiasm for working in the world of cinema, because he considers it 'a very significant, necessary and pleasant activity for a writer'. He explains that in writing the screenplay *Strogii iunosha* he worked 'as if I were writing a novel, a novella or a short story'.[4] Olesha implies that he feels film work to be as significant, and demanding, as any other literary endeavour. Although Olesha's text provoked much criticism, again, of both form and content, at least it reached the public. Room's film was shelved for more than thirty years. In part, the difference in fates is due to changes in political circumstances, but it was also due to the differing reception of each medium, to the greater immediacy of film's impact.

OLESHA, FILM AND LIGHT

Iurii Olesha was fascinated by the cinema. This fascination operates on multiple levels: the most fundamental of these is that of technology. This forms part of a broader interest in the modern and the mechanical. As a schoolchild Olesha was enthralled by one of cinema's precursors, the Magic Lantern, which he found the most enticing object in a toy shop:

you were simply awestruck, looking at them! . . . and if you had been able to light the lamp inside it, and if it was dark in the place, then you could have put it into action right away: the plate would appear on the wall in the form of a rosy, greenish, carmine illuminated picture of some fairy tale which all children knew.[5]

The device is referred to in Olesha's *Tri tolstiaka* (*The Three Fat Men*), when Doctor Gaspar looks down from the top of a tower, thinking: 'all this looked like a Magic Lantern picture. The sun was shining brightly, the green was blazing'.[6] Olesha is captivated both by what he sees, and by the Lantern itself, as a technological invention.

As with the Magic Lantern, so with the cinematograph. Olesha admires moving pictures as an art, but he is also impressed by the requisite paraphernalia of cinema, which enables these pictures to move.[7] He describes how intrigued he was by the rays of light coming from the projector, as well as how he would watch both the events on screen and the actual projection of the films with equal fascination, dividing his attention 'between what was taking place on the screen and the rays moving above my head'.[8]

In 1896, Gorky famously referred to the cinema as the 'kingdom of shadows', thereby summarising its essence in the interplay of light and shade, which occurs both on the film itself, and subsequently on the screen.[9] Just as light is the life force of cinema, without which there could be no shadows, so it is a crucial factor in Olesha's literature. For Olesha, the sun is the ultimate light, and the closing words of *Ni dnia bez strochki* (*No Day Without a Line*) confirm how obsessive his attitude to the sun is, in life, as in art: 'There was nothing in my human life which could have taken place without the sun's participation, whether fantastic or concealed, whether actual or metaphorical.'[10]

The sun, and light in general, work in two different ways in Olesha's scheme of things, as they often do in the cinema; light either plays with the surface of objects, or people, or appears to radiate from within.[11] Olesha's eye for tricks of the light, his detailed observation and eloquent recording of what he sees, steer his prose towards the diametric realms of poetry and science in terms of content, and towards that of cinema in terms of form.

Olesha conveys fleeting instances of sunlight-play on the page, in the same way that a photographer might capture it on film. This can be seen in numerous examples. Simple versions, such as the image of 'a bright summer's day' recur in variations in many works.[12] In 'Natasha' we read: 'the day was bright and hot' ('iarok i svetel den''); in 'Pervoe maia' ('The First of May') the boulevard is described as 'sun-drenched' ('Zalityi solntsem'); in 'Zrelishche' (The Spectacle) we read that 'The whole picture had a very summery quality' ('Vsia kartina nosila ochen' letnii kharakter').[13] Yet, for all the 'cinematic' qualities of this device, Olesha gives literature as the source of inspiration for it; in 'Pervoe maia' he recalls stories he liked as a child, explaining that 'The colouring of these stories is summery' ('Kolorit etikh skazok – letnii.')[14] In 'Beseda s chitateliami' (A Conversation with my Readers) he says that Wells' *The Invisible Man* is the influence behind the summer colours which pervade *Zavist'* (*Envy*).[15]

In addition to the examples above, there are more complex scenes involving light being refracted through or being reflected from objects. In the story 'Natasha' Olesha describes, as if in passing, a domestic still-life: 'the glass in its holder with a blindingly burning ray of sun on the spoon' ('stakan v podstakannike s oslepitel'no goriashchei v solnechnom luche lozhechkoi').[16] Two other instances of beautifully observed detail, which convey the magical quality of the sun, seem particularly filmic. The first comes from his memoirs: 'And in the blaze of the setting sun a spider's web burns into my eye socket – and it burns like a rainbow. . . A tiny, short rainbow on the circumference of my eye . . .' ('I v bleske zakhodiashchego solntsa zagoraetsia v glaznitse pautina – i ona gorit radugoi . . . Malen'kaia korotkaia raduga stoit na kruge glaza . . .').[17] The second is part of 'Ia smotriu v proshloe' ('I Look into the Past'): 'I open my eyes and in the midst of the blue sky I see a rainbow, because I have tears on my eyelashes' ('Ia otkryvaiu glaza i sredi sinego neba vizhu radugu, potomu chto na resnitsakh u menia slezy').[18] In Olesha's eyes, and in those of his perceptive characters, the everyday becomes special simply through the effect of light. This, as emphasised above, is a device typically employed by painters and filmmakers.

The foregoing discussion focuses on superficial radiance. The following discussion will show the significance of the sun and light, on a metaphorical level, in the work of Olesha. In *Zavist'*, and subsequent works, Olesha uses the sun as an emblem of the 'radiant future', the Communist future. He realises the metaphor by having the sun shine dazzlingly on its representatives (see below). However, Olesha's portrayal of these supposedly ideal young people is not always entirely free from irony. This led many to suppose, rightly, that the writer's sympathies lay more with the older, doubtful generation, that is, with those who were by no means convinced that the future would be ideal and who knew that it would have no place for them.

In his introduction to the play extract 'Chernyi chelovek' ('The Black Man'), which deals with questions of creativity and literature, Olesha sets out the problem of writing for propagandistic purposes, as opposed to creating spontaneously, in the context of his character Zand. Like the post-*Zavist'* Olesha, Zand wants to (or feels under pressure to) write 'a great work about construction, the proletariat, the new man, the life of the young world', which means renouncing a whole series of themes 'which for our times [. . .] are harmful, reactionary even if only because they are pessimistic'.[19] The key to Olesha's sun-symbolism lies here, in the statement that the book Zand longs to write should have a ' "sunny" theme' (' "solnech-n[aia]" tem[a]'), and be 'a work in which the whole of our new life would shine' ('tvorchestv[o], v kotorom siiala by vsia novaia zhizn').[20]

Olesha's cinema style of lighting, whereby certain characters are associated with certain kinds of light, is reflected in his frequent use of the verbs 'blestet'' and 'blistat'' – meaning 'to shine' (in the literal and the figurative sense) – and related words, which are not solely sun-inspired.[21] So, for instance, the description in *Zavist'* of the young Communist, Volodia Makarov, being lifted up after the football match is as follows: 'Diagonally over the crowd the shining, splashing nakedness of a body flew up.' [22] This is related to the idea of the ideal *komsomolets* as healthy, handsome and ideologically pure. Valia, the idealised female of the future, is linked to the sun in a similar way. Moreover, in the play based on *Zavist'*, *Zagovor chuvstv* (A Conspiracy of Feelings), Ivan Babichev explains that woman was the 'light' of the past, and that Valia had seemed to him, erroneously, to be the bridge between the future and the dying past. Although the image here is of light in general, not of the sun specifically, the symbolism is closely related in that Valia was to play the part of a guiding light. He had hoped that 'Valia will illuminate the dying age, she will light up its path to the great cemetery. But I was mistaken.'[23] She does indeed shine and radiate light, but not for him and the past, solely for the future.

FROM CRITICISM TO SCRIPTWRITING: OLESHA'S MOVE
INTO FILM

In the context of Olesha's use of cinematic devices in his literature, it is worth trying to understand the way in which he read other people's writing, and made connections between writing and cinema. An example of film and literature merging applies to a scene by Ernest Hemingway: 'The pace of this scene, the foreshortening, the colouring is so strangely attractive, that you cannot even work out whether you are reading a book, watching a film, dreaming a dream or witnessing an event which is actually taking place.'[24] Here, Olesha uses the terminology of the visual arts in speaking of foreshortening, as well as explaining how the images become moving pictures in the reader's mind.

Olesha is deeply interested in the relationship between film and literature, discussing it in various pieces of writing. In 'Razgovor v foie kinematografa' ('A Conversation in a Cinematograph Foyer'), the narrator expresses his view that cinema would kill the book.[25] This is explained by the idea that the cinema can do for us what we now do for ourselves – imagine. His logic goes as follows: 'We read and ask ourselves: what was it like? In the cinema I also read a book. And what I imagine is on the screen. The viewer in the cinema is a reader with a good imagination. Imagination is sold at the box office. The cinema will render the book redundant.'[26] In an unpublished text of the 1920s, 'Kino-filosofiia' ('Film-philosophy'), Olesha uses the same words, which indicates how important he felt them to be.[27]

In the article 'Beseda s chitateliami' Olesha speaks about the visual aspect of his prose, explaining that 'when I write, I think only about how to get across what I see with the maximum clarity'.[28] Elsewhere he says that while reading, when you close your eyes and imagine what it was like, 'you are working in a similar way to a camera. The imagination works cinematically – it creates frames.'[29] This is why Olesha feels that 'the cinema experience is closer to the act of reading than to that of watching a play'.[30]

Olesha was actively involved in the world of film from the 1920s onwards, as a scriptwriter. In 1921, he wrote two short film scenarios, 'Zolotoe iabloko' ('The Golden Apple') and 'Svoeiu sobstvennoi rukoi' ('By His Own Hand'), for the Khar'kov provincial political educational committee (gubpolitprosvet). These were not published, and the films were not made, but they show that Olesha was already writing for the screen before incorporating 'cinematic' techniques in *Zavist'* and in his short stories. Most significantly, in the Soviet Union in the 1930s a growing body of writers moved into script-writing in response to pleas that writers came to work for the screen, as there was a shortage of good filmscripts. The writers who responded include Il'f and Petrov, Isaak Babel', Iurii Tynianov (who, like Olesha, had already been writing scripts in the 1920s) and Iurii Olesha, with *Strogii iunosha*, in 1934. The same year in a speech on writing for the cinema, at the First All-Union Congress of Soviet Writers, the prominent director and scriptwriter Natan Zarkhi defined the script as a literary work, and as the main factor determining the success of Soviet film. At the Congress, Zarkhi discussed Olesha's scenario in particular, commenting that although the dialogues work on the page, and would work on stage, 'they need a scriptwriter to translate them into cinema language'.[31] Olesha, for his part, published an article about screenplays, 'Kardinal'nye voprosy' (Cardinal Questions), in 1935, in which he explained that he felt he was inventing a new genre with his play for the cinema: 'When I write a scenario, [. . .] I am writing a completely independent work of literature. [. . .] This is [. . .] neither drama nor fiction. It contains too much illustration for drama, and the composition is too bared for fiction. It is a form of its own.'[32]

In 'Kardinal'nye voprosy' Olesha writes that more and more films are being made on the basis of screenplays by writers, meaning that 'the sphere in which those people who paid less attention than anyone else to how the word used to work, is now under the influence of precisely those who specialise in words'.[33] In this essay, too, Olesha raises the question of whether or not a screenplay should be a work of literature in its own right. He gives various existing responses to these questions; for example Béla Balázs feels that a screenplay can never be considered a work of literature to be read in the same way as a short story or novel. There are those who believe a screenplay should be just the bare bones of a film, leaving the details to be decided by the director and cameraman; others, however, believe that a writer should give the director as complete a picture as possible, to provide him/her with a full vision to realise on screen.

Olesha's personal feeling is that he himself is unable to write an inspired screenplay without doing it as an independent literary work. He hastens to add that 'of course [. . .] I do not forget for a second that what I am writing must be transformed into visual images'.[34] It is precisely through this dual aim that, in Olesha's view, a new genre comes about: 'This is neither drama nor fiction. There is too much painting here for drama, and the composition is too exposed for fiction.'[35]

Perhaps unsurprisingly, Olesha attempted a cinematic plan for
Zavist' (in 1928–9). The treatment was never published and the film
was never made, but brief extracts of the plan do exist. These reveal
something of Olesha's vision.[36] As in the novel, the writer emphasises the play of light on objects, as well as reflections and unusual
perspectives. What appears to be the opening scene features a white
door: 'A white high door, taking up almost the whole of the screen';
bright lighting and the use of a close-up are the significant factors
here.[37] A few lines further on light again plays a key role: 'A wall,
with a sink next to it. [. . .] a thick mirror [. . .] a strong lamp.
Everything sparkles in this light: the sink, the mirror, metal bits and
pieces on the sink, scent-bottles.'[38] Finally, although crossed out by
Olesha, the following lines further indicate that for him perspective
and light are of major importance to the composition of a shot: 'A
bright sunny background of sky. At the bottom of the screen, on the
side, taking up only part of this empty background, a little platform
is visible, evidently, at a great height.'[39] In the novel the equivalent
scene is indicated, less graphically, but effectively, simply by: 'The
balcony hangs in mid air.'[40]

Although many critics and readers were impressed by Olesha's
striking literary style in *Zavist'*, and many sympathised with his
ambiguous attitude to the Communist world being built up around
him, the book quickly came to be seen by the authorities as
ideologically subversive and its style overly complex for the general
reader and therefore elitist. Olesha was shocked by the severity of
the criticism, and decided that he would try to write a more
ideologically straightforward and positive work, one which would be
more accessible to a broader readership in terms of structure and
imagery. Consequently, in his speech at the Congress of Soviet
Writers, Olesha said: 'I want to create a type of young man who will
represent the best of my own youth [. . .] Communism is not only an
economic but a moral system as well, and this aspect will be
embodied predominantly in its young men and women.'[41] He
proclaimed: 'I personally have set myself the task of writing about
young people. I will write plays and stories in which the characters
solve problems of a moral nature.'[42] This is precisely what Olesha
did in *Strogii iunosha*.

Strogii iunosha, Olesha's film script of 1934, is the culmination of the writer's decades-long enthusiasm for film; the text is an anthology of Olesha's cinematic techniques, and a demonstration of the meta-phorical resonance of these.

With *Strogii iunosha*, Olesha set out to write a work whose atmosphere would be suffused with sunlight; however, like Zand in 'Chernyi chelovek', he was unable to escape the darkening shadow of troubling questions, the 'chernaia tema-iashcheritsa' 'the black lizard-theme', as he called it.[43] Despite, or because of, such ideolo-gical shadows, Olesha declared, in various public interviews (most famously in his Speech at the Soviet Writers' Congress of 1934) that he would try to look forward, to write about young people as the hope of the future, in short, to be positive.

Typically, in *Strogii iunosha*, Masha's first encounter with the handsome young Communist, Grisha, takes place in the sun, where it is specifically and symbolically associated with him: 'a young man stands in front of Masha now, on the grass, amongst the daisies, in the bright glare of the sun'.[44] To the same end, Grisha's friend 'Diskobol', another example of the perfect *komsomolets*, and therefore a man of the Communist future, is vividly bathed in sunlight: 'His tanned body shines in the sun'.[45] Also in 1934, in a journalistic article, revealingly entitled 'Krasota sily' ('The Beauty of Strength'), Olesha describes a festive parade full of beautiful young people, about to work on constructing the metro system, and the whole scene is sun-drenched:

The town, the factories, the construction sites, the metro tunnels – and right in the middle of town, on the square, drenched in sun, are the young people, many of whom today will go down into the tunnels to perform something which is equal, in its beauty, gracefulness and accuracy, to the circus or the ballet.[46]

Significantly, in Olesha's *Strogii iunosha*, Masha's husband, the bourgeois *intelligent* Dr Stepanov, never shines. In a transparently symbolic scene, Grisha and Masha catch sight of each other in a crowd, outside. Stepanov sees Masha and wonders 'Why is her face shining? [. . .] Stepanov wants to know what is making Masha's face shine.'[47] This is because a boy is directing rays of sunlight with a mirror. He shines it on to Stepanov's face, but instead of reflecting it, the Doctor is temporarily blinded, and cannot see Grisha when he tries to see what Masha is looking at. All this light play led one critic to mock Olesha's obsession: 'the stunning game with brilliant and dazzling objects, that is what captivates Olesha, like a child. He has rushed to the cinema to captivate everyone with this game.'[48] This scene is omitted from the filmed version, perhaps because it is too obvious as an image, or perhaps because it is too complex to film.

One of the most frequent applications of Olesha's cinematic style of writing is to descriptions of stadiums, as the subject-matter offers obvious opportunities to play with perspective and sunlight.[49] The sports stadium plays a significant role in *Strogii iunosha*, as it is where the young people gather to train and talk; it is a symbol of striving towards mental and physical perfection. In Olesha's text the size of the playing field is emphasised by the description of Diskobol and Masha, on separate occasions, appearing to be small figures in the distance to someone looking down at them. In the filmed version, the stadium is filmed from above, looking huge and deserted, as a lone figure walks across it. Such cinematic vision is typical of Olesha's prose, and recalls his description of some film footage of a Spanish bullfight. The bullfight film draws his attention both for its content and for the way in which it is shot. His description of it is revealing as much for what Olesha focuses on as for the imagery with which he chooses to describe what he sees. Many elements which characterise Olesha's style of writing can be found in this extract, from the mention of sunlight to the interest in perspective.

Olesha introduces the recollection with a general observation on contemporary documentaries: 'Contemporary documentary films are shot very epically, employing the techniques of feature films (foreshortening, close-ups).'[50] This already reveals the writer's eye for camera techniques, and what they can achieve. As for the content, Olesha describes it using metaphorical language to maximum visual effect. Describing the stadium, Olesha sees it in a way others would be unlikely to: 'At first I saw a section of a circus, of some sun-drenched coliseum, which, since it was shown in wide-angle view, resembled a cut watermelon with swarms of seed people.'[51] Moving on to animate objects, cinematic devices continue to feature in the analysis as the scene becomes still more vivid: 'Then there was a fleeting close up of two near-naked, sun-drenched Spanish women fanning themselves. Then I saw a medium shot of a picador on a horse, which he was making stand almost on the spot, and take compressed, springy steps in anticipation of the bull.'[52] Finally, Olesha shows how disorientating a close-up can be, making the objects almost unrecognisable because of their unnatural size: 'And suddenly almost the entire length and breadth of the frame was taken up by two figures – that of the bull and the matador!'[53] This is the kind of perspective Olesha uses in his own work.

These examples reveal Olesha's use of cinematic techniques to some extent, but his most explicit use of cinematic imagery occurs in a simile, in which he compares a moment in a football match, when the ball has been kicked into the crowd and the players watch in utter surprise, to a freeze-frame from a film: 'Thus a motion picture stops all of a sudden at the moment of a break in the film, when the light has already been switched on in the auditorium, but the projectionist has not yet managed to turn off the light, and the audience sees the strangely whitened screen and the contours of the hero, absolutely motionless in that pose, which speaks of the most rapid movement.'[54]

Further evidence of Olesha's interest in film techniques can also be found in a particularly effective passage from *Strogii iunosha*, which adopts the characteristics of early, silent, moving pictures. Here, a jealous Dr Stepanov watches Masha and Grisha flirting in the distance, through binoculars, longing to know what they are talking about. On the page, as on screen, it is *his* view which is given: 'He sees: lips moving. Masha is laughing. One would suppose loudly. But Stepanov cannot hear anything. For him it is silent cinema.'[55] In a different vein, in 'Liubov'' (Love), Olesha has Isaac Newton (in a dream) see 'his grey, photographic world through glasses'.[56] The words which describe his vision echo those of Olesha's narrator from 'Razgovor v foie kinematografa', as he identifies a paradox of early films, the ability to make what looks artificial seem natural: 'nature, people, objects, everything is bathed in one and the same grey, photographic colour, and everything is silent, everything is grey and everything is silent – and this does not disturb us, does not amaze and irritate us? Herein lies the power, the secret of art. A lie becomes truth.'[57] This passage reveals much about Olesha's intentions in his own work, as well as intensifying the underlying link with film. If early films seem unreal because of their lack of colour, Olesha's descriptions sometimes seem unreal because of their intensity of colour. Yet, ultimately, at their best, both are convincing.

STROGII IUNOSHA

The film *Strogii iunosha* was the result of a collaboration between a writer and a filmmaker, both of whom had achieved a certain notoriety in the late 1920s in their respective fields. The collaboration between filmmaker and writer was initiated by Olesha. He wrote the screenplay with Room in mind and expressly chose him to direct it. This may seem strange, given that Olesha was explicitly trying to reach an accommodation with political demands. Room had already had some difficulties, as a film director, with the authorities of the time. Nonetheless, Olesha's political and artistic ambitions were met with some degree of goodwill in the official film world and the picture was given the biggest budget of the year at Kiev's Ukrainfil'm studio.

As in Olesha's case, with *Zavist'*, 1927 was the year Room made his first impact on the public, with the excellent film *Tret'ia Meshchanskaia*.[58] Like Olesha, again, his work is about the old and the new, and the struggle to change bourgeois attitudes. Co-scripted with Viktor Shklovskii, it concerns a ménage-à-trois, in which the pregnant heroine chooses freedom over both possible fathers, her husband and her lover, leaving them to live together happily ever after without her. Questions of contemporary morality, social and sexual issues are all present here, as in *Strogii iunosha*, although in the latter film political ideology plays the greatest role.

After *Tret'ia Meshchanskaia* Room made nineteen more films. In 1933 he began work on *Odnazhdy letom* (*One Day in Summer*), Il'f and Petrov's adaptation of their novel *Zolotoi telenok* (*The Golden Calf*), but in March 1934 The Ukrainian Directorate for the Cinema and Photographic Industry, VUKFU, removed Room from *Odnazhdy letom* and struck him off the list of filmmakers intended for future projects.[59] Then, when it came to *Strogii iunosha*, the State Directorate for the Cinema and Photographic Industry, GUKF, warned Ukrainfil'm that they were taking a risk by allowing Room to make such a serious film, but the studio supported him – to its cost.[60]

The plot of *Strogii iunosha* concerns a romantic triangle, in which a young *komsomolets*, Grisha, is in love with Masha, wife of a celebrated surgeon, Doctor Stepanov. This is no mere private issue, however, since it is complicated by ideology. Seeing that the doctor is favoured by the authorities, Grisha feels that it would be *anti-Soviet* to steal his wife. His friends, fellow Komsomol members, try to persuade him that the doctor is committing a crime against socialism by abusing his power over another man, in trying to keep Grisha away from Masha (such 'possessiveness' was also considered to be a negative, bourgeois trait). However, Grisha disagrees, claiming that the doctor's power is pure, because he is a genius and therefore deserves special treatment. There is also a parasitical hanger-on, Tsitronov, who lives at the Stepanovs', who represents the worst of decadent bourgeois lifestyles. The culmination of the film's ideological message comes when one of the young women falls ill and the doctor saves her life, thereby *serving Communism*. During her recovery he talks to the young people and is won over by their words. He is amazed to hear that Komsomol members, who talk about aiming to raise themselves to the level of the best, include in this category not just engineers, but also those who create science, technology, music and who struggle with nature, such as doctors. This is the real message, that the intelligentsia have a place as long as they work with, rather than against, the creators of the radiant, socialist future. The notebook kept for Room by his assistant Lelekov during the filming of *Strogii iunosha* suggests that the film recounts how the moral and ethical outlook of an old member of the intelligentsia, Stepanov the doctor of genius, is transformed under the influence of the new young people.[61]

CRITICAL RESPONSES TO *STROGII IUNOSHA*

Olesha often said he wanted people to debate his work, but perhaps even he would have wished for less controversy. His screenplay 'Strogii iunosha' was discussed in Moscow and Kiev even before being published in *Novyi mir* in August 1934. In Moscow there were meetings at both the Dom sovetskogo pisatelia and the Dom kino. The participants of the former included Vsevolod Meierkhol'd, to whose then wife Zinaida Raikh the work was originally dedicated, and who, it was hoped, would play a minor part in the film (which he did not), Aleksandr Fadeev and Viktor Shklovskii. Shklovskii felt that the work would be fine if only Olesha were not trying to pass it off as a scenario. Meierkhol'd, with a touch of playfulness, said Olesha must be *implored* not to work directly for the cinema, but to write a story and get those who understand the nature of film better to translate it into the language of the screen. Yet the article in *Sovetskoe iskusstvo* of July 1934 reporting on this meeting claimed that all those taking part unanimously stressed that *Strogii iunosha* was a great creative success. The journalist explained that in his cine-play Olesha had for the first time examined the important issue of the new person, new socialist feelings and relations, concluding that in terms of his concept Olesha's cine-play was a literary work of profound philosophical significance.[62] Olesha was trying to create a new literary genre with his 'play for the cinematograph'. It was to have a dual function, acting as a guideline to the filmmaker, but also serving as a work of literature, worthy of being read in its own right.

As soon as it was published, Olesha's *Strogii iunosha* provoked much more negative criticism than this. In 1935, in an article entitled 'O geroiakh' ('On heroes'), although praising Olesha for understanding that the new hero needs new moral and philosophical principles, the critic N. Zhdanov condemned him for making the characters so unlifelike and abstract.[63] That same year, in 'O chuvstvakh sotsialis-ticheskogo cheloveka' ('On the feelings of socialist man'), another critic, Kulikov, said: 'Instead of the richness and brightness of socialist individuality, instead of living people, *Strogii iunosha* has dead outlines, dry abstractions, shadows with no flesh. Their spiritual life is extremely simplified and primitive. They are neither worried nor joyful and do not stir the reader.'[64] He also pointed out that the characters' abstraction was emphasised by the generalised names some of them are given, such as 'the discus thrower', 'the girl', 'the sailor'. Clearly these were meant to represent 'types' of idealised Soviet youth, but it was considered a problem because it was thought young people would not be able to identify with these characters, and the script's propagandistic potential would be lost.

A further problem was that although the script was meant to be set in the future, it portrayed a world very close to contemporary reality. This upset those who felt there could be no place for the intelligentsia in the future. The discussions about genius and equality were considered pretentious. One supremely biting reviewer, Dmitrii Maznin, wrote a long review in *Literaturnaia gazeta* in the style of the screenplay. Here the characters bemoan the lines and roles they have been given. For example, Stepanov, discussing who the reader will worry about at the end of the play, says it will be 'about me. That's clear. Ol'ga has recovered now, Grisha Fokin has stopped being stubborn, it's clear Masha loves him [. . .] but what will become of the old *intelligent*, of the husband who had so recently been a happy husband, whose dazzling wife has betrayed him?'[65] Elsewhere

Masha says that it is ridiculous that the problem should be whether Grisha might be destroying the happiness of a genius – in such a situation it is not Grisha's and Stepanov's characters which are being tested. For it is not they who can settle the question, but Masha alone.[66]

In 1936, in a speech to 'scenario writers and writers working in film', Olesha looks back on the fate of his script and Room's film. Here, under still greater political pressure than at the time of writing, he explained that he came to realise the script's flaws in the subsequent two years, but that he felt that the film based on it did contain worthwhile elements. For this reason, Olesha felt that the film should not have been taken off the screen. The writer further explained that neither he nor Room know why the film was not shown, but Olesha puts it largely down to the change in political circumstances between his starting the script in 1933, and the film's making in 1935: 'In two years much had changed. There was much I had not understood when I wrote the scenario. All the same, it seemed to me that it was worth showing it, because there were some accurate things there.'[67] It is clear, therefore, that although the idea of a sophisticatedly literary, yet functional, 'play for the cinematograph' was exciting, particularly for a writer who had hitherto been working to 'improve' other people's second-rate film scripts, in practice it very soon came up against significant problems.

On reading Olesha's work for the production department at Ukrainfil′m, Iukov, the official responsible for guiding the filmmakers who were making the film, produced his 'Conclusion regarding Iu. Olesha's scenario *Strogii iunosha*'. This contains complaints that the moral code discussed by Grisha is too removed from social concerns; the character of Masha is too superficial; the ending is too ambiguous (Masha and Grisha kiss, then she goes back to her husband); there is too little emphasis on Stepanov's behaviour as a leading representative of the intelligentsia.[68] The criticism, then, is that ideologically the film does not convey the desired, inspiring message, that it does not convince the viewer of a radiant Communist future. More seriously, Olesha's characters' discussions about genius and equality were considered pretentious, and, in general, *Strogii iunosha*'s underlying idea that suffering is part of the human condition under any political system was deemed to be 'philosophical pessimism directed against the Communist ideals of the revolutionary proletariat', as phrased by the director of Ukrainfil′m, Tkach.[69]

Nor was the scenario the only controversial element in *Strogii iunosha*. On a page headed 'Reshitel'no borot'sia s brakom v kinoproizvodstve' ('Doing decisive battle with shoddy workmanship in the film industry'), the newspaper *Kino* published a piece on the film *Strogii iunosha* in July 1936, entitled: 'Pouchitel'naia istoriia' (An instructive story). It explained that the screenplay's thematic complexity and its weaknesses should have instigated the head of Ukrainfil'm to ensure that Abram Room was particularly careful in his work as director, and corrected the failings of Olesha's text. But, the commentary continues, not only did Room not improve Olesha's text, but the film actually emphasised the text's ideological shortcomings. It celebrated 'the idea of a technocracy, of mankind being doomed to suffer, the opposition between the hero and the masses'. He summed up by stating that 'The director realised the film's impoverished ideological content in an extremely aestheticised form. As a result, the film, which has taken nearly two years to make and cost about two million roubles, has turned out to be ideologically and artistically shoddy.'[70] Similar views are expressed in *Radians'ke kino*, where the commentator Iurchenko also argued that the positive aspects of Olesha's script had been removed, yet the faults remained. He added that even the cameraman Ekel'chik's professional expertise and skill had only played a negative role in the film.

We can see, then, that Room's *Strogii iunosha*, like Olesha's, was severely criticised for its form, as well as its content. Just as the writer's prose was seen as overly stylised and metaphorical, so the look of the film was regarded as excessively decorative and glamorous. A large part of the film's generous budget went towards the construction of magnificent sets. These included a swimming pool, expertly used in Grisha's dream sequence. This scene was very much in the extravagant style of Hollywood, designed to achieve a fantastic, impressive effect. Ultimately, however much guidance Olesha gave to Room in his text, it was the director who had to find ways to realise such seemingly impossible visions, and to convey the ethereal quality of the scene in a way not necessary for Olesha. It was the stylised sequences, such as the dream, which provoked criticism of the film's style, and caused some to brand it 'formalist'. Ideologically, therefore, many critics deemed it pointless and empty, although there were those who admitted that, aesthetically, the film had spectacular moments.[71]

FROM THE 'CINEMATIC' TO THE CINEMA: ROOM AS INTERPRETER OF OLESHA'S TEXT

With all adaptations, one of the key factors which alter the author's original conception is the director's agency.[72] Any film version of a literary text is an interpretation, adding something of the director's vision to the text. Often, literary commentators see this in terms of a loss of sophistication; but, in fact, a gifted director (like any other talented individual) interprets creatively, not only stripping away detail, but also enhancing and augmenting the original text.

With the case of a writer whose work is itself self-consciously 'cinematic', a very particular process of collaboration comes about. Olesha's language centres on creating visual images, revolving around optical points of interest, particularly unusual perspectives and light play, which would, to the uninitiated eye, appear to act almost as directions and natural bridges to the director and the lighting and camera operators. Yet, in practice, any attempt to recreate such effects on screen is likely to be problematic. This is partly because 'cinematic' effects drawn from pre-existing film may seem hackneyed and predictable when transferred to the screen, but it also emanates from the status of 'cinematic' devices in the literary text, the fact that they are perceived as 'quotations' from another artistic mode. Such citations of cinematic language in the literary text are an important case of what Bakhtin named as *chuzhoe slovo*, or 'the word of the other'; the identical device, put back on the screen, becomes merely part of the everyday language of film. Finally, there is the fact that 'cinematic' light effects may make technical demands that are in fact unrealisable in terms of actual cinema technology.

It is important to remember that Olesha intended *Strogii iunosha* not only as a guide to the filmmaker, but also as a text suitable for private reading. This explains why it contains several entirely unfilmable passages. The clearest example of this is the description of the characters. With Olesha's characteristic admiration of the male body, Grisha is described as follows:

'There is a type of male appearance which has developed as a result of the evolvement of technology, aviation, sport. From under the leather peak of a pilot's helmet, a pair of grey eyes, as a rule, look out at you. And you may be sure that when the pilot takes off his helmet it will be fair hair that gleams before you. [. . .] Light eyes, fair hair, a thin face, a triangular torso, a muscular chest – such is the modern type of male beauty. This is the beauty of the young men who wear the 'GTO' badge on their chests. It comes about from frequent contact with water, machines and gymnastic equipment.'[73]

Only some of this can be conveyed on screen, although much is typical of literary and filmic stereotypes of the 1930s.

However, Room's interpretation indicates his determination to remain faithful to the visual world of *Strogii iunosha* in a broad sense and to the governing motifs in Olesha's imagery.

Instances of how Room and his cameraman, Iurii El'chik, adapted and intensified Olesha's 'cinematic' devices are made manifest by the notes taken by Room's assistant following viewing of the rushes for the opening scenes, which provide insights into the process of achieving the film's idiosyncratic style. One note comments that plot elements should be cut in favour of atmospheric shots of water and light-play. A case in point is the scene of Masha bathing:

Move away from the impression that Tsitronov is observing Masha bathing and significantly shorten this in favour of her bathing and her walk in favour of the sea and 'shadows'.[74]

A second instance of creative adaptation concerns close-ups. In keeping with the writer's affection for this device *per se*, rather than any specific directions at given points of his script, the director and cameraman make use of this technique at various stages to great effect. As the note book puts it, the desired effect was 'a pictorial hermeticism of elements, so for example the dog can be incomplete in the frame, the head incomplete, the hand incomplete, the cigar incomplete [. . .] but just the start of them, a part of them, half of them, so that there is a world beyond the frame, so that objects do not end in the frame and so on. The next frame is linked to this one.'[75]

Other visually striking aspects of the film are also adapted from hints in Olesha. For example, the description of the Stepanovs' luxurious surroundings is broken down shot by shot: 'Through the interlacing wrought-iron bars of the fence, he sees: an orchard. Clumps of trees. A dacha. A kitchen-maid, running with a tray. On the tray there gleams a bucket containing ice and bottles of wine'.[76] This method is explained in the following way: 'Although it is transparent, the style of filming gets across the confused lines of the subjects' contours: it recalls Japanese drawings on silk.'[77]

8.1 A scene from *Strogii iunosha* (A Strict Youth), showing a light-saturated image shot behind decorative metal-work ('the interlacing wrought-iron bars of the fence'). Dovzhenko Film Studio Museum, Kiev.

If the visual richness of Olesha's text is still further enhanced by Room's filming, the psychological atmosphere of the household is also conveyed through the music. Like the other elements of the film, this is very carefully chosen for its metaphorical resonances: 'Waltz-like jazz. The tender, resounding strains of harps interweave. It is a musical characterisation of the dacha, of Tsitronov, which reflects the confusion and opacity of relations in the Stepanov household.'[78] Like the music, the light creates an atmosphere which perfectly conveys the emotional and psychological timbre of Olesha's text: 'The light must convey an impression, the emotional side, the colour of the film – which is poetic. It is realistic, yet unrealistic. The hot day does not penetrate. Evidently, we need something sort of dappled, moving trees, something a little fantastic.'[79]

The technical mastery of Room's *Strogii iunosha* is apparent in many instances, including the task of filming white on white. For example, this meant white plates on a white tablecloth, or figures dressed in white against a white background. Such scenes require

8.2 The dream sequence from *Strogii iunosha*, showing the metal flowers attached to cork floating on water. Dovzhenko Film Studio Museum, Kiev.

great lighting and photographic skill, in order to avoid looking washed out or simply indistinct. Even the critics who condemned the content of such aesthetic scenes as politically pointless usually did not fail to acknowledge the masterful photography and technique.

Room's and Ekel'chik's cinematographic skill and imagination are, though, most evident in Grisha's daydream sequence, where he kisses Masha. Although there is no specific description of the dream-like atmosphere, only of people and objects, in Olesha's text, Room conveys the unreality and beauty of the shimmering fantasy (see ill. 8.2). To this end, chairs and columns were mounted on to poles rising from the pool, and a 'path' was similarly supported, so that when the water was still it looked like a mirror. Then the water rippled, by means of a kind of water-mill, the furniture folded and was submerged and metal flowers attached to cork were released from the bottom of the pool. The sets were more than six storeys high; over 5000 metres of gauze were used to film through to achieve a surreal, hazy effect, more than 400 lights were used. At the centre of this mirror-like platform are Masha and Grisha, and Dr Stepanov by a piano, which is being played. When Stepanov tells his wife to leave as she is in the way, Grisha comes to her defence, saying she cannot be in the way as 'She is music itself.'[80] To prove this he lifts her arm: 'Her arm sings'; he strokes her hair: 'Her hair sings'; he lays his head on her breast: 'Her heart sings' and he kisses her, revealing that 'Her kiss sings.'[81] When he kneels at her feet, kissing and embracing her: 'All of her sings', and the music becomes 'Masha's melody'.[82]

An important aspect to be considered in regard to the transformation from book to film is the abstract nature of the word. Perhaps the most characteristic trait of Olesha's prose is his use of imagery, simile and metaphor. His comparisons are often quite idiosyncratic, impossible to realise on screen (other than in surreal animation, perhaps), intended for the individual imagination alone. Faced with such a text, the film director must do what he can, sometimes keeping to the original idea, at other times inventing filmable equivalents of his own.

Given that one of the main criticisms of Olesha's screenplay was its abstraction from reality, it had generally been expected that Room would correct these perceived errors of the script. Instead, Room intensified them, making the characters still more symbolic. In the written text, for example, Grisha is described as getting off the train 'brushing off, as it were, traces of the crush in the railway carriage. It's as if he were straightening out his crumpledness.' As contemporary critics were quick to point out, this passage could not be filmed as it was, with its metaphoric language. More than this, one would expect there to be crowds at the station. Instead the young man is shown emphatically alone, in quite an unnatural way, partly to emphasise his outsider status in the world he has come to visit. This can be compared to the scene showing Masha swimming. In the written text other bathers are mentioned walking past her as she goes home. In the film, again, she is strikingly alone. With both Masha and Grisha, the viewer's first glimpse of them is from behind, therefore faceless, symbolically generic rather than realistically specific.

Grisha is further shown as less 'real' than in the text, because he does so little. In the 'silent cinema' scene described above, Grisha fixes the Stepanovs' car when it breaks down as Masha is driving him to the station. Room, on the other hand, makes the young man watch passively, as *Masha* repairs the engine. As the critic Iurchenko mocked, Grisha is always impeccably shaven, his trousers carefully pressed, and is afraid to dirty his hands and ruin his suit![83] Finally, in Olesha's text, Grisha is shown fixing a tram cable. To paraphrase Iurchenko again, Room, the director, and Ekel'chik, the cameraman, deprive Grisha of this possibility of rehabilitating himself. Instead, they show him and his friend chariot racing, in a scene totally absent from the literary original. This emphasises them as classical 'types', removing them further from everyday existence.[84]

A key scene, in which Grisha expounds his ideas of morality, is filmed as a series of tableaux, with semi-naked, athletic, young men and women posing as they talk. Iurchenko condemns Room's use of retardation of movement in this scene, as well as its statuesque quality. He says the figures turn into pseudo-classical sculptures in light and shade. This makes them unreal and ineffective as images of Soviet youth. Their dialogue is unnatural and unconvincing; like-wise, their athletic posturing and idealised physiques.

The undertone of irony that both Olesha and Room employed with respect to their portrayal of these supposedly idealised young people suggests that any public statements about embracing the new world wholeheartedly should be carefully considered, rather than taken at face value. One example of an ironic depiction of the young protagonist involves Grisha, who is less than the ideal courageous *komsomolets*, hiding from the woman he loves out of fear. His friend, Diskobol, asks him: 'Which moral quality, according to your theory, are you putting into practice at this moment? Shyness? In my opinion it's cowardice.' He then decides to carry out Grisha's principle of honesty and tells Masha and her husband, who have turned up at the stadium, that Grisha is in love with her. As Grisha arrives and hears what is going on, Doctor Stepanov points out with dignity: 'Masha, I think this conversation is stupid',[85] leaving the young people looking foolish.

A further example of such irony shows Stepanov coming to apologise to Grisha for having jealously banned him from his party, and re-inviting him. Once more, Grisha hides, leaving his comrades to deal with the situation. Eager to let him hear the good news that Masha also wants him to come, his friend reveals his hiding place: the wardrobe, as in all good farces:

[Grisha] FOKIN: I will not come. A Komsomol member should have pride.
STEPANOV: A man is standing in a cupboard and talks about pride. A
  Komsomol member should have a sense of humour . . .[86]

The future has little chance of radiating moral and physical perfection if this is a typical example of the young Communist building it.

Another tongue-in-cheek scene involves Doctor Stepanov, who is
due to go to a medical conference in London, and his assistant, who
asks the doctor to bring him back a hat. Stepanov is outraged at the
suggestion that he should be racing around the shops, 'Me, a
member of the English Academy.'[87] The real offence here, in the
eyes of Tkach, director of Ukrainfil'm, was that Stepanov invokes the
English Academy as a symbol of his standing, as if the Soviet
Academy of Sciences were not impressive enough![88] Olesha's and
Room's sense of irony was far from being shared by all.

Given the 'formalist' character of Room's film, and its failure to
'correct' Olesha's text in an ideological sense, it is entirely predictable that the official 'Decision of the Ukrainfil'm Trust on the
banning of the film *Strogii iunosha*' includes criticism of Room for not
improving Olesha's script, but rather adding to its flaws. In addition
to this, the 'Decision' condemns the work for 'the crudest deviations
from the style of Socialist Realism'. It states that Room is to be
dismissed from the post of director; Ekel'chik is to be reprimanded,
and Neches, director of the studio while the film was in production,
is to be brought before the 'direktivnye organy' (directive bodies).
The studio's deputy director was also removed from his post. In spite
of all the problems caused for him by the banning of *Strogii iunosha*,
Abram Room did not leave Kiev, but he did not make any films in
1937 or 1938, having been demoted to assistant. Room directed his
next film, a war film, *Eskadril'ia N⁰· 5 (Squadron no. 5)*, in 1939.[89]

CONCLUSION

Iurii Olesha was clearly fascinated by film, and the influence of
cinematic techniques can be found throughout his work. Having
taken the bold step, with *Strogii iunosha*, of trying to create his own
type of film script, which he intended to stand as an independent
piece of literature too, Olesha raised important questions regarding
literary adaptation. Room's film of *Strogii iunosha* confirmed that

there were difficulties in transposing a work from one medium to the other, yet it also proved that, if inspired and determined, a director and cameraman can create their own vision, which is at once independent from and close to the original source.

The literary critic V. Pertsov wrote of Olesha's text that: 'The play for the cinematograph *Strogii iunosha* awaits its adaptor, some great artistic director. A. Room's interesting attempt has not exhausted its profound content';[90] however, he does not provide any convincing substantiation for this, and from a non-ideological viewpoint there is no doubt that Abram Room did succeed in making a visually ravishing film, developing stylistic qualities which Olesha merely hinted at. At the same time, Room took up Olesha's sense of irony and humour and used them to great effect, retaining the playfulness which made the original story more than a mere schematic outline of moral and political issues. Yet, when political constraints are imposed, from without and within, as they were on Olesha, and to an even greater degree on Room, and the artists constrained, aesthetic qualities cannot fail to be severely threatened. If, in such circumstances, the artists attempt to put creative experimentation before ideological content, as Olesha and Room did, they risk denying their public access to their work, since it is likely to be banned. A 'safer' film might have been a more successful one; a diluted version of formalism would have reached the public more easily than Room's and Olesha's collaboration.

But this would have been to deny the experimental ambition of this creative team. The greatest significance of both these versions of *Strogii iunosha*, then, lies not in their content, or even in their form, although both are formally innovative, but, above all, in the fact that they mark transitional stages in their creators' lives, and are courageous and complex attempts to reconcile art and politics, as well as to fuse literature and film.

NOTES

1 On this and related issues see Peter Kenez, *Cinema & Soviet Society 1917–1953* (Cambridge, 1992), pp. 79–83.
2 For detailed surveys see S. D. Gurevich, *Sovetskie pisateli v kinematografe (20–30-e gody)* (Leningrad, 1975) and Jerry Heil, 'Russian writers and the cinema in the early 20th century – a survey', *Russian Literature* 19 (1986), 143–73.

3 See Jerry Heil, 'Jurij Tynjanov's film-work. Two filmscripts "Lieutenant Kize" (1927, 1933–34) and "The Monkey and the Bell" (1932)', *Russian Literature* 21 (1987), 353–5.

4 'Stenogramma soveshchaniia kinodramaturgov i pisatelei, rabotaiush-chikh v kino. *Sektsiia dramaturgov.* 23 November 1936'. RGALI, SPSSSR (Soiuz pisatelei SSSR), f. 631, op. 2, ed. khr. 173.

5 Iurii Olesha, *Izbrannoe* (Moscow, 1974), pp. 359–60. For a more detailed account of Olesha's experiences of, attitude towards and influence by the cinema see Milena Michalski, 'Iurii Olesha: Cinematic Interests and Cinematic Influence', *Slovo* (London), 8/2 (November 1995), 33–43.

6 Olesha, *Izbrannoe*, p. 100.

7 The physical and technological aspects of early cinema-going are vividly described in an unpublished article by Olesha: Iu. Olesha, 'Zhizn' moia zamechatel'na uzhe tem . . .', RGALI, f. 358 (Olesha), op. 2, ed. khr. 451.

8 Ibid.

9 'Maxim Gorky, The Lumière Cinematograph (Extracts)', in Richard Taylor and Ian Christie (eds.), *The Film Factory: Russian and Soviet Cinema Documents 1896–1939* (Cambridge, Mass., 1988), p. 25.

10 Olesha, *Izbrannoe*, p. 558.

11 Elizabeth Klosty Beaujour suggests that the difference in meaning is as follows: 'Surface light is laughing light, but real blessedness is usually represented by Olesha in terms of an object's or person's ability to absorb light, hold it, and thus possess it. Surface light is playful.' See *The Invisible Land: A Study of the Artistic Imagination of Iurii Olesha* (New York and London, 1970), p. 60. Beaujour also discusses H. G. Wells' image of the idyllic garden in 'The Door in the Wall', seeing it as using light in a similar way. As will be shown, Olesha cites Wells as an influence in this very respect too.

12 Olesha, *Izbrannoe*, p. 310.

13 Ibid., pp. 221, 218, 262 and 274 respectively. In the last of these quotations, the word 'kartina' could suggest a film as well as a painting.

14 Ibid., p. 259.

15 Olesha, 'Beseda s chitateliami', *Literaturnyi kritik* 12 (1935), 157.

16 Olesha, *Izbrannoe*, p. 263.

17 *Vstrechi s proshlym. Sbornik materialov Tsentral'nogo Gosudarstvennogo Arkhiva Literatury i Iskusstva SSSR* 6 (Moscow, 1988), p. 310.

18 Olesha, *Izbrannoe*, p. 225.

19 Olesha, 'Chernyi chelovek' in Iu. Olesha, *P'esy. Stat'i o teatre i dramaturgii* (Moscow, 1968), p. 272.

20 Olesha, *P'esy*, p. 272.

21 *The Oxford Russian–English Dictionary* (Oxford, 1985), p. 33. This also offers: 'to glitter', 'to sparkle', again not only in the literal sense.

22 Olesha, *Izbrannoe*, p. 87.

23 Ibid.

24 Ibid., p. 509.

25 Kazimiera Ingdahl, *A Graveyard of Themes: The Genesis of Three Key Works by Iurii Olesha* (Stockholm, 1994), p. 147. Here, Olesha explains that Victor Hugo saw buildings as having been like books in that they were repositories of knowledge, they used to be decorated with statues, bas-reliefs, characters, and people used to learn from buildings.

26 Ibid., p. 147.

27 Olesha, 'Kino-filosofiia', RGALI, f. 358, op. 2, ed. khr. 407.

28 Olesha, 'Beseda s chitateliami', 155.

29 Iurii Olesha, 'Zakaz na strashnoe', *30 dnei* 2 (1936), 34.

30 Ibid.

31 'First Congress of Soviet Writers (Extracts)', in Taylor and Christie (eds.), *The Film Factory*, p. 332; *Pervyi Vsesoyuznyi s"ezd sovetskikh pisatelei 1934. Stenograficheskii otchet* (Moscow, 1934), pp. 464–6.

32 Iu. Olesha, 'Kardinal'nye voprosy', *30 dnei* 12 (1935), 46.

33 Ibid., 45.

34 Ibid., 46.

35 Ibid.

36 See Jerry Heil, *No List of Political Assets: The Collaboration of Iurii Olesha and Abram Room on "Strogii iunosha"*, [A Strict youth (1936)], Slawistische Beiträge, vol. 248 (Munich, 1989), p. 97. Heil writes that the plan was written with Evgenii Cherviakov, who was supposed to direct it, in the late 1930s, but the extract at RGALI is dated as 1928–9 by the archivists. For more on Evgenii Cherviakov (director, actor and script-writer, 1899–1942), see S. I. Iutkevich (ed.), *Kino: entsiklopedicheskii slovar'* (Moscow, 1986), p. 482.

37 Iurii Olesha, 'Belaia vysokaia dver', zanimaiushchaia pochti ves' ekran', RGALI, f. 358, ed. khr. 199, op. 2, p. 1.

38 Ibid., p. 2.

39 Ibid.

40 Olesha, *Izbrannoe*, p. 15.

41 *Pervyi vsesoyuznyi s"ezd sovetskikh pisatelei*, p. 236.

42 Ibid. Strangely, Olesha did not mention his screenplay *Strogii iunosha* here; an extract had already been published a month earlier in *Novyi mir*, and the complete work was to appear there six days later.

43 Olesha, *P'esy*, p. 272.

44 Olesha, *Izbrannoe*, p. 304 (section 11). Hereafter, references to *Strogii iunosha* will be given using page and section numbers, but omitting the word 'section'.

45 Ibid., p. 311 (22).

46 Iurii Olesha, 'Krasota sily', *Vecherniaia Moskva* 169 (25 July 1934), 1 (unnumbered).

47 Olesha, *Izbrannoe*, p. 331 (40).

48 Dmitrii Maznin, 'Grisha Fokin otmezhevyvaetsia. Konferentsiia geroev "Strogogo iunoshi" ', *Literaturnaia gazeta* 143 (459) (24 October 1934), 2 (unnumbered).

49 For example, in the story 'Stadion v Odesse' ('A Stadium in Odessa'), a stadium is explicitly linked to the idea of optical special effects (Olesha, *Izbrannoe*, p. 258). Similarly, in *Zavist'*, a football pitch viewed from above is vividly bright and filmic (Olesha, *Izbrannoe*, p. 82). Finally, in the unpublished article 'Doroga na stadion' ('The Way to the Stadium'), Olesha again gives a view of a stadium from above and uses the idiosyncratic play of sunlight to give the impression of waching a film. Yet Olesha uses a simile which could never be adequately conveyed on screen, despite sounding cinematic: 'The stadium suddenly opens out in all its glory. Through one of the arches you go out onto a stand and the stadium lies before you. It is below you and in the distance and all around. It is a giant place full of people. The side opposite you looks like the high bank of a river, strewn with shining pebbles. Those are the spectators' (Iurii Olesha, 'Doroga na stadion', RGALI, f. 358, op. 2, ed. khr. 375, pp. 4–5).

50 Olesha, *Izbrannoe*, p. 462.

51 Ibid.

52 Ibid.

53 Ibid.

54 Ibid., p. 86.

55 Ibid., p. 308 (19).

56 Ibid., p. 200.

57 Ingdahl, *A Graveyard of Themes*, p. 148. This was part of a draft chapter for *Zavist'*, but was not included in the final version.

58 For more on Abram Room's life and works, see I. Grashchenkova, *Abram Room* (Moscow, 1977).

59 'Reshitel'no borot'sia s brakom v kinoproizvodstve. Pouchitel'naia istoriia', *Kino* (28 July 1936), 2.

60 Ibid.

61 Lelekov's notebook is in Room's files at the Dovzhenko Film Studios in Kiev.

62 ' "Strogii iunosha" – Pervaia kinop'esa Iu. Oleshi', *Sovetskoe iskusstvo* (5 July 1934).

63 N. Zhdanov, 'O geroiakh', *Literaturnyi sovremennik* 9 (1935), 159–60.

64 I. Kulikov, 'O chuvstvakh sotsialisticheskogo cheloveka', *Volzhskaia nov'* 8–9 (1935), 88.

65 Maznin, 'Grisha Fokin otmezhevyvaetsia', 2.

66 Ibid.

67 'Stenogramma soveshchaniia kinodramaturgov i pisatelei, rabotaiush-chikh v kino. *Sektsiia dramaturgov.* 23 November 1936'. RGALI, SPSSSR (Soiuz pisatelei SSSR), f. 631, op. 2, ed. khr 173.

68 Iukov, 'Zakliuchenie na stsenarii Iu. Oleshi "Strogii iunosha"' (28 July 1934) in 'Partitura postanovki fil'ma "Strogii iunosha"' held at the Dovzhenko Film Studios.

69 Tkach, 'Postanovlenie tresta Ukrainfil'ma o zapreshchenii fil'ma "Strogii iunosha" ', *Kino* (28 July 1936), 2.

70 *Ibid.*

71 Scenes in Grigorii Aleksandrov's 1936 film *Tsirk* were also similar to those created in Hollywood; the cameraman on *Tsirk*, Vladimir Nil'sen, and some other members of the Soviet film industry had actually been taken to Hollywood, in 1935, by Boris Shumiatskii, head of the film union and notoriously anti-'formalist', to see how things were done. However, there is a crucial difference between the use of a Hollywood style in these two films: the content of Aleksandrov's scenes 'proved' that the Soviet Union was not only as developed, artistically and technologically, as the United States, but even better, because it was ideologically superior. In *Strogii iunosha* the desired effect was purely aesthetic pleasure.

72 For consideration of this question with reference to the theatre, see Cynthia Marsh's chapter in the present volume.

73 There were many films made about pilots during the 1930s, the most famous of which is Raizman's *Letchiki* of 1935, reviewed by Olesha, which also glorified such 'types'. The 'GTO' (Gotov k Trudu i Oborone: Ready for Labour and Defence) was a young Communists' physical training group; Olesha has Grisha invent a list of moral qualities which all 'GTO' members should adhere to; this is fictitious.

74 'Partitura postanovki fil'ma "Strogii iunosha" ', p. 3.

75 Ibid., p. 97.

76 Ibid., p. 47.

77 Ibid., p. 22.

78 Ibid., p. 22.

79 Lelekov's notebooks on the filming of Room's ' "Strogii iunosha" ', p. 99.

80 Olesha, *Izbrannoe*, p. 322 (32).

81 Ibid.

82 Ibid. A similar image and concept is used seven years earlier by Olesha, in *Zavist'*, as Kavalerov hallucinates feverishly about Valia being literally transported by an orchestra into his arms: 'The sound of the instruments held her in the air. The sound carried her . . . The last passage threw her to the top of the stairs and she fell into Volodia's arms. Everybody stepped aside. The two of them alone remained in the circle' (Olesha, *Izbrannoe*, p. 92). This passage seems absurd on the page, yet it is easily visualised by the reader.

83 I. Iurchenko, 'Za sotsialisticheskuiu narodnost' kinoiskusstva', *Radians'ke kino* 6 (1936), 7.

84 Ibid.
85 Olesha, *Izbrannoe*, p. 313 (23).
86 Ibid., p. 333 (41).
87 Ibid., p. 327 (37).
88 M. Tkach, ' "Strogii iunosha" i ne strogie rukovoditeli', *Kino* (26 July 1936).
89 Grashchenkova, *Abram Room*, p. 175.
90 V. Pertsov, *'My zhivem vpervye'. O tvorchestve Iuriia Oleshi* (Moscow, 1976), p. 63.

CHAPTER 9

Meaningful voids: facelessness in Platonov and Malevich

Andrew Wachtel

As the fin de siècle approaches, one question that comes up with increasing urgency in Russian studies is: what artists or works expressed the quintessential truth about Russia's cruel experience in the twentieth century? Many plausible candidates can and have been proposed: the fantastic and grotesque visions of Mikhail Bulgakov in *The Master and Margarita*, the pathos of Osip Mandelstam's late lyrics, the monumental litany of suffering recounted in Aleksandr Solzhenitsyn's *Gulag Archipelago*, the passionate agony of Dmitrii Shostakovich's string quartets, or the wistful poignancy of Boris Pasternak's *Doctor Zhivago*. In this essay, I advance the candidacy of Kazimir Malevich (1878–1935) and Andrei Platonov (pseudonym of Andrei Klimentov, 1899–1951): in particular, I will be focusing on what I see as the analogous works they produced in the period from 1928 to 1935 – in the case of Malevich a series of figurative paintings, his first since well before the Revolution of 1917; and in the case of Platonov his great novels *Kotlovan* (*The Foundation Pit*) and *Chevengur*, as well as some shorter stories. In this period, I will argue, both artists attempted to find an adequate expression for Soviet reality, a reality they accepted and in which they probably believed. Most probably unaware of each other's work, through a parallel use of devices of depersonalisation and depsychologisation – figured variously in their different media, of course – they created a series of profoundly troubling, ambiguous works which have not lost their power to move viewers or readers to this day, works that can stand as monuments to their century.

In 1928 Kazimir Malevich embarked on a cycle of paintings that differed radically from the work he had produced in his previous period. Turning away from the abstract, geometric shapes of his suprematist paintings, Malevich returned to figurative art in a series of canvases which, for the most part, depict volumetrically shaped peasant figures *en face* against spartan backgrounds. The figures themselves are distinguished by the bright colours of their clothing as well as by a complete (or, in some cases, almost complete) lack of facial features.[1] What interests me is why Malevich chose to produce paintings of this sort and how they should be interpreted. As far as interpretation goes, the key question to be answered concerns the significance of the faceless figure. To understand these paintings, I propose first to ask what artistic trends and pressures might have led the artist to return to figurative painting at this time. Next, I will focus on the device of facelessness both in Malevich's painting and in analogous literary works by Platonov. I will try to elucidate both what Malevich and Platonov thought their works were about, and explain why and how it is that these works express so much more than they intended.

The first interpretive step is to note that in the context of Russian art of the late 1920s a return to figurative painting provided a potential route for Malevich to integrate his work with mainstream artistic trends. As any student of Soviet culture is aware, the period stretching from immediately after the Revolution of 1917 until the mid-1920s was one of remarkable artistic ferment; avant-garde trends existed cheek by jowl with proletarian art movements and incipient Socialist Realism. In the latter half of the 1920s, however, this pluralism gradually disappeared, and artistic movements that succeeded in linking communist ideology with more traditional (nineteenth-century for the most part) artistic forms began to get the cultural and political upper hand.[2] For avant-garde and modernist writers who had remained in the Soviet Union the pressure to become 'Soviet' artists intensified, both because publication and exhibition were gradually closed to those outside the official fold, and also because in many cases these artists genuinely wished to assist in the creation of the new society. The trick was how to do so without sacrificing their artistic principles entirely. Malevich undoubtedly faced something of this dilemma. His suprematist work had come increasingly under attack in the Soviet Union by the mid-1920s, and we know that he left much of it in Germany after his 1927 European shows, at least in part for safekeeping. Yet we also know that he was basically sympathetic to the goals of the new regime and, like his poetic counterparts Mandelstam and Pasternak,[3] he both needed and desired to play a role in the artistic development of the Soviet Union.[4] To do so, he would have to come to some kind of accommodation with officially approved artistic currents which, in the world of visual art, would have meant first and foremost a return to figurative painting.[5]

Malevich's specific choice of subject-matter in this period can also be understood, at least in part, as an attempt to carve out a place for himself in the world of Soviet art (see e.g. ill. 9.1). To be sure, scenes of peasant labour had been important for the artist in his pre-suprematist work, and it is therefore possible to see these new paintings as a personal synthesis of his primitive (in subject-matter) and suprematist (in colour and form) periods.[6] But even if partly traceable to the internal factors of Malevich's biography, such a synthesis surely had external causes too, given that peasant scenes were quite acceptable, even common, in the politically correct artistic work of the day, and the achievements of collectivisation (which was just getting under way at the time Malevich began his new peasant series) was a favoured theme in mainstream Soviet art. Even in their anti-perspectival monumentality, Malevich's peasant figures do not flout Soviet conventions. If anything, they seem to be a response – perhaps parodic, perhaps not – to contemporary works like G. Riazhskii's *Delegate* (1927) and the peasant paintings of Sergei Gerasimov.[7] Thus, as regards their theme, their concern with figuration and their monumentality, Malevich's second series of peasants can be read as an attempt by the artist to find a compromise with the leading trends of Soviet art.

If this was his goal, however, it did not entirely succeed. Even had he wanted to, Malevich probably could not have produced work acceptable in official circles. For Soviet official criticism was not interested in compromise with independent artistic thinkers; the abject subjection of hacks was far preferable. Nevertheless, just as Mandelstam and Pasternak, in their attempts to become Soviet artists, produced poems that resembled in some respects the work of official writers and that differed significantly from what they had done before, so Malevich changed and adapted his art in the direction of mainstream trends without joining them. What most strikingly sets Malevich's paintings apart from the works of his socialist realist counterparts, of course, is the absence of facial features on his peasant figures, an absence that is central to the impression they produce.

The primary feeling that strikes me in looking at Malevich's canvases of this period is one of disorientation. At first glance, there appears to be enough information present to read them. We have to do with a venerable genre: the rustic scene (we recognise the rural setting, the peasant clothes, and even the peasant bodies). But traditional rustic scenes show peasants labouring (this was true, for example, of Malevich's earlier series of peasant paintings). In these works, however, the people are usually standing still, *en face*, often without so much as a tool in hand. Actual farm labour, if it is figured at all, is relegated to the background, while static figures dominate the foreground. Thus, based on their poses, it appears as if the foregrounded subjects of the paintings think they are the subjects of an entirely different genre: the portrait.

The portrait is, of course, one of the oldest genres in painting, but it remains ever-popular because it serves both as an illustration of how individuals are viewed in a social context and as a focus for changing conceptions of personal identity. What do we expect from a portrait, and what do we see in it, particularly if it is not a portrait of ourselves? Most obviously, when seeing the face of an individual in all of his or her particularity, we attempt not only to interpret his or her personality, but we find in the portrait an affirmation of our own. That is to say that for the viewer, the portrait functions equally to call attention to the existence of others and to remind us of the very possibility of selfhood. As Richard Brilliant puts it: 'Making portraits is a response to the natural human tendency to think about oneself, of oneself in relation to others, and of others in apparent relation to themselves and to others. "To put a face on the world" catches the essence of behavior in the social context; to do the same in a work of art catches the essence of the human relationship.'[8] Malevich's faceless paintings function precisely to disturb this central interactive aspect of the portrait situation. Instead of providing a window on to the soul, the blackness of the face in *Krest'ianka* (Peasant Woman, 1928–32) (ill. 9.1), for example, seems an impenetrable, even terrifying shield. We are staring not at a person, but at the shell of a person, a void. And that void reflects back on us, calling into question our own existence as a self. The impression is, if anything, even stronger in group portraits like *Devushk: v pole* (Girls in the Field (1928–32), because the individual empty faces of the collective's members are echoed by the absence of interaction (see also ill. 9.2).[9]

Are these paintings optimistic or pessimistic, tragic or comic?[10] To be sure, the emptiness of the faces and landscapes produces a feeling

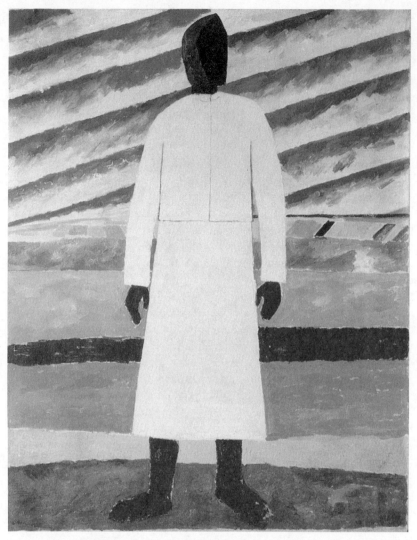

9.1. Kazimir Malevich, *Krest'ianka* (*Peasant Woman*, 1928–32), oil on canvas, 98.5 × 80 cm. Russian Museum, St Petersburg.

9.2. Kazimir Malevich, *Tri zhenskikh figury* (*Three Female Figures*, 1928–32), oil on canvas, 47 × 63.5 cm. Russian Museum, St Petersburg.

of existential hopelessness, even terror. But the bright colours of the clothing and the land lend a certain brightness to the scene, which serves partially to balance the depression evoked by the blank faces. The flatness and emptiness of the background suggest an inhospitable environment, a place in which starvation – a reality of the time in any case – is lurking about. Yet the volumetric, heavy bodies of the peasants do not seem threatened in any immediate way. Indeed, their very monumentality suggests they have conquered the land. In the end, all we can say is that the world depicted by Malevich is one in which bodies are present but minds have no place, a world devoid of psychology and selves. But what does this world mean?

At this juncture it is worth considering other faceless portraits to see whether the device in and of itself produces the emotions I am describing. Let us look, to begin with, at the work of Giorgio di Chirico, who produced a whole gallery of more-or-less faceless

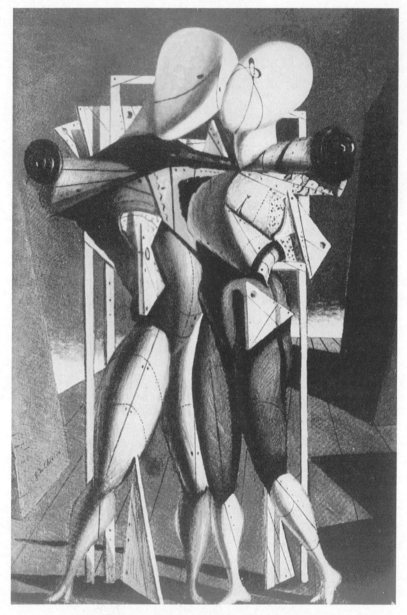

9.3. Giorgio de Chirico, *Ettore e Andromache* (*Hector and Andromache*, 1946).
Oil on canvas. 82 × 60 cm. © Foundation Giorgio de Chirico.
Licensed by VAGA, New York

(although none has a completely blank face as far as I have been able to ascertain) figures between 1914 and 1917.[11] In the case of *Hector and Andromache* (1946, Gianni Mattioli Foundation, Milan, ill. 9.3), we perceive not a psychological blank but a love story which is all the more concentrated by the lack of faces. What is important here (and absent in Malevich's faceless portraits) is the interaction of bodies. We feel a dichotomy between dead matter (the tailor's dummies of which the figures are composed) and living passion, a favourite theme of modernist art (the ballet *Petrushka*, for example).[12] In the case of *Troubadour* (1917, Collection Carlo Frua de Angeli) we are struck by the detailed background of the building and attracted by the mystery of the shadow that is falling across the right foreground. Is the troubadour being punished (that is, is he attached to the pillar against which he stands), or is he in revolt against matter (his forward-striding 'futurist' gait, reminiscent of Boccioni's sculpture of a male figure in the Museum of Modern Art in New York)? Whatever the interpretation one prefers, there is no lack of psychology here despite the absence of facial features, nor are the works unreadable. If anything, the blank faces concentrate our attention on other aspects of the paintings, making them easier to interpret.

Matisse also experimented with faceless portraiture, although, again, his works produce quite a different effect from those of Malevich. Take, for example, the 1916 painting *Le Peintre et son modèle* (ill. 9.4). The artist is shown in three-quarter view, but his features cannot be seen. The model is seen face on (we also see her uncompleted portrait from the same angle), equally devoid of facial features. The absence of faces here does not appear to be a commentary on the inner psychology of the two figures, however, but rather a device to focus the viewer's attention on the act of portrait painting. What is more, the blankness of the faces is offset by other details which are lacking in the Malevich works under consideration: the carefully rendered landscape seen out of the window, the oriental mirror over the model's head, and the painter/model interaction all speak, even if the faces do not. One could read this painting as a commentary on the unimportance for the artist of the individuality of his model (her nullity, in a sense). But the fact that Matisse produced a number of highly psychologised portraits of individuals (for example, the *Portrait de Madame Greta Prozor* or *Les Trois sœurs*, both of 1916) in this same period undercuts such an interpretation.[13]

The most 'Malevich-like' painting of Matisse's *œuvre* of this time is

9.4. Henri Matisse, *Le Peintre et son modèle* (*The Painter and His Model*, 1916–17).
Oil on canvas, 146 × 97 cm © 1999 Succession H. Matisse, Paris/Artists
Rights Society (ARS) New York.

Les Demoiselles à la rivière (1910–17).[14] This work does approach the
blankness of Malevich's paintings from the 1920s, but even here
there are important differences. We have a title and landscape that
point to the women's activity. The central figure seems to be
preparing to dive into the water, while the figure on the left appears
to be shaking water off herself. Nevertheless, in their opaqueness to
psychological interpretation these figures do produce an effect somewhat analogous to that produced by Malevich's peasants, although
not as far-reaching. Some of Matisse's work from the 1930s (most
notably his definitive version of *La Danse* (in the Barnes Collection,
1932–3) again features faceless figures, but here the facelessness is
easily explicable by the artist's desire to have us concentrate on the
painting's subject. This is not a portrait of an individual or individuals but of the dance itself; as a result, facial features are
unnecessary.

A few years after Malevich's experiments, René Magritte used featureless faces, but again his treatment of this subject produces a completely different impression than does Malevich's. In the painting *L'éternité* (1935) Magritte depicts a blank bust between busts representing Jesus and Dante. The point is clearly not the blank portrait itself, but its relationship to the figures that surround it. We are meant to wonder who should occupy that blank space, or whether the busts of 'real' people are more full of content than the blank one. We should also note in this context Magritte's portraits of Edward James, *The Pleasure Principle* and *La Réproduction interdite*, both of 1937. Here I would agree with A. M. Hammacher, who says that 'In the two portraits Magritte made of James [. . .], this ultra-individualistic, eccentric Englishman did not become "the man without a face" but rather "the man with the hidden face".'[15]

The point of this survey is to show that although the faceless portrait was a fairly common device in European art of the 1910s, 1920s and 1930s, it is a device with a multitude of potential meanings. If we wish to interpret the faceless portraits of Malevich recourse to comparisons with superficially similar works by his European contemporaries will not be of much help, because their paintings do not produce anything like the same effect as Malevich's, As a way into a more satisfying interpretation, I propose to turn away from Malevich, as well as from visual art altogether. I will try to demonstrate that the closest analogy to Malevich's faceless paintings can be found in the depsychologised human portraits omnipresent in the prose of his Russian contemporary, Andrei Platonov.[16] Recognition of this parallel may perhaps lead us to a satisfactory interpretation of both Malevich's and Platonov's work.

Even more than Malevich, Andrei Platonov welcomed the Russian Revolution, and put his artistic and intellectual abilities at its disposal. Although most scholars now agree that Platonov deserves a central place in the canon of twentieth-century Russian literature, there is little agreement about how to classify or interpret him.[17] I do not wish to propose an overall interpretation of Platonov's work here, but I would like to point out a few aspects of it that seem relevant to an examination of Malevich's painting from 1928 to 1932. These are: (1) the consistent linkage of future socialist happiness with psychological emptiness in Platonov's work; and (2) an avoidance of the devices of traditional psychological prose. The

latter feature has been identified by at least one scholar as the
central distinguishing feature of Platonov's prose: 'In my view, what
is evident in Platonov's prose is a refusal to project events, plot lines,
and plans of behavior . . . What is represented is deprived of
traditional novelistic props: it is depersonalized, depsychologized,
and not definable by any inner teleology.'[18]

The result, in Platonov's prose as in Malevich's paintings, is not
merely a formal break with the expected narrative conventions of
the chosen genre, but an even more vertiginous refusal to allow the
reader to identify with the characters, and, thereby, to discover his or
her own self. The contrast between how Platonov's characters act
and what readers do has also been noted: 'The Platonov gaze
externalizes any event, even those that by their nature must belong
only to inner measurements of the world and of human beings. Even
the most thoughtful of Platonov's characters are more akin to sage-
automatons than to living, sensible people who are responsible for
their actions – like us, the "normal" readers.'[19]

The main character of Platonov's novella *Kotlovan* (1929–30) is
Voshchev, a man whose central trouble is thinking too much. When
we first meet Voshchev, he has just been fired from his job for 'the
growth of weakliness in him and for thoughtfulness amidst the
general tempo of labour'.[20] He wanders off to discover the meaning
of life, and his travels bring him first to a group of workers who are
digging a gigantic foundation pit for the future house of the
proletariat, and then to a farm in the process of collectivisation.
Ultimately, he returns to the pit and, apparently, becomes a kind of
leader of the working masses in their increasingly futile effort at
'socialist construction'. What is significant for us is the extent to
which happiness in the novel is identified with psychological emptiness. In the passage that follows, Voshchev observes a group of
workers eating. The men are seen as a generalised mass, distinguished by no particular features, as opposed to the observing
Voshchev: 'Although they knew the meaning of life, which is
equivalent to eternal happiness, their faces were nevertheless gloomy
and thin, and instead of the peace of life, they possessed exhaustion'
(p. 13). This description could almost serve as a caption to one of the
Malevich paintings we have seen. Of cardinal importance is its
oxymoronic character; instead of the joy or at least the tranquillity
we might expect to see on the faces of these men, there is a chillingly

empty blankness. The inexplicable contrast between the emotions they are said to feel and their external appearance is analogous to the vertiginous combination of vibrant colours and static bodies with completely blank faces in Malevich's peasant paintings. Also analogous is the narrator's refusal to enter into their minds, to tell us what they are thinking, as a way to resolve this contradiction. It should be noted that in contradistinction to the practice of nineteenth-century novels, this refusal cannot be chalked up to the status of the men as secondary characters. Rather, it appears that they simply do not have any psychology to treat.

The correlation between happiness and emptiness is repeated in a passage that appears somewhat later in the novel. Here, Chiklin (one of the workers from the construction brigade) and Voshchev have gone to the countryside to help collectivise a village.

– Is everything good now, comrades? – Chiklin asked.
– It is, replied the entire Org-courtyard. – We don't feel anything now. Only dust remains in us.
Voshchev was lying to one side and he just could not go to sleep lacking the tranquillity of truth within his own life, and then he stood up from the snow and went amidst the people.
– Hello! – he said joyfully to the kolkhoz. – You have now become like me. I am also nothing. (p. 83)

The Soviet men of the future, it appears, reach happiness by draining themselves of all desire, leaving nothing but matter – 'only dust remains in us'.[21] Again, the collective is identified with happiness and blankness simultaneously.

The position of Voshchev here is curious. He, we know, has been searching for the meaning of life, not by emptying his mind but by intense thought. At this point, it appears that he has reached the same level of happiness as the collective, but by a diametrically opposite path; he has literally thought his way through to emptiness. *Kotlovan* can thus be seen as a novella in which a psychologised individual is brought into contact with a world lacking psychology. Voshchev's paradoxical quest, therefore, has been to achieve the level of happiness, equivalent to psychological emptiness, that the masses appear to possess naturally. At the end of the novel, however, Voshchev's route to happiness is called into question. Nastia, the child who has symbolised that ideal future world for which the foundations are being dug, dies, and the building task of the collective becomes transformed from construction to burial. As Voshchev parts with the child, the narrator tells us: 'Voshchev would have agreed to know nothing again and to live without hope and in the nebulous desires of a vain mind, if only the girl were to be whole again, ready for life, even if she did need to suffer in the course of time. Voshchev lifted Nastia into his arms, kissed her swollen lips and hugged her with the greediness of happiness, finding more than he had searched for' (p. 113). This passage again indicates that Voshchev has indeed found what he had taken to be happiness – before, he had known nothing but now, presumably, he knows something of importance. The death of the child calls the value of this knowledge into question, however. The opaque final gestures – the hug of happiness and the final kiss – along with the cryptic hint of the attainment of a new level of knowledge, beyond what Voshchev had ever consciously sought, hint that he has perhaps achieved a final stage of unconscious happiness.[22] He has merged with the collective of diggers, no longer alienated from them because of his psychological fullness. But if he has finally drained his mind completely and found happiness, he has found it in death, a state that is not (cannot be?) expressed. At this moment, I believe, Voshchev has become analogous to one of Malevich's blank-faced peasants. He has purchased life in the world of the future at the price of psychological blankness in the present; in so doing, he becomes a human shell.

In other works of Platonov the revolution is seen even more directly as having depsychologised the world. In the novel *Chevengur*, for example, Kopenkin and Dvanov wander over the steppes of Russia looking for Communism. Although the narrator describes the thoughts and actions of his heroes continually, it is difficult for the reader to create a mental portrait of either of them. This is because the physical descriptions he provides are almost totally featureless, exact analogues to Malevich's peasant paintings of the same period. Here, for example, is the narrator's description of Kopenkin: 'Kopenkin thought gloomily. His international face did not express any feelings now, and, in addition, it was impossible to imagine its origins – was it from the barge-haulers or the trade unions – the traits of his personality had already been rubbed away by the revolution.'[23] The revolution creates entirely new people who can be characterised ideologically, but who lack any trace of distinctive appearance or personal psychology.

The physical world that surrounds the two men is marked by the same emptiness that characterises each of them. And that emptiness is seen precisely as the guarantee of future growth.

In his soul he [Dvanov] loved ignorance more than culture: ignorance – is a fallow field, while culture is an overgrown field where the salts of the earth are taken up by plants and where nothing else will grow. That is why Dvanov was happy that in Russia the revolution had emptied completely the few places of growth where there had been culture, and the people were, as they had been, a fallow field – not a ploughed one but an empty fertile place. (p. 148)

As in *Kotlovan*, the metaphors are of blankness and emptiness, and Platonov's opaque prose only deepens the feeling of deadness. To be sure, the central characters and the narrator seem convinced that life will arise, phoenix-like, from this deadness, but it is hard for the reader to believe in these assurances, particularly since no life ever does appear. Hard as it may be to believe, the characters described above are the most fully realised psychological portraits in Platonov's novel. For Kopenkin and Dvanov constantly interact with a group of characters called the *prochie* (perhaps best translated in this context as 'miscellaneous'). Whereas Kopenkin and Dvanov do act (although it is generally impossible to follow the inner logic of their action), the 'miscellaneous' merely exist, in a kind of permanent vegetative state.

But by far the most far-reaching faceless portrait in the work of Platonov is the story 'Reka Potudan'' ('The River of Potudan', 1937). This story has been identified as a central one for Platonov's 'socialist realist' period.[24] In many ways, however, until its requisite happy ending (accompanied, tellingly, by a certain amount of psychological portraiture), it can be seen as a continuation and deepening of the anti-psychologism that marked Platonov's work from the period of *Chevengur* and *Kotlovan*. The story is set in the early 1920s and describes a demobilised soldier, Nikita Firsov, who returns to his home village after the Russian Civil War. Like the characters in Platonov's earlier works, the former soldiers are characterised as having been completely emptied by their experience: as *tabulae rasae*: 'They were going now to live as if for the first time, barely remembering themselves as they were three or four years ago.'[25] In drawing his portrait of Firsov, the narrator deliberately gives us a largely featureless face, and then proceeds to prevent us from interpreting even the few features he provides. The landscape is as blank as the person in it, and the whole produces a distinctly melancholy impression:

This was a man of about twenty-five, with a modest, seemingly always saddened face, but this facial expression proceeded, perhaps, not from unhappiness but from the measured goodness of his character or from the normal concentration of youth. His blond, long uncut hair descended from under his cap about his ears, his big gray eyes looked with gloomy intensity at the peaceful, boring world of the monotonous countryside, as if the walker was not from these parts.[26] (pp. 579–80)

Still more importantly, Platonov's narrator eschews any technique that would give the reader access to Firsov's inner life, particularly the favourite tool of psychological novelists, *style indirect libre* (free indirect style). Instead, the narrator simply observes Firsov as if through the unblinking lens of a motion picture camera.[27] This technique is used not only in the passage cited but almost constantly throughout the work.

The scene of Firsov's return to his childhood home, one that would seem to cry out for an exploration of what the character is feeling, is resolutely blank: 'Nikita walked into his room, with its bed and low ceiling, with its one small window facing the street. It smelled the same as it had in his childhood, the same as it had three years before when he went off to war; even the smell of his mother's skirts could be sensed – this was the only place in the whole world. Nikita took off his pack and his cap, slowly undressed and sat on the bed' (pp. 581–2). The absence of any internal monologue is practically spooky, as if a corpse had come in and sat down. And in fact, a living corpse has arrived, in a psychological if not a physical sense.

This is not to say that the story completely lacks glimpses of Nikita's psychology, but these glimpses are reduced to a minimum in the early chapters. Eventually, Nikita marries a woman whom he had known before the war, but he is unable to consummate their relationship for fear of hurting her. In this, the most psychologised section of the story, Nikita realises that he is making Liuba miserable. Even here, though, the psychological portrait is primitive and deliberately unclear: 'He did not know himself why he did not go to work today, – it seemed to him that it was now shameful to live and, perhaps, completely unnecessary: why then bother to earn money for bread? He decided somehow to live out his life, until he pined away from shame and angst' (p. 597).

Ultimately, Nikita decides to run away from his wife. He escapes to a neighbouring town and arrives at the marketplace, 'where he sat in the shade behind a covered market stall [runduk], and stopped thinking about Liuba, about the problems of life, and about himself' (p. 601). As often happens in Platonov's work, this emptying of the mind creates the preconditions for a transformation to what is identified as happiness. In this case though, the emptying is far more radical than in the earlier works:

Nikita lived for a long time at the town market-place. Having first got out of the habit of talking, he also began to think, remember, and torment himself less . . . He now felt like himself only rarely and thought little; thoughts only came to him accidentally. By fall, most probably, he would completely forget who he was, and seeing the world's activity around him, he would no longer have any idea of it; let it seem to everyone that this person lives in the world, while in fact he would only be found here and exist unconsciously, with an empty mind, without feelings. (pp. 602–3)

It is precisely this portrait of a human being without any feelings, thoughts, or emotions, that seems most analogous to the figures we saw earlier on the canvases of Malevich.

However, what makes this story an example of Platonov's version of Socialist Realism, as opposed to the earlier works, is its unambiguous ending. After having emptied his mind, Firsov is discovered by his father, who informs him that Liuba has attempted to commit suicide because he has disappeared. The recognition that Liuba does indeed need him appears to jolt Firsov into a new state of mind, and he is able to return to his wife, consummate his marriage and, we assume, live happily ever after.

This story, too, evokes parallels with some Malevich paintings. In the last two years of his life, Malevich created a series of portraits that in certain ways approach more closely the ideals of Socialist Realism while still recalling the faceless portraits that have interested us here. In *Rabotnitsa*, for example, Malevich provides a fully realised physiognomy, but the bright colours of her clothing, stiff pose and volumetric body still nevertheless recall the faceless figures he had painted earlier. Thus both Malevich and Platonov, as they evolve toward their own interpretations of Socialist Realism, create works that recall the eerie ambiguity of their earlier phases, even as they abandon it, through their refusal to psychologise.

Let us suppose, for the moment, that I am correct, and that Malevich's faceless paintings and Platonov's pre-socialist realist prose depict depsychologised individuals. What we still need to know is, why would they do so? To answer this question, we must again consider certain trends in Russian art and literature both before and after the Revolution of 1917. The second half of the nineteenth century was marked, of course, by the great achievements of Russian psychological prose in the novels of Turgenev, Dostoevskii, and Tolstoi, and in the stories and plays of Chekhov. The focus of each of these writers was the complex motivation of human action, and their works can be seen as a hugely diverse psychological portrait gallery.[28] Although Russian painters of this period are a bit less well known, the members of the so-called Wanderer school achieved a similar degree of ability to depict complex psychology through physiognomy. If we look, for example at portraits like Ivan Kramskoi's *Lev Tolstoi* or Vasilii Perov's *Dostoevskii* (ill. 9.5) we feel that we know and understand these men, as well as we know Natasha Rostova or Rodion Raskol'nikov. The same can be said even when we do not possess any outside biographical information about the portrait's subject, as is the case, for example, with Valentin Serov's *Girl with Peaches*. The point is that a portrait tells us a psychological story about its subject, a story which we read primarily from the face that looks out at us from the canvas. The assumption underlying such works is that individual psychology is in and of itself valuable, an assumption that came to be generally accepted in European culture only in the eighteenth century, although a look at portraits by Rembrandt or Titian is sufficient to show that at least some artists believed this to be so more than a century earlier.

Paintings of Russian peasants dating from the second half of the nineteenth century reveal that techniques of psychological portraiture were felt to be equally applicable to lower-class subjects. A painting like Il'ia Repin's celebrated *Burlaki na Volge* (*The Barge-Haulers*, 1873, ill. 1.1) for example, shows us carefully delineated physiognomies, each of which is as expressive as those of the writers and intellectuals who sat most frequently for the Wanderers. Repin's own description of the Boatmen from his autobiography illustrates the extent to which he attempted to understand the boatmen as psychological subjects.

Gloomy faces, once in a while a heavy glance flashed from beneath the locks of matted hanging hair; their sweaty faces shine and their shirts are blackened through . . . But what do I see! these sodden horrible monsters

9.5. Vasily Perov, *Portret F. M. Dostoevskogo* (*Portrait of F. M. Dostoevskii*, 1872), oil on canvas, 80.5 × 99 cm. Tret'iakov Gallery, Moscow. From A. A. Fedorova-Davydova, *V. G. Perov* (Moscow, 1934).

look at the idle well-dressed gentry with a kind of good, childish smile, and they lovingly observe them and their fine clothes. And then the lead boatman lifted up the tow rope with his gigantic sunburned black arm when he passed by a ladder so that the beautiful sylph-like young girls could float down below.[29]

The period just before and after the Russian Revolution saw a major re-evaluation of previously regnant canons of artistic expression. In particular, there was a waning of the belief that an adequate artistic depiction of the world could be achieved through the application of the psychologically oriented techniques that the artists of the nineteenth century had perfected. This was particularly true after the Revolution, when the task of art was felt to be the depiction (or even the creation) of the new Soviet person. In the 1920s, the notion that psychological art was passé became almost a commonplace. Perhaps the most provocative statement on the subject was made by Osip Mandelstam in his essay 'The End of the Novel' (published in 1928 in *On Poetry*, but most likely begun in 1923):

All of this leads us to speculate about the link between the fate of the novel and the role of the individual in history at a given time [. . .]

It is clear that as soon as we enter the epoch of powerful social movements and organised mass actions, the efficacy of the individual in history wanes, and so does the influence and strength of the novel . . . The measuring stick of the novel is the individual biography or the system of biographies [. . .] thus, the novel always presents us with a system of phenomena organised through a biographical connection, evaluated by a biographical measure [. . .]

The future fate of the novel will be nothing more than this history of the breaking apart of biography as a form of individual existence; not just the breaking apart but the catastrophic destruction of biography [. . .]

For today, Europeans are cast out of their biographies, like pool balls onto a table, and the laws of their interaction, like the collision of pool balls, are governed by one principle: the angle of incidence equals the angle of reflection. A human being without a biography cannot be the pivot of a novel, and the novel, at the same time, is senseless without an interest in individual human fate – the plot and everything that accompanies it. Furthermore, the concern with psychological motivation (by which the decadent novel, already perceiving its impending doom, cleverly attempted to survive) has been ripped from its roots and has been discredited by the powerlessness of psychological motives in the face of those real forces which become crueller by the hour.

The contemporary novel was deprived simultaneously of the plot, that is the actions of an individual at a given time, and psychology, since it no longer forms the basis of any actions.[30]

In his essay, of course, Mandelstam was talking about the reality of the revolutionary period, but his words apply even more aptly to the Stalinist Soviet Union which, with its increasingly faceless and

terrifying bureaucracy, its mass actions, five-year plans and collectivisation efforts, was certainly a place in which the individual was
being 'radically undermined and discredited by the growing impo-
tence of psychological motives in the confrontation with the forces of
reality'. The task of prose writers, in this view, was to find a way to
construct fictional texts without psychology, or, at the very least, to
produce successful works of fiction that would undermine the central
position of individual psychology in the world of the novel. And this
is precisely what Platonov does in his major novels: Voshchev,
Kopenkin or Dvanov are by no means the pivots of novelistic action.
Instead, they are men without psychological biographies (that is to
say, they participate in various events, but they do so in a mechanical
way whose causal wellsprings are opaque, both for us and them),
billiard balls rolling over the face of Soviet reality. Malevich, in my
view, was driven by an analogous desire to depict the reality of the
world around him, a world that could no longer be adequately
captured by the use of traditional techniques of psychological
portraiture. It could equally not be captured by pure avant-garde
techniques, however. What he invented was his series of faceless
portraits – deindividualised individuals.[31] It was a desire to depict
the new Soviet world, I believe, that drove both the prose of Platonov
and the figurative painting of Malevich from 1928 to 1932 and led
them to produce the faceless portraits we have been examining.

Analogy, however, is not interpretation, and it still behoves us to
say what the analogous devices we have identified here mean.
Malevich's paintings have, as it turns out, been interpreted in a
bewildering variety of ways, despite the fact that they have been the
subject of study for a relatively short period.[32] Some Malevich
specialists were quick to provide straightforward political interpretations based exclusively on the blankness of the faces. Thus, for
example, the French art historian Valentine Marcadé 'assumes that
they illustrated the helplessness of the bewildered peasants faced
with the mechanization and collectivization to which they were
brutally subjected at the time'.[33] The distinguished Russian art
historian Dmitry Sarabianov agrees with this view in part, but
modifies it with reference to specifically aesthetic criteria:

The second peasant series, from the late 1920s and early 1930s, provided
Malevich with a highly idiosyncratic way out of nonobjective painting into
a new kind of figuration. But this series was not only a response to the
tragic situation that had developed in Russia by that time. Works such as

'Peasant Woman', 'Sportsmen', and 'Complex Premonition' are remarkable in their expressivity, for they still contain those ideas that Malevich
discovered during the 'cosmic period' of his creativity.[34]

However, the French scholar Serge Fauchereau rejects political
interpretations based on the device of the faceless portrait entirely,
noting that such works are common in twentieth-century art even in
the works of painters who did not share Malevich's experience and
could not have shared anything resembling his political point of
view, whatever it might have been.[35] Instead, he provides a purely
formal interpretation (here of the painting entitled *Peasant*): 'Rather
than search for symbolic significance in the blackness of the face and
extremities of this flat figure dressed in white, I would be more
inclined to see a metamorphosis of a suprematist figure in which the
white and black retain their preeminence.'[36] John Bowlt agrees with
the need to see a relationship between the late peasant paintings and
the work of Malevich's suprematist period, but, using somewhat
syllogistic logic, he proposes that we consider form and ideology
inseparable; that is to say, if Suprematism was meant to depict the
ideal men of the future and if the peasant pictures grow out of
Suprematism, then they, too, are ultimately positive statements:
'Malevich – in his late peasant pictures – was also celebrating the
abundance, strength and optimism of a new race for whom the
portals and porticos of Stalin's new palaces were the symbols of their
massive strength and limitless endurance.'[37]

There are, it seems to me, a number of problems with existing
interpretations. First, it is hard to feel satisfied with purely formal
readings. These paintings undoubtedly share the colours and shapes
of the artist's suprematist period, but they are not simply extensions
of those works; the sudden jump from non-objective to figurative art
seems too large to be explained in evolutionary terms.[38] Furthermore, although it is reasonable to note that the mere presence of
faceless figures is not sufficient grounds on which to base a political
interpretation, since the device can have a multitude of meanings,
this does not relieve one of the responsibility of interpreting these
particular faceless portraits, especially since they seem to cry out for
interpretation in human terms.

At the same time, those who believe that Malevich was making a
direct negative comment on the political situation in the contemporary Soviet Union seem quite naive. First of all, whatever his
opinions might have been, the artist avoided making direct political

statements in his art. Thus, although he appears to have supported the Bolshevik cause unreservedly in its early days, he never produced unambiguously pro-Soviet art, unlike many of his erstwhile artistic colleagues such as Maiakovskii and Meierkhol'd. What is more, even if we think that the paintings represent a political statement, there is no evidence from any of Malevich's writing that he felt any conscious enmity towards the regime in this period; certainly he considered himself a Soviet artist to the end of his life. In any case, and most significantly, were these paintings straightforwardly negative statements about Soviet reality they would not be as evocative as they are; for their continuing power derives precisely from the haunting balance they strike between elements that can be interpreted negatively and others that seem positive.

Though Bowlt's assertion that Malevich probably thought he was creating positive representations is surely well-founded, my objection to Bowlt's interpretation follows similar lines. I agree with him that as Malevich thought of himself as a communist he may well have thought also that he was depicting the new Soviet man in the process of construction, and that he would have seen the works in question as ultimately optimistic statements (and the same can be said for Platonov). Indeed, one could push Bowlt's claim further by claiming that just as the formal devices of Malevich's and Platonov's work from this period show a family resemblance to the devices favoured by their socialist-realist counterparts (e.g. a concern with the human figure rather than a focus on pure abstraction, a thematic treatment of collectivisation, of peasants and workers), so the overt ideology of the works echoes the optimism of incipient Socialist Realism. This is quite obvious in Platonov's prose, in which the bright socialist future, the happiness of all humankind or individual humans, are constantly invoked, albeit frequently juxtaposed to elements that appear to contradict them directly. But it is also present in the bright colours and 'cosmic' suprematist echoes in Malevich's canvases. But even so, it is impossible to accept Bowlt's overall line of interpretation because, when we view these paintings – or read Platonov's prose – today, authorial intent is neither the only nor the most important relevant interpretive category. It is as impossible to ignore the simultaneous presence of ominous elements in these works as it is to forget our post-factum knowledge that the blank slate produced by the Revolution was eventually, and what is worse, inevitably, filled not by the bright socialist future but by the unprecedented suffering of millions of people. If we already see that suffering here, and I think we cannot avoid seeing it, then we must view the psychological voids Platonov and Malevich gave us rather differently than they were intended.

In coming to an interpretation of these paintings from a position of hindsight, it seems clear that in their works of the late-1920s and early 1930s Malevich and Platonov succeeded better than any other Soviet artists in rising to the challenge Mandelstam had set in his essay 'The End of the Novel' (cited above). Their non-psychological human portraits are the most effective description I know of a populace that had, after years of war and ideological struggle, been deprived of individuality. These are, in the deepest sense, realist works, insofar as they reflect a world in which individual psychology had lost its place. Because they depict a time in which many people were willing to abandon the individual as a step towards the creation of a utopia, we now recognise these works as tragic, both in their subject-matter and in their revelation of their creators' psychology. On the one hand we have to do with artists who supported and continued to support the Revolution and its goals, who wished to be part of Soviet art and who included echoes of its ideals in their work. But on the other, either consciously or unconsciously, they sensed that the void the Revolution had created, its destruction of the possibility for individual action (and therefore the futility of psychology as an artistic device), was leading to misery rather than utopia. The depression and deep sadness produced in the viewer or reader by these faceless portraits is the result of their ability (most likely despite their authors' conscious desires) to capture what was perhaps the greatest tragedy of our century – the blindness of those who hoped for happiness built on the abnegation of their own individuality, of people who 'stepped on the throat of their own song', and who in so doing helped to bring unheard of misery to themselves and to millions of others.

NOTES

1 Not all of Malevich's peasant paintings from this period are so extreme. In *Plotnik* (The Carpenter, 1928–32), for example, he shows a peasant holding a hatchet and a nail in front of a fairly detailed village backdrop. The paintings I will discuss here, however, are the most disturbing of this series, as well as the most radical.

2 For a collection of the manifestos of proto-socialist realist groups in the
1920s, see John Bowlt (ed.), *Russian Art of the Avant-Garde* (London, 1988),
pp. 265–97. See also summaries and excerpts of manifestos from less
well-known groups in P. Lebedev, *Russkaia sovetskaia zhivopis'* (Moscow,
1963), pp. 65–90.

3 In his discussion of Pasternak's work of this period, Lazar Fleishman
says that it 'indicated Pasternak's readiness to accept Soviet reality as
an inevitable and lawful model of socialism. No matter how much this
model differed from the utopian prognoses expressed by the poet in his
"Dialogue" of 1917, he gave the benefit of the doubt to this unprecedented social experiment.' See *Pasternak. The Poet and His Politics*
(Cambridge Mass., 1990), p. 164. Gregory Freidin, in *A Coat of Many
Colors* (Berkeley, 1987), notes that 'Mandelstam's commitment to the
"revolution", however naive and utopian it may appear to us now, was
long-standing and entirely serious' (p. 228). As a result, his 'poems of
1931–32 display an ambiguous attitude to the Stalin revolution.
Although much of what he saw he found repulsive, he was nevertheless
unwilling to declare himself squarely against the changes taking place'
(p. 229).

4 See Charlotte Douglas, *Kazimir Malevich* (New York, 1994) for excerpts
from Malevich's letters of this period. The most poignant of them,
addressed to an old friend, then high-up in the Ministry of Culture,
contains the following plea: 'Let's proceed with an analysis of the
problems of art; let's return power to the innovators. I and Tatlin and
Filonov and many others – and also the youth who do actually want to
create a great Art – will become shockworkers . . . Am I needed or not
needed?' (p. 36). Here we see best Malevich's principled refusal to give
too far on the artistic front, coupled nevertheless with a desire to play a
role in the artistic life of the country understood in Bolshevik terms
(e.g., shockworkers).

5 It is, of course, anachronistic to speak of 'officially approved' art in the
late 1920s because no single artistic method had been officially chosen
as uniquely appropriate for Soviet art at this time. Nevertheless, it was
not hard to tell which way the cultural winds were blowing, and it was
obvious to all that the period of formal experimentation was over and
that some form of realism was on the rise.

6 This is the opinion of Jean-Claude Marcadé, who says ' "The Carpenter" is part of the cycle of works that recall the subjects of the
countryside in the primitive cubo-futurist period and subject them to a
post-suprematist treatment.' *L'avant-garde Russe. 1905–1925* (Catalogue
of an Exhibition at the Musée des Beaux-Arts de Nantes, 1993), p. 188.

7 As one very Soviet art historian tells us: 'The exhibition "Life and
Activities of the Peoples of the USSR" opened on May 3, 1926 . . .
Most of the works in the exposition reflected the first triumphs of our
fatherland in the areas of socialist industrialisation, the new life of the

city and countryside, co-operation, working class and agricultural movements' (Lebedev, *Russkaia sovetskaia zhivopis'*, p. 83.) For reproductions of the works of Riazhskii and Gerasimov, see Lebedev, *Russkaia*, pp. 86, 68.

8 Richard Brilliant, *Portraiture* (Cambridge Mass., 1991), p. 12.

9 Again, Malevich seems deliberately to be subverting the genre rules here. As Brilliant notes: 'Group portraits are not random collections of persons but deliberate constructions of the significant relations among them.' *Portraiture*, pp. 92–3. In works like *Women in a Field* Malevich makes it impossible to see any relation, calling into question not just the possibility for interaction in the subjects depicted, but the possibility of any meaningful human interaction. It has been suggested to me that in these portraits Malevich was echoing the stiff poses that peasants (and not just Russian ones) generally adopt when being photographed. This may well be the case but if it is, the lack of facial expression and 'props' becomes all the more striking; for in anthropologists' photos, the goal is to show the faces as well as the accoutrements of the subject, even if a sense of them as actors is lost. In transforming the photograph to the painted portrait (if this is what he did), Malevich appears to have emptied the genre of its *raison d'être*, creating again a mysterious absence, as if the camera did indeed steal the souls of his subjects (a widely held fear in non-photographically literate societies).

10 Malevich himself appears to have said very little about these works. Indeed, the only record appears in the 1934 diary of L. Iudin: 'Nonobjective artists and partial images [poluobrazy] (like my peasants) have the greatest significance for the time. They have the strongest effect.' Quoted in Evgenii Kovtun, 'K. Malevich: His Creative Path', *Malevich. 1878–1935* (Moscow–Amsterdam, 1988), p. 171.

11 Malevich knew di Chirico's work extremely well by the late 1920s and evidently admired it very much (see Douglas, *Kazimir Malevich*, p. 35 for details).

12 For more on this theme in Petrushka see Andrew Wachtel, 'Introduction. Petrushka in the Context of Russian Modernist Culture', in Andrew Wachtel (ed.), *Petrushka. Sources and Contexts* (Evanston, Illinois, 1998).

13 Brilliant provides an interesting analysis of this work in the context of the (stylistic) self-portrait (see *Portraiture*, pp. 142–3).

14 Serge Fauchereau discusses analogies between this work and Malevich's *Sportsmen* in *Kazimir Malévich* (Paris, 1991), p. 182.

15 A. M. Hammacher, *René Magritte* (London, 1986), p. 34.

16 The interconnections between Malevich's art and the literary work of his Russian contemporaries have been studied in detail by a number of scholars. Most such work has, however, concentrated on the relationship between Malevich and his futurist colleagues and sometime collaborators, Maiakovskii and Khlebnikov (see, for example, such

excellent studies as Juliette Stapanian, 'Mayakovsky's "Street-" and an "Alogical" Cubo-Futurist Painting by Malevich', in Lauren G. Leighton (ed.), *Studies in Honor of Xenia Gasiorowska* (Columbus, 1983), pp. 99–110, and Jiří Padrta, 'Malévitch et Khlebnikov', in Jean-Claude Marcadé (ed.), *Malévitch. 1878–1978* (Lausanne, 1979), pp. 31–46. As far as I am aware, however, there is only one study that has focused on Malevich's later period. This article, 'Babel' i Malevich' by Alexander Flaker (*Wiener Slawistischer Almanach*, 10 (1982), 253–69), examines 'Red Cavalry', which is perhaps the most anomalous painting of the period I am considering.

17 For a detailed survey of this problem, see Thomas Seifrid, *Andrei Platonov. Uncertainties of Spirit* (Cambridge, 1991), pp. 14–18.

18 Valery Podoroga, 'The Eunuch of the Soul', *Late Soviet Culture. From Perestroika to Novostroika*, ed. Thomas Lahusen with Gene Kuperman (Durham, NC, 1993), p. 190.

19 Ibid., p. 191. Surprisingly enough, at least from my point of view, the visual artist with whom Podoroga chooses to compare Platonov is Pavel Filonov. He points to Filonov's tendency to reverse the expected weight of background and foreground as analogous to Platonov's narrative technique (pp. 199–200).

20 Andrei Platonov, *Kotlovan, Iuvenil'noe more* (Moscow, 1987), p. 1. Further references to *Kotlovan* will be made in the main text by page number from this edition.

21 For a detailed discussion of the role of desire in Platonov's work, see Eric Naiman, 'Andrei Platonov and the Inadmissibility of Desire', *Russian Literature* 23 (1988), 319–67.

22 The images here – silent kiss, dead child, questing hero – clearly connect Voshchev with Alesha Karamazov. But whereas Dostoevskii provides Alesha's transformation with detailed and careful psychological motivation, Platonov demonstratively refuses to do so.

23 Andrei Platonov, *Chevengur* (Moscow, 1988), p. 112. Further references to *Chevengur* will be made in the main text by page number from this edition.

24 Seifrid, *Andrei Platonov*, pp. 194–7.

25 Andrei Platonov, 'Reka Potudan'', *Izbrannye proizvedeniia* (Moscow, 1983), p. 579. Further references to the story will be made in the main text by page number from this edition.

26 The refusal to attempt psychological portraiture through the device of ignorance (i.e., the presentation of multiple possible reasons for an action, any one of which might be the cause but none of which is chosen) is frequent in Platonov's work. See, for example, the story 'Dzhan' (A. Platonov, *Sobranie sochinenii* vol. ii (Moscow, 1985), pp. 34–5).

27 Podoroga presents a detailed discussion of analogies between Platonov's prose and the work and thought of Dziga Vertov on pp. 205–8. A

classic example of style indirect libre from Russian prose is in Chekhov's famous story 'Dama s sobachkoi' (The Lady with the Little Dog) as Gurov sits with Anna looking out over Yalta: 'The monotonous, hollow sound of the sea, coming from below, spoke of peace and the eternal sleep that awaits us. It resounded like that before Yalta or Oreanda existed, now it still resounds and it will go on resounding long after we are dead' (chapter 2).

28 For a discussion of the development of psychological portraiture in the Russian novel see Lydia Ginzburg, *On Psychological Prose*, trans. Judson Rosengrant (Princeton, 1991) and Andrew Wachtel, 'Psychology and Society in the Russian Novel', in Malcolm Jones and Robin Miller (eds.), *The Cambridge Companion to the Classic Russian Novel* (Cambridge, 1998), pp. 130–49.

29 Il'ia Repin, *Burlaki na Volge (Vospominaniia)* (Moscow, 1944), p. 8.

30 O. Mandel'shtam, 'Konets romana' in his *Sobranie sochinenii*, vol. III (New York, 1971), pp. 267–9.

31 In *Kazimir Malevich, The Climax of Disclosure* (London, 1993), Rainer Crone and David Moss discuss these paintings as a subversion of narration (p. 178). They certainly are, but this to me is secondary to their subversion of individual psychology, the absence of which makes narrative in a conventional sense impossible.

32 Many if not all of the paintings were known during Malevich's lifetime. Some were apparently exhibited at the artist's one-man show in the Tret'iakov Gallery in 1929, and a number of others appeared at the show entitled 'Artists of the RSFSR over the last XV Years' at the Russian Museum in 1932. What is more, they can be seen hanging on the walls of his room in the photographic portrait of Malevich on his deathbed (this photo is reproduced in Fauchereau, *Kazimir Malévitch*, p. 214). However, the artist's family gave them to the Russian Museum for safe keeping in 1936, and they remained sequestered in the Museum's vaults until the late 1970s. Thus, they have been discussed in the scholarly literature only since then.

33 Paraphrased in Serge Fauchereau, *Malevich*, trans. Alan Swan (New York, 1993), p. 34.

34 D. Sarabianov, 'Kazimir Malevich and his Art, 1900–1930', in Kovtun, *Kazimir Malevich 1878–1935*, p. 165.

35 'The faceless man is present in all modern movements because of the diversity of interpretation which he can be given' (Fauchereau, *Malevich*, p. 34).

36 Fauchereau, *Kazimir Malévitch*, p. 174.

37 John E. Bowlt, 'Body Beautiful. The Search for the Perfect Physique', in John E. Bowlt and Olga Matich (eds.), *Laboratory of Dreams. The Russian Avant-Garde and Cultural Experiment* (Stanford, 1995), p. 58.

38 It is, however, a mirror image of Malevich's break with figurative art.

For unlike, say, Picasso, whose abstract art grew from a slow and evolutionary move away from figurations, Malevich's Suprematism appears quite suddenly, as a sharp break with his previous primitivist and cubist work.

CHAPTER 10

Painted mirrors: landscape and self-representation in Russian women's verbal and visual art

Pamela Chester

The modernist era was, in the words of literary historian Charlotte Rosenthal, the time of a great creative outburst for women in literature.[1] Marina Tsvetaeva and Anna Akhmatova were only the most lastingly famous of a pleiad of talented poets, including Elena Guro, Liubov' Stolitsa, Sofiia Parnok, Poliksena Solov'eva, Anna Prismanova and Vera Zviagintseva. The prose writers Ol'ga Forsh and Nina Berberova, and such versatile figures as Zinaida Gippius (poet, dramatist, prose writer, and literary journalist) and Lidiia Zinov'eva-Annibal (prose writer and dramatist) fill out this remarkable picture. While women writing in other genres were hampered by the absence of a conscious continuity with the work of earlier generations, women poets could build on an established tradition of women's creativity going back to the late eighteenth century.[2] Preceding the tremendous achievements of female modernist artists, on the other hand, were two generations of women who had managed to obtain academic training. Beginning in the 1850s, women were admitted directly into the Academy of Arts in St Petersburg, which offered the sole route to official credentials for an artist. The arts academies were accorded lower status than universities (to which women were not admitted in the nineteenth century), and, perhaps for that reason, they were more porous to outsiders, including both women and lower-class men.[3] In some respects, the entrance to the world of visual art was less jealously guarded than the realm of verbal authority. It is true that attitudes were at first somewhat condescending. In his memoirs, the famous painter Il'ia Repin recalled women at the Academy in the 1860s as peripheral: 'dainty little aristocratic figures' going past in a cloud of perfume, and 'a plump lady – then still a great rarity at the Academy' sitting in a drawing class.[4] Even hard-won success in the Academy's examinations did not necessarily confer respect in the outside world.

Sof'ia Sukhovo-Kobylina remained a marginal figure despite the fact that she not only came from a distinguished St Petersburg family, but was the first woman to be awarded a gold medal, in 1853.[5] The artistic establishment of the 1860s, 1870s and 1880s remained resolutely male; not a single woman was a member of the Peredvizh-niki (Wanderer) group, the most important force in realist painting from the 1860s to the 1890s. The absence of prominent women realists contrasts with the measure of recognition accorded to women painters in Western Europe, and in Finland, then part of the Russian Empire. The sense that women who tried their hand at art were likely to be charming amateurs at best was partially caused by the Academy's appeal to lower-class young men who added to their artistic talents a clear understanding of the institution as a path to social mobility (it was this social group from which the Peredvizhniki was drawn).[6] Significantly, no major woman artist was ever to emerge from the Academy, even after reforms in 1893 went some way towards de-bureaucratising the institution.

But there was also a flourishing tradition of women amateur artists, producing portraits and interior scenes, and occasional exceptional women managed to evade the restrictions on advanced study by training abroad (a case in point was Mariia Bashkirtseva, whose work will be considered briefly below), or by training with established painters (as was done by Mariia Iakunchikova, who was a pupil between 1886 and 1889 of Elena Polenova). The Academy's less conservative and repressive sister school, the Moscow School of Painting, Sculpture and Architecture, founded in 1843, had some important alumnae to its credit, among them Anna Golubkina, Nadezhda Udal'tsova and Nataliia Goncharova. But the upsurge in talented women artists in the late nineteenth and early twentieth centuries is attributable above all to opportunities outside the state system. Some women (Sof'ia Kramskaia-Veber, Zinaida Serebria-kova) came from families of artists. Others trained directly in the studios or at classes held by major painters (as was the case with Liubov' Popova). Most important of all, perhaps, was access to the growing number of private art schools in Moscow and St Petersburg: Varvara Stepanova attended the Stroganov school in Moscow, Ol'ga Rozanova the Zvantseva school in St Petersburg and Aleksandra Ekster the Academy in Kiev. In fact Stepanova, like her future husband Rodchenko, was able to obtain her first formal training in Kazan' before coming to Moscow, emphasising the extent to which

academic art training was decentralised by this period. Many of the
women artists mentioned were later to establish international repu-
tations, and all took a full part in the artistic life of their time,
exhibiting widely, attracting critical attention, and in some cases
controversy (Nataliia Goncharova was the defendant in a renowned
trial for pornography in 1910).[7] Among the modernists, in fact,
female visual artists held a place at least as significant as women
writers among their literary peers.

   This essay is concerned with two of the best-known figures in
literature and the visual arts respectively: Marina Tsvetaeva
(1892–1941) and Nataliia Goncharova (1882–1962). Born only a
decade apart, the two also had much else in common, as Tsvetaeva's
biographical essay 'Nataliia Goncharova' delightedly emphasised.[8]
Both came from well-off upper-middle-class families in Moscow:
indeed, the two families had grown up as next-door neighbours on
the same street in the Arbat. Both were, in imaginative terms,
strongly affected by their early contacts with the Russian countryside. Tsvetaeva's family traditionally spent their summers in Tarusa,
south of Moscow, while Goncharova had spent her early childhood
on a family estate in Tula Province, also south of the city. Both
women were later to become part of the Paris emigration; Goncharova had been stranded there by the outbreak of the First World
War and stayed put after the Revolution, while Tsvetaeva moved
there from Prague in 1925. However, my discussion here is not
primarily concerned with the two women's biographical contacts (in
any case, the two met for the first time only in the late 1920s, after
most of the works that I shall be discussing were completed). Rather,
I am concerned to establish formal affinities between the two in
terms of their representation of landscape and of the self's relation
to landscape (I use the term 'landscape' in the broadest sense, to
include interior views and cityscapes as well as panoramas of the
Russian countryside). I shall hypothesise that it was precisely in the
representation of space that these two exemplary women modernists
established separate territory from their male colleagues, and that in
some ways their presentation of landscape bears a covert and
probably unconscious relation to representation of landscape in the
work of women writers and painters from an earlier generation,
such as Mariia Bashkirtseva, Evgeniia Tur and Mariia Iakunchikova.

   This essay has grown out of my work on the landscapes of male artists and writers, and in particular out of my contention that nineteenth-century male writers and painters sought in the landscape of childhood a restoration of Eden, a connection with Mother Earth and a nurturant female presence. The novelist Lev Tolstoi, like the poet Wordsworth and the painters Constable and Isaak Levitan, saw landscape as feminine, linking it with the mother or the beloved, and perceiving contact with nature as a means of escape from post-lapsarian ills (mortality, illness, melancholy, guilt) into transcendence and ideal reality. Therefore, both Levitan's canvasses and Tolstoi's autobiographical novel *Detstvo* (Childhood) offer glimpses of the high central Russian sky, and of a horizon that seems to promise a way into the sublime.[9]

The explicit gendering of the approach adopted here does not mean that my discussion rests on acceptance of a hard-and-fast and simplistic distinction between 'masculine' and 'feminine' traditions. I follow Bridget Elliott and Jo-Ann Wallace, who have argued in their study of Western women modernists (French, British and American) that there is a need 'to *trouble* or *make messy* any easy narrative of literary or art history, whether traditional or feminist'.[10] The work of Tsvetaeva and Goncharova has obvious parallels not only in the work of their male contemporaries, for example, Goncharova's longterm partner Mikhail Larionov, or Tsvetaeva's epistolary friend Boris Pasternak, but also in the proto-modern features to be found in the work of Dostoevskii, whose treatment of space depends upon multiple perspective and upon an idiosyncratic understanding of reality drawn ultimately from the Russian icon.[11] It is also possible to adduce sociological and political reasons for this resemblance: Dostoevskii's status as a social outsider (*raznochinets*), on the margins of his society, placed him, in some ways, as far outside the cultural mainstream as women artists, while his Slavophile convictions led him to feel more suspicious than did liberals or radicals of his day of *obshchestvo*: 'civil society' or 'the public domain'. But although gender must be considered one among many signifiers of identity, along with ethnic, social, cultural or political affiliation, it was of vital importance to Russian modernists themselves because of the widely held belief that there were essential differences between 'the masculine' and 'the feminine', a belief fostered by contemporary interest in the writings of Weininger, Nietzsche and Vladimir Solov'ev. Both Tsvetaeva and Goncharova felt uncomfortable about being labelled 'women artists', yet the work of both was informed by a strong sense

of 'feminine' identity. Goncharova's gender is by no means the least
of the reasons why Tsvetaeva, in 'Nataliia Goncharova', perceived
her as a 'double', even though the main purpose of her essay is to see
Goncharova as an masculine 'anti-double' to her namesake, 'the
other Nataliia Goncharova', the embodiment of the 'purely feminine'
character of the total beauty, who combines destructiveness and
intellectual nullity with sexual magnetism. Similarly, in her angry
sketch of a 'poetesses' evening' held in Moscow in 1918, Tsvetaeva
concluded a diatribe against the denomination 'poetess' and against
the feminist movement with a list of women's causes and famous
women of the past that she was prepared to take an interest in: these
included not only The Women's Battalion of Death, the last line of
resistance against the storming of the Winter Palace by the Bolshe-
viks, but also the figure of Mariia Bashkirtseva.[12] And Goncharova
herself was explicitly aware of the existence of a women's tradition in
the visual arts, even though she was not prepared to be limited by
what were conventionally considered 'female subjects', painting
male nudes and pagan idols as well as such 'gender-appropriate'
subjects as flower paintings and portraits.

TSVETAEVA AND GONCHAROVA'S LOCATION WITHIN MODERNISM

The landscapes of Goncharova and Tsvetaeva do not purport to be
windows on to a scene faithfully reproduced from nature. Rather,
these two women modernists created scenes in paintings and prose
that reflect their sense of their situation as artists, as Russians, and,
to varying degrees, as females whose creation of art made their
cultural status anomalous. To some extent, this sense of situation is
traceable to the general concerns of the modernist movement, and
to the move away from the conventions that nineteenth-century high
realism used in order to legitimate its illusionistic representation of
the world, and most particularly the all-embracing, panoramic,
'omniscient' viewpoint on the one hand, and the viewing of the
world 'through the eyes' of a single character or from a particular
and discrete viewpoint on the other. In Levitan's canvases we behold
the Russian landscape as if from a balcony or high river bank, and
Repin overwhelms us with over-life-sized figures of barge-haulers
and icon-bearers that tower above and around us (see ill. 1.1);
conversely, in realist portraits, such as Repin's painting of the

composer Musorgskii or Perov's of Dostoevskii (see ill. 9.5), we engage in intimate dialogue with a single and unique individual.[13] Equally, Tolstoy's viewpoint in *War and Peace* and in *Anna Karenina* alternates between the distant and the intimate, moving from the battle of Borodino to Natasha's first experience of the opera, from the local government elections to Anna's own immediate impressions, presented as stream of consciousness, in the hours before her suicide. On the other hand, modernist writers such as Nabokov, Belyi, Blok and Tsvetaeva always make their readers aware of their own presence in the text, their perceptions shaping and filtering our perceptions, their representations demanding our active participation in the deciphering of meaning. And in the paintings of Larionov, Tatlin, Konchalovskii or Goncharova, just as in post-impressionist art generally, there is no single point from which we view the scene as we do (or assume we do) in the material world. We must assemble a sense of space and its meaning based on the contradictory planes the artist has created. Space becomes a powerful trope, taking on symbolic and even spiritual dimensions.

If we consider realist art as a window through which the reader or viewer sees an illusionistic space from a single fixed viewpoint, then modernist art is by contrast a mirror reflecting back both artist and audience, who must collaborate in conceiving the space represented in the work of art. The writer and critic John Berger, in his essay 'The Moment of Cubism', describes the Cubists' revolutionary breakthrough by saying, 'The Cubists created the possibility of art revealing processes instead of static entities. The content of their art consists in various modes of interaction: the interaction between different aspects of the same event, between empty space and filled space, between structure and movement, *between the seer and the thing seen*.'[14] A case in point would be Picasso's *Composition avec tête de mort* (Still Life with Skull, 1908). The painting is a collage of object fragments – edges of book-covers, the corner of a painting, part of a palette, a distorted skull – whose employment of multiple planes defies the viewer to select an 'optimal' viewing-point. There is a powerful sense of kinesis – the fragments appear to be spun round kaleidoscopically, never coming to a final resting-point – and the presence of a schematically rendered work of art within the work of art (contrast the carefully rendered, and recognisable, works of art in Vermeer's interiors) emphasises the anti-illusionistic purpose of the piece. Similarly, *Trois femmes* (Three Women, 1908) transforms the three bodies into one another by visual paranomasia (geometrical representations of limbs allow a leg to become a shoulder to become part of a side). The flaring edges of a shawl have as much apparent depth, as much 'character', as the limbs of the human beings against which they are placed.

Both these Picasso paintings were held in Sergei Shchukin's collection in Moscow, one of the most important holdings of modernist art in Europe.[15] Picasso's 'cubist' mode influenced Russian artists directly: as Beverly Kean has demonstrated, Goncharova's *Prachechnaia* (The Laundry, 1912) is a reworking of motifs from Picasso's *La Bouteille d'anisette* (Bottle of Pernod), right down to citation of the proprietary pastis label.[16]

However, Russian Modernism had native as well as foreign roots. The response to multiple perspective was particularly warm because the broken space that Western modernists depicted had affinities with the representation of space and spiritual reality in icon painting. Like the icon, the modernist image, whether verbal or visual, is non-material; it could never exist in actuality, and has its reality in the world beyond, and also in the psyche of the one perceiving it. As Ouspensky says, 'when we look at [the icon], we not only know but also see that we stand not before the person or the event itself, but before its image'.[17] This insistence on the status of the representation as image and not as illusion, with the concomitant demand that the audience enter into the work of making sense of that image, is a shared feature of modernists, writers as well as painters. In his brilliant treatise 'On Reverse Perspective', Father Pavel Florenskii defended icon-painters against progressivist accusations that they had not employed geometrical perspective because they were ignorant of its existence; on the contrary, he argued, they had deliberately flouted the rules of geometrical perspective because their purpose was not simplistically illusionistic.[18] And modernist painters – Tatlin, Petrov-Vodkin, Malevich, Chagall – employed references to the icon not only thematically (as had been done in the work of their late-nineteenth-century predecessors, such as Nesterov and Vasnetsov), but also compositionally. In this context, Goncharova's imitations of the icon (as in her designs for the ballet project *Liturgie*) were very much in the artistic mainstream, just as was Tsvetaeva's multiple-perspective reworking of imagery from the Orthodox Hymn to the Virgin (Akathistos) in her *Poema lestnitsy* (The Staircase Poem) (Tsvetaeva, SS, vol. III, 120–31.)

If the icon mediated between Cubism and Russian traditional painting, there were also Russian localities where 'archetypes and magic signs from the field of "Primitive Art" [which] show the modern movement the way to elementary form' could be looked for.[19] Picasso's fascination with African masks and sculptures was matched by Russian artists' enthusiasm for 'primitive' materials that were to be found on the territories of the Russian Empire: pre-Christian idols, Tatar barrows, Scythian gold, peasant crafts and legends. Here, again, Tsvetaeva and Goncharova were very much part of the mainstream. Where Kliuev asserted his descent from members of the 'Flagellant' group of Russian sectarians, and Kandinskii's mythological autobiography included a great-grandmother who was a Mongol princess, Tsvetaeva, in some of her memoirs, traced her descent through the female line to peasant roots, emphasising her closeness to 'primitive' Russia.[20] Where Larionov and Goncharova, Boris Grigor'ev and Mstislav Dobuzhinskii drew on the *lubok*, popular print, and on painted shop-signs as sources for their art, writers such as Valerii Briusov, Aleksei Remizov and Evgenii Zamiatin exploited the legends, tales and popular religious beliefs of Central Russia for their writings, and Tsvetaeva used the classic folk-tale collection of Afanas'ev, 'the Russian Grimm', in several of her works (for example *Tsar'-Devitsa* (The Tsar-Maiden), and 'Dom u starogo Pimena' (The House at Old Pimen), which contains a tale about a vampire-mother in Afanas'ev's collection). And where the broad brush-strokes and unintegrated blocks of colour characterising Russian popular painting found their way into modernist art, so 'folk' lexicon, metrics, proverbs and sayings found their way into prose and verse of the time.

Yet even when this background is taken into account, there still seems something in the work of Goncharova and Tsvetaeva which is not entirely explicable in terms of modernist concerns generally. If one compares Tsvetaeva's 'Dom u starogo Pimena' with Belyi's autobiography *Kotik Letaev*, one notes a far greater emphasis on constricted space in Tsvetaeva. To be sure, Belyi's text is concerned with the claustrophobic nightmare of upbringing in an haut-bourgeois Moscow household peopled with sinister aunts and an authoritarian mother. Yet, at the same time, a symbolic sense of relief is afforded by narrative interruptions that return the narrator to the moment of his birth, or to the delirium of his bout with dysentery, scarlet fever and measles:

the passageways, rooms, corridors that arose before me in the first moments of consciousness relocate me into the most ancient era of life, the caveman period; I live a life of black emptinesses hollowed out of the mountains with beings running about in the darkness gripped with fear, and with fires; the beings hide out in the depths of these holes because at their entrances are winged monsters; I experience the cave era; I experience the catacombs; I experience . . . Egypt beneath the pyramids, and we're living inside the body of the Sphinx; the rooms and corridors are the hollows inside the bones of the Sphinx's body; if I should bore through the wall, I wouldn't come out on the Arbat, and I wouldn't come out in Moscow at all; perhaps . . . I would see the expanse of the Libyan desert; and among it a Lion lying in wait for me . . .

Imagine the human skull,

it's enormous, enormous, enormous, exceeding all measure and all temples; imagine . . . It rises up before you, its nostrilled whiteness rises up like a temple chiselled into a mountain; this mighty temple with its white cupola emerges from the gloom before you; the curves of its walls are inimitable; its honed flat surfaces are inimitable; and inimitable are the architraves of the columns at its entrance, as of a colossal, honed mouth; the multitoothcolumned mouth opens the way to the immeasurable gloom-shrouded halls, the compartments of the skull, the rocky peaks rising to the gloom of the vault, the bony vaults call to each other with a hollow noise; and lower their embraces; and they form an enormous polyphony, the cosmos coming into being; and the ledges fall away ponderously and perpendicularly; the leer and grimace of the precipices make multiseeing holes, fall away, descending in rapid criss-crossings to the labyrinth of the semicircular canals; you go out into the place of the altar, above the ossis sphenodei . . . To this place the priest will come; and you await; before you is the interior of the frontal bone, and suddenly it splits asunder, and into the breach in this grey-black, whistled, wind-licked world rush walls of light and torrents; and in whorls of clamouring, singing rays they fall, they start lashing your face:

'He's coming, he's coming, here he is'

– and tumbling away from beneath your feet are the flowing locks of a diamond torrent, into the cave-whorls of the brain . . . [21]

There is no such moment of epiphany in Tsvetaeva's autobiographi-cal texts, such as 'Mat' i muzyka' (My Mother and Music), or 'Dom u starogo Pimena', but rather an unmitigated sense of constraint and closure. Compare her sense that far from being separated from her mother by birth, she is condemned to bear her mother 'buried alive inside [her] unto life eternal' (SS, vol. v, p. 14). Just so does one note the sense of lowering horizon and of cut-off space in some of Goncharova's paintings. *Posadka kartofelia* (Planting Potatoes, c. 1908),

10.1 Natal'ia Goncharova, *Posadka kartofelia* (*Planting Potatoes*, 1908–9), oil on canvas, 111 × 131.5 cm. Gift of USSR to France. Centre Georges Pompidou, Paris, AM 1988–879. © 1999 Artists Rights Society (ARS), New York/ADAGP, Paris.

for example, (ill. 10.1) shows a line of peasant women, shawled and huddled, clustered together against a landscape cross-hatched by fences and divided by trees. The purely notional line of sky along the top of the painting affords no sense of release or of an alternative world. Particularly interesting, so far as Goncharova's *Posadka karto-felia* is concerned, are contemporaneous landscape views by her partner, Mikhail Larionov, with whom Goncharova had worked closely since the early 1900s. Just as Goncharova's landscapes of 1908–9 depict her family's estate at Polotnianyi zavod, Larionov's work of the same period shows scenes characteristic of his childhood home, Tiraspol. *Siniaia svin'ia* (*The Blue Pig, c.* 1909) (ill. 10.2) shows a scene that is ostensibly closed off, by a pallet fence to the foreground of the picture. But in fact a gap in the fence offers glimpses of a distant house beyond, as well as of a female figure half-metamorphosed into a tree-trunk; this figure, as well as the blue pig to the left

10.2 Mikhail Larionov, *Siniaia svin'ia* (*The Blue Pig*, 1909–1910), oil on
canvas, 65.5 × 75.5 cm. Centre Georges Pompidou, Paris, AM 1976–16.
© 1999 Artistis Rights Society (ARS), New York/ADAGP, Paris.

and a peasant placing swill for the pig at left, offer lyrical punctua-
tion of what is by no means a constricted view.

Interestingly, the sense of constricted space is also a point picked
up in Tsvetaeva's essay on Goncharova. Goncharova is glimpsed
herself for the first time in a confining landscape: the *ulichka/ushchel'e*,
alley/gorge, in which she lives in Paris:

Not an alley, a gorge: better yet: a defile. So entirely not a street that each
time forgetting, each time expecting a street ! there is a street name, there is
a house number! – I skip past it, and fetch up right by the Seine again. And
so back – to look. But the street deviates – the deviations of gullies – just
ask any hill-dweller! – so, flailing, I bang around – is that it? No: that's a
house opening out into a courtyard as wide as a square – no, it's a gateway
from which the draft of ages is blowing – no, that's an ordinary street, with
shop-fronts, with motor-cars. It's not there. It's melted into thin air. The hill

has sunk into itself, swallowing up Goncharova and all her treasures. I shan't get to Goncharova today, I shall end up getting lost. (SS, vol. IV, p. 64)

Given her own growing interest in childhood and in the remembered garden, Tsvetaeva elicited from her subject information that no other biographer would think to ask for. And one of the crucial childhood memories cited is of a restricted scene rather than a large panorama – green shoots under the ice:

I spent my whole childhood in the country, but I don't remember any of the winters. I must have been taken for walks and so on, but I don't remember a thing. *This* I do remember, though. Spring on the threshing floor. I'm being led by the hand, through the puddles. And from the puddles (her voice drops, her eyes sparkle, she's looking straight at me but not seeing me, she's seeing this) from under the ice and snow – shoots. Green pointed shoots. Lots of grain gets scattered on a threshing floor: these were the first shoots to break through. [. . .] Don't those green shoots – afterward – grow all the way through the book of her creation: of her genesis? (SS, vol. IV, p. 76)

Tsvetaeva's assertion of affinity was not simply wishful thinking. The motif of constricted landscape is found elsewhere in her work. *Poema Gory* (Poem of the Mountain, 1924), for example, ends with an apocalyptic vision of the mountain covered by dachas as the city encroaches into the landscape (SS, vol. III, p. 28). The sense of constrained landscape is accompanied by a questioning of the automatic assumption 'natural = good' that persisted in the work of Russian modernists, perhaps most strikingly in Nabokov's story 'Vesna v Fialte' (Spring in Fialta) and his memoir *Speak, Memory*. If Nabokov's writings about early childhood are Edenic (as in Tolstoi, even childhood erotic encounters retain innocence, in no sense presaging a lapse from grace), Tsvetaeva's are anti-Edenic. Indeed, her autobiographical piece 'Chert' (Devil, 1934), makes explicit reference to the Eden myth: 'In my half-sister Valeriia's room, transformed into a bookcase, stood the Tree of the Knowledge of Good and Evil' (SS, vol. V, p. 36). In Tsvetaeva's poetic cycle, 'Moi Pushkin' (My Pushkin, 1937), this myth is again evoked and fleshed out. Now the 'forbidden fruit' is identified specifically as a volume of Pushkin's *Collected Works*, which she reads 'in the bookcase, with my nose in the book and in the shelf, in near darkness and nearly touching it and even a bit suffocated by its weight, which comes down right on my throat [. . .]: I read Pushkin directly into my breast and directly into my brain' (SS, vol. V p. 65).

This child's pre-lapsarian state is no paradise, in fact: the tree has become the crafted wood of a bookcase, and the flowers in her childhood world are carved into the music stand on her piano. She is stuck in a domestic interior, not a garden. Further, the girl seems never to have been at ease; not surprisingly, the fall into knowledge is celebrated, not nostalgically regretted. It feels more like a break-out than an exile when she leaves the childhood garden.

In the centrepiece of her autobiographical cycle 'Dom u starogo Pimena', similarly, constriction inheres in the setting as much as, or perhaps more than, in the human relationships: 'Their home, the house itself, oppressed them [. . .] The house oppressed them with its walls as thick as a citadel's, with its deep window alcoves [. . .] with its garden. O, most of all with its garden, with its illusory freedom.' The children of this house 'were cast down by their parents into the netherworld, under actual *vaults . . .* of Hades' (SS, vol. v, pp. 117–18).

'Anti-Edenic' elements were present in Goncharova's childhood recollections too. As recorded by Tsvetaeva, Goncharova's memories of school were of senseless repression, a repression contested by her rebellious and naturally curly hair, which, wetted down to make it decorously straight and flat, kept springing back into tendrils again. By contrast, her painting *Zavtrak* (Breakfast), here seen through the eyes of Tsvetaeva, turned the family at breakfast in a garden, which cliche would have as serene *rus in urbe*, into a hellish vision in which claustrophobia, greed and intellectual inertia are combined with hints of the ultimate post-Edenic sin – incest:

The big canvas – *Breakfast*. A green garden, a table with the remains of breakfast. Against a background of the summer tropics – a family. The centre of attention is a moustachioed profile, with his moustache aimed at two people at once: wife and non-wife, blue and pink, one a deceiver and the other deceived. The blue woman's cigarette is being lit by the pink, the pink woman holds the matches with a puffy hand. The air above these three is – concupiscence. Opposite the pink woman, at the other end of the table, a puny 'eedjit' in a straw boater, with no jacket. His red hands have dug into the weave of the chair back. He is bowlegged. Also a profile, though not the same one. Moustache – moustacheless. Dark – pale. Base – stupid. He looks at the pink woman (his mother or sister) but sees the white one, whom he can't look at, awaiting the hour when he too will gaze like a child, he looks at two women at once. (SS, vol. IV, p. 126)

Significantly, in this scene, 'there are no children; there could be no children. There's a dog – not a hound, but a demon' (SS, vol. IV,

p. 127). This is not the childhood garden, with its ambiguous joys and its promise of future creativity, but a vision of hell. The figures in this tableau have not only fallen from innocence but chosen to sink into self-absorption and degradation.

Constricted, haunted by visions of sin, Tsvetaeva and Goncharova's landscapes are post-Edenic in another way too: their emphasis on work, the biblical curse ('in the sweat of thy face shalt thou eat bread' (Genesis 4:19)). *Posadka kartofelia* deserts the lyrical neo-pastoral of Larionov's figures in landscape (soldiers, individual peasants feeding animals) for a vision of serious labour; similarly, Tsvetaeva's 'Muza' (Muse, 1921) represents this normally ethereal and paradisaical figure of allegory as a peasant woman in gaping, broken shoes and dirty homespun skirt. These motifs are strikingly similar to those in poetry and painting by other Russian women of the period. Zinaida Serebriakova's paintings of peasant women, such as *Obestsvechivanie l'na* (Bleaching Linen), shows a line of stocky, preoccupied figures hauling cloth under a sky itself bleached and shrunken, pierced by the dead black of leafless trees. And an untitled poem written by Akhmatova in 1913 takes as its setting the 'Tverskaia skudnaia zemlia' (the scanty earth of Tver' province):

> Журавль у ветхого колодца,
> Над ним, как кипень, облака,
> В полях скрипучие воротца,
> И запах хлеба, и тоска.

> И те неяркие просторы
> Где даже голос ветра слаб,
> И осуждающие взоры
> Спокойных загорелых баб.

> A crane juts above an old well,
> And above it the clouds boil;
> In the fields are creaking gates,
> And the smell of grain, and sadness.

> And those dim distances,
> Where even the wind's voice is feeble,
> And the condemnatory gazes
> Of calm, sunburnt peasant women.[22]

Here there is no cultivated garden; the broad expanses of the Russian landscape are not so much constricted as unwelcoming. The speaker feels constrained by a sense of her own guilt and of her alienation from the peasant women who gaze at her accusingly. Whereas both Tsvetaeva and Goncharova return repeatedly in their art to the landscape of their girlhoods, representing their own origins amidst ostensible freedoms constrained by their emerging identity as artists, this region is not the scene of Akhmatova's own childhood, and accordingly she includes no trace of creation myth in her depiction of it. The elements here – unfreedom (*nevolia*), dim prospects (*neiarkie prostory*) and a sense of sin, expressed in the 'condemnatory glances' of the watching women – make this vision of nature, too, claustrophobic and anti-idyllic, if not anti-Edenic in quite the sense of Tsvetaeva's or Goncharova's.

THE FEMININE 'ANTI-EDEN': TSVETAEVA AND GONCHAROVA'S ANCESTORS

I believe that it is possible to trace a similar sense of constricted space with added symbolic dimensions in the work of women like Mariia Bashkirtseva and Evgeniia Tur in the 1880s, whose paintings and writings offer a similar contrast with the work of their male contemporaries. So far as Bashkirtseva is concerned what is at first striking is the dominance of cityscapes and interior scenes when compared with the work of male contemporaries such as Repin, Savrasov or Kuindzhi. There are practical reasons for this, of course; as a respectable young lady, she could not go anywhere without a chaperone, and the constant presence of her governess, mother or devoted aunt was understandably cumbersome and irritating; and as her tuberculosis progressed, her family, equally understandably, tried to prevent her from sketching outdoors during wet or cold weather. Figure-painting and portraits were, in the circumstances, simply more accessible. But practical causes are not the only explanation for the dominance of portraits and figure-paintings in her œuvre, which is also traceable to aesthetic preferences. On 27 July 1880, after having been able to attempt some landscapes during a stay at a health spa away from Paris, Bashkirtseva noted in her diary that she had ended by 'knocking down the canvas' in frustration and exclaiming, 'How can one prefer anything in the world to the figure?' [23]

Equally remarkable are the differences between Bashkirtseva's few completed landscapes and those of her male contemporaries, such as Shishkin and Savrasov. In the paintings of the Peredvizhniki artists, the natural landscape represents a space more lasting than human values, a counter-image to the corruption of rural life that was a topos of painterly critical realism. *Rozh'* (Rye, 1881) by Aleksei Savrasov (1830–97), shows a golden crop-field bordered by clumps of wild flowers. A twisting path, its outlines picked out in places by bronze areas of standing water, stretches towards a distant and expansive horizon. More than half the canvas consists of a view of the sky, with pewter, henna, grey-mauve and turquoise rain-clouds just lifting to show a clearing blue sky and great banks of pinkish-cream cloud lit by the sun that will soon shine down unimpeded.

It has been asserted that 'the theme of a road disappearing into the distance [. . .] and the moving picturesqueness of form, are trademarks of Savrasov.' [24] However, both these features are very widespread in landscape painting by other male artists of the 1870s and 1880s. In the paintings of Ivan Shishkin (1832–98), such as *Lesnoe boloto* (Forest Swamp, 1873), or *Niva* (Wheatfield, 1875) or *Khvoinyi les v solnechnyi den'* (A Coniferous Forest on a Sunny Day, 1895: ill. 10.3), a path stretching towards the horizon and lost in mysterious distance is also a standard feature; and in Shishkin, too, a sense of emotional space is conferred by the use of enormous expanses of sky (for example, *Zaria* (Dawn, 1883)). Shishkin also liked to employ the motif of a forest glade, a place of light and sunshine amidst the dark of trees, and, in symbolic terms, somewhere outside time, a place avoiding the oppressive sense of trees closing in, with their metaphorical connotations of imprisonment and of mortality.

In Bashkirtseva's work, on the other hand, the landscape, so far from being transcendent, is generally inhabited by human beings. In *Le Printemps* (Spring), for example, a young woman sits at the foreground of the landscape; rather than her appearing an allegory of the natural season, the spring landscape is a backdrop to her intense contemplation. And above all the space is subject to constriction. *Paysage* (Landscape) contains a central diagonal element in the form of a path, in a manner superficially reminiscent of Shishkin and Savrasov. But rather than leading into the depth of the landscape, drawing the viewer's eye to the horizon, the road disappears into the trees; similarly, the sky is pallid and undramatic, offering no possibilities of escape. So, in *Le Printemps*, though the path leads on beyond the young woman placed at the front, it ends in a dark tangle of undergrowth. The distant vista could hardly be less sublime.

10.3 Ivan Shishkin, *Khvoinyi les v solnechnyi den'* (*Coniferous Forest on a Sunny Day*, 1895),
oil on canvas, 137 × 103 cm. Russian Museum, St Petersburg.

This 'female' tradition in 1880s landscape painting can be matched by a 'female' tradition in landscape writing. Evgeniia Tur's semi-autobiographical novel *Semeistvo Shalonskikh* (The Shalonskii Family, 1880), shares significant elements with Bashkirtseva's canvases in the treatment of women's space. Her heroine and alter ego Liuba, on a visit to her grandmother's estate in the country, is sent out with her cousins to get apples from the orchard:

'Why have you fallen silent, girls?' grandmother says [. . .] 'you know, the *Arcadian* apples have already ripened, the little white ones, so pretty. Go find the gardener Spiridon, ask for the ones he has picked [. . .].

We run to the garden, but can't find Spiridon right away, he has gone home. We deploy ourselves decisively, the smaller children climb into the hut's narrow little window, built in the middle of the parterre to store apples, which had been carefully sorted by varieties on the shelves. My brothers and male cousins, and the little girls, are scooping the apples into their caps, scattering them everywhere, laughing, passing them out the window to us. Inside the dark hut there is laughter, crashing, talk: the apples are rolling from shelf to shelf and falling like hail onto the floor. Finally, having amused themselves to the full, all the children crawl out and gallop home with their booty. An ineffable joy seizes us, and our merriment knows no bounds. To cap it all, Spiridon, who has been walking along slowly with the keys to the hut, comes to a halt on the path, and stands stock still. [25]

When the gardener complains of their behaviour, however, Liuba, the newcomer in the group, is singled out for punishment. In fact, she herself did not trample or mix the apples, and had no part at all in an earlier incident in which her cousins had dragged the gardener's netting. Yet she is the only one punished for the theft of the apples. Afterwards, the narrator says, 'I sat silently at my grandmother's feet the whole day, and this prank has remained ineradicably in my memory – it was the last. With it I also bade farewell to my childhood.'[26] Again, the landscape motif is associated with sin and with labour (in this case, the gardener's), rather than with joy and freedom.

The distinction between 'masculine' idyll and 'feminine' anti-Eden persisted into the work of the next generation of landscape painters and writers too. The most prominent of the painters, Isaak Levitan (1860–1900), is renowned for his lyrical visions of the Russian countryside, such as *Zolotaia osen'* (Golden Autumn, 1896), in which late sun transforms a stretch of Russian river bank (the river again acts as a path to the horizon) into a place of mediterranean

light and colour. In *Reka Oriat* (The Oriat River, 1890) by Vasilii
Polenov (1844–1927), a sky of high cloud, occupying more than one-
third of the canvas, is dappled mauve, gold and blue; a great swathe
of broad river, lit to silver-grey, cuts across the painting from the
bottom left, tracking up banks of golden sand and fluffy green trees
before disappearing at upper left, beyond which tracks of woodland
carry the impulse onwards to a line of purple upland bordering the
horizon. In the work of Mariia Iakunchikova (1870–1902), on the
other hand, a similar palette is employed to quite different emotional
effect. In a letter to her sister, Natalia Polenova, written in 1889,
Iakunchikova had spoken of her impulse to landscape painting as an
urge to capture time before it moved on: 'One must hurry with life
or everything will pass.'[27] Rather than an escape from time and
from the transient human experience, though, she had seen painting
as a necessary record of the passage of time. Longing for escape
from self, she had seen this as a near-impossibility: 'What if it were
possible to get outside one's fate and one's deserts, to cut the threads
binding us to our lives, to step aside, be forever an observer rather
than a participant? Well? I think this would be quite a bearable
condition, though what a difficult one!'[28] Iakunchikova's *V okno
starogo doma. Vvedenskoe* (From the Window of the Old House.
Vvedenskoe, 1897) expresses precisely this anxiety of participation
and transience. It shows a view constricted by the looming neo-
classical columns of the old house, which slice the landscape
panorama into sections and off-centre these in compositional terms.
Departing light shows to the left of the painting and is picked up in a
small irregular area of standing water to the right, but no track leads
up to the horizon. Bushes from which the light has totally disappeared dominate the front of the painting, standing like charred
remains after a forest fire; the sense of destruction here underlines
the buried association between classical columns and ruins that was
established in Picturesque works of the late eighteenth and early
nineteenth centuries. And Iakunchikova's *Bois de Boulogne* (1896)
turns a tamely suburban scene into an image of forbidding gloom,
with shadowy trees hemming in path and river that move into
darkness rather than into light.[29]

Goncharova and Tsvetaeva's 'anti-Edenic' handling of landscape
can, then, be seen as a transmutation of a tradition established by
their female predecessors in painting and writing. M. N. Yablonskaya
has asserted that 'it is with [Mariia Iakunchikova] that we can first

10.4 M. V. Iakunchikova and V. V. Vul'f, *Vecher na bal'kone: Zakat* (*Evening on the Balcony: Sunset*, 1911), appliquéd fabric. Tret'iakov Gallery, Moscow.

trace the expression of a specifically female creative perception',[30] but I would suggest that Iakunchikova is herself heir to a 'creative perception' expressed by Mariia Bashkirtseva and Evgeniia Tur. Indeed, Iakunchikova forms, with Polenova, a kind of 'missing link' between the realist art of the 1880s and the modernist work of Goncharova and Tsvetaeva. These painters, both members of the Abramtsevo circle of arts and crafts enthusiasts, differed from their male peers, who used folk art as source material for motifs in their canvases, in adopting the techniques of folk artists – embroidery,

wood-carvings, and so on – and the world-vision associated with
them. Polenova, for example, painted landscapes which abstracted
the natural scenes around her as much as the decorative elements of
peasant embroidery and carving did.[31] And Iakunchikova, in collaboration with V. V. Vul'f, in *Vecher na balkone* (Evening on the
Balcony) (ill. 10.4), produced a landscape whose jarring effects are
attributable to techniques as well as to compositional devices. The
picture represents a terrace overlooking a park with stands of trees;
the view is cut off by objects (according to Iakunchikova's customary
method), in this case a row of planters. At first, these planters appear
to lead the eye to the horizon, suggesting the lines converging at
vanishing point that are required by classic exercises in post-
Renaissance geometrical perspective. The clouds, though, stop our
eye at the picture's surface and make obvious their shallow texture
and two-dimensionality. The work only *appears* to be a painting: it is
in fact an appliqué, with pieces of fabric forming large areas of
colour and stitching forming the finer lines.

CONCLUSION: 'ANDROGYNOUS' ART?˘

The discussion so far has sought to trace a 'female' tradition of
landscape painting from Realism to Modernism. It would equally be
possible to trace a 'male' tradition. For example, Larionov's *Vecher.
Posle dozhdia* (Evening After the Rain, 1909) is an intriguing modernist reworking of an established theme in Realist landscape painting.
Behind trees that are rendered anything other than naturalistically
(they stand like comical gangly wooden forks decorated with cactus-
like blobs of notional foliage), is a sky that picks up and deepens the
purples and mauves of Polenov's *Reka Oriat*.

   But for all that, to over-emphasise gender homogeneity would be
to travesty the greater freedom that Modernism made available to
women painters and writers, and its liberating effects on gender
boundaries more generally. To be sure, Tsvetaeva and Goncharova
shared the sense of constricted possibilities open to women in the
works of their predecessors. Many of the dynamics in the autobiographical writings of Tur and Tsvetaeva are similar: the girl is not
alone in her transgression, but she takes the whole blame. The figure
in authority is female. The girl does not die, though the episode does
mark the death of childhood. And like Tsvetaeva, Tur's narrator
does grow up to be a writer. However, Tur provides a male frame

narrator to 'discover' his aunt's neglected manuscript and choose to publish it. Her garden does not live up to the promise of freedom and pleasure which the 'Arcadian' apples seem to offer, and the rewards of transgression are less significant than they are when Tsvetaeva buries herself in Pushkin. What is more, Tsvetaeva has a clear sense of an overbalancing art which rewards transgressions. In 'Dom u starogo Pimena', a central chapter of her autobiographical prose cycle, Tsvetaeva shows one of the fruits of this artistic initiation: she represents the woman poet as a creator, moving through space and time, conferring life on the dead. The domestic interiors in this house, inhabited by her step-grandfather and his family, connect directly with Hades, and Tsvetaeva, like a more powerful Orpheus, moves back and forth between the two domains with impunity. As a poet, Tsvetaeva exercises power over the forces of both life and death: 'Dear Nadia, having seen [from the next world] all that the future holds, in following me, a little girl, were you perhaps following *your own* poet, the one who is now resurrecting you, almost thirty years later?' (SS, vol. v, p. 133.) If the constraints of childhood 'Anti-Eden' included linear time (the inescapable necessity of the fall later remembered forever), then the surviving adult is also granted the power to return to the past at will.

Equally, Goncharova was a far more versatile and resilient painter than Bashkirtseva or even Iakunchikova. Her memories of childhood included serene moments, as well as moments beset by intimations of imprisonment; indeed, her first memories, if not as nostalgia-laden as Tolstoi's, are peaceful and joyous; she recalls sitting at age two at a round table with her brother, looking at a thick book of pictures, in a scene combining domestic comfort with rich intellectual exploration. And, as Tsvetaeva pointed out, her adult feeling for landscape veered between constraint and enormity. This paradox is metaphorically represented in 'Nataliia Goncharova' by an ocean wind that howls down the narrow gully–alley of her studio, rattling the iron window-grates opposite that Tsvetaeva fancifully associates with those outside a Spanish seraglio. If Goncharova, in Tsvetaeva's view, shared a peasant's fear of expanses, she also shared a peasant's delight in these:

On Goncharova's country-ness. When I say country, I naturally include estates as well. I take that whole free flood: of spring, longing, pastures, rivers and work in the fields – all that surging sea of song. The country not in a caste sense, but as a cast of mind: not the izba itself so much as the steppe that rushes in through the door of the izba, flooding it, sweeping it away. An intriguing coincidence: Russian peasants are still nomads – in sleep. Today it'll be the porch, tomorrow the shed, the next day the hayloft. If it's hot, they'll sleep outside; if it's cold, they'll climb on the stove. – Pure nomadism. – Goncharova with her camp bed (the last word in technology!) that suddenly shoots out from under the table – from under the table today, from behind an easel tomorrow – with her ease of moving about – with her unsettled way of sleeping – is an obvious nomad, an obvious peasant. Her most fundamental – habitual – gesture is to take any object that's in her way – a book, a plate, a hat – and put it down on the floor. Without any contempt for either object or floor, the floor's simply the most natural place (the earth being the first floor) – the table just isn't essential for her (except as somewhere to work: a workbench) – nor is the chair (standing by the table); feeling a passion for the fire, the hearth – the living fire! the scarlet hearth! – needing no servants, her hands being sufficient (craftsman, apprentice, sweeper-up – Goncharova has two hands: her own): all this and everything else makes Goncharova an obvious part of the country, the Orient – from which latter she has, by the way, inherited her cheekbones. (SS, vol. IV, pp. 102–3)

Three years before she painted *Planting Potatoes*, Goncharova repre-sented a quite different landscape, that of her childhood years at Lodyzhino. The overwhelming effect of the scene is of joy and openness, though in fact the spatial planes within the picture are broken and fairly flat. Goncharova is here far from the constricted world of Bashkirtseva and Iakunchikova; though the manner of applying paint and the compositional conventions are utterly differ-ent from Levitan's, her rich tonalities recall his, and the brilliant turquoise of the sky seems almost to touch the boughs of the trees. While not leading the eye to the horizon or to a distant vista, Goncharova has suggested space and light *within* her constricted scene. It is no coincidence that Tsvetaeva sees Goncharova, with her passionate devotion to art, her single-minded pursuit of her training and her vocation, as the '[male] descendant by the male line' of her great forebear Pushkin; her early years are perhaps more boyhood than girlhood.

One interesting measure of comparison for the women painters is their literal self-portraits: Bashkirtseva (*c.* 1883) represents herself at the easel, on a dark, almost empty background, while Goncharova (1907) shows herself holding a sheaf of yellow lilies but enclosed in the shallow space of a room whose walls are lined with canvasses – presumably her own. The resolutely non-avant-garde Serebriakova

(1909), by contrast, shows herself at her mirror, and the brush in her hand is a hairbrush and not a paintbrush. The room behind her, reflected in the glass, is spacious and full of light. She seems to assert that her gender is no bar to her identity as a painter.

What is more, the sense of 'constricted space' seemed in itself less peculiar, less marginal, in the 1900s, 1910s and 1920s than it had before 1900. The great majority of modernists, whatever their gender, depicted space as broken, non-continuous, non-illusionistic. The generation that witnessed the Russo-Japanese War and the Russian Revolution of 1905, and then the still greater cataclysms of war and revolution that followed, saw not a photographic or even impressionistic image of a world with integrity, but a multi-planed image of a world coming apart, or a fragmentary glimpse of a world closing down. Goncharova's series of etchings on the subject *Voina* (War) can be placed alongside the wartime and post-war works of painters such as Wyndham Lewis or David Bomberg in Britain, Otto Dix in Germany, and against Picasso's famous study of destruction *Guernica*. Similarly, Tsvetaeva's poems that are addressed to the painful fracturing of the identity endured by those in emigration, such as 'Rodina' (Motherland), have more in common with the work of Vladislav Khodasevich than they do with the writings of Evgeniia Tur. Regardless of gender, the artists, in their agony at the loss of humane values, felt marginalised by an increasingly violent society.

In the final analysis, then, Tsvetaeva and Goncharova created a body of original work which cannot in justice be excluded from the modernist canon. As the training available to women and men artists began to equalise towards the end of the nineteenth century, the dramatic differences in the treatment of space which we saw in comparing Bashkirtseva and Levitan, Tur and Tolstoi, Iakunchikova and Polenov, and Letkova and Chekhov began to disappear.

Yet for both Tsvetaeva and Goncharova, as for the British painter Vanessa Bell, like their Russian female forerunners, the domestic setting is of necessity prominent in their art works, and their sense of their ambiguous femininity, of the constraints as well as the rewards of this constricted domain, shapes their representation of a space physically narrow but opening into other, non-material worlds. They bring to their 'unwomanly' vocation an artistry which acknowledges but does not accede to the limits society would impose on their gender. They represent themselves both directly, in the painted mirrors of self-portrait and autobiography, and obliquely, in the space which they carve for their landscapes, as creators with authority but without illusions about their own access to paradise. If Tolstoi and Shishkin, Polenov, Nabokov and Levitan, created a golden Mother Russia who holds up a Lacanian mirror to tell them they are loved, worthy, perhaps even immune to death, these women offer – and seek – no such assurances. They focus on the immediate, on the patterns of the surfaces around them, on the human rather than on the natural or supernatural world. They express less anxiety about their mortality (even in the case of Bashkirtseva, whose journal indicates that she was aware in her last years that she was dying). Their fear is, rather, that they will be shunted aside from the art to which they feel called before they have realised their gifts to the full extent. The world that they show us is unidealised, anti-nostalgic: the children are dirty and neglected, the women are heavy and engaged in heavy, clearly post-lapsarian labour. The space does not open out to infinite distance or hover timelessly like the sacred space of one of Shishkin's forest glades. In Goncharova's work, the flattened plane so characteristic of the work of modernist artists implies a coinherence of the physical and the spiritual; there is no place here for the horizon's liminal zone. I would offer as a tentative explanation for this commonality the women's shared experience of girlhood as anti-Eden, a condition whose constraints are not balanced by joy and ease but by the stern rewards of Art; and their focus on the artist as one whose Fall brings the possibility of craft and creativity, and thus of a chance to attain another sort of immortality.

NOTES

This essay has benefited from the work and the comments of many friends and colleagues, and I would like to thank them all, without of course implicating them in any errors of fact or interpretation which I may have committed. I am especially indebted to Roger Anderson, whose ability to draw fresh and startling connections among texts, and among different artistic media, continues to provide food for my own thoughts on writers and painters. My understanding of Tsvetaeva has profited greatly from the work of Sibelan Forrester. The painter and teacher John Norton supplied helpful insights into Modernism, as well as bibliographic references; Prof. Edythe Haber generously shared her collection of books on the art of this period. Discussions with the scholar and writer Patricia Sollner have also sharpened my awareness of the connections between Tsvetaeva's texts and the works of modernist painters. Jehanne Gheith first introduced me to the writings of Evgeniia Tur, and supplied me with copies of her novels, out of print since the 1880s; her deep knowledge of Tur's life and work, and her ongoing work on 19th-century women writers, has been a help and an inspiration in my own work. Catriona Kelly's extensive editorial comments have significantly improved the structure and content of this piece. To them and to the other colleagues and students whose comments have helped to catalyse my analysis of this problem and to clarify its weaknesses, I offer belated thanks.

In cases where authors have spelled their own names without regard to Library of Congress transcription, I have naturally retained their spelling. In citing from texts, I indicate my own ellipses with square brackets as well as three dots [. . .]; this serves to distinguish them from Tsvetaeva's frequent ellipses.

All translations are mine unless otherwise indicated.

1 C. Rosenthal, 'Introduction', in M. Ledkovsky, C. Rosenthal and M. Zirin (eds.), *Dictionary of Russian Women Writers* (Westport, CT, 1994), p. xxxiv.

2 C. Rosenthal, 'Achievement and Obscurity: Women's Prose in the Silver Age' in T. Clyman and D. Greene (eds.), *Women Writers in Russian Literature* (Westport, CT, 1994), p. 151.

3 See Elizabeth Kridl Valkenier, *Russian Realist Art* (New York, 1989), who points out that university graduates entered the civil service four ranks above academy graduates (p. 12). Women were admitted to post-secondary education in the Vysshie zhenskie kursy only in the 1860s, and in isolation from male students, and women's medical courses were authorised only in 1873 (and suspended from time to time thereafter).

4 I. Repin, *Dalekoe – blizkoe* (Moscow and Leningrad, 1937), p. 172.

5 In the context of my later discussion, it is of some interest that Sukhovo-Kobylina was awarded the medal for landscape painting, and that she was the sister of Evgeniia Tur. See Jehanne Gheith, 'Tur, Evgeniia' in Ledkovsky, Rosenthal and Zirin, *Dictionary of Russian Women Writers*, p. 603.

6 See Valkenier, *Russian Realist Art*, esp. pp. 10–13.

7 See Jane A. Sharp, 'Redrawing the Margins of Russian Vanguard Art: Natalia Goncharova's Trial for Pornography in 1910', in J. Costlow, S. Sandler and J. Vowles (eds.), *Sexuality and the Body in Russian Culture* (Stanford, 1993), pp. 97–123.

8 Marina Tsvetaeva, 'Nataliia Goncharova', *Sobranie sochinenii v 7 tomakh* (Moscow, 1994–6), vol. IV, pp. 64–129. (Future references to this collection as SS, vol. and p.)

9 See P. Chester, 'The Landscape of Recollection: Tolstoy's *Childhood* and the Feminization of the Countryside', in P. Chester and S. Forrester (eds.) *Engendering Slavic Literatures* (Bloomington, Indiana, 1996), pp. 59–83. Simon Schama's *Landscape and Memory* (New York, 1995),

pp. 6–7 and pp. 236–37, bears out my hypothesis dramatically, if unintentionally. He repeatedly points to the human urge to find in landscape an Eden, without considering whether there are gender constraints upon this habit, though his juxtaposing of the images of the water cave and the female pudenda in Courbet's *The Source of the Loue* (1863) and *The Origin of the World* (1866) leaves little doubt that male artists, or at least art historians, have at times sexualised the landscape.

10 See B. Elliott and J.-A. Wallace, *Women Artists and Writers: Modernist (Im)positionings* (London, 1994), p. 16.

11 See Roger Anderson, 'The Optics of Narration: Visual Composition in *Crime and Punishment* ', in Anderson and Paul Debreczeny (eds.), *Russian Narrative and Visual Art: Varieties of Seeing* (Gainesville, 1994), pp. 78–100; and Konstantin Barsht's essay in the present volume.

12 M. Tsvetaeva, 'Geroi truda', SS, vol. IV, p. 38.

13 On the latter point, see also Andrew Wachtel's comments on realist portrait-painting in the present volume.

14 John Berger, 'The Moment of Cubism', in *The Moment of Cubism and Other Essays* (New York, 1969), p. 23. My emphasis.

15 See Beverly Whitney Kean, *French Painters – Russian Collectors* (London, 1994), plate section between pp. 202 and 203.

16 See *ibid.*, print section between pp. 234 and 235.

17 L. Ouspensky, 'The Meaning and Language of Icons', in *idem* and V. Lossky, *The Meaning of Icons* (Crestwood, NY, 1982), p. 39.

18 P. Florenskii, 'Obratnaia perspektiva', *Sobranie sochinenii*, vol. I (Paris, 1986), pp. 117–92.

19 S. Wichmann, 'Foreword', *World Cultures and Modern Art: The Encounter of Nineteenth- and Twentieth-Century European Art and Music with Asia, Africa, Oceania, Afro- and Indo-America* (Munich, 1972), n.p.

20 See N. Kliuev, 'Avtobiograficheskaia zametka' in *Sobranie sochinenii* (2 vols., Munich, 1969), vol. I, pp. 211–12; Peggy Weiss, *Kandinsky and Old Russia: The Artist as Ethnographer and Shaman* (New Haven, 1996), p. 9; Tsvetaeva's lyric 'U pervoi babki–chetyre syna' dates from 1920.

21 A. Belyi, *Kotik Letaev* (Petersburg, 1922), pp. 33–5. This translation is by G. S. Smith: see Catriona Kelly (ed.), *Utopias: Russian Modernist Texts, 1905–1940* (London, 1999).

22 Anna Akmatova, 'Ty znaesh', ia tomlius' v nevole', *Stikhotvoreniia i poemy* (Leningrad, 1977), p. 69.

23 M. Bashkirtseva, *The Complete Journal of Marie Bashkirtseff* , trans. A. D. Hall (Chicago, 1913), Part II, p. 35. On Bashkirtseva's biography, see also A. Cahuet, *Moussia: the Life and Death of Marie Bashkirtseva*, trans. K. Wallis (New York, 1929), Dormer Creston, *Fountains of Youth: the Life of Marie Bashkirtseff* (London, 1936), Mathilde Blind, 'A Study of Marie Bashkirtseff', in André Theuriet, *Jules Bastien-Lepage and His Art: A Memoir* (London, 1892) and Rosenthal, 'Achievement and Obscurity:

Women's Prose in the Silver Age' in Clyman and Green, *Women Writers*, esp. pp. 151, 159, 166.

24 See caption to plate 77, p. 147, in E. K. Valkenier (ed.), *The Wanderers: Masters of Nineteenth-Century Realist Painting* (Dallas, 1990).

25 E. Tur, *Semeistvo Shalonskikh: iz semeinoi khroniki* (St Petersburg, 1880), pp. 40–2; my emphasis.

26 *Ibid.*, p. 43.

27 Cited in M. N. Yablonskaya, *Women Artists of Russia's New Age, 1900–1935* (London, 1990), p. 15, p. 235 n. 6.

28 Letter from M. V. Iakunchikova to E. D. Polenova, 31 May 1889: see Yablonskaya, *Women Artists*, p. 20.

29 Both these paintings are reproduced in Yablonskaya, *Women Artists*, plate 1, plate 17. A rather different sense of constriction is expressed in Ekaterina Letkova's realist fiction of the 1890s: her emphasis is on winter rather than summer, and the 'bleak' landscape adds to the sense of deprivation. It would be instructive to compare Chekhov's fiction, for example 'Step'' (The Steppe), 'Student', or 'Sluchai iz praktiki' (A Doctor's Case-Notes), but such an analysis lies outside the bounds of this study.

30 Yablonskaya, *Women Artists*, p. 11.

31 O. I. Arzumanova, A. G. Kuznetsova, T. N. Makarova, V. A. Nevskii, *Muzei-zapovednik 'Abramtsevo'. Ocherk-putevoditel'* (Moscow, 1989), pp. 79–80.

Select bibliography

GENERAL AND THEORETICAL WORKS

Bakhtin, M., *Rabelais and His World*, trans. Hélène Iswolsky, Cambridge, Mass., 1968.

'Problema soderzhaniia, materiala i formy v slovesnom khudozhestvennom tvorchestve', in *Voprosy literatury i estetiki*, Moscow, 1975.

'Forms of Time and of the Chronotope in the Novel: Notes Toward a Historical Poetics', in *The Dialogic Imagination: Four Essays by M. M. Bakhtin*, ed. M. Holquist, trans. C. Emerson and M. Holquist, Austin, 1981.

Barish, J., *The Antitheatrical Prejudice*, Berkeley, 1980.

Berger, J., *The Moment of Cubism and Other Essays*, New York, 1969.

Braun, E., *The Director and the Stage*, London, 1990.

Butler, C., *Early Modernism: Literature, Music and Painting in Europe, 1900–1916*, Oxford, 1994.

Elliott, B. and Wallace, J.-A., *Women Artists and Writers: Modernist (Im)positionings*, London, 1994.

Emerson, C., *Boris Godunov: Transpositions of a Russian Theme*, Bloomington and Indianapolis, 1986.

Florenskii, P., 'Obratnaia perspektiva', in *Sobranie sochinenii*, vol. 1, Paris, 1986.

Ginzburg, L., *On Psychological Prose*, trans. J. Rosengrant, Princeton, 1991.

Heffernan, J. A. W. (ed.), *Space. Time. Image. Sign: Essays on Literature and the Visual Arts*, New York, 1987.

Likhachev, D. S., *Chelovek v literature drevnei Rusi*, Moscow, 1958.

Poetika drevnerusskoi literatury, 3rd edn., Moscow, 1979.

Lotman, Iu., 'The Theater and Theatricality as Components of Early Nineteenth-Century Culture', trans. G. S. Smith, in A. Shukman (ed.), *The Semiotics of Russian Culture*, Ann Arbor, 1984.

'The Stage and Painting as Code Mechanism for Cultural Behaviour in the Early Nineteenth Century', trans. J. Armstrong, in A. Shukman (ed.), *The Semiotics of Russian Culture*, Ann Arbor, 1984.

McFarlane, B., *Novel to Film: An Introduction to the Theory of Adaptation*, Oxford, 1996.

Ouspensky, L. and Lossky, V., *The Meaning of Icons*, Crestwood, 1982.
Pigarev, K., *Russkaia literatura i izobrazitel'noe iskusstvo*, Moscow, 1972.
Praz, M., *Mnemosyne: The Parallel Between Literature and the Visual Arts*, Princeton, 1970.
Rokem, F., *Theatrical Space in Ibsen, Chekhov and Strindberg*, Ann Arbor, 1986.
Soja, E., *Postmodern Geographies: The Reassertion of Space in Critical Social Theory*, London, 1985.
Tynianov, Iu. N., *Poetika. Literatura. Kino*, Moscow, 1977.
Weisstein, U., 'Literature and the (Visual) Arts: Intertextuality and Mutual Illumination', in I. Hoesterey and U. Weisstein (eds.), *Intertextuality: German Literature and Visual Art from the Renaissance to the Twentieth Century*, Columbia, SC, 1993.
Zis', A. Ia., 'Teoreticheskie predposylki sinteza iskusstv', in D. D. Blagoi *et al.* (eds.), *Vzaimodeistvie i sintez iskusstv*, Moscow, 1978.

PRIMARY TEXTS

Aikhenval'd, Iu., *Otritsanie teatra*, in *V sporakh o teatre*, Moscow, 1914.
Akhmatova, A., *Stikhotvoreniia i poemy*, Leningrad, 1977.
Annenskii, I., 'Chto takoe poeziia?', in *Knigi otrazhenii*, Leningrad, 1979.
Belyi, A., *Kotik Letaev*, Moscow, 1920.
  Peterburg, Moscow, 1928.
Blok, A., *Liricheskie dramy*, in *Lirika, teatr*, Moscow, 1982.
Bowlt, J. (ed.), *Russian Art of the Avant-Garde*, London, 1988.
Briusov, V., 'Nenuzhnaia pravda (Po povodu Moskovskogo khudozhestvennogo teatra)', *Mir iskusstva* 4 (1902).
Chekhov, A. P., *Polnoe sobranie sochinenii i pisem*, 30 vols., Moscow, 1974–82.
Dostoevskii, F. M., *Polnoe sobranie sochinenii v tridtsati tomakh*, Leningrad, 1972–90.
Evreinov, N., 'Apologiia teatral'nosti', in *Teatr kak takovoi*. Berlin, 1923.
  Revizor, in M. Poliakov (ed.), *Russkaia teatral'naia parodiia XIX–nachala XX veka*, Moscow, 1976.
Golomshtok, I. and Siniavskii, A., *Pikasso*, Moscow, 1960.
Griboedov, A., 'Po povodu "Goria ot uma"', in *Sochineniia v stikhakh*, Leningrad, 1987.
Gumilev, N., *Akteon*, in *Sobranie sochinenii*, vol. III, Washington, 1966.
Kelly, C. (ed.), *Utopias: Russian Modernist Texts 1905–1940*, London, 1999.
Khlebnikov, V., *Sobranie proizvedenii Velimira Khlebnikova*, ed. N. Stepanov and Iu. Tynianov, 5 vols., Leningrad, 1928–33.
Khlebnikov, V., *Tvoreniia*, M. Poliakov *et al.* (eds.), Moscow, 1986.
Mandel'shtam, O., *Sobranie sochinenii v 3 tomakh*, New York, 1971.
Markov, V. (ed.), *Manifesty i programmy russkikh futuristov*, Munich, 1972.
Meierkhol'd, V., *Meyerhold on Theatre*, trans. and ed. E. Braun, London, 1969.
Nabokov, V., *Speak, Memory*, Harmondsworth, 1969.
  The Annotated Lolita, ed. Alfred Appel Jr., London, 1995.

Olesha, Iu., *P'esy. Stat'i o teatre i dramaturgii*, Moscow, 1968.

　Izbrannoe, Moscow, 1974.

Pasternak, B., *Sochineniia*, ed. G. P. Struve and B. A. Filippov, 3 vols., Ann Arbor, 1961.

　Stikhotvoreniia i poemy, Moscow, 1965.

　Doktor Zhivago, Ann Arbor, 1967.

Platonov, A., *Izbrannye proizvedeniia*, Moscow, 1983.

　Sobranie sochinenii, 3 vols., Moscow, 1984–85.

　Kotlovan. Iuvenil'noe more, Moscow, 1987.

　Chevengur, Moscow, 1988.

Prismanova, A., *Sobranie sochinenii*, Leyden, 1990.

Repin, I., *Dalekoe – blizkoe*, Moscow and Leningrad, 1937.

Rozanova, O., 'Osnovy novogo tvorchestva i prichiny ego neponimaniia', *Soiuz molodezhi* 1 (1913).

Siniavskii, A., *Ivan-Durak: ocherk russkoi narodnoi very*, Paris, 1991.

Siniavskii, A., [as 'Abram Tertz'], *Fantasticheskii mir Abrama Tertsa*, New York, 1967.

　Golos iz khora, London, 1973.

　Spokoinoi nochi, Paris, 1984.

　Sud idet, in *Sobranie sochinenii v dvukh tomakh*, vol. 1, Moscow, 1992.

　'Puteshestvie na Cherniuiu rechku', *Sintaksis* 34 (1994).

Stanislavskii, K.S., *Moia zhizn' v iskusstve*, in *Sobranie sochinenii v vos'mi tomakh*, vol. 1, Moscow, 1954.

Teatr: Kniga o novom teatre, St Petersburg, 1908.

Tsvetaeva, M., *Stikhotvoreniia i poemy*, Leningrad, 1990.

　Sobranie sochinenii v 7 tomakh, Moscow, 1994–96.

Tur, E., *Semeistvo Shalonskikh: iz semeinoi khroniki*, St Petersburg, 1880.

Tynianov, Iu. N., *Arkhaisty i novatory*, Leningrad, 1929.

Voloshin, M., 'Oslinyi khvost', *Apollon* 7 (1912).

Zoshchenko, M., *Sobranie sochinenii v trekh tomakh*, Leningrad, 1987.

　Uvazhaemye grazhdane. Parodii. Rasskazy. Fel'etony. Satiricheskie zametki. Pis'ma k pisateliu. Odnoaktnye komedii, ed. M. Z. Dolinskii, Moscow, 1991.

SECONDARY LITERATURE: RUSSIAN LITERATURE AND THE
OTHER ARTS, 1860–1960

Al'fonsov, V., ' "Chtoby slovo smelo poshlo za zhivopis'" ' (V. Khlebnikov i zhivopis')', in A.I. Iezuitov (ed.), *Literatura i zhivopis'*, Leningrad, 1982.

Anderson, R. and Debreczeny, P. (eds.), *Russian Narrative and Visual Art: Varieties of Seeing*, Gainesville, Florida, 1994.

Barnes, C., *Boris Pasternak: A Literary Biography: Volume 1 1890–1928*, Cambridge, 1989.

Bartlett, R., *Wagner in Russian Culture*, Cambridge, 1994.

Basker, M., 'Gumilev's *Akteon*: a forgotten manifesto of Acmeism', *Slavonic and East European Review* 63 (1985).

Beaujour, E. K., *The Invisible Land: A Study of the Artistic Imagination of Iurii Olesha*, New York and London, 1970.
Bowlt, J. and Matich, O. (eds.), *The Laboratory of Dreams: The Russian Avant-Garde and Cultural Experiment*, Stanford, 1996.
Boym, S., *Death in Quotation Marks*, Cambridge, Mass., 1991.
Braun, E., *Meyerhold: A Revolution in Theatre*, 2nd ed., London, 1995.
Carnicke, S. M., *The Theatrical Instinct: Nikolai Evreinov and the Russian Theatre of the Early Twentieth Century*, New York, 1989.
Chester, P., 'The Landscape of Recollection: Tolstoy's *Childhood* and the Feminization of the Countryside', in P. Chester and S. Forrester (eds.), *Engendering Slavic Literatures*, Bloomington, Indiana, 1996.
Clayton, J. D., *Pierrot in Petrograd: The Commedia dell'arte/balagan in Twentieth-Century Russian Theatre and Drama*, Montreal, 1994.
Compton, S., *The World Backwards: Russian Futurist Books 1912–16*, London, 1978.
Russian Avant-Garde Books 1917–34, London, 1992.
Davies, R. (ed.), *Leonid Andreyev: Photographs by a Russian Writer*, London, 1989.
Flaker, A., 'Babel' i Malevich', *Wiener Slawistischer Almanach* 10 (1982).
Fülöp-Miller, R. and Gregor, P., *The Russian Theatre: Its Character and History*, London, 1930.
Golub, S., *Evreinov: The Theatre of Paradox and Transformation*, Ann Arbor, 1984.
Gremislavskii, I.Ia., *Kompozitsiia stsenicheskogo prostranstva v tvorchestve V. Simova*, Moscow, 1983.
Gurevich, S. D., *Sovetskie pisateli v kinematografe (20–30-e gody)*, Leningrad, 1975.
Heil, J., 'Russian Writers and the Cinema in the Early 20th Century – A Survey', *Russian Literature* 19 (1986).
'Jurij Tynjanov's film-work. Two filmscripts "Lieutenant Kiže" (1927, 1933–34) and "The Monkey and the Bell" (1932)', *Russian Literature* 21 (1987).
No List of Political Assets: The Collaboration of Iurii Olesha and Abram Room on 'Strogii iunosha' [A Strict Youth (1936)], Slawistische Beiträge, vol. 248, Munich, 1989.
Holmgren, B., 'Gendering the icon: marketing women writers in fin de siècle Russia', in H. Goscilo and B. Holmgren (eds.), *Russia: Women: Culture*, Bloomington, Indiana, 1997.
Hutchings, S. C., *Russian Modernism: The Transfiguration of the Everyday*, Cambridge, 1997.
Janecek, G., *The Look of Russian Literature: Avant-Garde Visual Experiments 1900–1930*, Princeton, NJ, 1984.
Jangfeldt, B., *Majakovskij and Futurism, 1917–1921*, Stockholm, 1977.
Kleberg, L. and Nilsson, N. A., *Theater and Literature in Russia 1900–1930*, Stockholm, 1984.

Leach, R., *Directors in Perspective: Vsevolod Meyerhold*, Cambridge, 1989.
  Vsevolod Meyerhold, Cambridge, 1993.
  Revolutionary Theatre, London, 1994.
Lodder, C., *Russian Constructivism*, New Haven, CT, 1983.
Mandelker, A., *Framing Anna Karenina: Tolstoy, the Woman Question, and the Victorian Novel*, Columbus, Ohio, 1993.
Marsh, C., 'Chekhov's "Modernist" Theatre', in C. Marsh and W. Rosslyn (eds.), *Russian and Yugoslav Culture in the Age of Modernism*, Nottingham, 1991.
Men'shutin, A. and Siniavskii, A., *Poeziia pervykh let revoliutsii: 1917–1920*, Moscow, 1964.
Michalski, M., 'Iurii Olesha: Cinematic Interests and Cinematic Influence', *Slovo* (London) 8:2 (November 1995).
Padrta, J., 'Malévitch et Khlebnikov', in J.-C. Marcadé (ed.), *Malévitch. 1878–1978*, Lausanne, 1979.
Ripellino, A., *Majakovski et le théâtre russe d'avant-garde*, Paris, 1965.
Rudnitskii, K., *Russkoe rezhisserskoe iskusstvo, 1898–1907*, Moscow, 1989.
  Russian and Soviet Theatre, London, 1988.
Russell, R. and Barratt, A. (eds.), *Russian Theatre in the Age of Modernism*, Basingstoke, 1990.
Sherel, A. (ed.), *Meierkhol'dovskii sbornik: Vypusk pervyi*, 2 vols., Moscow, 1993.
Stapanian, J. R., *Mayakovsky's Cubo-Futurist Vision*, Houston, 1986.
Styan, J. L., *Chekhov in Performance*, Cambridge, 1971.
Tikhvinskaia, L., *Kabare i teatry miniatiur v Rossii. 1908–1917*, Moscow, 1995.
Tsivian, Yu., *Early Cinema in Russia and Its Cultural Reception*, trans. A. Bodger, London, 1994.
Weststeijn, W. (ed.), *Velimir Chlebnikov (1885–1922): Myth and Reality*, Amsterdam, 1986.
Woodward, J., 'From Brjusov to Aikhenvald: Attitudes to the Russian Theatre, 1902–1914', *Canadian Slavonic Papers* 1 (1965).

Index of names

Index of concepts

absurdism, 192
Acmeism, 10, 59–60, 75
adaptations, 4–5, 11
  to screen, 5, 228
  to stage, 4–5, 161–5
architecture, 33, 50, 207–8
autobiography, 60, 68–77, 100–7

boundaries
  between visual and verbal culture, 5–8,
    14–16, 58–60
  overcoming of these, 1–6
bricolage, 14
byt, 11, 97, 119–20
  fusion with art, 15

cabaret, 11, 154–65 *passim*
calligraphy, 38–54 *passim*
Christianity, 26, 28, 41–3, 68–9, 110–11
  in art, 26, 33, 41–3
  Russian Othodoxy, 9, 54, 110–11
chronotope, 11–12, 26, 48, 55
  in theatre, 120, 172
cinema, 5, 12–13, 16, 220–44
  filmic style in literature, 5, 96, 223–5, 229–31
  parody of, 164
classicism, 3, 95, 97
close-ups, 5, 221, 230–1, 238
collaboration
  in cinema, 220–2, 237–44
  across different art forms, 1–3, 11, 172–3,
    192–3
  in theatre, 4, 172–93 *passim*
collage, 5
colours, 6, 91, 96, 202
Constructivism, 4, 15
Cubism, 60, 81–3, 283–4
Cubo-Futurism, 4

director

role of, 152, 160–1, 237
doodles, 9, 43–54, 200

ekphrasis, 5, 59, 71
eye(s), 10, 12, 197–8, 211–15

facture, 5, 83
the fantastic, 95, 97–8
folk art, 79, 102, 124, 211–12, 297–8
Formalism, 5
Futurism, 96, 202–3
  parody of, 157–8

Gesamtkunst, 3
Gothic, 33, 46–7, 49–51, 75, 94
the grotesque, 74–6, 97–8

hieroglyphics, 12, 203–6

icons, 19–20 n. 27, 27, 64, 102, 107, 110,
    201–2, 204, 281, 284–5
  violation of, 37
illustrations, 4, 15–16, 91–2, 96
intertextuality, 8, 11, 83, 123–7, 131–8, 175–6

landscape, 10, 13–14, 72–83, 181–2, 191,
    280–302 *passim*
  and identity, 280–2, 285–302
light, 222–5
  in cinema, 12, 222–5, 228, 229–30,
    239–40
  in theatre, 123–4
  used symbolically/metaphorically, 123–4,
    126, 129
lik (the face), 9, 23–4, 25–6, 27, 29, 31, 32,
    36–7, 52, 54, 64, 72
  facelessness, 13, 250–72 *passim*

memory, 29–30, 74–7, 160, 289
metaphor, 10, 93–4, 101–2, 106–10, 224

Middle Ages, 19–20 n. 27, 26, 33, 38–9, 92, 95, 188–9, 212
mimesis, 5, 9, 202
Modernism, 1–16, 88, 283–5
  fusion of art and life in, 14–15
  relationship to realism, 1, 14, 58–9, 150–3, 208, 282–3
  and women, 13–14, 60, 278–80, 298–9
montage, 5, 14
music
  in film, 239, 241
  in poetry, 58–9, 83, 199

narrative
  in Modernism, 2, 5, 106–7
naturalism, 12, 176, 182, 183–92 *passim*
neo-primitivism, 4, 80–1, 206, 285
'primitive' art, 94, 106–10, 111–13, 285
nihilism
  in aesthetics, 35, 43
numbers, 200, 203–4, 208

opera, 11, 123–7, 133–7, 150

painting, 5, 32–6, 62–4, 90, 103–6, 119
  relationship with literature, 2, 5–8, 80–4, 90
  relationship with theatre, 181
parody, 98, 187–92
  in theatre, 11, 154–8, 172–3, 190–2
performance
  attitudes to, 7, 11, 149–51
photography, 3, 28, 30, 31, 121, 136–7, 274 n. 9
portraits, 9–10, 20 n. 27, 24–5, 27–8, 29–32, 41–3, 47, 253–9, 266–9
  of poets, 9–10, 266–9
  and psychology, 24–5, 266–9

realism, 5–7, 9, 14, 54, 58–9, 150–3, 158, 208, 266–9, 282–3, 297–8
  in painting, 279

in theatre, 12, 82–92 *passim*, 150–3
Renaissance, 33, 95
Romanticism, 3, 54, 78, 97–8

scriptwriting, 220–1, 226–7
self
  constructions of, 11, 25–6, 67–8, 70–1, 280–2
  undermining of, 2, 119–21, 122–3, 137–8, 253–5
self-portraits, 10, 68–9, 203–4, 300–1
sketches, 4, 9, 38–54 *passim*, 200
Socialist Realism, 10, 13, 14, 88, 92, 95, 97, 243, 251–2, 263, 265, 271
space
  and identity, 13–14, 72–80, 280–301
  on manuscript page, 44–51
  in theatre, 4, 175–93
  versus time, 8, 184–5, 208–9
stage design, 4, 11–12, 172–81
Suprematism, 4, 208, 251, 270
Symbolism, 7, 151–2
synaesthesia, 3, 191, 203–4

theatre, 4, 11, 149–65
  attitudes to, 11, 149–53
  reflected in literature, 119–38
  teatral'nost', 153–4
typography, 4, 96, 202–3, 205–6

viewpoint, 2, 5, 282–4
visual punning, 10, 81–3

women
  sense of self, 13–14, 65, 67–8, 70–1, 280–2, 285–302
  in the visual arts, 9–10, 278–80
  as writers, 60, 67–8
word-paintings, 10, 201–2, 202–4

zaum', 12, 198, 206